Cambridge IGCSE®

Economics

STUDENT'S BOOK

Also for Cambridge O Level

James Beere,
Karen Borrington, Clive Riches

William Collins' dream of knowledge for all began with the publication of his first book in 1819.

A self-educated mill worker, he not only enriched millions of lives, but also founded a flourishing publishing house. Today, staying true to this spirit, Collins books are packed with inspiration, innovation and practical expertise. They place you at the centre of a world of possibility and give you exactly what you need to explore it.

Collins. Freedom to teach.

Published by Collins

An imprint of HarperCollins*Publishers*
The News Building, 1 London Bridge Street, London, SE1 9GF

HarperCollins*Publishers*
Macken House, 39/40 Mayor Street Upper, Dublin 1 D01 C9W8, Ireland

This book contains FSC™ certified paper and other controlled sources to ensure responsible forest management.

For more information visit: www.harpercollins.co.uk/green

Browse the complete Collins catalogue at
www.collins.co.uk

© HarperCollins*Publishers* Limited 2018

10 9 8 7

ISBN 978-0-00-825409-4

British Library Cataloguing in Publication Data

A catalogue record for this publication is available from the British Library.

Authors: James Beere, Karen Borrington, Clive Riches
Reviewer: Colin Harber Stuart
Development editor: Hetty Marx
Commissioning editor: Lucy Cooper
In-house editors: Alexander Rutherford, Letitia Luff
Project managers: Elina Helenius, Amanda Harman
Copyeditor: Philippa Tomlinson
Proofreader: Write Communications Ltd
Cover designers: Kevin Robbins and Gordon MacGilp
Cover illustrator: Maria Herbert-Liew
Internal designer / Typesetter: Jouve India
Production controller: Tina Paul
Printed in India by Multivista Global Pvt. Ltd.
® IGCSE is a registered trademark.
All exam-style questions and sample answers have been written by the authors. In examinations, the way marks are awarded may be different.

The authors and publishers would like to thank the following teachers for providing material for some of the case studies:
Diarmaid Gallagher of the British School of Costa Rica, San Jose, Costa Rica
Ms. Akshika Bansal, Economics and Business Studies Faculty at International Pioneers School, Bangkok, Thailand
Sanne Schobbe, St. George's School, Cologne, Germany

Contents

Introduction

Welcome to Collins Cambridge IGCSE Economics which has been carefully designed and written to help you develop the knowledge and skills you will need to succeed in the *Cambridge IGCSE Economics* course or *Cambridge O level Economics* course.

Economics is the study of economies and how they use the limited resources they have available to satisfy as many people's needs and wants as possible. The *Cambridge IGCSE Economics* course covers both micro economics and macro economics.

Micro economics is the study of smaller economic issues faced by individual consumers, workers and firms. It aims to answer questions like:

- Why do people consume too much fast food and not enough flu vaccinations?
- Why are wages very high for some workers but very low for others?
- Why might having a single (monopoly) seller in a market be good and bad for consumers?

Macro economics is the study of larger economic issues faced by countries at national and international level. It looks at questions like:

- Why are some countries rich and other countries poor?
- What causes extreme poverty and how can it be eradicated?
- Who gains from globalisation and international trade and who loses?

By the end of this course you should have the knowledge and skills to not only succeed in the *Cambridge IGCSE Economics* course but also to better understand the many important economic issues facing the world in which you live. Good luck with your study of economics!

How to use this book

This Student's Book covers all the content for the *Cambridge IGCSE Economics* syllabus. It is divided into six chapters – one for each of the areas of the syllabus. Each chapter is divided into units which cover the essential knowledge and skills you need as specified by the syllabus. Each of the units is organised in the same way and has the following features:

- **Learning objectives** list the key knowledge and skills you need to acquire.
- **Starting point** questions allow you to check your understanding of previous topics and help you to understand the links between topics.
- **Exploring** questions ask you to think about the content you are studying in a broader sense and can be considered across the course of the unit.
- **Key terms** and **key knowledge** boxes provide summaries and definitions of important terms and concepts for at-a-glance reference and to support your understanding.
- **Questions** within the text allow you to check your understanding of key concepts or encourage you to come up with an answer before it is explained in the text.
- **Extension questions** marked with an Ⓔ are designed to be more challenging to stretch you and encourage you to further your understanding of Economics.

- **Case studies** focus on different areas of the world and help to provide a real life context for applying many of the ideas which you have investigated in each unit. These include questions to help develop your understanding of the impact of economic concepts around the world.

- A range of **diagrams** help to develop your core skills in analysis and manipulation of data.

- **Application tasks** allow you to apply what you have learnt in a variety of economic settings.

- **Worked examples** take you through economic concepts step by step and help you to understand the topic. They demonstrate how a problem or question can be addressed and what constitutes a good response.

- **Project work** at the end of each unit provides an opportunity to bring together your learning. You will be asked to collate and analyse data, produce individual text and drawings, write and deliver presentations and solve problems.

- **Knowledge check questions** at the end of each unit allow you to check your knowledge and understanding of the material in the unit. To the right of each question is a number in square brackets, for example [2]. This indicates the number of marks available for that type of question.

- **Check your progress** helps you to evaluate how you are doing.

- **Extension topics** provide opportunities for you to extend your knowledge beyond the scope of the syllabus. You do not need to read this material to understand the rest of the text.

The Student's Book also includes two other sections to support your knowledge and understanding of the syllabus content:

- **Chapter reviews** allow you to practise what you have learnt in the chapter with exam-style questions designed to help you prepare for examination.

- A **glossary** explains and defines the key terms highlighted in the text. Words in bold throughout the book can be found in the glossary. (You may come across these words before they are defined in detail in a later unit. Remember to make frequent use of the glossary.)

The basic economic problem

1

In this first chapter you will learn some of the underlying, fundamental ideas and concepts that form the basis of the study of economics. You will begin by exploring the nature of the economic problem and the fact that resources are scarce. You will then look in more detail at the nature of the economic resources available for production. Finally, you will develop your understanding by looking at choices and opportunity cost. These are illustrated using a production possibility curve, and you will explore the significance and interpretation of these diagrams.

1.1 The nature of the economic problem

1.2 The factors of production

1.3 Opportunity cost

1.4 Production possibility curve diagram (PPC)

The nature of the economic problem

Learning objectives
By the end of this unit, you should be able to:
* define what is meant by finite resources
* explain what is meant by unlimited wants
* give examples of the economic problem in different contexts
* explain the difference between an economic good and a free good.

Starting point

Complete these tasks in pairs:

1 Write a list of five goods or services you need to survive.

2 Now write a list of 10 goods or services you would buy if you won $500.

3 Explain why you can't have all 10 goods or services.

Exploring

Discuss these questions in pairs:

1 What materials do you need to make a car?

2 Will any of the resources you listed in question 1 eventually run out?

3 Will any of the resources you listed in question 1 always be available in the future?

4 Why are some resources likely to be available in the future whereas other resources are likely to run out?

5 What can be done to make resources last longer and not run out as quickly?

Developing

Finite resources and unlimited wants

Everyone has **basic needs** to survive, such as food, clean water and shelter. However, all people will have a never-ending list of goods or services they *want* – such as cars, fashionable clothes and holidays. What is the difference between a need and a want?

Key term

Basic needs – what is needed for survival, such as food, shelter, water and clothing

A **need** is necessary for survival but a **want** is something that is not needed for survival.

Resources are used to produce goods and services to satisfy these needs and wants. They include natural resources (land, soil, timber), human resources (farm workers, factory managers) and manufactured resources (robots, tractors, factory buildings).

Some of these are **finite resources**, which means that there is a limited amount available in the world and they will eventually be used up. Examples of finite resources are oil, coal and uranium.

Other resources are **renewable resources**, which means that they can be replaced. Examples are timber, fish, grain and meat. However, if we use these resources faster than they are being renewed or replaced then they will run out as well. For example, if fish are caught in too large numbers then there will not be enough fish left in the oceans to replace those caught. This would mean that fish are no longer renewable and will eventually die out. This is why it is so important today that resources are replaced at the same rate as they are being used. For example, new trees can be planted to replace those that have been cut down for timber.

Both finite and renewable resources are used to produce goods and services. However, there are never enough of these resources, even the renewable ones, to produce all the goods and services to satisfy everyone. This is because people, or consumers, have **unlimited wants**.

The economic problem

The economic problem is that there are limited resources and unlimited wants, which leads to a problem of scarcity. **Scarcity** means there is a lack of resources available to produce all the goods and services to satisfy these unlimited wants. Therefore, choices have to be made about what goods and services to produce, how to produce the goods and services and who will be able to consume those goods and services (this is covered in more detail in Unit 2.2).

The economic problem applies to more than just consumers. It applies to all areas of the economy, as shown in Figure 1.1.1.

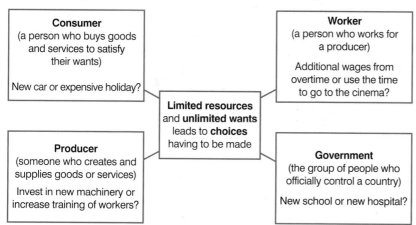

Consumer
(a person who buys goods and services to satisfy their wants)

New car or expensive holiday?

Worker
(a person who works for a producer)

Additional wages from overtime or use the time to go to the cinema?

Limited resources and unlimited wants leads to **choices** having to be made

Producer
(someone who creates and supplies goods or services)

Invest in new machinery or increase training of workers?

Government
(the group of people who officially control a country)

New school or new hospital?

Figure 1.1.1 The economic problem applies to all areas of the economy

Consumers will always want more goods and services, such as more clothes, more furniture, new electrical items or to eat in restaurants more often. They will have to make choices between the goods and services they want.

 1 Can you think of examples of other choices that consumers, workers, producers and government might make?

Economic goods and free goods

Goods that are produced and sold at a price are called **economic goods**. A price is charged for these goods because they are scarce relative to demand. However, there are some goods that are unlimited in supply and are therefore free, such as air, pebbles on a beach and sand in the desert. **Free goods** are goods which are not scarce relative to demand.

 2 Is water free? What are the costs to both individuals and the economy of supplying water?

CASE STUDY 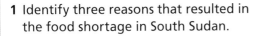 **Famine hits South Sudan**

Although rising living standards in many countries are lifting people out of poverty, there are frequent reminders of the fundamental problem of scarcity. In 2017, for example, a famine was declared in South Sudan. In recent years this African country has suffered civil war, low rainfall, increasing prices and disrupted farming. Now nearly half the population, about 5 million people, are struggling to survive and 100 000 are close to starvation.

1 Identify three reasons that resulted in the food shortage in South Sudan.

2 Describe the choices people in South Sudan could make as to where they spend their money.

3 Describe two choices the government could make as to where it could spend its money.

Applying

Project work

Using the internet, find out about the resources in your country, and across the world.

1. Find five examples of resources in your country that are finite.

2. Find five examples of resources in your country that are renewable.

3. Are any of these renewable resources being used up more quickly than they are being replaced?

4. Is renewable energy used in your country?

5. (E) Is there anything being done by governments to stop resources being used up more quickly than they are being replaced?

6. (E) Is there anything being done by governments to encourage the use of renewable energy?

Knowledge check questions

1 What is meant by the economic problem? [2]

2 What is the difference between a need and a want? [2]

3 Explain why some resources are finite resources and some resources are renewable. [4]

4 Describe an example of the economic problem for producers. [2]

5 Explain why some goods have a price while some goods are free. [4]

6 (E) Analyse why, if you wanted sand, you may sometimes have to pay a price and sometimes it is free. [6]

Check your progress

Read the unit objectives below and reflect on your progress in each.

- Define what is meant by finite resources.

- Explain what is meant by unlimited wants.

- Give examples of the economic problem in different contexts.

- Explain the difference between an economic good and a free good.

▲ I struggle with this and need more practice.

▲ I can do this reasonably well.

▲ I can do this with confidence.

The factors of production

Learning objectives
By the end of this unit, you should be able to:
- define the four factors of production
- give examples of each of the factors of production
- identify the rewards that go to the factors of production
- explain what affects the mobility of factors and whether the factors can be moved to other industries
- explain what causes changes in the quantity and quality of the factors.

Starting point

Answer this question in pairs:

1 You want to build a wooden house for your younger brother or sister to play in. What resources will you need to do this?

Exploring

Discuss these questions in pairs:

1 A person wants to start his or her own business making ice cream. What resources will they need to do this?

2 What resources will be needed to build a textiles factory and manufacture clothes?

Developing

Factors and their rewards

All the resources you have identified in the tasks above can be put into four main categories. These are called the **factors of production**. The four factors of production are **land, labour, capital** and **enterprise**.

- **Land** – anything natural that is used to produce goods and services. This includes land itself but also natural resources that come from land, such as cotton, timber or cocoa. The payment made to the owner for the use of land as part of the production process is the rent paid.

- **Labour** – human resources used to produce goods and services. This can be physical or mental effort. The payment of wages rewards the work carried out as part of the production process.

- **Capital** – manufactured resources used to produce goods and services. Capital includes machinery, equipment, factory and office buildings, and automated production lines. The payment made for borrowing money to buy capital is called interest.

- **Enterprise** – brings together all the other factors so that production of goods and services can take place. Without

Key terms

Factors of production – land, labour, capital and enterprise

Land – includes all natural resources

Labour – includes all human resources

Capital – includes all man-made resources

Enterprise – brings all the other factors together to produce a good or service

enterprise there would be no production. Enterprise is carried out by the entrepreneur, and the reward gained by the entrepreneur is profit.

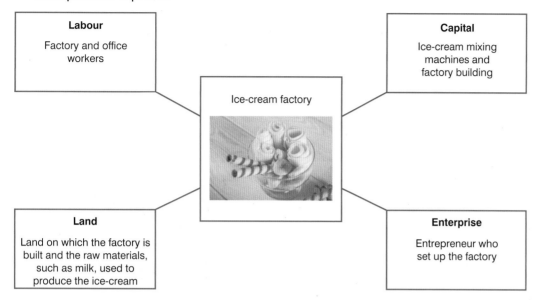

Figure 1.2.1 Factors of production for an ice-cream factory

Mobility of factors of production

1 What happens to the factors of production when a business closes?

2 Can the factors of production be sold and transferred to another industry?

For some factors the answer to question 2 is yes, but for others it may be very difficult to sell and move them. A coal mine with machinery used to extract coal is probably not useful for any other industry. However, computer systems or factory buildings could be used in another industry and are therefore considered to be **mobile**.

Land can often be adapted for other uses and labour can often be retrained to carry out other jobs. Capital can be more difficult to move to an alternative use. The more specific the capital, the less mobile it is. For example, if machinery is made especially to carry out a particular purpose as part of the production process then it will probably not be able to be used for anything else. An example is a robot on a car production line that welds the car body together. Enterprise, on the other hand, can be moved to alternative industries if the entrepreneur has some knowledge of the alternative industry.

Key knowledge

Land	Natural resources
Labour	Human resources
Capital	Manufactured resources
Enterprise	Brings together all the other factors of production to produce goods and services

Key term

Mobility of factors of production – how easy or difficult it is for factors of production to be transferred to alternative industries

Application task

Copy and complete the table below. Which of the factors of production could be easily changed to an alternative industry? Give reasons.

Factor of production	Is it mobile? Yes/No?	Reason for your answer of Yes or No
Power station		
Lorry (truck)		
Field used for growing rice		
Manager of a factory		
Computer		
Shop		
Electrician		

Causes of changes in the quantity and quality of the factors of production

How do the factors of production enable production of goods and services to be increased and allow economic growth?

The economic resources can be increased in quantity. If there are more economic resources, as in the following examples, then the economy can produce more output:

- More labour – due to an increase in the population or immigration.

- More land – for example, an increase in the natural resources available to an economy, such as the discovery of more oil.

- More capital – for example, due to businesses purchasing more machinery and equipment.

The quality of the resources can be improved, such as in the following cases:

- Land can be made more productive by using fertilisers to increase the output from farming land.

- Education and training improve the quality of labour and make it more productive.

- Improvements in technology increase the quality of capital.

- Entrepreneurs can become more skilled through education to manage the other factors of production in a more efficient way.

So an increase in output and economic growth is usually because there are more factors of production available for the production of goods and services and/or the quality of the factors of production has been improved.

Introduction of the steel mini-mill

The increase in productivity in the US steel industry can be directly linked to the introduction of a new production technology: the 'mini-mill'. The mini-mill plants are significantly more productive than traditional steel plants, and this higher productivity has resulted in mini-mills replacing the older technology plants. The use of new capital has increased output by about 33% in the steel industry's total output.

1 Which factor of production has improved in quality?

2 Explain why output of steel has increased.

3 What do you think will happen to the price of steel?

4 Explain the benefits to other industries that buy steel from these mills.

Applying

Project work

Using the internet, find out more about training in your country.

1. Research the training courses provided at your local college or university.

2. Does the government provide any of these training courses?

3. How will these training courses help firms in your area?

4. How has the available training helped your country to increase the production of goods and services?

5. (E) Analyse why some training courses are more effective than others at increasing output in the economy.

Knowledge check questions

1 Define the **four** factors of production. [4]

2 Give an example of each factor of production. [4]

3 Explain what affects the mobility of factors of production. [4]

4 Explain how the quality of the factors of production might be improved. [4]

5 (E) Discuss the extent to which the government can increase the factors of production in an economy. [8]

Check your progress

Read the unit objectives below and reflect on your progress in each.

- Define the four factors of production.

- Give examples of each of the factors of production.

- Identify the rewards that go to the factors of production.

- Explain what affects the mobility of factors and whether the factors can be moved to other industries.

- Explain what causes changes in the quantity and quality of the factors.

I struggle with this and need more practice.

I can do this reasonably well.

I can do this with confidence.

Opportunity cost

Learning objectives

By the end of this unit, you should be able to:

- define opportunity cost
- give examples of opportunity cost in different contexts
- explain how opportunity cost influences decision making by consumers, workers, producers and governments when allocating resources.

Starting point

Answer these questions in pairs:

1 What is the economic problem?

2 Why can you not have all the goods you want?

Exploring

Discuss these questions in pairs:

1 How do you decide which goods and services to buy and which ones not to buy?

2 Think of four things you would want to buy that cost approximately $5. Place these items in order of preference with the most preferred at the top (1) and the least preferred at the bottom (4). Explain why you would not buy the items ranked 2, 3 and 4.

Developing

Opportunity cost

In Unit 1.1 it was explained that there are not enough resources to provide goods and services to satisfy all the wants in an economy. Wants are unlimited but the ability to satisfy these wants is limited due to resources being scarce, so choices have to be made. Much of what you will study in economics is about the choices behind using scarce resources to satisfy as many of these unlimited wants as possible.

When making a choice between wants, something has to be given up. This is known as **opportunity cost.** Opportunity cost is the next best alternative foregone when making a choice. It is a cost because it is something that has been given up in favour of the first choice.

For example, you have a birthday and you are given $50 to spend. You go to the shops and decide to buy either a new pair of jeans or a new jacket. You decide to buy the jacket – so what have you given up?

You have given up the jeans as they were the next best alternative foregone or, in other words, the alternative choice you decided to give up. So the opportunity cost of purchasing a new jacket is the pair of jeans that you didn't buy.

Key term

Opportunity cost – the next best alternative foregone when making an economic decision

1 Can you think of other opportunity cost examples when you faced a choice and gave up buying something or doing something else instead?

Opportunity cost is not just relevant when you are buying goods or services. It can also apply when you choose between doing particular activities; a money cost is not always involved. You may have been asked by friends to go and play basketball while some other friends asked you to play tennis. If you choose to play basketball what have you foregone? You have given up playing tennis. So the opportunity cost of you choosing to play basketball is playing tennis because you have given up playing tennis.

The following table has examples of choices that have been made and the opportunity cost of these choices.

	Choices: the alternatives to choose between	First choice	Opportunity cost: the next best alternative choice that has been given up
Consumer	Buy a new watch or buy concert tickets	Concert tickets	A watch
Worker	Work overtime or spend time with your children	Spend time with your children	Additional wages from working overtime
Producer	Increase advertising expenditure or increase training	Increase training	More advertising
Government	Pay higher pensions or higher wages for government employees	Higher pensions	Higher wages for government employees

2 What might change to cause each of the items ranked as the next best alternative choice to be chosen instead?

CASE STUDY **Aldi – investment in staff leads to global growth**

Aldi is a global discount supermarket chain. It has more than 8000 stores worldwide and continues to open new stores in Europe, North America and Australia. Aldi aims to provide its customers with high quality products at competitive prices. One of the ways it achieves this is by focusing on the training and development of its employees. Aldi has spent some money advertising its brand in the UK as this is a very competitive market and it wants to increase its market share. In America it has a low number of employees in each store relative to other supermarkets.

1 What else could Aldi spend its money on instead of training and advertising?

2 What is the opportunity cost of Aldi choosing to invest in its employees?

3 Why do you think Aldi made this choice?

Applying

Project work

In groups of three or four, carry out the following tasks:

1. Ask your parents for examples of choices they have made. Ask them why they made the choice they did and why they rejected the next best alternative.

2. Ask someone who works in a business for examples of choices they have made. Ask them why they made the choice they did and why they rejected the next best alternative.

3. Ask someone who owns a business for examples of choices they have made. Ask them why they made the choice they did and why they rejected the next best alternative.

4. Research examples of choices the government has made. Why do you think it made the choice it did and why did it reject the next best alternative?

5. Present your findings to the rest of the class.

Knowledge check questions

1   What is meant by opportunity cost?   [2]

2   Give an example of opportunity cost for a consumer.   [2]

3   Why do you think they made this choice?   [2]

4   Give an example of opportunity cost for a worker.   [2]

5   Why do you think they made this choice?   [2]

6   Give an example of opportunity cost for a producer.   [2]

7   Why do you think they made this choice?   [2]

8   Give an example of opportunity cost for the government.   [2]

9   Why do you think it made this choice?   [2]

10   Why is opportunity cost part of the decision-making process in these different contexts?   [2]

11   (E) Analyse why there would be no economic problem if there was no opportunity cost.   [6]

Check your progress

Read the unit objectives below and reflect on your progress in each.

- Define opportunity cost.

- Give examples of opportunity cost in different contexts.

- Explain how opportunity cost influences decision making by consumers, workers, producers and governments when allocating resources.

🔺 I struggle with this and need more practice.

🔺 I can do this reasonably well.

🔺 I can do this with confidence.

Production possibility curve diagram (PPC)

Learning objectives

By the end of this unit, you should be able to:
- define what is meant by a production possibility curve (PPC)
- draw a production possibility curve
- interpret a PPC diagram
- explain the significance of the location of production points on the diagram
- explain opportunity cost and movements along the PPC
- explain the causes and consequences of shifts in the PPC in terms of an economy's growth.

Starting point

Answer these questions in pairs:

1 If a farmer had six fields and could grow either wheat or rice in the fields, which should the farmer grow?

2 What could affect which crop the farmer chooses to grow?

Exploring

Discuss these questions in pairs:

1 A car company can manufacture two models of car in its factory. Should it manufacture only one model or should it manufacture some of both models?

2 What are your reasons for this choice?

Developing

Production possibility curve

The **production possibility curve (PPC)** shows in diagram form how much of two goods or services could be produced with a given amount of resources in a stated time period. It assumes that all the resources are used efficiently. As a diagram has only two axes, no more than two goods or services can be compared at any one time – one good or service goes on each axis. The PPC can be drawn as a curve or a straight line.

For example, a farmer has four fields and can grow only two crops on the land. If the farmer uses all the fields to grow only wheat then the output is 100 units of wheat and no rice. If the six fields are used to grow only rice and no wheat then the output is 200 units of rice.

Key term

Production possibility curve (PPC) – shows the maximum possible output for two goods or services with a given amount of resources

Alternatively, the farmer could use some fields to grow wheat and some to grow rice in order to produce both crops, as shown below:

Output (units) of wheat	100	75	50	25	0
Output (units) of rice	0	50	100	150	200

If these combinations of output for the two crops are plotted on a graph, it will look like Figure 1.4.1.

The farmer could choose to use half the fields to grow wheat and the other half to grow rice. This would produce an output of 50 units of wheat and 100 units of rice. This is point A on the PPC.

If the farmer then chose to move one field from growing wheat to growing rice, we move to point B on the PPC. This change will mean the farmer grows 25 fewer units of wheat but gains 50 units of rice. The farmer has given up growing some wheat to gain some units of rice, and this is called the opportunity cost (see Unit 1.3).

The opportunity cost for the farmer is one unit of wheat for two units of rice. The opportunity cost remains the same all the way along the PPC.

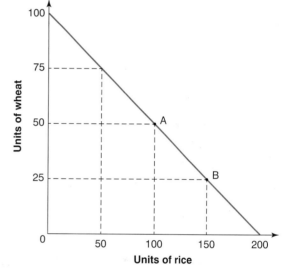

Figure 1.4.1 The PPC for a farmer with constant opportunity cost

 Why do you think that is the case? Do you think all four fields are equally suitable for growing both crops?

No! Some fields will be more suitable for growing wheat and some will be more suitable for growing rice. This may be because the soil is more suited to growing one or the other.

A new PPC curve (see Figure 1.4.2) can be drawn from the following information.

Output of wheat	100	90	75	55	30	0
Output of rice	0	60	90	120	140	150

When the fields that are better for growing wheat are changed over to growing rice they will not be as productive. Less rice will be produced from these fields than from those fields which are more suited to growing rice. There is an opportunity cost when a field is changed over to the production of another crop.

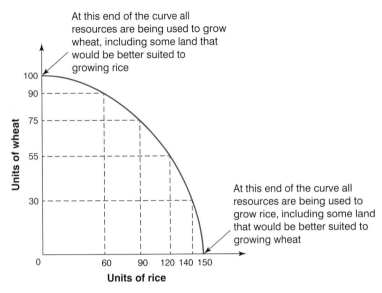

At this end of the curve all resources are being used to grow wheat, including some land that would be better suited to growing rice

At this end of the curve all resources are being used to grow rice, including some land that would be better suited to growing wheat

Units of wheat

Units of rice

Figure 1.4.2 The PPC for a farmer with opportunity cost that is not constant

2 What is the opportunity cost of wheat when one field is changed over to growing rice?

The answer can be found below:

Output of wheat (units)	100	90	75	55	30	0
Output of rice (units)	0	60	90	120	140	150
Opportunity cost of increased rice output		10 units of wheat	15 units of wheat	20 units of wheat	25 units of wheat	30 units of wheat

3 Why is the PPC in Figure 1.4.2 not a straight line?

4 What is happening to the opportunity cost of foregone wheat when more fields of rice are being grown?

It changes and it increases. This is because fields that are more suitable for growing rice will be used to grow rice first and so not much wheat is foregone at the start. But as more and more fields are changed over to growing rice then the fields that are more suitable for wheat will be changed over to growing rice, and the opportunity cost in terms of wheat will be higher. If the fields were equally suitable for both crops then the opportunity cost would stay the same and the PPC would be a straight line.

Production possibility curves for an economy

The production possibility curve can be used to show the choices made in an economy about what to produce.

The resources for the whole economy could be used entirely to produce goods for consumers to buy (for example, televisions) or entirely to produce goods for producers to buy (for example, machinery). The PPC will look the same as it does for an individual producer deciding how much of two goods to produce.

What is the opportunity cost for each capital good foregone? If the country moves from producing 120 consumer goods to 140, it will reduce production of capital goods from 80 to 70 (see Figure 1.4.3). For one capital good it gives up it will gain two consumer goods at this point on the curve. Therefore the opportunity cost of two additional consumer goods is one capital good foregone. You can also say that in this case one consumer good has an opportunity cost of 0.5 capital goods.

5 Would it be a wise decision for an economy to produce only consumer goods and no capital goods?

6 How do you think the PPC diagram could help individuals, firms or governments to make decisions?

Individuals, firms and governments can all use the PPC diagram to weigh up choices and their opportunity costs. For example, the government could decide to spend more money on healthcare if it seems better than spending more money on building new motorways. This was covered in more detail in Unit 1.3.

Location of production points on the diagram

Is production always on the PPC? No, it can be inside the curve. Look at point X in Figure 1.4.4. This position indicates that some of the resources in this economy are not being used efficiently or there are unemployed resources, such as people not working.

The PPC is assumed to represent the maximum output possible using all scarce resources available in an economy.

However, there can always be unused resources or those that are not working at their full efficiency. In fact this is probably more likely for most economies in the real world.

7 Is the economy in the photograph operating at point X or Y?

An economy could be producing at points X or Y, but could it achieve output at point Z? The answer is no! There are not enough resources in the economy to produce this level of output.

So how could this economy achieve output at point Z? It could increase the quantity and/or quality of its resources (see Unit 1.2).

Moving the PPC

To move from Y to Z on Figure 1.4.4, the economy would have to achieve economic growth. One way of achieving economic growth would be to increase production of capital goods (for example, by moving from point Y on the curve to point W). By producing more capital goods, the economy is then able to produce more consumer goods in the future, and so move to point Z.

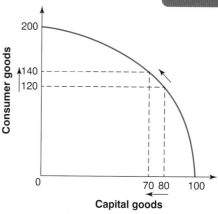

Figure 1.4.3 PPC showing the opportunity cost of consumer goods in terms of capital goods foregone for an economy

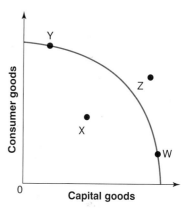

Figure 1.4.4 PPC for an economy showing obtainable and unobtainable output

The economy would now have increased its ability to produce both consumer goods and capital goods. This would mean the PPC curve will move outwards.

 8 What will move the PPC curve to the right?

Developments that could move the PPC curve to the right include:

- additions to resources, such as more available labour from immigration
- training of labour in the form of improvements to education
- improvements in technology, such as more efficient equipment.

Application task

Consumer goods

Copy the table below. In the first column, place the following movements on the PPC shown in Figure 1.4.5 against the correct explanation:

- Y to X
- Y to Z
- Z to Y
- X to Y

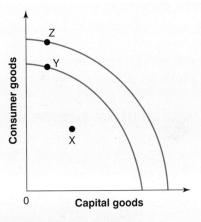

Figure 1.4.5 A shift of the PPC

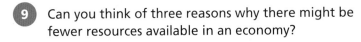

Movement on the PPC in Figure 1.4.5	Explanation of the movement
	Increase in unemployment
	Increase in workers leaving the country to work abroad
	Improvements in technology for factory machinery
	Spare capacity in factories gets used up and now factories are working at full capacity

The PPC curve can also move inwards to the left.

9 Can you think of three reasons why there might be fewer resources available in an economy?

An economy's available resources can be reduced in the face of destruction from a war or natural disaster or when labour migrates away to other countries. This reduces the economy's maximum output as it will now have fewer resources or they may be working less efficiently.

Key knowledge

Positions on the PPC

- A position on the PPC indicates all resources are being used efficiently.

- A position inside the PPC indicates there are unemployed resources or an inefficient use of resources.

- A position beyond the PPC is impossible because the economy does not have sufficient resources to produce this combination of products. For the PPC to reach this new position, there needs to be either an increase in productive potential from an increase in available resources or an increase in the efficiency with which the available resources can be used.

CASE STUDY **High rates of economic growth in China**

China has continued to enjoy high rates of economic growth for the last 30 years and is now the second largest economy in the world. It produces nearly 15% of the world's output. It exports many products all over the world.

China has the largest population in the world, with over 1.3 billion people, and it is still increasing slowly. Education is compulsory for the first nine years and many students go on to university. China now has over two thousand universities, which has been important for its economic growth, scientific progress and social development. It is also seeing high levels of investment including the construction of factories and housing in cities and towns and the development of new motorways and high-speed trains.

1 What has happened to China's PPC over the last 30 years?

2 How has China moved its PPC?

Project work

1. Research what is happening to your country's economic growth. Is economic growth increasing and if so at what rate? Are more goods and services being produced in your country?

2. Are there more people working in your country? What is happening to unemployment – is it increasing or decreasing? What can you say about the migration of workers?

3. Are firms in your country using more advanced technology in factories? Are there examples of industries that are using advanced technology such as robots?

4. Does this suggest that the PPC is shifting inwards or outwards? If so, what are the main factors making it move?

Knowledge check questions

1 What is meant by a production possibility curve? [2]

2 Draw a PPC diagram (remember to label the axes). [3]

3 Explain why the PPC curve shows opportunity cost. [4]

4 Analyse how an increase in investment can result in economic growth. Illustrate your answer with a PPC. [6]

5 (E) Analyse how a country's PPC can shift outwards. [6]

6 (E) Analyse, using a PPC diagram, how an economy suffering from unemployment will be affected by an increase in labour productivity. [6]

Check your progress

Read the unit objectives below and reflect on your progress in each.

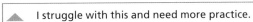 I struggle with this and need more practice.

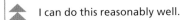 I can do this reasonably well.

 I can do this with confidence.

- Define what is meant by a production possibility curve (PPC).

- Draw a production possibility curve.

- Interpret a PPC diagram.

- Explain the significance of the location of production points on the diagram.

- Explain opportunity cost and movements along the PPC.

- Explain the causes and consequences of shifts in the PPC in terms of an economy's growth.

Chapter review

Multiple-choice questions

1 Scarcity in an economy means that:

   A all resources are finite.   **B** people must make choices.

   C people's wants are limited.   **D** there are no free goods.

2 Which is the best description of the economic problem?

   A limited wants, limited resources   **B** limited wants, unlimited resources

   C unlimited wants, limited resources   **D** unlimited wants, unlimited resources

3 Which is **not** a factor of production?

   A land   **B** machinery   **C** money   **D** workers

4 Which is an example of a free good?

   A air   **B** healthcare

   C roads   **D** waste collection

5 Which is a finite good?

   A copper   **B** fish   **C** trees   **D** water

6 Which is an opportunity cost of a person choosing to spend $30 of birthday money on a pair of shoes?

   A buying a new car   **B** spending the day with friends

   C the cost of a meal at a restaurant   **D** working an extra two hours at work

7 Which positions on the production possibility diagram on the right are attainable?

   A ABC

   B BCD

   C CDA

   D DAB

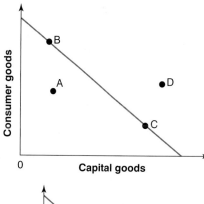

8 Which position on the production possibility diagram on the right shows that the economy is inefficient?

   A A

   B B

   C C

   D D

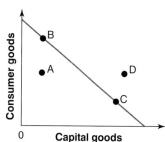

9 Which position on the production possibility diagram on the right shows where the economy is **likely** to be in the future after a period of high economic growth?

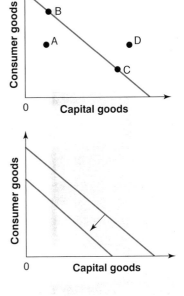

A A

B B

C C

D D

10 What could have resulted in the production possibility curve moving inwards?

A   An earthquake destroys power stations.

B   Firms borrow more money.

C   Firms invest in more training.

D   There is high immigration.

Structured questions

1   Germany's population

A record 2.14 million people moved to Germany in 2015. Around 45% were citizens of other European Union countries, 13% were from non-EU European countries, 30% were from Asia, and 5% were from Africa.

Source: 'Refugees lead to record German immigration: statistics office', Reuters, 14 July 2016

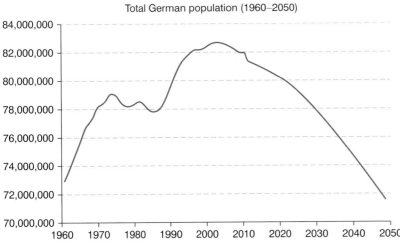

Total German population (1960–2050)

Germany's population is expected to shrink by 10 million people between 2014 and 2050 – that's more than the entire population of Sweden! The 10 million includes Germany's 4 million expected immigrants. Without immigration, Germany is expected to shrink by 14 million people by 2050. However, German industry does use a lot of machinery when producing goods and this will help output to increase to higher levels. The German government will have to consider how it spends its revenue from taxation. It has several choices to make on what to spend it on such as education and new roads. It may also consider whether to reduce taxation rather than increase government spending.

Source: Anne Roback Morse, 'Germany to shrink by 10 million people by 2050', Population Research Institute, 30 September 2014

(a)   Identify **two** factors of production mentioned in the article.   [2]

(b)   Explain **two** examples of opportunity cost for the German government.   [4]

(c)   Analyse, using a diagram, how immigration is likely to affect the PPC of Germany.   [6]

(d)   Discuss whether immigration is always beneficial for an economy.   [8]

The allocation of resources

2

In this chapter you will learn about the decisions behind what products get made, what consumers can buy and how prices are determined. You will learn to draw and interpret diagrams that show demand and supply for a market and to identify where the market price will be. You will explore how changes in demand and supply affect prices and also how much demand and supply are responsive to changes in price using the concept of price elasticity. Finally, you will consider the causes and consequences of a market failing to work correctly.

2.1 Micro economics and macro economics

2.2 The role of markets in allocating resources

2.3 Demand

2.4 Supply

2.5 Price determination

2.6 Price changes

2.7 Price elasticity of demand (PED)

2.8 Price elasticity of supply (PES)

2.9 Market economic system

2.10 Market failure

2.11 Mixed economic system

Micro economics and macro economics

Learning objectives
By the end of this unit, you should be able to:
- explain the difference between micro economics and macro economics
- identify the decision makers involved in each.

Starting point

Perform these tasks in pairs:

1 What affects the demand for cars? Discuss this with your classmate.

2 Identify four different groups of people who are affected by an increase in the production of cars.

3 In what ways will an increase in car production affect the government?

Exploring

Discuss these questions in pairs:

1 Do you think saving some of your income is a good idea?

2 How would a family benefit if everyone in the family saved a little more of their income?

3 How would retailers be affected if everyone in the economy started saving a higher proportion of their income?

Developing

Micro economics and macro economics

Economics can be divided into two main areas of study. **Micro economics** is the study of the actions of individual consumers and producers. It focuses on what happens in individual firms and the markets in which they operate. For example, an economist may study the market for cars. This will involve looking at the behaviour and decisions of firms which produce cars as well as the consumers who buy the cars.

Key term

Micro economics – the study of the economic behaviour of individuals and businesses

Other groups that influence this market will be studied, such as:

- firms which supply components to car companies

- banks that lend money to car companies or to consumers so they can buy the cars

- governments, as they make regulations and impose taxes (see Chapter 4 for more on government intervention).

Macro economics is the study of the whole economy. This includes looking at the results of each market added together and the impact on the whole economy instead of just one particular market. The study of macro economics includes, for example, the nature and causes of unemployment, economic growth, inflation, imports and exports, international trade and government economic policy.

Micro economics is the study of economics on a small scale, whereas macro economics is the study of large-scale economic issues. Micro and macro economics might seem different from one another, but the issues studied in each part often overlap. For instance, a macroeconomic study could investigate how increased economic growth might affect consumer spending, while a microeconomic study would cover its effect on the demand for cars.

Most of what you will study in Chapters 1, 2 and 3 will be concerned with microeconomic issues. Most of the issues covered in Chapters 4, 5 and 6 involve the study of macroeconomic issues.

Key term

Macro economics – the study of the whole economy

Application task

Copy the table below. Explain whether micro economics or macro economics is being studied in each example.

Include which decision makers are being affected: individuals, consumers, firms, workers, the government, or others that make sense to include. The first example is filled in for you.

Economics studies the effects of:	Micro economics or macro economics?
Bad weather affecting the rice harvest	Micro economics, as rice farmers and consumers are affected. It only affects one market and not the whole economy.
Unemployment increasing	
An increase in your parents' wages	
The government raising income tax	
The invention of a new machine to clean floors more quickly	
Rising wages for all workers across the country	
An increase in the price of cocoa	

Housing market in Singapore in 2017

In the Singapore private residential property market there has been an increase in house purchases and house prices have been rising. This is despite a slowdown in economic growth, with a wide range of companies announcing job losses. For example, Singapore Press Holdings, a media company, announced that it was planning to reduce its workforce by 10% over the next two years. The Government warned that unemployment may increase. As people lost jobs and wage increases were low, you might expect to see a reduced demand for housing; however, house sales actually increased over this period.

1 Identify which parts of the article refer to microeconomic issues.

2 Identify which parts of the article refer to macroeconomic issues.

Applying

Project work

1. Find the figure for the inflation rate in your country. Inflation measures the general increase in prices across the economy.

2. How has the inflation rate changed over the last five years?

3. Inflation is a macroeconomic issue. How will microeconomic decision makers be affected by changes in the inflation rate in your country? Think about examples of firms producing particular products and about the consumers of these products.

Knowledge check questions

1   What is meant by micro economics? [2]

2   What is meant by macro economics? [2]

3   Give **two** examples of decision makers who are involved in micro economics. [4]

4   Give **two** examples of decision makers who are involved in macro economics. [4]

5   (E) Analyse whether there is always a clear distinction between micro economics and macro economics when studying issues in economics. [6]

Check your progress

Read the unit objectives below and reflect on your progress in each.

- Explain the difference between micro economics and macro economics.
- Identify the decision makers involved in each.

 I struggle with this and need more practice.

 I can do this reasonably well.

 I can do this with confidence.

The role of markets in allocating resources

Learning objectives

By the end of this unit, you should be able to:

- explain what is meant by the market system
- describe how markets determine the allocation of resources
- describe the economic problem
- explain how the price mechanism determines the answers to the following key questions about resource allocation:
  - what goods and services to produce
  - how these goods and services should be produced
  - who should be able to purchase and consume these goods and services.

Starting point

Answer this question in pairs:

1 Identify where you can buy the following goods or services:

fruit and vegetables

currency – for example, US dollars

tickets for a sporting event or concert

a football shirt.

Discuss these questions in pairs:

1. A newspaper headline states: "The price of a popular new wooden toy to rise as demand grows more than expected." This is because consumers want more of this particular product. How would firms that produce the wooden toy respond to the increase in demand?

2. What is the likely effect on firms that supply wood to these toy manufacturers?

3. After the increase in demand for the product, what happens to workers who are employed by the toy manufacturers?

Developing

The market system

A **market** is made up of buyers and sellers. Consumers want to buy goods and services, and businesses want to sell the goods and services they have produced. The market is where buyers and sellers meet to exchange goods or services for money. Markets do not have to be in a single physical location. They can be anywhere buyers and sellers come together – at a street market, online, on the telephone or in retail shops.

In a **market economy** the **price mechanism** allocates resources. In a **planned economy**, however, the government decides how to allocate resources. The characteristics of a market economy are:

- many buyers and sellers (the market is competitive)
- buyers seeking maximum satisfaction from consuming goods and services
- sellers seeking to maximise profit
- **economic resources** mostly privately owned
- the government playing only a small role in the economy
- resources allocated via the price mechanism.

1. Look at the photograph below. What makes this a good place to sell products?

2. How are prices determined in this market?

Key terms

Market – where many buyers and many sellers come together

Market economy – also called a 'free market economy', an economy in which goods are bought and sold, and prices are determined by the free market without intervention by the government

Price mechanism – a system that enables buyers and sellers to trade with each other at an agreed price

Planned economy – an economy in which all decisions concerning production, investment, prices and incomes are determined by the government

Economic resources – land, labour, capital and enterprise

The price mechanism

The price mechanism is the key to matching buyers with sellers. If buyers want to buy a greater quantity of chocolate bars than sellers are offering for sale, what will happen to the price of chocolate bars?

3 Would you expect the price of chocolate bars to increase?

As sellers can make more money from selling chocolate bars, what might happen to the number of people who want to start selling chocolate bars?

4 If there is a greater quantity of chocolate bars offered for sale than the quantity of chocolate bars wanted by buyers, what will happen to price?

This time you would expect the price of the chocolate bar to fall.

5 Why is this?

6 What might happen to the number of sellers of chocolate bars if the amount earned from selling chocolate were to fall?

When the price that buyers are willing to pay for a certain quantity of chocolate bars is just equal to the quantity of chocolate bars sellers are willing to offer at that price, we have reached **market equilibrium**. This means that, unless something else changes, the market has stabilised at a particular price for the chocolate bar – the **equilibrium price**.

It is the role of the price mechanism to ensure that buyers and sellers of goods are at the market equilibrium. If the quantity buyers want to buy at a given price is the same quantity as sellers are offering to sell at that price, everyone is happy.

However, a market can get knocked out of equilibrium if there is a change in market conditions. This state is called **market disequilibrium**; this is where the quantity demanded and quantity supplied of a good or service are not equal.

Consider a $100 ticket for a football match at a stadium with a fixed number of seats. There will be a disequilibrium if a lot more people want to buy tickets (quantity demanded) than there are tickets available for sale (quantity supplied).

Allocation of resources

As we saw in Unit 1.1, the economic problem is that there are limited resources and unlimited wants by consumers, leading to a problem of scarcity. Therefore choices must be made about what goods to produce, how to produce the goods and who will be able to consume the goods that are produced.

Economic resources, or the factors of production – land, labour, capital and enterprise (see Unit 1.2), are used to produce the

Key terms

Market equilibrium – where the quantity demanded by consumers and the quantity supplied by producers are equal

Equilibrium price – the price at which the quantity that buyers want to buy is equal to the quantity that sellers are prepared to sell

Market disequilibrium – where the quantity demanded by consumers and the quantity supplied by producers are not equal

Allocation of resources – the way resources are allocated to the production of the goods and services most wanted by consumers

goods and services bought by consumers. But how are these scarce resources allocated? The answer is the price mechanism in a market economy.

Land	Labour	Capital	Enterprise

There are three key questions that are answered by the price mechanism when allocating scarce economic resources. They are:

- *what* goods or services to produce?
- *how* to produce the goods or services (which method of production to use)?
- *who* consumes the goods or services produced?

How does the price mechanism answer these key questions in a market economy?

What to produce

Businesses produce the goods or services that earn them the highest profit. If consumers want more of a product, they are often willing to pay higher prices. This increases the profit made from selling these goods and so firms produce more of these goods or services (Unit 3.7 covers firm's profits and costs in more detail).

Firms that produce goods or services that are not wanted as much by consumers will see prices fall and so profit decreases and firms produce fewer of these goods or services.

How to produce

When firms are competing they need to find ways to produce goods or services at the lowest cost per unit so that their prices will remain competitive. If a firm does not keep the unit cost low by using the most efficient methods of production then competitors will take their customers. The price mechanism helps to make sure that firms use the most efficient ways of making products. By keeping down unit costs, they are more able to maintain competitive prices.

Who consumes the goods and services

Successful businesses that experience increased levels of demand can afford to pay their workers higher wages, and their owners (entrepreneurs) can earn higher profits. Less successful businesses experiencing falling demand for their goods or services will pay lower wages, and the owners will earn lower profits.

If the demand for mobile phones increases, for example, then production should increase, which means more workers are needed to make the phones. What will happen to the wages paid to these workers? Their wages will increase and they can now buy more goods and services.

7 If demand for DVDs falls and then production of DVDs falls, what will happen to employment levels and wages for the workers who produce them?

Fewer workers will be required and so employment and wages will fall. As a result, the workers will be unable to buy as many goods and services as before. In this way the price mechanism determines who is able to consume more or less of the goods and services produced.

CASE STUDY | ## Silver is losing its shine!

The demand for silver to use in photography has fallen as most of the industry has switched from using printed photography to using digital photographs. The demand for silver jewellery has also fallen, particularly in China as higher incomes have led to increased demand for other luxury items such as designer goods and travel. This has led to a fall in the demand for silver ore.

1 Why has demand for silver ore been falling?

2 Why do you think demand for silver jewellery has fallen?

3 What do you think will happen to the number of employees and their wages at businesses that make silver jewellery?

4 What do you think will happen to factories that make silver jewellery?

5 Which products are consumers buying instead of silver jewellery?

Project work

Use the internet to support your work:

1. Find an example of a firm that has recently seen a fall in the quantity of products that it sells. Offer an explanation for this decrease. Is it related to the demand for its products, for example, or is the firm not competitive on price any more?

2. Find an example of a firm that has recently seen an increase in the quantity of products that it sells. Offer an explanation for this increase. Is it related to the demand for its products, for example, or has the firm become more competitive on price?

3. Find out what has happened to the quantity of goods or services sold, the number of employees, and the number of factories or retail outlets for the firms in questions 1 and 2.

4. Present your findings as a written report that explains why some firms have seen a fall in the quantity of products that they sell and why some firms have seen an increase.

Knowledge check questions

1 What is meant by a market? [2]

2 What are the **three** key questions in determining the allocation of resources? [3]

3 Explain how the price mechanism moves resources towards making products that experience increasing demand and away from making products that experience falling demand. [4]

4 (E) Analyse how the price mechanism rewards professional sportspeople more than it rewards street cleaners. [6]

Check your progress

Read the unit objectives below and reflect on your progress in each.

- I struggle with this and need more practice.

- I can do this reasonably well.

- I can do this with confidence.

- Explain what is meant by the market system.

- Describe how markets determine the allocation of resources.

- Describe the economic problem.

- Explain how the price mechanism determines the answers to the following key questions about resource allocation:

  – what goods and services to produce

  – how these goods and services should be produced

  – who should be able to purchase and consume these goods and services.

Demand

Learning objectives

By the end of this unit, you should be able to:

- define demand
- draw a demand curve and illustrate movements along the curve
- understand the link between an individual's demand and market demand
- explain what causes a shift in the demand curve and show this on a diagram.

Starting point

Complete these tasks in pairs:

1 Write a wish list of 10 things you would like to have.

2 Consider whether you will be able to have all 10 items in the future.

3 If not, then explain why not.

Exploring

Discuss these questions in pairs:

1 The photo shows a busy fruit and vegetable market. Can you think of possible reasons why people might buy more or less of particular fruits or vegetables?

2 What might happen to the quantity of meat people buy if the price of fish increases?

3 What might happen to the amount of vegetables people buy if their incomes increase?

Developing

The demand for goods and services

Demand is not the same as the desire or need for a product. Why might just wanting something not have any effect on the market for that product? Consumers must have the ability to pay for the product as well as wanting or needing it for this to qualify as demand. This is why economists are interested in **effective demand**, which means wanting to buy a product but also having an ability to pay for the product. Demand does not cover something a consumer wants but is too expensive for them to buy.

Demand refers to the quantity of a good or service that consumers are willing and able to buy at given prices in a particular time period.

Key terms

Demand – the quantity of a good or service that consumers are willing and able to buy at given prices in a particular time period

Effective demand – consumers' desire to buy a good, backed up by the ability to pay

The law of demand and the shape of the demand curve

Economists have studied markets and found that, for most products, as the price increases fewer items will be demanded, and as the price decreases then more products will be demanded. It is possible to study how a single individual reacts to price changes.

 1 Why does an individual buy fewer items when the price increases or more items when the price falls?

An individual's demand information can be shown in a **demand schedule**. This is a table that gives the quantities demanded at a range of prices. The table below shows an individual's demand schedule for chocolate bars:

Demand schedule (individual)

Price of chocolate bars ($ per unit)	Quantity demanded per week (units)
5	3
4	5
3	8
2	10
1	12

Key term

Demand schedule – a table that gives the quantities demanded at a range of prices

This demand schedule shows that the lower the price the more chocolate bars the individual will buy each week.

When the demand of each individual is added together then the market demand for a product can be determined.

For example, an individual buys 1 kg of sweet potatoes a week. Adding together each individual's demand for sweet potatoes each week at the current price gives the market demand for sweet potatoes each week. Perhaps this is 2000 kg of sweet potatoes.

This market information can also be shown in a demand schedule. The table below gives the quantities demanded for sweet potatoes each week at a range of prices.

Demand schedule (market)

Price of sweet potatoes ($ per kg)	Quantity demanded per week (kg)
5	1000
4	1500
3	2000
2	2500
1	3000

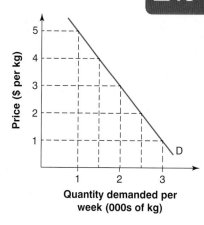

Figure 2.3.1 Market demand curve for sweet potatoes

The **law of demand** means that as the price of a good or service falls, the quantity demanded increases. This relationship between the price and the quantity demanded for a product is shown in the demand schedules for chocolate bars and sweet potatoes.

The **demand curve** plots the information in the demand schedule on a graph with the price on the vertical axis and the quantity demanded on the horizontal axis. This is shown in Figure 2.3.1 using the data on the market for sweet potatoes above.

In analysing the effect of a change in price on quantity demanded, it is usually assumed that all other possible factors affecting demand do not change. For example, the weather can affect the sales of ice cream. On a very hot day people want to buy more ice cream even if the price is the same. For the purpose of our analysis, such factors that can affect the position of the demand curve are assumed to stay the same. Economists refer to this as *ceteris paribus*, which means all other things remain the same.

It is only *price* that is being considered when the demand curve is drawn and not any other factors that could affect demand.

A fall in price leading to an increase in quantity demanded is known as an **extension in demand**. On Figure 2.3.2 this is shown as a fall in price from 80 cents to 60 cents for a can of cola, which leads to an extension in demand from 300 to 500 cans per week (a movement along the demand curve from point A to point B).

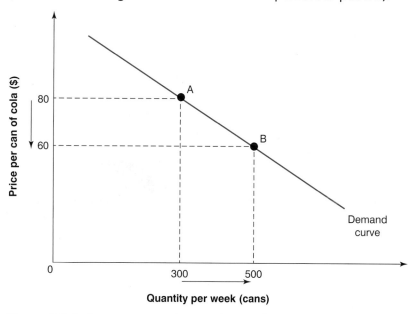

Figure 2.3.2 A movement along a demand curve – an extension in demand

An increase in price resulting in a fall in quantity demanded is known as a **contraction in demand**. On Figure 2.3.3 this is shown as a price increase from P to P_1, which leads to a contraction in demand from Q to Q_1 (a movement along the demand curve from point X to point Y). The labels 'P' and 'Q' are often used on demand diagrams, rather than actual prices and quantities.

Key terms

Law of demand – as the price of a good or service falls, the quantity demanded increases, and vice versa

Demand curve – a graph plotting the quantities of a product demanded at a range of prices

Ceteris paribus – all other things remaining the same

Extension in demand – an increase in quantity demanded as a result of a fall in price

Contraction in demand – a decrease in quantity demanded as a result of a rise in price

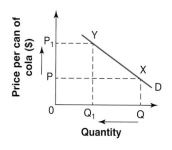

Figure 2.3.3 A movement along a demand curve – a contraction in demand

Application tasks

The market for coffee

Coffee is a product consumed widely around the world. Demand for coffee is influenced by price and also other factors known as the conditions of demand.

1 Using graph paper, construct a demand curve diagram to show the following information about the world demand for coffee:

Price of coffee ($ per kg)	Quantity of coffee demanded per week (kg)
18	150 000
15	200 000
12	250 000
9	300 000
6	350 000
3	400 000

2 What does your diagram show? Explain to your classmates the relationship between the price of coffee and the quantity of coffee demanded.

Shifts of the demand curve

Be careful not to confuse a movement along a demand curve with a shift of the demand curve itself. The only variable that leads to a movement along a given demand curve is a change in the price of that good or service.

Figure 2.3.4 shows a movement along a demand curve from X to Y and Figure 2.3.5 shows a movement or shift of the whole curve from D to D_1.

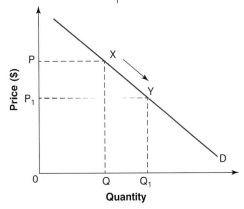

Figure 2.3.4 A movement along a demand curve – an extension in demand

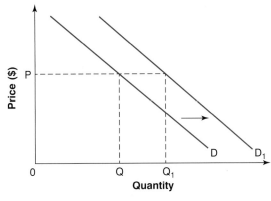

Figure 2.3.5 An increase in demand

Factors that lead to a shift in the position of the demand curve are referred to as the **conditions of demand**. These are non-price factors, which are any factors that affect demand for a good or service that do not include changes in the price itself.

These non-price factors include the following:

- **Real disposable incomes:** in other words, changes in the incomes of individuals after the effects of inflation and taxation have been taken into account. If incomes rise then consumers will have more money and may increase their demand for goods and services.

- **Tastes and preferences (trends and fashion):** the popularity of goods and services is often influenced by changes in society's preferences and may be influenced by the media, advertising and technological change. If a good or service goes out of fashion then its demand will fall.

- **Population:** the size, age and gender composition of the population will affect the market for many products. If more babies are born then there is likely to be an increase in the demand for baby food, for example.

- **Prices of substitute goods:** substitute goods are those that may be seen as close alternatives to a particular product or service. If the price of cola increases then the demand for lemonade is likely to increase. The better or closer the **substitute**, the greater the effect on demand.

- **Prices of complementary goods:** complementary goods are those in joint demand, which is to say that they are consumed together and therefore demanded together (for example, cars and petrol). If the price of a complementary good increases then the quantity demanded will decrease, and the demand for its complementary good will also decrease – smaller quantities of both goods are now consumed.

Key term

Conditions of demand – factors other than the price of the good or service that lead to a change in position of the demand curve

Key concept

A change in price will result in an extension or contraction in demand but a change in any of the non-price factors that affect demand will shift the whole demand curve.

Key terms

Substitute good – a good that is consumed as an alternative to another good

Complementary good – a good that is consumed together with another good

Conditions of demand

Factor	Example and effect
Real disposable income	If income tax falls, it leads to more money available to spend, which is likely to result in an increase in demand for most goods, such as cars.
Tastes and preferences (trends and fashion)	Increased advertising for a particular brand of mobile phone is likely to lead to an increase in demand for it.
Population	An increased population is likely to lead to an increase in demand for most goods.
Prices of substitute products	A fall in the price of tea may lead to a decrease in the demand for coffee.
Prices of complementary products	An increase in the price of coffee may lead to reduced demand for milk.

1 Give your own example for each of the conditions of demand listed in the table.

If any of these factors change then the demand curve for the good or service will change. This leads to either a rightward shift or a leftward shift of the demand curve, as shown in Figure 2.3.6.

A rightward shift from D to D₁ illustrates an **increase in demand**, whereas a leftward shift from D to D₂ illustrates a **decrease in demand**. A rightward shift means that a greater quantity of a good or service is demanded at any given price, whereas a leftward shift means that a lower quantity of a good or service is demanded at any given price.

Key terms
....
Increase in demand – a rightward shift in the demand curve showing that a greater quantity is demanded at each price than was previously

Decrease in demand – a leftward shift in the demand curve showing that a smaller quantity is demanded at each price than was previously

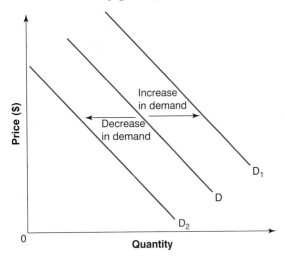

Figure 2.3.6 Shifts of the demand curve

Application task

Copy the table below. For each of the changes listed, put a tick in the box to show whether the change will lead to an extension or a contraction in demand (a movement along the demand curve) or an increase or a decrease in demand (a movement of the whole curve). You should only tick *one* of the four options.

Change	Extension in demand	Contraction in demand	Increase in demand	Decrease in demand
Price of oranges increases				
Orange juice drinks become more popular				
A popular new film has been released – how will the cinema market be affected?				
Price of jeans decreases				
How does a decrease in income tax affect the demand for holidays?				
There is an increase in the number of babies born. How is the demand for nappies affected?				

CASE STUDY

Coffee drinking becomes more fashionable

Over the last 10 years it has become much more fashionable for people to drink coffee. Major multinational coffee houses such as Starbucks and The Coffee Bean have expanded their ranges of drinks, made their cafés very pleasant places to sit and relax, and have provided free internet and mobile phone charging facilities. These trends have led to an increase in the demand for coffee on the world market at every given price.

Price of coffee ($ per kg)	Original quantity of coffee demanded per week (kg)	New quantity of coffee demanded per week (kg)
18	150 000	300 000
15	200 000	350 000
12	250 000	400 000
9	300 000	450 000
6	350 000	500 000
3	400 000	550 000

1 Go back to the demand curve you drew in the first application task in this unit. Now draw a new demand curve on your previous graph, based on this information.

2 Using the case study, explain three factors that may have led to an increase in the demand for coffee.

3 Explain how this change in demand for coffee might affect demand for substitutes such as tea or hot chocolate.

Applying

Project work

Using the internet, research prices for airline flights from your home country to four other countries. Find out if the prices change with the time of year that you might want to fly. Check if the prices are different during school holidays. Try to explain any changes you find.

Write a one-page report to your head teacher on why the prices of airline flights vary at different times of the year. Recommend when the school should take an overseas school trip if it wants to keep the cost of the trip low.

Knowledge check questions

1 What is meant by effective demand? [2]

2 Draw a diagram to show an extension and a contraction in demand. [3]

3 Explain **two** factors that may lead to an increase in demand. [4]

4 Illustrate, using a diagram, the difference between a movement along a demand curve and a shift in the demand curve. Explain what causes each of these two changes in demand. [6]

5 (E) Analyse how an increase in the price of ice cream will cause a contraction in demand, whereas an increase in the demand for ice cream will cause the whole demand curve to shift. [6]

Check your progress

Read the unit objectives below and reflect on your progress in each.

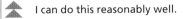 I struggle with this and need more practice.

I can do this reasonably well.

I can do this with confidence.

- Define demand.

- Draw a demand curve and illustrate movements along the curve.

- Understand the link between an individual's demand and market demand.

- Explain what causes a shift in the demand curve and show this on a diagram.

Supply

Learning objectives

By the end of this unit, you should be able to:

• define supply
• draw a supply curve and illustrate movements along the curve
• understand the link between an individual's supply and market supply
• explain what causes a shift in the supply curve and show this on a diagram.

Starting point

Answer these questions in pairs:

1 If your school is going to hold a charity event, which products would you sell to raise money for your chosen cause?

2 Why did you choose these products and reject others?

Exploring

Discuss these questions in pairs:

1 Why might a firm want to sell a particular product rather than alternatives?

2 Why might a farmer want to increase the quantity of some crops and reduce the quantity of other crops?

Developing

The supply of goods and services

In a market economy, firms (otherwise known as producers) combine the factors of production to produce goods and services. **Supply** refers to the quantity of a good or service that producers are willing and able to supply to a market at a given price. If the price is higher, will producers want to supply more or less to the market? Generally, the higher the price of a good or service in a market the more suppliers are willing and able to supply to the market.

Why do firms supply more goods or services to a market if the price rises? This is because at higher prices firms can earn higher profits, so there is an incentive to supply more of the good or service to the market. The higher price will allow firms that have higher costs to be able to enter the market. These firms will be able to make a profit even though they have higher costs than the firms that are already in the market.

Key term

Supply – the quantity of a good or service that producers are willing and able to supply at a given price in a particular time period

1 Why is wanting to supply a good or service to a market not the same as supply?

The law of supply and the shape of the supply curve

The supply from each individual firm in a particular market is added together to determine the market **supply curve** for a product. For example, if each firm in a market is willing and able to supply 1000 cans of cola each week at current prices, and if there are 100 firms supplying cola to the market, then the market supply at the current price will be 100 000 cans per week.

The individual and market supply can be shown on a **supply schedule**.

Supply schedule

Price ($ per unit)	Quantity supplied per week (units)
5	3000
4	2500
3	2000
2	1500
1	1000

The **law of supply** means that as the price of a good or service falls, the quantity supplied decreases, and vice versa. This relationship between the price and quantity supplied of a good or service is shown in Figure 2.4.1. In analysing the effect of a change in price on quantity supplied, it is usually assumed that all other possible effects on supply do not change. You may remember from Unit 2.3 that this is known as *ceteris paribus*.

The supply curve is drawn from information in a supply schedule.

An increase in price that leads to an increase in the quantity supplied is known as an **extension in supply**.

Key terms

Supply curve – a diagram showing the quantities of a product supplied at a range of prices

Supply schedule – a table that gives the quantities supplied at a range of prices

Law of supply – as the price of a good or service falls, the quantity supplied decreases, and vice versa

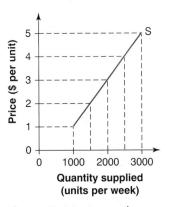

Figure 2.4.1 A supply curve

Key terms

Extension in supply – an increase in the quantity supplied in response to an increase in price

Contraction in supply – a decrease in the quantity supplied in response to a decrease in price

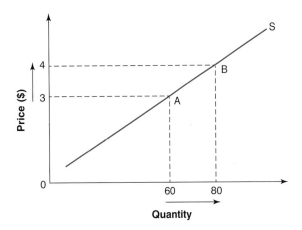

Figure 2.4.2 A movement along a supply curve – an extension in supply

On Figure 2.4.2 an increase in price from $3 to $4 results in an increase in quantity supplied from 60 to 80. An extension in supply is shown as a movement along the supply curve from point A to point B as a result of the change in price.

In Figure 2.4.3 a fall in price from P to P_1 results in a decrease in quantity supplied from Q to Q_1. The quantity supplied contracts from Q to Q_1 and is referred to as a **contraction in supply**. This is a movement along the supply curve from point X to point Y as a result of the change in price.

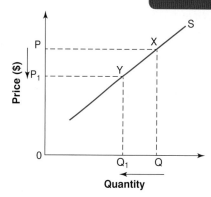

Figure 2.4.3 A movement along a supply curve – a contraction in supply

Application tasks

The market for coffee

Coffee is a product supplied from many different countries around the world. The supply of coffee beans is influenced by price and other factors known as the conditions of supply.

1 Using graph paper, construct a supply curve diagram to show the following information about the world supply of coffee beans:

Price of coffee ($ per kg)	Quantity of coffee beans supplied per week (kg)
18	400 000
15	350 000
12	250 000
9	200 000
6	150 000
3	100 000

2 What does your diagram show? Explain to your classmates the relationship between the price of coffee and the quantity of coffee supplied.

Shifts of the supply curve

Be careful not to confuse movement along a supply curve with a shift of the whole supply curve. The only variable that leads to a movement along a given supply curve is a change in price of that good or service. Any change that makes it more expensive for the firm to supply each good or service to the market will decrease supply. Any change that makes it cheaper for the firm to supply each good or service to the market will increase supply.

Figure 2.4.4 shows movement along the supply curve from X to Y and Figure 2.4.5 shows a movement of the whole curve from S to S_1.

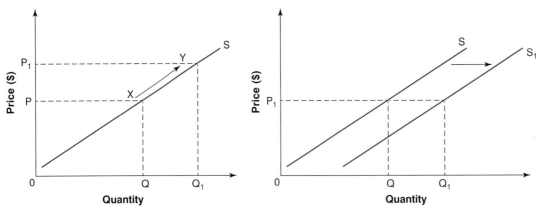

Figure 2.4.4 A movement along a supply curve – an extension in supply

Figure 2.4.5 An increase in supply

Factors that may lead to a shift in the position of the supply curve are referred to as the **conditions of supply**. These are non-price factors, which are any factors that affect the supply of a good or service that do not include changes in the price itself.

If any of these factors change, then the supply curve of the good or service in question will change. This leads to either a rightward shift or a leftward shift of the supply curve, as shown in Figure 2.4.6.

 If supply decreases, does the supply curve shift to the left or to the right?

A rightward shift from S to S_1 illustrates an **increase in supply**, whereas a leftward shift from S to S_2 illustrates a **decrease in supply**. A rightward shift means that a greater quantity of a good or service is supplied at any given price, whereas a leftward shift means that a lower quantity of a good or service is supplied at any given price.

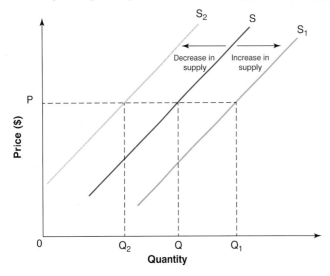

Figure 2.4.6 Shifts of the supply curve

Key concepts

A change in price will result in an extension or contraction in supply. However, a change in any of the non-price factors that affect supply will move the whole supply curve.

Key terms

Conditions of supply – factors other than the price of the good or service that lead to a change in position of the supply curve

Increase in supply – a rightward shift in the supply curve showing that a greater quantity is supplied at each price than was previously

Decrease in supply – a leftward shift in the supply curve showing that a smaller quantity is supplied at each price than was previously

Non-price factors that affect the cost of producing a good or service include the following:

- **Change in the cost of factors of production:** if there are changes in the cost of producing a product, such as an increase in wages, then supply will decrease (the supply curve will shift to the left). This is because it will now cost more to supply the good at any given price.

- **Improvements in technology:** if there are improvements in technology that result in more output with the same factors of production, then supply will increase (the supply curve will shift to the right). This is because the firm can now supply more goods at any given price.

- **Imposition of an indirect tax or subsidy:** an **indirect tax**, such as VAT, will increase the cost of supplying the good to the market and will cause supply to decrease. It has the same effect as an increase in the costs of the factors of production. A subsidy (see Unit 2.11) has the opposite effect as it reduces the cost of supplying the good to the market and therefore increases supply.

- **Weather conditions:** agricultural products are often affected by good or bad weather which may affect the harvest or output of a crop. If the weather is favourable then supply is likely to increase, and if the weather is unfavourable then supply is likely to decrease.

- **Changes in the prices of other products:** a firm may have the choice of producing two different products. If the price of one of the products increases, the firm may find it more profitable to increase production. This will mean the firm has to reduce the production and supply of the alternative product.

- **A change in the number of suppliers to the market:** if more firms decide to enter the market and start supplying a particular good or service, supply will increase. This does not usually happen in the short term. The time taken to enter a market will vary a lot depending on the type of product being produced. For example, it will not take long to set up a shop selling fruit and vegetables but it will take a lot longer to set up a factory making motorbikes.

Key term

Indirect tax – a tax on expenditure, such as sales tax or VAT

3 Give three more examples of factors that would affect the cost of producing a good or service.

Conditions of supply

Factor	Example and effect
Change in the cost of factors of production	An increase in wages, interest rates, and the prices of raw materials, power or rent leads to higher costs of production, so supply will decrease.
Improvements in technology	Improvements in the technology used on a production line will increase efficiency and lower the unit cost of production, leading to an increase in supply. The improvements could include: more technologically advanced machinery; improvements in the organisation of the factory and management techniques, leading to increased efficiency; improved communications; any changes that lead to increased efficiency that lower the costs of producing each unit.
Imposition of an indirect tax or subsidy	An increase in indirect taxes will lead to a decrease in supply. A subsidy will lead to an increase in supply.
Weather conditions	Good weather conditions are likely to lead to a good harvest causing the supply of agricultural products to increase.
Changes in the prices of other products	Take, for example, a farmer who produces wheat and barley. If the price of wheat increases, the farmer will grow more wheat and plant fewer fields of barley, leading to a decrease in supply of barley.
A change in the number of suppliers to the market	If farmers decide to start supplying more coffee, for example, then there will be an increase in the supply of coffee to the market and the supply curve will shift to the right.

Application task

Copy the table below. For each of the changes listed in the table put a tick in the box to show whether the change will lead to a contraction or an extension in supply (a movement along the supply curve) or an increase or a decrease in supply (a movement of the whole curve). You should only tick *one* of the four options.

Change	Extension in supply	Contraction in supply	Increase in supply	Decrease in supply
Price of tea increases				
Wages of tea pickers increase				
More efficient machinery developed to process tea leaves				
Very hot weather causes a poor harvest				
Government increases a subsidy on tea				
An increase in the number of growers harvesting tea				

CASE STUDY | ## The global supply of sugar in 2017

Sugar production in Mauritius is expected to fall by 7% in 2017 due to poor rainfall between October 2016 and January 2017. However, Russia is expected to experience an increase in sugar output due to good weather conditions. The Indonesian government has introduced new incentives to boost sugar production, and Brazil, the largest producer of sugar in the world, is predicted to have a record harvest.

1 Draw a diagram to show the change you expect to see in the world supply of sugar in 2017.

2 Explain the changes you have shown on the diagram.

Applying

Project work

Use the internet to research:

- which countries produce oil
- what factors affect the world supply of oil
- what has happened to the world supply of oil over the last five years.

Give reasons for the changes in supply.

Produce a one-page newspaper article titled "Changes in the world supply of oil".

Knowledge check questions

1 What is meant by supply? [2]

2 Draw a diagram to show an extension and a contraction in supply. [3]

3 Explain **two** conditions that may lead to an increase in supply. [4]

4 Explain **one** condition that may lead to a decrease in supply and show this on a diagram. [4]

5 (C) Analyse how an increase in the price of mobile phones will lead to an extension in supply, whereas an improvement in technology used to manufacture mobile phones will cause the whole supply curve to shift. [6]

Check your progress

Read the unit objectives below and reflect on your progress in each.

- Define supply.

- Draw a supply curve and illustrate movements along the curve.

- Understand the link between an individual's supply and market supply.

- Explain what causes a shift in the supply curve and show this on a diagram.

▲	I struggle with this and need more practice.
▲	I can do this reasonably well.
▲	I can do this with confidence.

Price determination

Learning objectives

By the end of this unit, you should be able to:

- define what is meant by market equilibrium
- draw demand and supply schedules and curves and identify the equilibrium price and sales in a market
- draw demand and supply schedules and curves to identify disequilibrium prices, shortages and surpluses in a market.

Starting point

Answer this question in pairs:

1   Have you or your family ever sold any products that you had already used? If so, how did you decide what price to charge?

Exploring

Discuss these questions in pairs:

1   How do sellers of fruit and vegetables in a street market decide the prices to charge for their products?

2   What might happen if a trader charges a higher price than all the other sellers in the street market?

3   What might happen if a trader sells at a lower price than all the other sellers in the street market?

Developing

Equilibrium

In a free market where there is no government control over prices, what determines the price of goods or services? The price of goods or services will be determined by demand and supply. If you put the demand curve and the supply curve on the same diagram then they usually cross at some point, which is the market equilibrium (see Unit 2.2). This is shown in Figure 2.5.1.

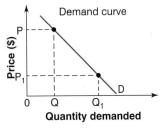
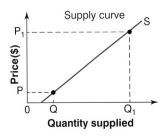
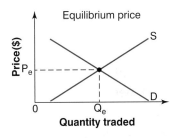

Figure 2.5.1   A demand and supply curve put together to determine the equilibrium price

The equilibrium price is where the quantity demanded and the quantity supplied are equal. The quantity of a good or service that consumers are willing and able to buy equals the quantity of that good or service that producers are willing and able to sell. This is called an equilibrium because at this point there is nothing causing the price to change, as long as all the other conditions of demand and supply (non-price factors) stay the same.

Figure 2.5.2 shows where the demand curve and the supply curve cross, and that the equilibrium price is at P. Where the curves cross is the point at which the quantity demanded equals the quantity supplied. The equilibrium quantity traded (sales) is Q units.

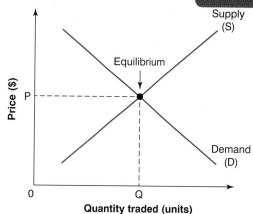

Figure 2.5.2 Equilibrium price and quantity where quantity demanded = quantity supplied

Key knowledge

The equilibrium price is where quantity demanded equals quantity supplied. If there is excess demand then the price should increase, and if there is excess supply then price should fall, until the price is at the equilibrium price.

Application tasks

The market for coffee

Coffee is a product consumed widely around the world. The demand for it and its supply are influenced by price and also other factors known as the conditions of demand and supply. The actual price set in the market for coffee is determined by demand and supply.

1 Copy the demand and supply schedule below. Complete the schedule using the information in the demand schedule for coffee in Unit 2.3 and the supply schedule for coffee in Unit 2.4.

Price of coffee ($ per kg)	Quantity of coffee demanded per week (kg)	Quantity of coffee supplied per week (kg)
18		
15		
12		
9		
6		
3		

2 Using graph paper, construct a demand and supply diagram to show the information in the demand and supply schedule about the market for coffee.

3 What does your diagram show? Explain to your classmates the relationship between the price of coffee and the quantity of coffee demanded and supplied.

4 If the price is $18 per kilogram, how much is demanded and supplied? Do you think the price will stay at $18? If not, why will the price change?

5 If the price is $6 per kilogram, how much is demanded and supplied? What do you think will happen to the price? Why will the price change?

Disequilibrium

Figure 2.5.3 shows that if the price is above $60 there will be a **surplus** of the product on the market because quantity supplied is greater than quantity demanded. If the price is below $60 then there will be a **shortage** of the product because quantity demanded will be greater than quantity supplied. These are both examples of a market disequilibrium (see Unit 2.2).

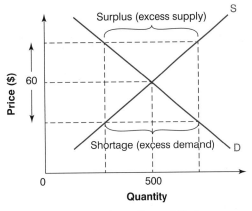

Figure 2.5.3 Market disequilibrium

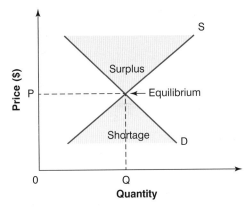

Figure 2.5.4 Surplus and shortage

Figure 2.5.4 shows that at prices above the equilibrium price, P, there will be a surplus of the product and at prices below the equilibrium price there will be a shortage.

1 How will the price mechanism eliminate a surplus or a shortage?

This is not a stable position in the market and there will be forces to move the price so that the market is no longer in disequilibrium. For example, if producers cannot sell everything they have for sale because the price is too high, they will reduce the price to try to clear the excess supply of unsold products. As producers lower their prices, consumers will want to buy more of the product. The effects of both suppliers lowering prices and consumers buying more at the lower prices will bring the market back to equilibrium.

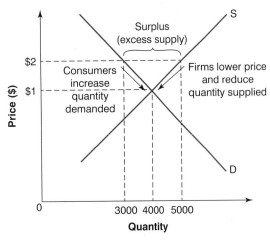

Figure 2.5.5 Adjustment towards equilibrium as a result of a surplus (excess supply) in the market for bananas

Figure 2.5.5 shows what happens when the price of bananas is too high relative to demand. The result is a **surplus (or excess supply)** of 2000 bananas at a price of $2. The price of a bunch of bananas will therefore fall from $2 to $1 as farmers lower price to clear their surplus stock. As price falls there will be a lower quantity supplied as farmers provide fewer bananas to the market. Quantity supplied falls from 5000 per week to 4000 per week. As the price falls, a higher quantity will be demanded by consumers as bananas are now cheaper. The quantity demanded will increase from 3000 per week to 4000 per week.

The result is an equilibrium of 4000 bananas bought and sold at $1.

Figure 2.5.6 shows what happens to the price, P, when there is a **shortage (or excess demand)**. The price will rise from P to P_e and as it rises there will be a higher quantity supplied, from Q to Q_e, and a lower quantity demanded, from Q_1 to Q_e.

This will happen until quantity demanded equals quantity supplied at the equilibrium price P_e and the equilibrium quantity bought and sold will be Q_e.

Key terms

Surplus (or **excess supply**) – quantity supplied is greater than quantity demanded at a given price

Shortage (or **excess demand**) – quantity demanded is greater than quantity supplied at a given price

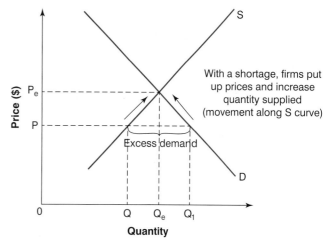

With a shortage, firms put up prices and increase quantity supplied (movement along S curve)

Figure 2.5.6 Adjustment towards equilibrium as a result of a shortage (excess demand) in a market

---

CASE STUDY **Food price controls in India, China and Venezuela**

India, China and Venezuela have tried different ways of controlling increases in the prices of basic food. This is in an effort to keep food affordable to people on low incomes. Putting a maximum price on basic foods will mean there is a disequilibrium in the market.

Street sellers in Venezuela sell basic products such as milk, toilet paper, coffee and soap for much higher prices than the maximum price set by the government. People have to queue to buy basic food and other products from supermarkets or pay high prices from the street sellers.

The government's 'fair' prices were set to help the poor, but in many supermarkets the basic products are not available and the shelves are empty. Supermarkets cannot afford to import these products and sell them at the price set by the government because it is not profitable.

1 Draw a supply and demand diagram to show what happens when prices are controlled and they are stopped from moving to the equilibrium price.

2 How are consumers and producers in this market likely to react to this disequilibrium?

Project work

Research what happens when tickets for popular sporting events are offered for sale.

1. Why is this evidence that the market is in disequilibrium?

2. Why can't the market equilibrium be achieved?

Share your findings with the rest of the class.

3. (E) Some people who have bought tickets then re-sell them to people who could not buy tickets. These tickets often sell for very high prices. Why is this?

Knowledge check questions

1   What is meant by equilibrium price?   [2]

2   Draw a diagram to show how the equilibrium price and sales are determined.   [3]

3   Draw a demand and supply diagram to show a shortage of a particular good in the market.   [3]

4   (E) Discuss whether government intervention can reduce disequilibrium.   [8]

Check your progress

Read the unit objectives below and reflect on your progress in each.

- Define what is meant by market equilibrium.

- Draw demand and supply schedules and curves and identify the equilibrium price and sales in a market.

- Draw demand and supply schedules and curves to identify disequilibrium prices, shortages and surpluses in a market.

 I struggle with this and need more practice.

 I can do this reasonably well.

 I can do this with confidence.

Price changes

Learning objectives

By the end of this unit, you should be able to:

- explain what causes the equilibrium price to change
- draw demand and supply diagrams to illustrate these changes in market conditions
- analyse the consequences of these changes in market conditions for the equilibrium price and sales.

Starting point

Answer these questions in pairs:

1 List three products which have prices that regularly change.

2 What do you think causes these price changes?

Exploring

Discuss these questions in pairs:

1 Why is the price of tickets for popular sporting events higher than the price for less popular events?

2 The prices charged by hotels in holiday resorts are usually lower during term time and higher when schools are closed. Why is this?

3 What happens to the price of mangoes when there has been good weather for growing them?

4 What would happen to the price of mangoes if there was a press report that stated eating mangoes improves your health?

Developing

The effects of changes in demand

The conditions of demand were explained in Unit 2.3. If one of these conditions changes, such as an increase in income resulting in the demand curve shifting to the right, this leads to a change in price.

The effects of an *increase* in demand, assuming nothing else changes, are that the price will rise and as a result there will be an extension in supply. The four steps in this process are shown in Worked example 1.

Worked example 1

The original equilibrium price for a 1 kg bag of apples is $2.00 (P) with 80 000 kg per day bought and sold (QS = QD).

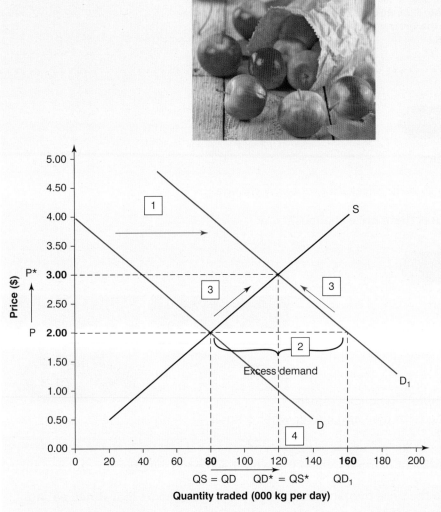

Figure 2.6.1 The adjustment of equilibrium price after an increase in demand

1 First, there is an increase in demand from D to D_1, possibly because the income of consumers has increased. This means the demand curve has shifted to the right.

2 Second, this leads to an excess demand for apples of 80 000 kg – the difference between 160 000 kg (QD_1) and 80 000 kg (QS) at the price of $2.00 per kilogram (P).

3 Third, the price rises, and as the price rises the quantity demanded for apples falls from 160 000 kg (QD_1) to 120 000 kg (QD*) and the quantity supplied increases from 80 000 kg (QS) to 120 000 kg apples (QS*) per day.

4 Finally, the new equilibrium price for apples will be $3.00 per kilogram (P*) and the new equilibrium quantity traded will be 120 000 kg of apples per day.

The original equilibrium quantity was at QS = QD and the new equilibrium is at QD* = QS*.

The effects of a *decrease* in demand, assuming nothing else changes, will cause the price to fall, and as a result there will be a contraction in supply. The four steps in this process are shown in Worked example 2.

Worked example 2

The original equilibrium price and sales for a 1 kg bag of apples is $2.50 (P) with 100 000 kg per day bought and sold (QS = QD).

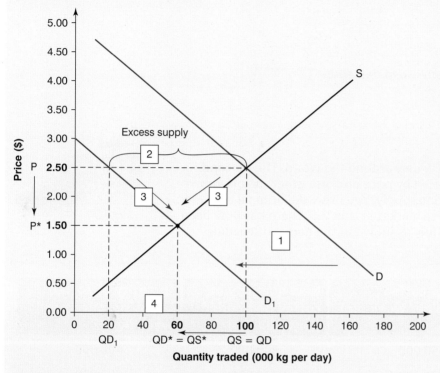

Figure 2.6.2 The adjustment of equilibrium price after a decrease in demand

1 First, there is a decrease in demand from D to D_1. This means the demand curve has shifted to the left.

2 Second, this leads to an excess supply of 80 000 kg – the difference between 100 000 kg (QS) and 20 000 kg (QD_1).

3 Third, the price falls, and as the price falls the quantity demanded rises from 20 000 kg (QD_1) to 60 000 kg (QD*) and the quantity supplied falls from 100 000 kg (QS) to 60 000 kg (QS*) per day.

4 Finally, the new equilibrium price will be $1.50 (P*) and the new equilibrium sales will be 60 000 kg per day. The original equilibrium quantity was at QS = QD and the new equilibrium is at QD* = QS*.

The diagram showing a decrease in demand can be simplified to indicate the original equilibrium price and quantity traded, P and Q, and the new equilibrium price and quantity traded, P_1 and Q_1, in Figure 2.6.3. The original equilibrium can be labelled as E, and the new equilibrium can be labelled E_1.

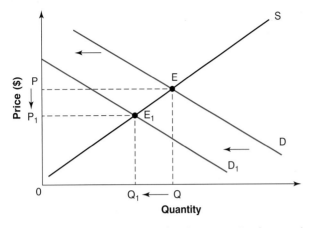

Figure 2.6.3 The effect of a decrease in demand

Application tasks

The market for coffee

Coffee is a product consumed widely around the world. The demand for and supply of coffee is influenced by price and also other factors known as the conditions of demand and supply. You drew the original demand and supply curves for the coffee market in Unit 2.5. There has now been an increase in demand for coffee, as shown in the demand schedule below.

Price of coffee ($ per kg)	Quantity of coffee demanded per week (kg)	New quantity of coffee demanded per week (kg)	Quantity of coffee beans supplied per week (kg)
18	150 000	300 000	400 000
15	200 000	350 000	350 000
12	250 000	400 000	250 000
9	300 000	450 000	200 000
6	350 000	500 000	150 000
3	400 000	550 000	100 000

1 Using graph paper, construct a demand and supply diagram to show the original demand and supply curves for coffee and the new demand curve for coffee. Identify the original equilibrium price and quantity traded and also the new equilibrium price and quantity traded.

2 What does your diagram show? Explain what has happened to price and quantity traded after the increase in demand.

The effects of changes in supply

The conditions of supply were explained in Unit 2.4. If one of these factors changes, such as change in the cost of raw materials, then the supply curve may shift, leading to a change in price.

The effects of an *increase* in the supply of chocolate bars, possibly due to a decrease in the cost of raw materials (assuming nothing else changes), are that the price will fall and as a result there will be an extension in demand. This is shown in Figure 2.6.4.

When the supply increases from S to S_1, there is a surplus or excess supply of the product at price P, which leads to a fall in price. As price falls, quantity demanded rises and quantity supplied decreases until equilibrium is restored at P_1Q_1 in Figure 2.6.4.

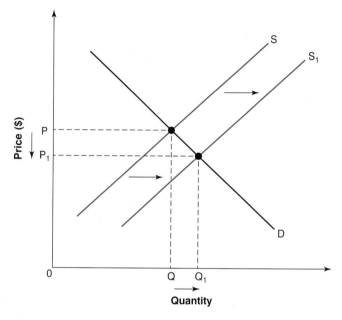

Figure 2.6.4 The effect of an increase in supply

1 Can you explain these steps for this increase in supply?

The overall effect is a fall in the equilibrium price from P to P_1 and a rise in the equilibrium quantity traded from Q to Q_1.

The effects of a *decrease* in supply, assuming nothing else changes, are that the price will rise and as a result there will be a contraction in demand. This is shown in Figure 2.6.5.

When the supply decreases from S to S_1 there is a shortage or excess demand for the product and this leads to the price rising. As price rises, quantity demanded falls and quantity supplied increases until equilibrium is restored at P_1Q_1 in Figure 2.6.5.

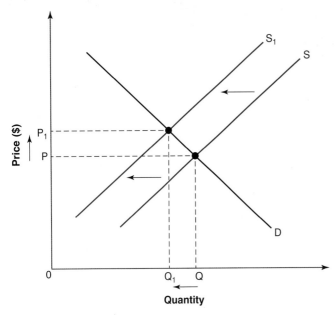

Figure 2.6.5 The effect of a decrease in supply

2 Can you explain these steps for this decrease in supply?

The overall effect is a rise in the equilibrium price from P to P_1 and a fall in the equilibrium quantity traded from Q to Q_1.

Application tasks

The market for coffee

You drew the original demand and supply curves for the coffee market in Unit 2.5. Earlier in this unit you also showed what happens when demand increases. There has now been an increase in the supply of coffee, as shown in a new supply schedule.

Price of coffee ($ per kg)	Quantity of coffee demanded per week (kg)	Quantity of coffee beans supplied per week (kg)	New quantity of coffee beans supplied per week (kg)
18	150 000	400 000	500 000
15	200 000	350 000	450 000
12	250 000	250 000	350 000
9	300 000	200 000	300 000
6	350 000	150 000	250 000
3	400 000	100 000	200 000

1 Using graph paper, construct a demand and supply diagram to show the original demand and supply curves for coffee and the new supply curve for coffee. Identify the original equilibrium price and quantity traded and also the new equilibrium price and quantity traded.

2 What does your diagram show? Explain what has happened to price and quantity traded after the increase in supply.

Key knowledge

Summary table of the effects of shifts in demand or supply

Change	Movement in the curve	Effect on price	Effect on quantity traded
Increase in demand	Moves right	Increase in price	Increase in quantity traded
Decrease in demand	Moves left	Decrease in price	Decrease in quantity traded
Increase in supply	Moves right	Decrease in price	Increase in quantity traded
Decrease in supply	Moves left	Increase in price	Decrease in quantity traded

Changes in both demand and supply

There can be changes in a market that result in both the demand curve and the supply curve moving. For example, visiting cafés and drinking coffee becomes more popular at the same time as a good harvest for coffee beans. The effect on the equilibrium price will be hard to judge. As you can see in Figures 2.6.6 and 2.6.7, the equilibrium price could remain the same or it could fall. Could the price actually rise? The answer is yes! The price would rise if the increase in demand that moves the curve to the right is greater than the increase in supply that shifts the supply curve to the right.

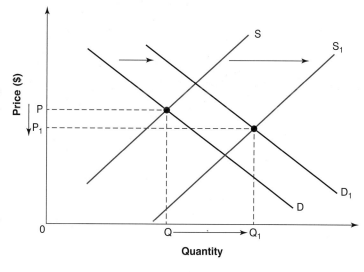

Figure 2.6.6 Increase in demand and supply – fall in price

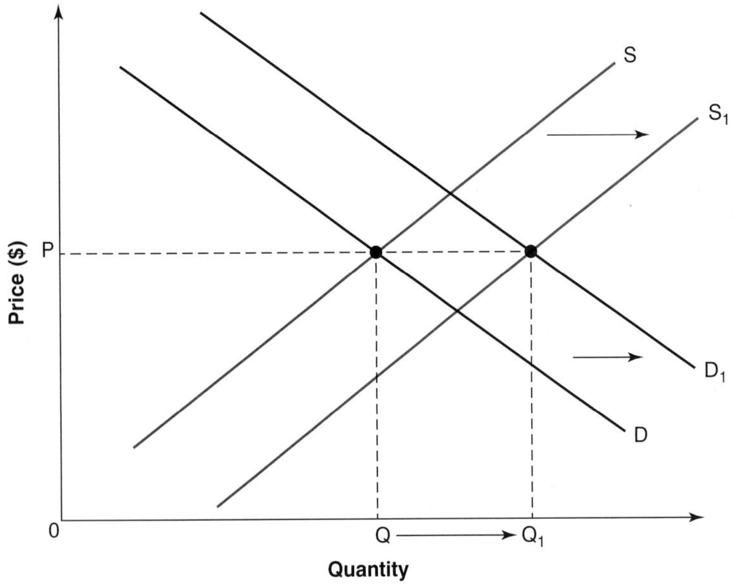

Figure 2.6.7 Increase in demand and supply – no change in price

3 Draw your own demand and supply diagram to show the price rising after both curves have increased.

CASE STUDY

The price of rice

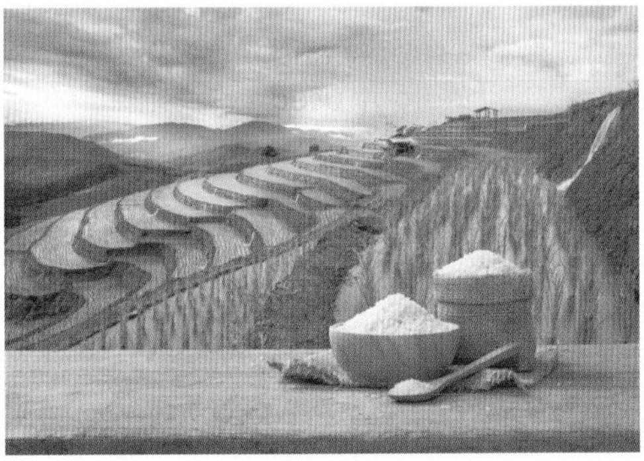

Global rice production in 2017 was expected to exceed output for 2016 by 9 million tonnes. Supplies at the beginning of 2017 were expected to be greater than in the previous year due to good weather conditions. However, demand for rice was also expected to rise due to increasing incomes in many developing countries and an increase in population. This increase in consumption was expected to be greater than the increase in supply and therefore lead to an increase in the price of rice.

1 Explain what was expected to happen to the world supply of rice in 2017.
2 Explain what was expected to happen to the demand for rice in 2017.
3 Draw a demand and supply diagram showing these changes in both demand and supply.
4 What happened to the equilibrium price shown on your diagram? Does it show an increase as the article suggests? If not, why not?

Applying

Project work

Using retail websites or shop price lists, find the price for different models of mobile phones.

1. What has happened to the price of these different models over the last two years?

2. Explain why there have been these changes to the price of different models.

3. Make a short news report of your findings, including a prediction of what you think might happen to the prices of the different models in the future.

Knowledge check questions

1 Identify **two** changes that could result in a different equilibrium price. [2]

2 Draw a diagram to show an increase in supply, and illustrate the consequences for the equilibrium price and quantity traded. [4]

3 Draw a diagram to show an increase in demand, and illustrate the consequences for the equilibrium price and quantity traded. [4]

4 Draw a diagram to show a change that results in a fall in the equilibrium price. [4]

5 (E) Using a supply and demand diagram, analyse the effects of a successful advertising campaign on the market for a breakfast cereal. [6]

6 (E) Using a supply and demand diagram, analyse the effects of improvements in technology used to produce televisions. [6]

7 (E) Using a diagram, analyse the effects on the market for DVD players if more consumers choose to download music and films from the internet. [6]

8 (E) Using a diagram, analyse the effects of the government putting an indirect tax on any products that contain high levels of sugar. [6]

Check your progress

Read the unit objectives below and reflect on your progress in each.

• Explain what causes the equilibrium price to change.

• Draw demand and supply diagrams to illustrate these changes in market conditions.

• Analyse the consequences of these changes in market conditions for the equilibrium price and sales.

 I struggle with this and need more practice.

I can do this reasonably well.

I can do this with confidence.

Price elasticity of demand (PED)

Learning objectives

By the end of this unit, you should be able to:

- define price elasticity of demand (PED)
- calculate PED using the formula and interpret the significance of the result
- draw and interpret demand curve diagrams to illustrate different PED
- explain the key influences on whether demand is elastic or inelastic
- explain the relationship between PED and total revenue, both in a diagram and as a calculation
- analyse the significance of PED for decision making by consumers, producers and the government.

Starting point

Answer these questions in pairs:

1 If the price of all drinks sold in school increased by 10%, would you still buy these drinks?

2 If the price of only Pepsi was increased by 10% and the prices of all other drinks remained the same, would you still buy Pepsi?

3 What factors might cause your decision to be different for questions 1 and 2?

Exploring

Complete these tasks in pairs:

1 List three goods or services where the price is a very important influence on whether or not consumers choose to buy them.

2 List three goods or services where the price is *not* a very important influence on whether or not consumers choose to buy them.

3 What is different about the goods or services on these two lists?

Developing

In Unit 2.3 you learned about the law of demand. It states that when the prices of goods and services increase consumers reduce the quantity of these goods and services they purchase, and when prices fall then consumers buy more of these goods and services. But firms and governments are interested in *how much* quantity demanded falls or increases when price changes. Why do you think they are interested in the size of the change in quantity demanded after a price change? Firms want to know how sensitive consumers are to changes in price so they can calculate the effect on sales and their sales revenue.

Knowing whether consumers are price sensitive or not price sensitive will help firms and governments make decisions about whether, and by how much, to change their prices. How will this help them? It will help them to see if the price change will have much effect on the amount consumers purchase.

The government may want to increase the price of some goods so that consumers are put off buying them. This could be the case for tobacco, where the government knows that smoking cigarettes is bad for consumers and therefore wants to encourage consumers to stop buying cigarettes.

A firm might consider a decrease in price to increase the quantity sold. However, if consumers are not sensitive to changes in price then there may only be a small increase in the quantity of products sold. The firm may feel the increase in quantity sold is not worth the reduction in revenue from the lower price.

1 A business discovers that consumers are not sensitive to changes in the price they pay for its product. Should the business increase or decrease the price? Explain your answer.

This sensitivity to price changes for a good or a service is called **price elasticity of demand (PED)**. PED can be calculated as a numerical value, and it affects the shape of the demand curve.

Price elasticity of demand (PED)

Price elasticity of demand is the responsiveness (or sensitivity) of the quantity demanded of a good or service to a change in its price.

PED is calculated by the following formula:

$$\frac{\text{percentage change in quantity demanded}}{\text{percentage change in price}}$$

The value for price elasticity of demand is negative because as price increases, quantity demanded does the opposite and falls; this is an inverse relationship between price and quantity demanded (an inverse relationship is simply where one variable increases as the other decreases and vice versa – that is, they go in opposite directions). It is not of any significance that PED is negative; it is the number calculated for PED that is important.

Key term

Price elasticity of demand (PED) – the responsiveness of quantity demanded to changes in price

NOTE

Quantity demanded in the formula refers to an extension or contraction of demand. It is not related to a movement of the whole demand curve.

Key knowledge

It is worth memorising the percentage change formula as you will need it to calculate the value of PED. To calculate percentage change you calculate the difference between the two numbers (the change) and divide this by the original number. Multiply the answer by 100 to turn it into a percentage.

For the PED formula this means you may need to calculate the following:

$$\frac{\text{change in quantity demanded}}{\text{original quantity demanded}} \times 100$$

and

$$\frac{\text{change in price}}{\text{original price}} \times 100$$

Worked example 1

A firm decreases the price of a bottle of water by 10% and sales of the water increase from 20 000 bottles per week to 21 000. What is the PED?

Quantity demanded changes by 1000 but it is the proportionate or percentage change that is important when working out the PED. The change is 1000 and the original quantity demanded is 20 000, so the percentage change in quantity demanded is:

$$\frac{1000}{20\ 000} \times 100 = +5\% \text{ (the value is positive because quantity demanded increases)}$$

The percentage change in price is –10% (it is a negative number because the price has been decreased).

Put this into the PED formula to give:

$$\frac{+5\%}{-10\%} = -0.5$$

1. What does this PED value tell you about how sensitive consumers are to price changes?

2. Should this firm increase its prices instead of decreasing them?

Worked example 2

A firm increases the price of a bottle of orange juice by 10% and sales of the orange juice decrease from 20 000 bottles per week to 15 000. What is the PED?

Quantity demanded changes by 5000 but it is the proportionate (or percentage) change that is important when working out the PED. The change is 5000 and the original quantity demanded is 20 000, so the percentage change in quantity demanded is:

$$\frac{5000}{20\ 000} \times 100 = -25\% \text{ (the value is negative because quantity demanded decreases)}$$

The percentage change in price is +10% (it is a positive number because price has been raised).

Put this into the PED formula to give:

$$\frac{-25\%}{+10\%} = -2.5$$

1 What does this PED value suggest about how sensitive consumers are to price changes?

2 Should this firm decrease its prices instead of increasing them?

Worked example 3

A firm increases the price of a bottle of coconut milk by 10% and sales of the coconut milk decrease from 20 000 bottles per week to 18 000. What is the PED?

Quantity demanded changes by 2000 but it is the proportionate or percentage change that is important when working out the PED. The change is 2000 and the original quantity demanded is 20 000, so the percentage change in quantity demanded is:

$$\frac{2000}{20\,000} \times 100 = -10\% \text{ (the value is negative because quantity demanded decreases)}$$

The percentage change in price is +10% (it is a positive number because the price has been increased).

Put this into the PED formula to give:

$$\frac{-10\%}{+10\%} = -1$$

1 What does this PED value suggest about how sensitive consumers are to price changes?

2 What, if anything, should happen to the price the firm charges?

Key knowledge

PED is about the proportionate or percentage change in quantity demanded and price, not the actual change in quantity or price.

For example, if the price is increased by $100 this would be very important for a product with a price of $200 but would be of little significance to a product that has a price of $100 000.

Similarly, if the quantity demanded decreased by 10 000 per week it is more important to a firm selling 30 000 products per week but less important to a firm selling 100 000 per week.

 Work out the different percentage changes for the price change and change in quantity demanded in the examples given in the Key knowledge box above.

PED and demand curves

The PED for most goods or services is classed as either **price elastic demand** or **price inelastic demand**. The following explains how the formula is applied and what the demand curve will look like for products that have a PED that is either price elastic or price inelastic.

Price inelastic demand

When demand for a product is price inelastic, the value of PED is between 0 and 1 (ignoring the minus sign). This will be the case for a good or service where consumers do not change their demand much if the price changes. They could be described as not being price sensitive, in other words price insensitive.

For example, the price of petrol increases from $10 to $15 per unit. This leads to a fall in quantity demanded from 500 to 450.

Key terms

Price elastic demand – the percentage change in quantity demanded is greater than the percentage change in price

Price inelastic demand – the percentage change in quantity demanded is lower than the percentage change in price

Percentage fall in quantity demanded = 50/500 × 100 = 10% (Q to Q_1 in Figure 2.7.1).

Percentage increase in price = 5/10 × 100 = 50% (P to P_1 in Figure 2.7.1).

So PED for petrol =

$$\frac{-10\%}{+50\%} = -0.2$$

The percentage change in price has led to a smaller percentage change in the quantity demanded, which means PED is inelastic as it is between 0 and 1 (ignoring the minus sign). In this case, consumers are relatively unresponsive to changes in price.

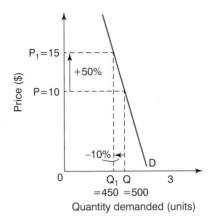

Figure 2.7.1 Price inelastic demand

An inelastic demand curve is shown in Figure 2.7.1. How different does this look to the demand curves you drew in Unit 2.3?

If PED is inelastic then the demand curve will tend to be drawn looking steep. This is because the percentage change in price is larger than the percentage change in quantity demanded.

What happens to the revenue that the firm receives in Figure 2.7.1?

For this petrol example, the original total revenue before the price rise was $10 × 500 = $5000.

(Total revenue is calculated using this formula: Total revenue = price × quantity sold)

The new total revenue after the price rise is $15 x 450 = $6750.

What has happened to the revenue from selling petrol after the price has been increased?

It has increased by $1750.

3 Why has revenue increased so much?

It has increased because the price increase is a higher percentage change than the percentage reduction in sales. Therefore, the revenue the firm loses from lower sales is more than made up for by the higher price charged for each unit of petrol.

Inelastic demand means that a price increase will result in an increase in total revenue for the firm and a price decrease will lead to a fall in total revenue.

4 What would you do to price if you knew the PED for the goods or services you produced was inelastic?

Price elastic demand

When demand for a product is price elastic, the value of PED is greater than 1 (ignoring the minus sign). This will be the case for a good or service where the consumers change the amount of a product they purchase a lot in response to a change in its price. They could be described as being price sensitive.

For example, a 10% reduction in the price of cars (P to P_1 in Figure 2.7.2) leads to a 15% increase in quantity demanded (Q to Q_1 in Figure 2.7.2).

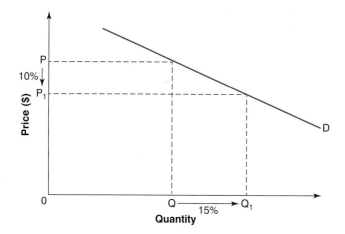

Figure 2.7.2 Price elastic demand

$$PED = \frac{+15\%}{-10\%} = -1.5$$

The change in price has led to a larger percentage change in the quantity demanded, which means PED for cars is elastic as it is greater than 1 (ignoring the minus sign). In this case, consumers are sensitive to changes in price.

An elastic demand curve is shown in Figure 2.7.2. The demand curve will usually look shallow if PED is elastic.

For the car example in Figure 2.7.2, what has happened to the revenue from selling cars after the price has been reduced?

The total revenue has increased because the price fall is proportionately smaller than the percentage increase in sales. Therefore, the revenue the firm loses from the lower price is outweighed by the increase in revenue it gains from the higher sales.

Elastic demand means that a price increase is likely to result in lower sales revenue for the firm while a price decrease is likely to lead to higher sales revenue. So how would you adjust the price if you knew this was the PED for the goods or services you produced?

5 What happens to the revenue received by the firm if the percentage change in price leads to the same percentage change in quantity demanded?

Summary of PED and the effect on revenue

Value of PED	Price change	Quantity change	Effect on total revenue
Inelastic PED	Price increase	Smaller percentage fall in quantity demanded	Total revenue increases
	Price decrease	Smaller percentage rise in quantity demanded	Total revenue decreases
Elastic PED	Price increase	Larger percentage fall in quantity demanded	Total revenue decreases
	Price decrease	Larger percentage rise in quantity demanded	Total revenue increases
Unit elastic PED	Price increase	Same percentage fall in quantity demanded	Total revenue is unchanged
	Price decrease	Same percentage increase in quantity demanded	Total revenue is unchanged

 How does this help firms when making decisions about price changes?

Special price elasticity of demand values

There are three special elasticities that are not usually found in the real world and are generally theoretical.

Unit elastic demand

When demand is **unit elastic**, the value of PED is exactly 1 (ignoring the minus sign).

For example: A 20% increase in the price of a mobile phone leads to a 20% decrease in quantity demanded.

$$PED = \frac{-20\%}{+20\%} = -1.0$$

The change in price has led to the same percentage change in quantity demanded, which means the PED is unit elastic as it is equal to 1. The revenue lost from sales is equal to the revenue gained from charging a higher price, and so the total sales revenue remains the same after the price change.

A unit elastic demand curve is shown in Figure 2.7.3.

Perfectly inelastic demand

When demand for a product is perfectly price inelastic, the value of PED is 0.

For example: A 10% increase in the price of a carton of milk leads to no change in quantity demanded.

Key term

Unit elastic demand – the percentage change in quantity demanded is the same as the percentage change in price

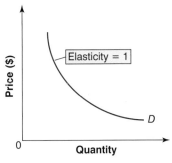

Figure 2.7.3 Unit elastic demand

$$PED = \frac{0\%}{+10\%} = 0.0$$

The change in price has led to no change in quantity demanded, which means consumers are not at all sensitive to the price change. PED is perfectly inelastic.

A perfectly inelastic demand curve is shown in Figure 2.7.4. It is vertical.

Perfectly elastic demand

When demand is perfectly elastic, the value of PED is infinity.

For example, an extremely small increase in the price of oranges sold from a farm leads to the quantity demanded falling to zero as consumers buy all their oranges from other farms that have not increased their prices.

The change in price has led to an infinitely large change in quantity demanded as consumers are so price sensitive that, even if the price rises by a very small percentage, consumers will stop buying it or buy from other suppliers.

A perfectly elastic demand curve is shown in Figure 2.7.5. It is horizontal.

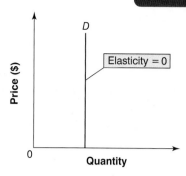

Figure 2.7.4 Perfectly inelastic demand

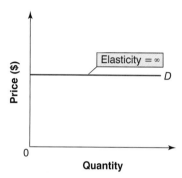

Figure 2.7.5 Perfectly elastic demand

Key knowledge

Summary of the values for PED

PED value	Interpretation
Between 0 and (–)1	Price inelastic demand
Greater than (–)1	Price elastic demand
Exactly 1	Unit elastic demand
0	Perfectly inelastic demand
Infinity	Perfectly elastic demand

Application tasks

You have researched the effect of price changes on the quantity demanded of various drinks that a local café sells. Your research has led you to the findings below:

Drink	Current price ($)	Current number sold per week	Estimated number sold per week if price is increased by 10%	Estimated number sold per week if price is decreased by 10%
Coffee	$2.20	1000	950	1050
Tea	$2.00	800	700	1000
Iced coffee	$2.50	500	450	525

1. Calculate the PED for coffee, tea and iced coffee following a price increase of 10%.

2. Calculate the PED for coffee, tea and iced coffee following a price decrease of 10%.

3. Recommend the price changes the café should make if it wants to increase revenue.

What affects PED?

Why do the consumers of some goods or services continue to buy them in similar amounts even when prices rise or fall? What do you think affects a consumer's price sensitivity? These are the main factors that affect the price elasticity of demand, but you may be able to think of other examples.

The number of substitutes

If there are a large number of alternative goods or services to buy then PED is likely to be elastic. Consumers will be price sensitive as they can easily swap to alternative goods or services if the price rises. If there are no close substitutes then PED is likely to be inelastic; when prices rise consumers have no alternative but to pay the higher price or go without the product. What do you think the PED for a local restaurant might be? If a local restaurant has many other similar restaurants nearby, then if it was to increase food prices consumers may go to eat at one of the other restaurants. Therefore, the PED is likely to be elastic.

Time period

Demand tends to be more elastic in the long run than in the short run. This is because consumers have time to adjust to price changes. For example, if the price of petrol increases, consumers will have little choice but to pay the higher price and so PED is inelastic. However, over time consumers will be able to purchase cars that use less petrol and so demand for petrol will become elastic in the long run.

Proportion of income spent on the good or service

If a good or service has a very low price and is a small proportion of consumers' income, then PED tends to be inelastic. This is because even if the price increases it won't take up much more income, and therefore consumers are likely to continue buying the good. For example, a box of matches is sold for a very low price, and even if the price increased by 50% consumers would still probably buy a similar amount to what they bought before the price increase.

This would be very different for a good or service that took up a large proportion of consumers' income. Buying car insurance is expensive and consumers will often compare several different insurance companies to make sure they are getting a good price. The PED is likely to be elastic, because an increase in price will see consumers compare other insurance companies in search of a better deal. After all, it involves such a large amount of money and a large proportion of their income.

Necessity/luxury/habit forming/fashion

If consumers feel they really want a good or service – perhaps because it is very fashionable or it involves an addiction (for example, cigarettes) – then PED will tend to be inelastic. Consumers are less sensitive to price changes for goods and services they really want. Advertising and the successful marketing of brand images can have a similar effect.

 7 Can you think of any goods or services that are examples of inelastic PED for this reason? Are there any products you would buy even if their prices increased by a large percentage?

CASE STUDY   ## Chocolate

Chocolate has been an extremely popular product in the West since around the mid-18th century. Nowadays it is a hugely popular component of desserts and may even be eaten as a meal substitute. In the last decade, chocolate has become more popular in Asian-Pacific countries and it has been discovered that certain types of chocolate have health benefits. These factors have led to even greater demand for chocolate both locally and globally.

Not only is chocolate extremely popular, chocolate consumers are relatively price insensitive. Chocolate is considered a luxury, but one that is affordable.

1 Explain what the article suggests about the price elasticity of demand for chocolate.

2 How will a knowledge of PED affect firms in this market?

3 Should one firm put up its prices for chocolate bars even if the rest of the firms in the market leave their prices unchanged?

4 Is PED for the chocolate bar of one firm the same as the PED for the market as a whole?

Project work

You have been asked by your school to advise which products to increase prices for and which ones to reduce prices for in order to increase the school's revenue from sales of drinks and food.

1. Carry out research among your classmates by asking them which food and drink products they will keep buying if prices are increased and which product prices should be reduced to encourage more sales.

2. Try to find at what price they will stop buying particular products.

3. Try to find out if lower prices will encourage more purchases of particular products.

4. Present your findings to the class and make recommendations as to which products should have their prices reduced and which products should have their prices increased. Explain why your suggestions should increase revenue.

Knowledge check questions

1   What is the formula to calculate PED? [2]

2   What is meant by an inelastic PED? [2]

3   Explain what it means for a firm if PED for its products is 2. [3]

4   Explain **two** reasons why demand might be price elastic. [4]

5   Analyse how a change in the price of a product with inelastic demand will affect the revenue earned. [6]

6   (E) Analyse why PED is important to a government when making decisions about which products to tax. [6]

7   (E) Analyse why PED is unlikely to be the same value at all points on a demand curve. [6]

8   (E) Explain why PED is not the same as the gradient of the demand curve. [4]

Check your progress

Read the unit objectives below and reflect on your progress in each.

- Define price elasticity of demand (PED).

- Calculate PED using the formula and interpret the significance of the result.

- Draw and interpret demand curve diagrams to illustrate different PED.

- Explain the key influences on whether demand is elastic or inelastic.

- Explain the relationship between PED and total revenue, both in a diagram and as a calculation.

- Analyse the significance of PED for decision making by consumers, producers and the government.

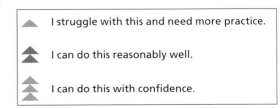

I struggle with this and need more practice.

I can do this reasonably well.

I can do this with confidence.

Price elasticity of supply (PES)

Learning objectives

By the end of this unit, you should be able to:

- define price elasticity of supply (PES)
- calculate PES using the formula and interpret the significance of the result
- draw and interpret supply curve diagrams to illustrate different PES
- explain the key influences on whether supply is elastic or inelastic
- analyse the significance of PES for decision making by consumers, producers and the government.

Starting point

Complete these tasks in pairs:

1 Discuss whether your school could easily find room if more students wanted to attend.

2 Explain how easily and quickly your school could accept more students into your year group.

Exploring

Discuss these questions in pairs:

1 How easily could a bicycle factory increase the number of bicycles it produces?

2 How quickly could a farmer produce more potatoes?

3 How easily could a restaurant serve more customers?

Developing

Price elasticity of supply (PES)

In Unit 2.4 you learned about the law of supply. It states that when prices increase, firms or individuals increase the quantity of goods and services supplied, and when prices fall then firms or individuals reduce the quantity supplied to the market. But how quickly can firms or individuals alter supply to the market? Does it matter how long it takes to alter quantity supplied? As shown in Unit 2.6, if the quantity supplied does not alter very quickly there will be excess demand or excess supply and price will change by a large amount.

For example, if there is an increase in demand for wheat to make bread, then the price will rise initially as there will be excess demand for wheat. Farmers will want to increase the quantity supplied as the price is higher and it is more profitable to supply wheat. However, it will take time to increase the number of fields planted with wheat. It will take time for quantity supplied to change and in the meantime prices will remain high until farmers can respond.

How easily and quickly quantity supplied can be changed is called **price elasticity of supply (PES)**. PES can be calculated as a numerical value. It also affects the shape of the supply curve.

PES refers to the responsiveness of the quantity supplied of a good or service to a change in its price.

The formula is stated as:

$$PES = \frac{\text{percentage change in quantity supplied}}{\text{percentage change in price}}$$

The value for price elasticity of supply is positive because changes in price and quantity supplied go in the same direction, which means that an increase in price will lead to an increase in quantity supplied and a decrease in price will lead to a fall in quantity supplied. It also means that if price increases, revenue will increase and if price falls, revenue falls.

 How is this different to PED and revenue?

When calculating PES, you may first need to calculate the percentage change in quantity supplied and the percentage change in price. This approach was explained in Unit 2.7.

Worked example 1

The price of paint increases from $10 to $15 per tin and the quantity supplied increases by 20%. What is the PES?

Price changes by $5 but it is the proportionate or percentage change that is important when working out the elasticity. The change is $5 and the original price is $10, so:

$\frac{\$5}{\$10} \times 100 = +50\%$ (It is a positive number because the price increases.)

The percentage change in quantity supplied is +20% (it is a positive number because quantity supplied increases).

Put this into the PES formula to give:

$$\frac{+20\%}{+50\%} = +0.4$$

What does this PES value suggest about how easily and quickly the firm can increase the quantity of paint it supplies to the market?

Worked example 2

The price of books decreases from $10 to $8 per book and quantity supplied decreases by 50%. What is the PES?

Price changes by $2 but it is the proportionate or percentage change that is important when working out the elasticity. The change is $2 and the original price is $10, so the percentage change in price is:

$$\frac{\$2}{\$10} \times 100 = -20\% \text{ (It is a negative number because the price decreases.)}$$

The percentage change in quantity supplied is –50% (it is a negative number because quantity supplied decreases).

Put this into the PES formula to give:

$$\frac{-50\%}{-20\%} = +2.5 \text{ (It is a positive number because a negative divided by a negative gives a positive.)}$$

What does this PES value suggest about how easily and quickly the firm can decrease the quantity of books it supplies to the market?

Worked example 3

The price of bread increases from $1 to $1.50 per loaf and quantity supplied increases by 50%. What is the PES?

Price changes by $0.5 but it is the proportionate or percentage change that is important when working out the elasticity. The change is $0.5 and the original price is $1, so the percentage change in price is:

$$\frac{\$0.5}{\$1} \times 100 = +50\% \text{ (It is a positive number because the price increases.)}$$

The percentage change in quantity supplied is +50% (it is a positive number because quantity supplied increases).

Put this into the PES formula to give:

$$\frac{+50\%}{+50\%} = +1$$

What does this PES suggest about how easily and quickly the firm can increase the quantity of bread it supplies to the market?

PES and supply curves

The PES for goods and services is classed as either **price elastic supply** or **price inelastic supply**. The following explains how the formula is applied and what the supply curve will look like for products that have a PES that is either price elastic or price inelastic.

Price inelastic supply

When supply for a good or service is price inelastic, the value of PES is between 0 and 1. This means that the percentage change in quantity supplied will be smaller than the percentage change in price.

For example, a 33% increase in the price of rented accommodation in a city ((10/30) x 100 in Figure 2.8.1) leads to a 7% ((1/15) x 100 in Figure 2.8.1) rise in quantity supplied.

$$\text{PES} = \frac{+7\%}{+33\%} = +0.21$$

> **Key terms**
>
> **Price elastic supply** – the percentage change in quantity supplied is greater than the percentage change in price
>
> **Price inelastic supply** – the percentage change in quantity supplied is lower than the percentage change in price

The change in price has led to a proportionately smaller change in quantity supplied which means PES is inelastic as it is between 0 and 1. In this case, producers are not price sensitive and will only increase their supply of rented accommodation by a relatively small amount after the price rise in the **short run**.

An inelastic supply curve is shown in Figure 2.8.1. It is a steep supply curve.

Price elastic supply

When supply for a product is price elastic, the value of PES is greater than 1. This means that the percentage change in quantity supplied will be greater than the percentage change in price.

For example, a 10% decrease ((3/30) x 100 in Figure 2.8.2) in the price of a child's toy leads to a 38% decrease ((30/80) x 100 in Figure 2.8.2) in quantity supplied.

$$\text{PES} = \frac{-38\%}{-10\%} = +3.8$$

(Remember, a negative number divided by another negative number equals a positive number.)

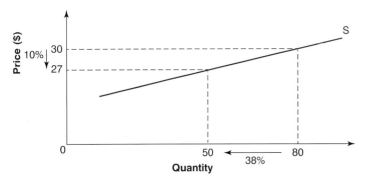

Figure 2.8.2 Price elastic supply

The change in price has led to a larger percentage change in quantity supplied, which means PES is elastic as it is greater than 1. In this case, producers are price sensitive and will be supplying a much smaller proportion of the toy to the market after the price falls.

An elastic supply curve is shown in Figure 2.8.2. It is usually a shallow supply curve.

Special price elasticity of supply

There are three special PES curves that are only found in the real world in special circumstances.

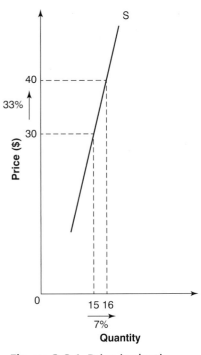

Figure 2.8.1 Price inelastic supply

Unit elastic supply

When supply is unit elastic, the value of PES is exactly 1.

For example, a 20% increase in the price of a mobile phone leads to a 20% increase in quantity supplied.

$$PES = \frac{+20\%}{+20\%} = +1.0$$

The change in price has led to the same percentage change in quantity supplied, which means it has a unit elastic PES as it is equal to 1.

Key term

Unit elastic supply – the percentage change in quantity supplied is equal to the percentage change in price

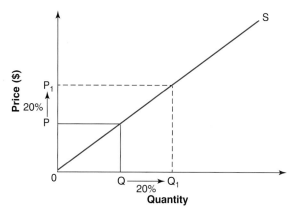

Figure 2.8.3 Unit elastic supply

A unit elastic supply curve is shown in Figure 2.8.3. It is a straight line that starts at the origin (0 on the graph).

Perfectly inelastic supply

When supply for a product is perfectly price inelastic, the value of PES is 0.

For example, a 10% increase in the price of water leads to no change in quantity supplied.

$$PES = \frac{0\%}{+10\%} = 0.0$$

The change in price to either P_1 or P_2 on Figure 2.8.4 has led to no change in quantity supplied, which means producers are not sensitive to the price change at all. They cannot or do not want to alter quantity supplied in response to the price change. PES is perfectly inelastic and is shown in Figure 2.8.4 as a vertical supply curve.

Perfectly elastic supply

When supply is perfectly elastic, the value of PES is infinity (∞).

For example, an extremely small increase in the price of a product leads to the quantity supplied falling to zero.

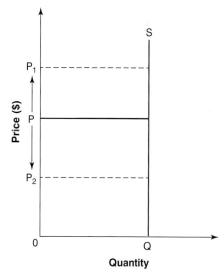

Figure 2.8.4 Perfectly inelastic supply

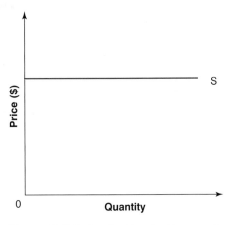

Figure 2.8.5 Perfectly elastic supply

As producers are so price sensitive even a small change in price will result in no supply being offered to the market.

A perfectly elastic supply curve is shown in Figure 2.8.5. It is a horizontal supply curve.

> **Key knowledge**
>
> **Summary of the values for PES**
>
> | PES value | Interpretation |
> |---|---|
> | 0 | Perfectly inelastic supply |
> | Between 0 and 1 | Price inelastic supply |
> | Exactly 1 | Unit elastic supply |
> | Greater than 1 | Price elastic supply |
> | Infinity | Perfectly elastic supply |

Application tasks

Work out the answers to these questions:

1. Hot weather increases the demand for ice cream and prices increase from $1.50 to $2.00. Quantity supplied increases from 1000 per day to 1200 per day. What is the PES for ice cream?

2. Wearing jeans has become more fashionable and prices increase by 25%. The quantity supplied to the market each week increases by 25%. What is the PES for jeans?

3. The price of chocolate bars fell by 10% while the quantity supplied stayed the same for the first week. What is the PES for the first week after the price falls?

4. Fruit juice has become more popular and prices have increased by 10%. The quantity supplied has increased by 30%. What is the PES for fruit juice?

Application task

As an economic adviser, you have been recruited by the Philippines Coffee Board to help the Philippines government plan the amount that coffee farmers will plant and grow over the next few years. Using the internet, research the coffee industry in the Philippines.

Write a report outlining how easily and quickly the supply of coffee from the Philippines could be increased if world prices for coffee were to increase.

2 How easily and quickly do you think the supply of the following items could be increased?

- copper
- wooden furniture
- luxury yachts

What affects PES?

How easily and quickly supply can be changed determines the PES. If quantity supplied can be quickly increased in response to an increase in price then PES will be elastic. For instance, a clothing factory that is not working at full capacity may be able to easily employ more workers to increase production. If it is difficult to increase quantity supplied quickly or easily then PES will be inelastic; it may take many years to build and increase the supply of electricity from a power plant.

So what factors do you think affect how easily and quickly quantity supplied can be increased? The following factors are the main ones that affect elasticity of supply, but you may be able to think of other examples.

The time period

Time is an important factor because even when prices increase many firms cannot increase quantity supplied straightaway, so PES will be perfectly inelastic in the immediate time period. This means that prices increase by a large percentage at first when demand increases. This is shown as S in Figure 2.8.6.

After a short time firms will try to increase quantity supplied by producing more of the good or service or selling any stocks they have. Thus, quantity supplied will become relatively inelastic but not perfectly inelastic. This is shown as S_1 on Figure 2.8.6. As this happens, the market price will start to fall.

Over the **long run** firms will have had a chance to change the scale of production and to expand in order to supply more of the good or service. This means that supply over the long run is elastic. This is shown as S_2 on Figure 2.8.6. Prices will have fallen again.

Key term

Long run – the time it takes to change the factors of production to expand and produce on a larger scale

Application task

Copy out Figure 2.8.6 and label the price changes as supply becomes less inelastic and more elastic as time passes following the increase in demand.

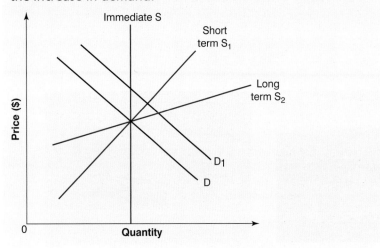

Figure 2.8.6 Elasticity of supply with changes in the time period

The amount of stock (inventories) or ability to store the stock (inventory)

Stock is also called inventory and it includes raw materials, components or finished products being held by the firm.

If a firm has a large amount of stock and it is easy to store the finished product then it will be easier and quicker to increase the quantity supplied to the market if demand increases and prices rise. Therefore, supply will be elastic as firms can easily respond to a change in price. If a firm does not hold much stock (inventory) because large items such as cars take up a lot of storage space, or because the inventory is difficult to store, like many foods that perish or rot over time, then supply is likely to be inelastic.

Level of spare capacity

If there is spare capacity in a factory, which means not all available space is being used or some machines are not being used all the time, then supply will be elastic. This is because it is easier for the firm to quickly increase production and supply more products to the market. If all the machines are being used and the factory has no space left to add more machines or workers, then supply will be inelastic because the firm is at full capacity and cannot quickly increase supply.

The mobility and cost of factors of production

The mobility of factors of production refers to how easily any of the factors of production (land, labour, capital or enterprise) can be transferred for use in alternative production processes. For example, it is not easy to change the machinery in a motorbike factory to produce anything other than motorbikes, but it could be adapted to produce different models of motorbike. A farmer can use land for growing different crops, so land may be quite mobile, although not for all crops, of course. If labour is unskilled, it can easily be transferred to alternative uses, but if the labour is skilled then it may be difficult and take a long time to train workers to transfer to alternative production. A shop worker who sells clothes, for example, could easily move to another type of shop that sells food, but an electrician could not easily become a computer programmer.

So the more mobile the factors of production are, and the cheaper it is to adapt or train them, then the more elastic the supply. The less mobile the factors of production are, and the higher the cost to move them to alternative production, then the more inelastic supply will be.

Significance of PES to decision making

	Significance of PES to decision making	Examples of decisions affected
Consumers	If demand increases and prices rise, how quickly can firms respond by increasing the quantity supplied to the market?	Demand for butter increases: it will take a long time for butter output to increase, and so there will be a sharp increase in price and this will affect consumer decisions about how much butter to purchase.
	If this takes a long time and PES is inelastic, then prices will rise by a much higher proportion than the increase in quantity.	
	The price change will affect the consumer's decision to purchase the product or service.	
Producers	If demand increases and the price is higher, how quickly can the firm take advantage of this higher price to try to increase revenue?	Demand falls for DVD players: therefore the price also drops. How quickly can firms reduce their supply of DVD players to the market? If PES is inelastic it will be difficult to reduce output quickly, and the firm may keep selling DVD players at lower prices while it tries to redirect its factors of production to alternative products.
	If PES is elastic then the firm can easily and quickly increase quantity supplied to the market and take advantage of the higher price.	
	The decision to respond to this higher price will enable the firm to benefit quickly from higher prices.	

	Significance of PES to decision making	Examples of decisions affected
Government	Decisions about the quantity of services to provide will be affected by PES. How quickly and easily could education or healthcare services be increased if the population increased? Recruiting the required skilled employees will take time if there are not enough trained people in the economy. If the government is planning to impose a tax or a subsidy on a product, then PES will affect how effective this will be. How quickly can the quantity supplied be decreased if a tax is imposed or increased if a subsidy is applied to a product? This may affect the decision about which products and services to tax and subsidise and how high the tax or subsidy should be.	An increase in the birth rate: this will increase the demand for education in a few years' time. The government will need to plan ahead to train the required number of teachers to fill the future job vacancies or it will find that demand will increase and the supply of teachers cannot meet this demand.

CASE STUDY   ## High demand for Google's Pixel smartphone

Pixel and Pixel XL smartphones were launched in October 2016. They are the first smartphones designed, developed and marketed by Google. However, demand for the phones far exceeded the company's expectations; by the end of the year many models were out of stock both at Google's online store and in the US Verizon outlets. Google was reported to be trying to restock as quickly as possible but was struggling to keep up with consumer demand. Online orders for the most popular models and colours were taking several weeks to fulfil.

1 What does the case study suggest about the elasticity of supply for Google's smartphones?

2 Explain what evidence there is in the case study to support your conclusion in question 1.

3 Explain what factors could be affecting the PES of Google's smartphones.

4 How does this elasticity of supply affect Google?

5 Could Google have avoided this problem with its smartphones?

Applying

Project work

Use the internet or research local firms to answer the following questions:

1. Research whether there are job vacancies in your country or local area that are not being filled. What sort of jobs are they: skilled or unskilled?

2. What problems are created for firms when job vacancies are not being filled and there are skills shortages?

3. What can firms do to overcome these problems?

4. What problems are there for the government when job vacancies are not being filled and there are skills shortages?

5. What can the government do to overcome or at least minimise these problems?

Knowledge check questions

1 What is the formula for price elasticity of supply? [2]

2 What is meant by price elastic supply? [2]

3 What affects PES? [2]

4 Calculate the price elasticity of supply of a product if a price increase of 20% leads to an increase in quantity supplied from 100 to 105 units. [2]

5 Draw the supply curve on a diagram for the product in question 4. [2]

6 Explain **three** factors that will cause PES to be inelastic. [6]

7 Analyse why PES is important to a government when making decisions about which industries to subsidise. [6]

Governments may use a buffer stock scheme where they buy up supplies of an agricultural crop when there has been a good harvest and then store this crop. Some or all of this stored crop can be supplied to the market when there has been a poor harvest.

8 (E) How will a buffer stock scheme affect the supply of the agricultural crop? [4]

9 (E) Analyse why a government might want to use a buffer stock scheme. [6]

10 (E) Analyse the impact of this intervention on farmers, consumers and the government. [6]

Check your progress

Read the unit objectives below and reflect on your progress in each.

- Define price elasticity of supply (PES).

- Calculate PES using the formula and interpret the significance of the result.

- Draw and interpret supply curve diagrams to illustrate different PES.

- Explain the key influences on whether supply is elastic or inelastic.

- Analyse the significance of PES for decision making by consumers, producers and the government.

▲	I struggle with this and need more practice.
▲▲	I can do this reasonably well.
▲▲▲	I can do this with confidence.

Market economic system

Learning objectives

By the end of this unit, you should be able to:

- define market economic system
- identify the difference between private and public sectors
- explain the advantages and disadvantages of the market economic system
- explain how market economic systems work in a variety of different countries.

Starting point

Complete these tasks in pairs:

1 List five products or services that are provided by businesses in your country.

2 List five products or services that are provided by your country's government.

3 List three products or services that are provided *only* by the government.

4 List three products or services that are provided by the government and also by businesses.

Exploring

Discuss these questions in pairs:

1 Can you name five firms that produce goods or services in your country?

2 Are these firms operating in markets where there are many competitors?

3 Why is the price a firm charges for its goods or services important to that firm if it has many competitors?

Developing

Market economic system

The **market economic system** is described in Units 2.1 to 2.8. In such a system, the price mechanism allocates resources to determine what goods and services should be produced, how they should be produced, and who should receive the goods and services produced. The market economic system has prices that are based on competition among private sector businesses and not controlled by the government.

A market economy has a **private sector** that is made up of individuals and privately owned businesses that make all the decisions in the economy. Most private sector organisations are

Key terms

Market economic system – a system with prices that are based on competition between private sector businesses; markets are not controlled by the government

Private sector – the part of the economy made up of individuals and privately owned businesses that make economic decisions assumed to have the aim of making a profit. Analysing just the private sector and ignoring the influence of the government makes it easier to understand the relationship between price and sales. There are no examples of countries that operate a pure market economic system with no government involvement; all countries have some government influence in the economy.

The characteristics of a market economy, also listed in Unit 2.2, are:

- many buyers and sellers (i.e. the market is competitive)
- buyers seek maximum satisfaction from consuming the goods and services they buy
- sellers want to maximise profit
- economic resources are mostly privately owned; for example, businesses are owned by private individuals and organisations
- the government only plays a small role in the economy
- resources are allocated via the price mechanism.

Examples of private sector businesses are small trader businesses that sell fruit and vegetables from street market stalls, companies that produce toys or clothing, and global mining companies that extract copper or diamonds. Most of the goods and services you buy will have probably been produced by private sector businesses.

Public sector examples will differ from country to country as some countries have a large public sector while others have a smaller public sector with more goods and services provided by the private sector. It is likely that basic education and basic healthcare will be provided by the public sector, as well as the armed forces, roads, and a legal system that includes the police, courtrooms and prisons.

Key term

Public sector – the part of the economy that is under the control of the government

Advantages of the market economic system

- **Increased consumer choice**. A market economy will provide the goods and services that consumers most want. There are many sellers in a market economy and therefore consumers will have a lot of choice about what to buy. There will be no government interference in the goods and services that are produced; it will be purely a matter of demand.

- **Competition leads to efficiency**. There is competition between firms in a market economy and this should keep costs low. Firms aim to produce at the lowest average cost so the difference between revenue and costs is as great as possible, which helps firms achieve their aim of maximising profits. Inefficient firms may go out of business if they cannot compete with their competitors on price. This too should keep prices as low as possible and ensure that consumers will not be exploited. Firms also have an incentive to be innovative because if they can find new ways to make or develop new products to sell they can make high profits for a short time. This will last until other firms copy them and supply increases.

- **Incentives to work**. In a market economy entrepreneurs can keep their profits and individuals can keep their wages, so there is an incentive to work hard. It is likely that there will be increased efficiency as a result of this incentive, and this supports economic growth and an increased standard of living for the population.

Disadvantages of the market economic system

- **Some goods will not be provided at all or not in a sufficient quantity** for the benefit of society. Goods such as education and healthcare are beneficial to the population, but in a pure market economy they will not be provided in sufficient quantities because the poor cannot afford to pay for them. These goods are known as merit goods (merit goods are discussed more fully in Unit 2.10). Defence of the country by the armed forces is an example of a service that will not be provided by the private sector and therefore will not be provided in a pure market economy. Such goods are known as public goods (public goods are discussed more fully in Unit 2.10). Therefore, the government will need to intervene in real world economies to overcome this disadvantage.

- **Income and wealth inequalities**. Even if there is increased economic growth and higher standards of living, these benefits may not be enjoyed by everyone in the economy.

1 Why are there likely to be 'winners' and 'losers' in a market economy and why will this lead to inequality?

Some people will be very successful and earn high incomes in a market economy. However, not everyone will be able to find a job, and there would be no help for poor people from the government. This will be discussed further in Unit 3.3.

- **Lack of concern for the environment**. The incentives will only be for profit and personal gain, and so harm to the environment will not be considered when decisions are made.

2 Why might a chemical producer pour waste into a river rather than clean it up?

Therefore, it is likely that environmental damage will occur in a market economy because there is no government taking into account wider considerations of the effects of production and consumption on society.

How the market economic system works in different countries

In some countries the market economic system is the main part of the economy, and the government has a smaller part in the economy. Countries like Singapore, the USA, Canada, Mexico, New Zealand and Switzerland have large private sectors and relatively smaller government or public sectors (see Figure 2.9.1c).

Countries that do not have a large market economy operating and have a large government or public sector are Cuba, North Korea, Venezuela, Republic of Congo and Eritrea (see Figure 2.9.1b).

Often the political system in an economy will have an influence on the economic system that is in operation. The more a government is involved in decision making in an economy, the less the market operates to allocate resources.

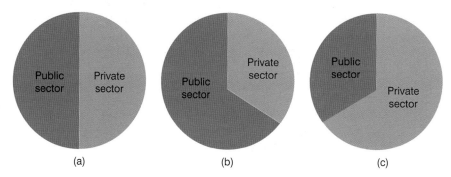

(a)   (b)   (c)

Figure 2.9.1 Proportion of public and private sectors in an economy

Country	Government spending as a % of GDP
Austria	52
Finland	57
France	57
Ireland	29
Italy	50
Japan	39
Norway	49
Sweden	50
Great Britain	43
USA	38
Germany	44

3 Why are there such big differences in the size of the government sector between the countries listed in the table?

Hong Kong – the world's freest economy

In 2017, for the 23rd consecutive year, Hong Kong was ranked the world's freest economy to do business in.

Each year, the Heritage Foundation rates 180 economies on a scale of 0 to 100, with countries scoring over 80 being considered free economies. Hong Kong scored 89.8. Only four other economies scored over 80. The least free economy was North Korea with only 4.9 points, while India was ranked 143rd.

Hong Kong's economy is strong and is supported by a government that promotes free trade and cooperation with its trading partners. It maintains an effective system of law and order and taxes are low and uncomplicated. These factors have helped Hong Kong maintain its impressive record as a great place in which to do business.

1 Why is Hong Kong considered to be an economy that is free to do business in?

2 What are the advantages to Hong Kong of this status?

3 Outline three policies that a government might adopt if it wishes to promote a free economy in which to do business.

Applying

Project work

1. Research which goods and services are provided by the government in your country.

2. Which goods and services are produced by private individuals and firms in your country?

3. Draw a pie chart to show approximately how much of your country's economy is private sector and how much is public sector. To what extent can your country be considered a market economy?

Knowledge check questions

1 What is meant by the market economic system? [2]

2 Identify **one** difference between the private sector and the public sector. [2]

3 Explain **two** advantages of the market economic system. [4]

4 Explain **two** disadvantages of the market economic system. [4]

5 (E) Analyse why a government might wish to increase the share of the private sector in the economy. [6]

Check your progress

Read the unit objectives below and reflect on your progress in each.

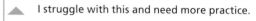

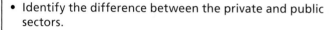

- Define a market economic system.

| | I struggle with this and need more practice. |
| I can do this reasonably well. |
| I can do this with confidence. |

- Identify the difference between the private and public sectors.

- Explain the advantages and disadvantages of the market economic system.

- Explain how market economic systems work in a variety of different countries.

Market failure

Learning objectives

By the end of this unit, you should be able to:

- define market failure
- define the following terms associated with market failure: public good, merit good, demerit good, social benefits, external benefits, private benefits, social costs, external costs and private costs
- explain how market failure can arise from public goods; merit and demerit goods; external costs and external benefits; the abuse of monopoly power; and factor immobility
- analyse the consequences of market failure with the overconsumption of demerit goods and goods with external costs
- analyse the consequences of market failure with the underconsumption of merit goods and those with external benefits
- analyse the implications of market failure on the misallocation of resources with either too many or too few factors of production being allocated by entrepreneurs to the production of these goods.

Starting point

Answer these questions in pairs:

1 What are three products that your parents/guardians encourage you to consume because they are 'good for you' but you do not want to?

2 Why do you think your parents/guardians think you should consume more of these goods?

3 What products might be harmful to people when consumed?

Exploring

Discuss these questions in pairs:

1 What costs are involved in driving a car?

2 How are individuals and firms affected by a large number of people driving cars on the roads?

3 Who is affected by road accidents? Explain how they are affected.

4 Why do some of the effects in question 3 cost money while others do not?

Developing

Units 2.1 to 2.9 discussed how markets work effectively to allocate resources. The price mechanism should ensure that firms and individuals in these markets supply the goods and services demanded by consumers. However, in practice there are many factors that interfere with the smooth working of the price mechanism. The result is an allocation of resources that produce goods and services in the 'wrong' quantities or, in other words, where there is market failure.

Market failure describes a situation where the market does not produce the goods and services that consumers most want and in a quantity that is required. This results in an inefficient allocation of resources. The market equilibrium that is reached has not taken into account all the costs and benefits associated with the production and consumption of the good and as such is the 'wrong' equilibrium. The correct equilibrium is at what is called the social optimum or **social optimum quantity**, where all the costs and benefits associated with the production and consumption of goods and services have been taken into account.

This unit explores the different types of market failure, what causes the different types of market failure to occur, and what consequences arise due to this failure.

Some types of market failure result in too few goods and services being produced and consumed, while others result in too many goods or services being produced and consumed. Another type of market failure would result in none of these goods or services being produced or consumed at all.

Merit goods

Some goods and services are considered beneficial for the consumer but the consumer may not realise just how beneficial these products are for them. When thinking about buying such products, the consumer does not take into account all the benefits that come from consuming them.

 1 Why is this an example of market failure?

It is an example of market failure because the wrong quantity is produced and consumed relative to the price and quantity that would lead to the social optimum quantity. For **merit goods**, do you think people underconsume or overconsume them?

The answer is that they are underconsumed because it is not known how beneficial it is to consume these goods and services, so consumers demand them at the 'wrong' level. This is the wrong quantity because if consumers had all the available information then there would be greater demand and a higher level of sales in the market – the social optimum.

Healthcare is a good example of a merit good.

 2 Why is healthcare an example of a merit good?

 3 Can you think of other examples of goods or services that are really beneficial to you but you probably do not fully appreciate how good they are for you?

Key terms

Market failure – a situation where the economy's resources are not efficiently allocated: the market does not produce the goods and services that consumers most want and in a quantity that is required

Social optimum quantity – the level of output where the social costs equal social benefits: the market equilibrium reached fully takes into account all the costs and benefits associated with the production and consumption of the good

Merit goods – a lack of information about how beneficial these products are for the consumer leads them to be underconsumed

Why are these goods and services better for consumers than they think?

Consumers often do not appreciate how beneficial it might be to get a health check-up, for example. A consumer might feel quite healthy and feel that a check-up is not necessary. They do not know whether or not a particular symptom is serious. Knee pain or frequent mild headaches may be a serious problem or not a problem at all. Consumers may also miss the benefit of vaccinations, education and eating certain types of food.

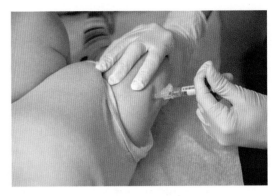

Demerit goods

Some goods and services are considered harmful but the consumer may not fully realise just how harmful the products are. This means that when consumers think about buying these products they do not take into account all the negative effects that result from consuming them. Why is this an example of market failure?

It is because the wrong quantity is produced and consumed relative to the market equilibrium price and quantity that would lead to the social optimum quantity. For **demerit goods**, do you think they are underconsumed or overconsumed?

The answer is that they are overconsumed because it is not known how harmful it is to consume these goods and services, so consumers demand them at the 'wrong' level. This is the wrong quantity because if consumers had all the available information then there would be lower demand and a lower level of sales in the market – consumption and production would be at the social optimum quantity.

Key term

Demerit goods – a lack of information as to how harmful these products are for the consumer leads them to be overconsumed

 Can you think of any examples of goods or services that are really harmful to you but you probably do not fully appreciate how bad they are for you?

Why are these goods and services more harmful for consumers than they think?

Consumers often do not appreciate how harmful it is to smoke cigarettes, for example. A consumer might feel quite healthy and feel that smoking will not cause much harm or that the harmful effects will be felt by someone else. This leads to overconsumption. Similar examples include certain unhealthy foods, alcohol and gambling.

Extension activity

1 (a) Draw a supply and demand diagram for a merit good, and then draw where the demand curve should be if the consumer has all the information about the product. Is this new demand curve at a higher or lower level than the original demand curve?

  (b) Indicate where the private or original equilibrium will be and where the social optimum level of sales should be. Is this output at a higher or lower level than the original output?

  (c) How does this show the existence of market failure?

2 (a) Draw a supply and demand diagram for a demerit good, and then draw where the demand curve should be if the consumer has all the information about the product. Is this new demand curve at a higher or lower level than the original demand curve?

  (b) Indicate where the private or original equilibrium will be and where the social optimum level of sales should be. Is this output at a higher or lower level than the original output?

  (c) How does this show the existence of market failure?

Public goods

Have you ever thought about why the government provides some goods and the private sector doesn't? You may have just thought the government is best at providing these goods. However, there are some goods that will not be produced at all by businesses, and therefore if the government does not produce them they will not exist.

Imagine you live in a village that is regularly flooded. Everyone in the village thinks it would be a good idea to build flood defences to stop the flooding. Will this happen? Everyone could pay a small amount and then the flood defences could be built. But will everyone pay towards the building of these defences? Some people in the village may decide not to pay, believing everyone else will pay. Their thinking goes that the flood defences will still be built without their payment so it will not matter that they have not contributed. These people are called 'free riders'. A free rider benefits from consuming a product or service that others have purchased. For example, people climbing onto the roof of a train as it is leaving the station will benefit from the ride but will not have paid. The problem is that if there are too many free riders there will be insufficient money to provide the good or service. In the case of flood defences, people in the village who have not paid towards the building of the flood defences cannot be excluded from having their houses protected from the floods, but there is no way to make these people pay. So the flood defences will not be built even though everyone agrees they are a good idea and that they would benefit everyone.

This is an example of what are called **public goods** (or **public services**).

So what makes something a public good? It must have two special characteristics – **non-excludability** and **non-rivalry**.

Non-excludability

The first characteristic of a public good is non-excludability. This means that even if someone has not paid for the good they cannot be excluded from consuming it. The people in the village who have not paid towards the building of the flood defences cannot be excluded from benefiting from them and will still enjoy protection from flooding.

Can you be excluded from eating a chocolate bar if you haven't paid for it? Yes, and this situation refers to **private goods** (or **private services**). Consumers who have not paid will not be able to enjoy the good or service. Most of the goods and services you buy are private goods because if you do not pay for them then you are excluded from consuming them.

 Can you be excluded from consuming the following goods and services if you have not paid for them?

(a) a jacket

(b) a beach

(c) a downloaded film

(d) a ferry journey

Non-rivalry

The second characteristic of a public good is non-rivalry. If you eat a chocolate bar it stops someone else from consuming the same chocolate bar. So there is rivalry for private goods. In the village example, however, if one person has their house protected from

Public goods (or **public services**) – goods that consumers cannot be excluded from enjoying even if they have not paid; everyone can equally enjoy consuming the good

Non-excludability – consumers who have not paid for a good (or service) cannot be excluded from benefiting from the consumption of that good or service

Non-rivalry – the consumption of goods by one individual does not prevent another individual consuming the good at the same time

Private goods (or **private services**) – goods that it is possible to exclude individuals from consuming if they have not paid and there is rivalry in the consumption of these goods

flooding it does not stop other people from having their houses protected as well. There is no rivalry and everyone can enjoy the benefit of the public good at the same time.

6 Can you consume the following goods and services without stopping someone else from consuming them at the same time, if you have not paid?

(a) a hospital bed

(b) crime prevention by the police in your local area

(c) a book

(d) a bicycle

7 Using the terms non-rivalry and non-excludability, explain why military defence for a whole country is a public good but providing a bodyguard for a VIP is a private good.

If the characteristics of non-excludability and non-rivalry do not apply, which is the case for most goods and services, then they are private goods (or services).

However, if both of these characteristics apply to the goods or services, then they are public goods and will be provided by the government or they will not exist. The government can make everyone pay by taxing them and using that money to build flood defences or street lights or military defence.

External costs

When you studied supply and demand in Unit 2.5, the only costs that were considered were **private costs**. These are the costs to an individual or business when they produce or consume something. The costs to a business of supplying a life-saving medicine, for example, will include wages, electricity, rent, the cost of raw materials, distribution costs and advertising. The cost to the individual to consume this medicine is the price they pay.

When a good or service is produced there are private costs to both the consumer and the producer.

In the case of medicine, the private costs will be:

* the costs of making the medicine

* the price paid by the consumer who buys the medicine.

Key term

....

Private costs – the costs to an individual or business when they produce or consume a good

However, these may not be the only costs involved. Look at the photograph of the factory. Who else does the factory affect when the medicine is being produced? The photograph shows that it is likely the air is being polluted, so all local people and nearby wildlife will be affected by breathing polluted air. Such costs that are borne by anyone else who is neither the producer nor the consumer are called **external costs**.

External costs affect others and are separate from the decisions made by producers and consumers. Those affected are third parties because they have had no say in the decisions about what to produce and consume. They are experiencing what are called **spillover effects** because the effects of production or consumption spill over onto others.

This means the full cost of producing a good or service includes both the private costs to the producer and any external costs to third parties. The total costs are called **social costs** as they include all the costs to society of producing a good or service.

+

A product may be overproduced and overconsumed if there are more social costs associated with the production and consumption of the good than are paid for as part of the price that was charged for it. So the product may have a lower price than it should have if all the costs, including the external costs, had been taken into account when the market price of the good was determined.

Demerit goods may also have external costs associated with their production and consumption. The external costs of consuming and producing them can spill over onto society. Take cigarettes, for example: smoking-related illnesses cost the National Health Service (NHS) in the UK approximately £2 billion (US$2.6 billion) a year to treat.

External benefits

When you studied supply and demand in Unit 2.5, the only benefits that were considered were **private benefits**. These are benefits an individual or business derives from producing or consuming something. They include the benefits to the business of supplying a good such as revenue. The benefit to the individual from buying a good or service is the enjoyment they get from consuming it.

When a good or service is produced and consumed it has benefits to both the consumer and the producer. However, these may not be the only benefits of this production.

Look at the photograph of the balcony with flowers on it. The consumer paid for the flowers to gain the benefit of displaying flowers on the balcony, and the supplier of the flowers benefited from selling them. Who else might be enjoying the flowers? Anyone who passes by the balcony and enjoys looking up at the flowers will enjoy a benefit. The flowers make the place more beautiful and third parties can enjoy them without having made any payment towards their production or consumption. The benefits of beautiful flowers spill over onto these passers-by.

The full benefits of producing a good or service include both the private benefits to the producer and any **external benefits** to third parties. The total benefits are called **social benefits** as they include all the benefits to society of producing and consuming a good or service.

social benefits = private benefits　　　+　　　external benefits

　　+　　

A product is underproduced and underconsumed if there are more benefits associated with the production and consumption of the good than are taken into account when deciding whether to buy the good. Equilibrium price and quantity are lower than they would be if demand was higher and reflected all the external benefits and not just those taken into account by consumers.

Merit goods may also have external benefits associated with their production and consumption. Businesses benefit from the spillover effects of healthcare and education in the form of a healthy and educated workforce.

Key terms

External benefits – the benefits to a third party from the production or consumption of a good or service

Social benefits – the private benefits plus the external benefits of producing a good or service

Application tasks

The government wants to build a new motorway to connect the airport to the capital city. It is important that this motorway gets built because the existing road is very congested and there are long delays for people and businesses getting to and from the airport. The motorway will lead to the destruction of forests and the removal of habitat for rare animals that attract foreign tourists.

1. Identify some of the private costs and benefits of building this motorway.

2. Identify some of the external costs and benefits of the motorway.

3. Do you think the social benefits (private benefits and external benefits) are greater than the social costs (private costs and external costs)? Should the building of the motorway go ahead?

Present your conclusion to the class.

4. (E) How could the external costs and external benefits associated with the building of the motorway be calculated?

5. (E) How should the decision to build the motorway be made?

Key knowledge

Summary of examples of market failure

Key term associated with market failure	Cause of the market failure	Consequence of the market failure	Examples
Merit good	A lack of information on how beneficial the product is when consumed	It is underconsumed relative to the social optimum level of consumption	Healthcare, education, certain foods that promote good health
Demerit good	A lack of information on how bad the product is when consumed	It is overconsumed relative to the social optimum level of consumption	Cigarettes, certain foods that cause health problems
Public good	Cannot exclude consumers who have not paid from enjoying these goods	These goods will not be provided in a market economy unless the government provides them	Street lights, military defence, lighthouses
External cost	Third parties have to pay a cost for the production and consumption of the good but they have no say over it	The product is overproduced and overconsumed as there are more costs associated with the production of the good and these are not paid for by the consumer	Air pollution, noise pollution, congestion, oil spills at sea, global warming, loss of rainforests
External benefit	Third parties enjoying the good cannot influence the decision to produce or consume it	The product is underproduced and underconsumed as certain benefits associated with the good are not taken into account by the consumer or producer	Gym membership, electric cars, healthcare, education

Other causes of market failure

Other examples of market failure include the abuse of **monopoly power** and factor immobility.

Abuse of monopoly power

If a market for a good or service only has a single supplier (or even a few very large ones) then that supplier might abuse the fact that there is no competition and charge a much higher price than if the market were competitive. The quantity supplied to the market may be restricted to keep the price higher, which translates into higher profits for the monopolist. This is market failure because consumers pay a much higher price for a lower quantity of the good or service than they would in a competitive market. The monopolist's greater profits come from an abuse of its position of power over the market.

Factor immobility

This is a cause of market failure because the factors of production do not move easily and quickly between different industries when consumer demand changes. Consumers may want less of one good and more of another good, and supply needs to increase for products where demand has increased and supply reduced where demand has fallen. Labour is a common example of factor immobility.

As demand changes, some industries will reduce in size and others may grow. The factors of production need to move from the industries that are decreasing supply to those that are increasing supply. These industries may be located in different parts of the country and may require different skills from their workers. Industries may face either geographical immobility of labour or occupational immobility of labour or both.

- Geographical immobility describes the situation faced by unemployed workers who live too far away from the areas with job vacancies. These workers remain unemployed while job vacancies remain unfilled.

- Occupational immobility describes workers with the wrong skills for available job vacancies. They may have the right skills for industries experiencing reduced demand, whereas the expanding industries require quite different skills. Again, these workers remain unemployed while firms cannot expand to produce the goods that are in higher demand. This is an example of market failure; the factors of production cannot be adjusted to meet the demand.

Key terms

Monopoly power – a single firm dominates the market and has the power to determine the market price

Factor immobility – the difficulties in transferring factors of production so that they may be used by an alternative industry

Soda and water usage

In March 2017, more than a million traders in India removed fizzy drinks produced by multinational companies, including Coca-Cola and PepsiCo, from their shelves. This was in protest against foreign exploitation of India's dwindling water resources.

The Indian Resource Centre, an NGO, has calculated that it takes 400 litres of water to make 1 litre of fizzy drink.

Vanigar Sangam is one of the two Indian trade associations leading the campaign. They claim that the level of water usage by MNCs in Tamil Nadu is unsustainable. The state is already suffering severe drought after low rainfall during the previous monsoon, and the farmers are struggling in difficult conditions.

1 Why are fizzy drinks produced?

2 Who benefits from the production and consumption of fizzy drinks?

3 Who are the third parties that are affected by the production of fizzy drinks in India?

4 Identify private and external costs associated with the production of fizzy drinks in India.

5 Should the government close businesses that create external costs?

Applying

Project work

Use the internet, individually or in groups, to research answers to the following questions:

1. What is meant by global warming?

2. What causes global warming?

3. Who is responsible for causing global warming?

4. Who is affected by global warming?

5. (E) Can global warming be corrected?

Present your findings to the rest of the class.

Knowledge check questions

1 What is meant by market failure? [2]

2 Explain the difference between a merit good and a demerit good. [4]

3 Explain the difference between a private good and a public good. [4]

4 Give **two** examples of external costs and **two** examples of external benefits. [4]

5 Analyse, using examples, how external costs are an example of market failure. [6]

6 Analyse why the social benefits of electric cars might be higher than the private benefits. [6]

7 Explain how monopolies can abuse their power. [4]

8 Analyse why immobility of labour causes market failure. [6]

9 (E) Analyse why the overconsumption of a demerit good is considered to be market failure. [6]

10 (E) Analyse why there are too few factors of production being allocated by entrepreneurs to the production of goods that have external benefits. [6]

Check your progress

Read the unit objectives below and reflect on your progress in each.

	I struggle with this and need more practice.
	I can do this reasonably well.
	I can do this with confidence.

- Define market failure.

- Define the following terms associated with market failure: public good, merit good, demerit good, social benefits, external benefits, private benefits, social costs, external costs and private costs.

- Explain how market failure can arise from public goods; merit and demerit goods; external costs and external benefits; the abuse of monopoly power; and factor immobility.

- Analyse the consequences of market failure with the overconsumption of demerit goods and goods with external costs.

- Analyse the consequences of market failure with the underconsumption of merit goods and those with external benefits.

- Analyse the implications of market failure on the misallocation of resources with either too many or too few factors of production being allocated by entrepreneurs to the production of these goods.

Mixed economic system

Learning objectives

By the end of this unit, you should be able to:

- define a mixed market economic system
- define minimum and maximum prices
- explain the effects of imposing maximum and minimum prices on markets in various contexts, such as product, labour and foreign exchange markets
- draw and interpret diagrams showing the effects of indirect taxation, subsidies, and minimum and maximum prices in product and labour markets
- define government microeconomic policy measures of regulation, privatisation and nationalisation, and the direct provision of goods
- discuss the effectiveness of government intervention in overcoming the drawbacks of a mixed economic system.

● ●

Starting point

Answer these questions in pairs:

1 What goods or services does your government provide for free?

2 What goods or services provided by your government do you have to pay to use?

Exploring

Discuss these questions in pairs:

1 What is the youngest age at which people can drive in your country?

2 What rules must you follow in your country in order to drive a car on the roads?

Developing

Mixed market system

As discussed in Unit 2.10, in a market economy not all goods will be produced and consumed in the 'right' quantities to arrive at the social optimum quantity. Market failure means that the government often chooses to intervene to reduce or correct market failure. A **mixed market system** is one that combines a market economy with government intervention.

Government intervention to reduce or correct market failure

The government tries to improve the way markets work in order to reduce market failure, and it can use several different policies to do this. These policies are microeconomic policies as they are aimed at individual markets and not at the economy as a whole.

Key term

Mixed market system – an economy that has both private sector firms and a government supplying goods and services

Three of these policies are:

- fixing a maximum or minimum price
- adding a tax to increase the price
- giving a subsidy to the producer to lower the price.

Maximum and minimum prices

Maximum price control is where the government puts a ceiling on how high prices can increase. It might do this because basic foods or energy are expensive and the government wants to make them affordable to low-income groups.

 1 What would happen if the maximum price is set above the equilibrium price? Draw a diagram to show this. At what price will the product be sold?

In Figure 2.11.1, if there is no government interference in the market, then the equilibrium price and quantity will be P_e and Q_e. This is where quantity supplied equals quantity demanded.

The government may feel that the equilibrium price at P_e is too high to be affordable to low-income groups. If the maximum price is set below the equilibrium price of P_e, the quantity supplied at this maximum price is Q_1 and the quantity demanded at this maximum price is Q_2.

This leads to excess demand of Q_1 to Q_2. The market cannot reach an equilibrium and therefore price and quantity will remain at a disequilibrium.

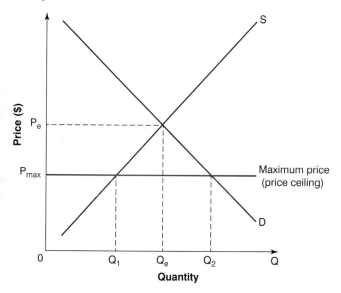

Figure 2.11.1 Effect of maximum price and rent controls in the housing market

An example of this arrangement is rent controls on housing. In this case the government steps in to protect people from having to pay very high prices to rent accommodation.

 2 How can you tell if the market for housing is in disequilibrium?

The consequences of applying a maximum price to rented accommodation is likely to be a shortage of this type of housing. Many people will be demanding rented accommodation but there will be too few properties available to rent. Without higher prices, property owners are not willing to supply more accommodation to the market for rent. The government accepts that the market will not reach an equilibrium. However, it believes this is better than having high rent, which leads to people on low incomes not having anywhere they can afford to live.

Maximum prices can also be placed on food so that people on low incomes can afford what they need to feed their families.

 3 What do you think is likely to happen if food has a maximum price put on it?

It is likely that there will be an illegal market for food because demand will outstrip supply. There will be shortages of food relative to the demand for it. People will queue to buy what little food is available in the shops. Illegal food markets would see sellers charge much higher prices than the maximum price and possibly higher prices than the equilibrium price, P_e. A maximum price will tend to lead to people trying to get round it in some way.

So the drawbacks of maximum prices are that there will probably be shortages and illegal markets with much higher prices than the free market would see. Some people will buy at the lower maximum price but many more people will not have their demand met unless they are prepared to pay a much higher price than the maximum price.

Minimum price control describes an arrangement where the government steps in to ensure prices do not fall below a certain level.

 4 Can you think of any examples of markets where minimum price controls might be a good idea?

In Figure 2.11.2 the equilibrium wage rate for a particular type of job will be W_1 if left to the market. This is where the demand for this type of labour is equal to the supply of workers willing to do this type of job. The wage rate of W_1 might be very low and workers may find it difficult to pay their household expenses. At a very low rate, workers may live in absolute poverty (see Unit 5.2).

In situations like this, the government can introduce a minimum wage so that all employers pay at least this much to workers.

Many countries have a minimum wage set for the whole country, such as in the UK, or for different regions, such as in China.

In Figure 2.11.2 the minimum wage is set well above the equilibrium wage. If it was set below the equilibrium wage, W_1, it would have no effect.

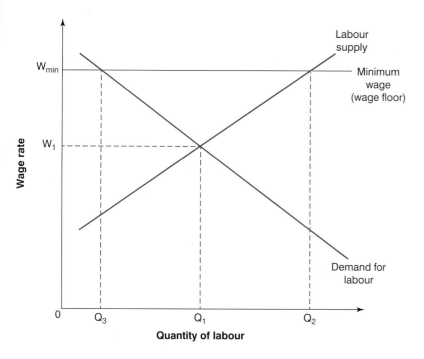

Figure 2.11.2 Effect of the minimum wage on the labour market

5 Why will a minimum wage rate set below W_1 have no effect?

The minimum wage in Figure 2.11.2 means that the quantity of labour demanded is Q_3 while the quantity of workers willing to supply their services to the market at this minimum wage is Q_2. There is an excess supply of labour in this market of Q_3 to Q_2. This means workers will be offering to work but there will be too few jobs available.

Again, this market will not move to the equilibrium wage of W_1 but instead will remain with an excess supply of people willing to work as long as the wage rate is not allowed to fall to W_1.

6 How can you tell that the labour market is not in equilibrium?

The impact of minimum wages on a labour market is likely to be that many workers will be looking for work and will remain unemployed because there are not enough jobs available at that wage rate.

Although the market will not reach an equilibrium, the benefit is that workers will not be exploited by low wages. The higher wage should cover necessities such as food and housing. Over time, higher wages from the minimum wage being imposed could create more spending in the economy and more jobs will become available. Unemployment may then fall as firms expand to meet the additional demand for goods and services.

The advantage of imposing maximum and minimum prices is their use in supporting government aims such as improving the market failure that arises from low-income families not being able to afford basic necessities. The disadvantage, however, is that the market won't move to an equilibrium so there will be either excess demand or excess supply.

Illegal markets often arise as producers or consumers attempt to get round the price restrictions. Suppliers may divert products to the highest bidder.

Exchange rates

Minimum and maximum prices can also be used to influence exchange rates. The government sets a minimum exchange rate for the currency not to fall below and/or a maximum exchange rate for it not to go beyond before the government itself intervenes to bring the exchange rate in line with the parameters it has set. This is a **fixed exchange rate system** (see Unit 6.3). By reducing the fluctuations of the exchange rate, the government makes importing and exporting more stable for individuals and firms.

Key term
....

Fixed exchange rate system – maintains a country's exchange rate within a very narrow band against other currencies

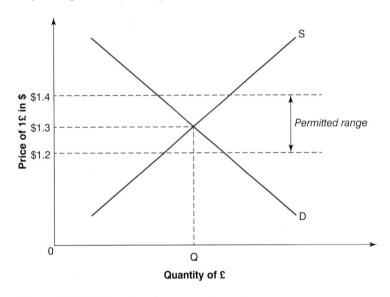

Figure 2.11.3 Fixed exchange rate system

In Figure 2.11.3 there is a maximum exchange rate of $1.4 to each £1 and a minimum exchange rate of $1.2 for each £1. The exchange rate can fluctuate between these two prices but if it starts to go above or below them then the government will intervene to buy or sell the currency to bring it back between the minimum and maximum. This is discussed in more detail in Unit 6.3.

Indirect taxation

The government may want to reduce the consumption of some goods such as demerit goods or those goods that have a lot of external costs associated with them. This can be a way of making consumers take account of the external costs involved in producing them. The government might impose an indirect tax on the goods or services to increase their price and reduce the quantity traded and thereby reduce market failure. An **indirect tax** is a tax on spending; it increases the price of goods and services (see Unit 4.3).

An indirect tax shifts the supply curve to the left and it moves up vertically by the amount of the tax, S to S₁ (see Unit 2.4). Figure 2.11.4 shows the effect of an indirect tax, raising the price from P to P₁ and reducing the equilibrium quantity from Q to Q₁.

Key term

Indirect tax – a tax on spending that increases the price of goods and services

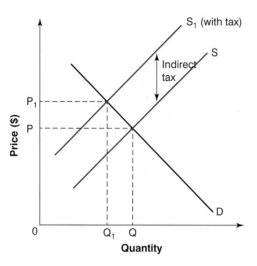

Figure 2.11.4 Effect of an indirect tax

Indirect taxes can be introduced to add costs that are equal to the external costs. This serves to reduce the quantity supplied and quantity demanded and moves them to the social optimum quantity. If adding the amount of the external costs of production is effective, then the market failure will have been corrected.

 Would an elastic or inelastic PED have the greatest effect on reducing sales if a tax is imposed on a good or service?

The impact of the indirect tax will be affected by PED for the good or service

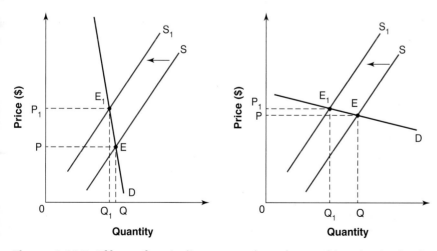

Figure 2.11.5 Effect of an indirect tax when demand is price inelastic and when it is price elastic

Figure 2.11.5 shows the effects of an indirect tax on price and quantity for two products with a different PED. The price rise is P to P_1 and sales fall from Q to Q_1.

An inelastic PED will result in a much higher percentage rise in price than the percentage fall in sales.

An elastic PED will result in a much smaller percentage rise in price than the percentage fall in sales.

8 Explain whether an elastic PED or an inelastic PED will raise the most revenue for the government when an indirect tax is imposed on a product.

9 Analyse why governments aim to place indirect taxes on products such as cigarettes and not on products such as chocolate.

How effective is taxation at reducing market failure?

Does a tax lower the quantity of cigarettes smoked? An indirect tax may reduce the number of people smoking but it is likely to reduce the quantity consumed by only a small percentage because smoking is addictive. Many people who smoke will continue to smoke and pay the higher price. The PED for cigarettes is inelastic and so the effectiveness of taxation in this example will be reduced. However, it may still be assumed to be better than imposing no tax at all and keeping the number of cigarettes smoked at the original quantity. Also the taxation revenue could be used to fund advertisements encouraging smokers to give up the habit, thus shifting the demand curve to the left.

Petrol and diesel are considered to have many harmful effects on the environment as they are used as fuel and burned in the engines of cars, trucks and buses. Many countries impose indirect taxes on petrol and diesel, both to raise revenue for the government and also to reduce the emission of exhaust fumes.

10 How effective is the indirect tax on petrol and diesel at reducing the external costs?

In this case the PED is inelastic, as petrol and diesel are required for driving. Many consumers will keep using petrol and diesel even if the prices are increased by indirect taxation. Over the longer term some consumers may switch to more efficient cars, trucks and buses, which will further reduce the consumption of petrol and diesel.

Economic growth can increase demand for petrol and diesel, which would drive up prices for them as well and in turn reduce quantity demanded. However, if the demand curve shifts due to economic growth and increased incomes then the higher price may have little overall effect on sales. If the government is still keen to adjust petrol consumption, the answer may be to make alternative fuels more attractive by supporting electric or hybrid cars, for example. Here, a subsidy is something to consider.

The advantages of imposing indirect taxes are that they raise revenue for the government and reduce the production and consumption of demerit goods and goods with high external costs.

The disadvantage of imposing indirect taxes is that they may not be very effective in reducing the consumption of demerit goods with inelastic demand.

Subsidies

A **subsidy** is like the opposite of an indirect tax. The government may want to increase the consumption of some goods such as merit goods or goods with high external benefits. It might apply a subsidy to reduce the price and increase quantity traded in order to reduce the market failure. A subsidy is an amount of money given to a firm to lower the costs of supplying the good or service so the market pays a reduced price.

Key term

Subsidy – an amount of money given to a firm to lower the cost of supplying the good or service to the market

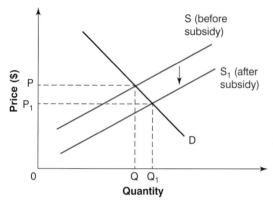

Figure 2.11.6 Effect of a subsidy

A subsidy shifts the supply curve to the right and it moves down vertically by the amount of the subsidy, S to S_1. This was mentioned in Unit 2.4. Figure 2.11.6 shows that the effect is to lower the price from P to P_1 and to increase the equilibrium quantity from Q to Q_1.

Subsidies are often given to firms to encourage consumers to buy more of the firm's good or service. This may increase the quantity produced and consumed of a merit good. The subsidy can also be applied to reduce the cost of goods or services by an amount equal to the external benefits of their production, increasing the quantity supplied and quantity demanded towards the social optimum quantity. If this is effective then the market failure related to a lack of knowledge of the external benefits will have been corrected.

How effective are subsidies at reducing market failure?

Will a subsidy increase the quantity of electric cars sold? A subsidy may reduce the price of electric cars but it is likely to increase the quantity traded by only a small percentage at the present time. This is because electric cars are still much more expensive than petrol cars and are still not very convenient to charge. This reduces

the effectiveness of a subsidy. However, it may still be better than not applying a subsidy at all and keeping the number of electric cars sold at the original quantity. Technological developments may well see this situation change. As more electric cars are sold, more firms may see an opportunity and want to develop and sell them. The advantage of subsidies is that they can increase the production and consumption of merit goods or goods with high external benefits. The disadvantage of subsidies is that they are expensive for the government and not very effective at increasing production and consumption for goods with inelastic demand.

 11 Can you think of other ways the government can influence consumers or producers of goods or services?

Government microeconomic policy measures

How else can the government influence the price and quantity produced and consumed of goods and services? It can impose regulations on how producers and consumers behave or it can directly intervene in the market to produce the goods and services itself.

Regulation

 12 Can you think of any regulations that your government has introduced to regulate how firms in your country behave or what goods or services you must use?

Regulation is the government imposition of rules backed by the use of penalties that are intended to modify the behaviour of individuals and firms in the private sector. There are many examples where governments have introduced regulations or restrictions, such as an age limit on driving a car and test requirements for driving alone. Governments have these regulations to protect the population.

However, there are other regulations that make certain things compulsory because they are seen as good for you and for society.

These include requirements to take out car insurance, wear a motorbike helmet and having to attend school up to a certain age. The advantages of regulations are that they instruct consumers and producers how they should behave and what they should do for the benefit of themselves and society. Demerit goods can be restricted and merit goods can be made compulsory to reduce market failure. Individuals and firms can be made to take into account external costs and benefits when they are producing and consuming goods. Forbidding firms from throwing waste into rivers and instructing consumers not to drop litter are just two examples.

The disadvantage is that regulations may not be followed. It costs the government money to investigate and prosecute individuals or firms that do not follow the regulations, and if regulations are not enforced then it may be a waste of time having them as they

Key term

Regulation – the imposition of rules by the government, backed by the use of penalties that are intended to modify the behaviour of individuals and firms in the private sector

will be ignored and market failure will persist. This will reduce the effectiveness of regulation and efforts to reduce market failure.

Privatisation and nationalisation

Privatisation is the transfer of ownership of property or business from the government to the private sector. **Nationalisation** is the opposite: it is the transfer of ownership of property or business from the private sector to the government. Some goods or services are considered to be so important that they are provided by the government. Examples include the generation of electricity, the provision of water and the maintenance of transport systems. In some countries it is thought to be better to rely on the private sector for goods and services because of the efficiencies and lower prices that come from competitive markets.

Direct government provision of goods

The government must provide public goods or they will not be provided at all, such as street lights or military defence. The goods and services that are directly provided by the government are often merit goods, and the government may want to increase the production and consumption of these goods and so provides them itself. Examples such as healthcare and education were considered in Unit 2.10.

One advantage of government provision is that the consumption of these goods and services should increase and be available to everyone, even the poor. Society may benefit from the increased consumption of merit goods such as healthcare. A healthy labour force will be more efficient when working for firms and it is better for the families themselves to be healthy. However, this is expensive and has an opportunity cost because the money could have been spent elsewhere in the economy. So there may be a conflict between different uses of government money. Also, if a merit good is free it may become overconsumed as people do not have to regulate their demand according to price. There could still be market failure if consumption is at the 'wrong' quantity.

Provision of information

Governments can also help to reduce market failure for merit and demerit goods by providing information as to how beneficial or harmful these goods are when consumed. This may help consumers make a better decision about their demand. However, the effectiveness of this approach depends on whether consumers receive this information and then act on it. Some foods are considered better for your health while other foods are considered harmful if eaten in large quantities. Government advertising in many countries is trying to encourage the population to have a healthier diet.

Key terms

Privatisation – the transfer of ownership (of property or a business) from the government to the private sector

Nationalisation – the transfer of ownership (of property or a business) from the private sector to the government

Challenges in waste management for India

Waste management rules in India mean local governments are responsible for reducing waste. With the expansion of cities in India more and more waste is produced, which causes increasing problems for its disposal. The Indian government has imposed regulations on local governments that they must keep cities clean. However, nearly all local governments dump the waste outside of the city in landfill sites and the space to keep doing this is running out.

Many people feel that there needs to be more emphasis on recycling to reduce the amount of waste that is dumped on these landfill sites. To do this effectively the waste needs to be separated before it is taken to landfill, so that it can be recycled. Most recyclable waste ends up in a landfill site due to the lack of efficient waste management.

Around 100 cities now have local governments that are planning in the long term to be able to process waste and not send it to landfill sites. To do this, households and firms will need to separate their waste so it can all be recycled or reprocessed. The aim is to get rid of landfill sites in 20 major cities in India. There is no spare land for dumping garbage, and the existing ones are almost full. It is reported that almost 80% of the waste at Delhi landfill sites could be recycled. So the challenge is to make this happen!

1 Why is garbage a problem?

2 Explain why garbage could be described as a demerit good.

3 What does the article suggest the government is doing to reduce the market failure?

4 How effective do you think this policy will be in reducing the problem of landfill?

Applying

Project work

Traffic congestion is a problem in many countries, especially in the cities. What problems are caused by too many cars on the road? Consider the problems caused for firms, consumers and emergency services.

Using the internet, investigate the different ways governments, such as those of China and Mexico, have tried to reduce this problem.

Recommend a way that would be most effective in your country.

Present your findings to the class.

Knowledge check questions

1 What is meant by a mixed market system? [2]

2 Draw a diagram to show the effect of a maximum price for food. [3]

3 Draw a diagram to show the effect of an increase in the minimum wage. [3]

4 Discuss whether raising indirect taxes is a good way of reducing market failure. [8]

5 Analyse, using a supply and demand diagram, the impact of applying a subsidy to a product. [6]

6 Explain **one** advantage and **one** disadvantage of using regulations to reduce market failure. [4]

7 What is the difference between privatisation and nationalisation? [2]

8 Explain why the government provides some goods and services free of charge. [4]

9 Analyse what affects how much the price rises and demand falls after an indirect tax is imposed. [6]

10 (E) Discuss the extent to which government intervention can overcome market failure. [8]

Check your progress

Read the unit objectives below and reflect on your progress in each.

	I struggle with this and need more practice.
	I can do this reasonably well.
	I can do this with confidence.

- Define a mixed market economic system.

- Define minimum and maximum prices.

- Explain the effects of imposing maximum and minimum prices on markets in various contexts, such as product, labour and foreign exchange markets.

- Draw and interpret diagrams showing the effects of indirect taxation, subsidies, and minimum and maximum prices in product and labour markets.

- Define government microeconomic policy measures of regulation, privatisation and nationalisation, and the direct provision of goods.

- Discuss the effectiveness of government intervention in overcoming the drawbacks of a mixed economic system.

Chapter review

Multiple choice questions

1 What would be studied in micro economics?

    A total amount of exports for the economy

    B total number of people unemployed in the economy

    C total output for the economy

    D total revenue from the sale of cars in the economy

2 What is the fundamental economic question that needs to be addressed by any economic system?

    A How should raw materials be paid for?

    B What goods and services are to be produced?

    C When should goods and services be produced?

    D Who should work in the economy?

3 Which diagram shows a contraction in demand?

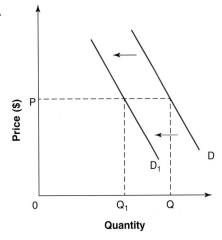

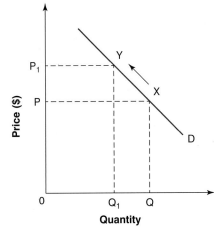

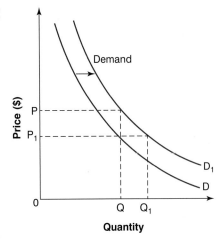

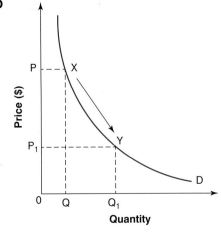

4 Which diagram shows what happens after a poor harvest?

A

B

C

D

5 A market is in a disequilibrium with excess demand. What is **likely** to happen in a market economy?

   A The price will fall.

   B The price will increase.

   C The quantity demanded will increase.

   D The quantity supplied will decrease.

6 Which diagram shows the effect of a successful advertising campaign for a new style of handbag?

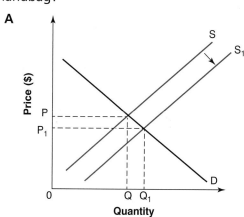

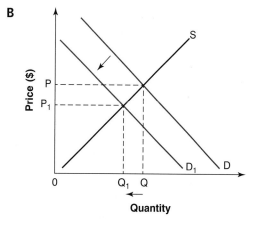

C

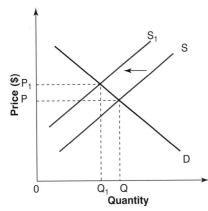

D

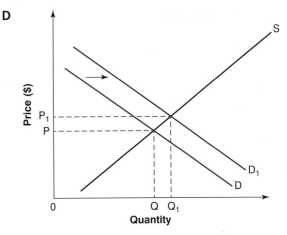

7 What will lead to an increase in revenue if PED is inelastic?

  A a fall in the price

  B an increase in quantity demanded

  C an increase in quantity supplied

  D an increase in the price

8 The price of a product falls by 10% and quantity supplied falls from 500 to 400. What is the PES for this product?

  A 2

  B 0.5

  C 50

  D 20

9 Which key term is associated with market failure?

  A private company

  B public company

  C public good

  D private good

10 Which is **likely** to be the result of an increase in the minimum wage on the labour market?

  A demand is greater than supply

  B fewer people want to work

  C supply equals demand

  D supply is greater than demand

Structured questions

1 The growth of fracking

According to a recent report from the US Energy Information Administration, 'fracking' – or, to give it its technical name, hydraulic fracturing – is now used to produce more than half of all crude oil in the USA. Fracking "has allowed the United States to increase its oil production faster than at any time in its history", with much of the new production coming from America's enormous shale oil deposits.

The dramatic increase in US oil output in the last ten years means that only Saudi Arabia and Russia supply more oil to the global market. It is also the main contributing factor to the current global surplus of oil and this excess supply is having an effect on the world price of oil.

(a)	Identify **two** non-price factors that affect the supply of oil.	[2]
(b)	Explain **two** reasons why the supply of oil may be inelastic in the short run.	[4]
(c)	Analyse, using a diagram, how fracking has affected the global price of oil.	[6]
(d)	Discuss whether a fall in the price of oil is likely to be beneficial to the US economy.	[8]

2 Environmental problems at fracking sites

Hydraulic fracturing, or fracking, involves the injection of frack fluid (a mixture of water and chemicals) under pressure to break up shale and other rock underground and release the oil it contains.

Increased use of this technology in the last decade has caused a huge increase in the amount of oil produced in the USA. This in turn has led to an increase in consumption. In addition, many jobs have been created and fracking companies have enjoyed increased revenues.

However, environmental campaigners have always had serious concerns about the fracking process. Much of the frack fluid returns to the surface and accidental spills, some of many thousands of litres, have been reported. There are also fears that the process can contaminate underground water supplies.

(a) Identity **two** private benefits from fracking. [2]

(b) Using the information in the extract, explain **two** external costs caused by fracking. [4]

(c) Analyse how fracking may cause market failure. [6]

(d) Discuss whether an increase in indirect taxes on oil producers will reduce the problems caused by fracking. [8]

3

Microeconomic decision makers

In this chapter you will learn about why people have to make decisions about what to buy. You will learn about money and banking before looking at how members of households decide what to spend, what to save and whether to borrow money. After that you will consider work, including what determines how much individuals earn and why workers usually specialise, as well as the role of trade unions. You will then think about firms, including how small firms can become larger and what is meant by economies and diseconomies of scale. You will look at what determines the demand for factors of production and why some firms use a lot of labour whereas others use a lot of capital. You will find out how to calculate the costs and revenue of firms and will consider the different objectives that firms can pursue, such as survival or profit maximisation. Finally, you will consider competitive marketplaces and monopolies.

3.1 Money and banking

3.2 Households

3.3 Workers

3.4 Trade unions

3.5 Firms

3.6 Firms and production

3.7 Firms' costs, revenue and objectives

3.8 Market structure

Money and banking

Learning objectives
By the end of this unit, you should be able to:
- describe the different forms that money may take
- explain the functions of money
- explain the characteristics of money
- analyse the role and importance of central banks for government, producers and consumers
- discuss the role and importance of commercial banks for government, producers and consumers.

Starting point

Answer these questions in pairs:

1 Which of the following do you consider to be money: bank accounts; bank notes; cheques; chickens; coins; gold bars; oranges; seashells; stocks and shares; water?

2 Why did you decide some were money and others were not?

3 What did those you decided were money have in common?

4 In addition to buying goods and services, what else might you use money for?

Exploring

Discuss these questions in pairs:

1 Find out which is the bank note with the highest value in your country's currency. If someone gave you one of these, where might you have difficulty using it?

2 If relatives all gave you money for your next birthday, what could you do with it? Which idea would be best?

3 If money did not exist, how might you obtain goods and services?

4 Why might you borrow money from a bank?

Developing

What are the forms of money?

Money is anything that is generally accepted as a means of payment for goods and services. It consists of notes and coins, and bank deposits in the form of both current and savings accounts. Cheques, debit cards and credit cards are not money. Cheques and debit cards allow money in the form of bank deposits in current accounts to be transferred between buyers and sellers. Credit cards enable the holder to spend money now and to pay it at a later point in time.

Key term

Money – anything that is generally accepted as a means of payment for goods and services

Before money was used people had to use **barter**. This involved what is called the 'double coincidence of wants' – the need to find someone who has products you want and is willing to exchange them for your goods or services. If, for example, a farmer wanted to sell chickens and buy a tractor, they would need to find someone who had a tractor to sell and wanted to buy chickens. Even if they could find such a person, it would still be difficult to decide how many chickens a tractor is worth.

Key term

Barter – the act of trading goods or services between two or more parties without the use of money

 Why has money replaced barter as a way of exchanging goods and services?

There are three main types of money:

- commodity money
- fiat money
- fiduciary money.

Type of money	Explanation
Commodity	Any commodity can be used as money. In many cases precious metals such as gold, silver and copper are used because they have value in their own right (intrinsic value). This is because they are scarce resources. In some parts of the world, commodities such as seashells (cowrie shells), beads, tea and tobacco have been used as money.
Fiat	Fiat money is the basis of all modern money systems. It consists of notes and coins. Although most coins were originally made from precious metals such as gold and silver and had intrinsic value, nowadays this is not the case. The value of fiat money is determined by the central bank and the amount that is issued by the government. The market forces of demand and supply determine the value of fiat money.
Fiduciary	Today's monetary system is highly fiduciary. This means that bank notes and coins are solely dependent for their value on the reputation of the issuer. Bank notes are backed either directly or indirectly by a country's central bank. Cheques are backed by the bank which issued them, as are debit cards.

What are the functions of money?

Money performs four important functions in an economy:

1. **Medium of exchange.** This is anything that sets the value of goods and services and is acceptable to all parties involved in a transaction. Money is generally widely accepted as the means of buying and selling products and is acting, therefore, as a medium of exchange. It overcomes the problems associated with the need to have a double coincidence of wants.

2. **Measure of value or unit of account.** This is the idea that money allows the value of different goods and services to be compared. The direct exchange of goods and services in a barter system made it very difficult to give a valuation to the different products being traded.

3. **Standard for deferred payment.** This enables people to borrow money and pay it back at a later date. It encourages, therefore, the provision of credit and so acts as an incentive to trade. Buyers are able to consume goods and services immediately, but the payment can be spread over a period of time. This was a major limitation of the barter system.

4. **Store of value.** This allows wealth to be stored in the form of money over time. Compared to the barter system, money does not deteriorate (unlike, for example, fruit, which goes rotten) and it is usually not expensive to store. This function of money, however, does face the problem of a possible deterioration in its value due to inflation (see Unit 4.8).

2 To what extent is 'standard for deferred payment' an important function in your country?

What are the characteristics of money?

For anything to be called money it has to have some essential characteristics to distinguish it from other pieces of metal, paper or plastic. These are shown in the table below. Note that you should be careful not to confuse characteristics with functions. Characteristics answer the question: 'What is money?' Functions answer the question: 'What does money do?'

Key terms

Medium of exchange – anything that sets value of goods and services and is acceptable to all parties involved in a transaction

Measure of value or unit of account – the idea that money allows the value of different goods and services to be compared

Standard for deferred payment – enables people to borrow money and pay it back at a later date

Store of value – allows wealth to be stored in the form of money over time

Characteristic	Explanation
Acceptable	Money needs to be accepted by everyone in an economy if it is going to be used to facilitate the exchange of goods and services.
Divisible	Money in an economy needs to be able to be divided into smaller units so that a range of prices can be offered for goods and services. The Malaysian currency, for example, is the ringgit, which is divided into 100 sens.

Characteristic	Explanation
Durable	Money needs to last for a reasonable amount of time if it is to be accepted. Paper money, in the form of bank notes, needs to be replaced after some time because the bank notes wear out. For this reason paper bank notes are being replaced, in many countries, by polymer bank notes which are much more durable.
Scarce	Money needs to be relatively scarce. If it is not scarce it would soon become worthless. This is a possible problem with commodity money because someone could discover and mine for the relevant metal.
Recognisable	Money needs to be easily recognisable in an economy. This contributes to confidence in it.
Stability of supply	Supply of money should only increase in line with economic growth. If it grows faster this will lead to inflation and loss of confidence.
Stability of value	It is important that money has a reasonable degree of stability of value or there will be a loss of confidence. However, inflation will diminish the value over time.
Uniformity	It is essential that every coin or note of a particular value used in an economy is the same. This is why coins have milled edges or special shapes and why bank notes have features such as watermarks, pictures or metal threads so the user has confidence in its value.

CASE STUDY   Food as money

Over the centuries there have been many strange forms of money. In some countries food has been used. Salt is one of the oldest examples, with the word salary coming from the Latin for salt. For many centuries it was used in East Africa and the Sahara desert, while in parts of Central America and Mexico the cocoa bean was a form of money. Among other foods, Parmigiano cheese was used in parts of Italy. Even into this century, turmeric spice wrapped in coconut fibres was an accepted currency in areas of the Solomon Islands.

1 What type of money would food be classified as?

2 Explain which of the characteristics of money food might have.

3 Analyse the extent to which food fulfils the functions of money.

An introduction to banks

Banks do many things. Their primary role is to take in deposits from those with money and lend to those who need funds. Those who deposit money (lend it to the bank) and borrowers (those to whom the bank lends money) include: individuals, households, firms and local and national governments. The amount banks pay for deposits and the income they receive on their loans is called interest.

The banking system and the roles the different banks play include: national central banks that issue currency and set monetary policy (see Unit 4.4), commercial banks that take deposits and make loans, and investment banks, which will *not* be considered here.

What is the role and importance of central banks for government, producers and consumers?

A **central bank** may be controlled directly by the government or may be able to determine policy independently of the government (see Unit 4.4). In most cases, however, they are wholly owned by the government.

The roles of the central bank include the following:

1 **To issue notes and coins:** in most countries only the central bank can issue notes. Coins are normally minted, or produced, by the government, but are issued through the central bank. Overall, the central bank supervises the supply of money in the economy.

2 **To control monetary policy:** the central bank decides the base rate from which other **interest rates** are set. If the central bank wishes, for example, to encourage borrowing and spending, it will reduce its **base rate** (or **bank rate**) which will usually be followed by the commercial banks lowering their interest rates. In recent years, many central banks have used **quantitative easing (QE)** to force interest rates lower (see Unit 4.4).

3 **To manage reserves of foreign currency:** the central bank manages the country's foreign exchange reserves and, depending on the foreign exchange system used by the country, intervenes in the foreign exchange market to influence the value of its currency (see Unit 6.3).

4 **To act as banker to the government:** the central bank keeps the revenue raised by the government and makes payments on its behalf. It also issues short-term and long-term government debt in order to raise extra funds for the government.

5 **To act as banker to commercial banks:** the central bank regulates the behaviour of commercial banks, including holding cash reserves equal to a set percentage of their total deposits. In holding these reserves it can control the ability of the banks to lend. In doing so it tries to ensure trust in the banking system is maintained. It also acts as **lender of last resort** to the commercial banks.

Key terms

Central bank – the bank of the government which is responsible for controlling a country's money supply, issuing notes and coins and setting the rules commercial banks must follow

Interest rate – the cost of borrowing money from a lender, and the reward for saving

Base rate (or **bank rate**) – the interest rate that a central bank will charge to lend money to commercial banks and on which other financial organisations base their interest rates

Quantitative easing (QE) – where a central bank buys financial assets from banks and other private sector businesses with new electronically created money

Commercial bank – a financial institution in which individuals and firms can save their money and also obtain loans

Lender of last resort – where the central bank gives loans to banks or other eligible institutions that are experiencing financial difficulty and may not be able to quickly borrow money elsewhere

The importance of central banks for government, producers and consumers

Government	The importance of the central bank is related to its roles of issuing currency, controlling monetary policy, managing foreign exchange reserves, and acting as banker to the government and the commercial banks – see above.
Producers	The two main areas of importance are interlinked. Changes in the rate of interest will affect producers' ability to borrow money for growth. If interest rates fall then producers are more able and willing to borrow money. In addition, the regulation of the commercial banks may also affect their ability to lend, while creating greater confidence in their survival. Actions such as **quantitative easing** will increase the ease of borrowing.
Consumers	As consumers deposit money with banks, the confidence element is very important. Changes in the rate of interest affect consumers in two ways: in the amount they have to pay for borrowing and in the amount they receive on their deposits.

 What are the advantages for the economy of the central bank being 'independent'?

What is the role and importance of commercial banks for government, producers and consumers?

The basic role of commercial banks is to take deposits or savings from customers and to use them to produce assets for themselves. They do this by lending to borrowers, or investing the money which has been deposited. They charge a rate of interest higher than base rate to borrowers, while normally giving savers a rate of interest lower than base rate.

The importance of commercial banks for government, producers and consumers

Government	Commercial banks are important to governments because they are the means by which monetary policy is transmitted to the rest of the economy. They also stimulate economic growth through lending money to producers.
Producers	The main importance is by taking the savings of many depositors and using them to provide loans to businesses so the businesses can expand. The length of these loans varies from country to country. In India, for example, the loans are usually for up to a year, but in Guatemala they can be for three years, while in South Korea they are for much longer periods. In addition the commercial banks finance trade, for example, by providing foreign exchange facilities to both exporters and importers. They also help people to set up their own businesses by lending money and giving advice.
Consumers	Consumers are provided with a safe place to save their money and to earn interest. Commercial banks also lend money so that individuals can buy expensive items such as cars, houses and refrigerators. Increasingly, they provide means such as mobile apps and debit cards for consumers to access accounts and pay for items without having to carry actual money. In addition, they may provide credit cards so consumers can borrow money for short periods to buy items immediately without waiting until they have enough money. They may also offer safe deposit boxes for very expensive items like jewellery, and important documents, as well as providing foreign currencies for tourists.

Applying

Project work

Use the internet to carry out the following tasks:

1. Research the central bank of your country. Find out its functions. Try to assess its importance for the government, for producers and for consumers. You may wish to split these three among your classmates. Discuss as a class what you have discovered.

2. Investigate one of the main banks online to find out about all the services they offer. Share your findings with the rest of the class to see if all banks offer the same services.

3. (E) Discuss how important commercial banks are for the economy.

Knowledge check questions

1	Define money.	[2]
2	Define barter.	[2]
3	Explain the **four** functions of money.	[8]
4	State **six** characteristics of money.	[6]
5	Explain **two** of the characteristics you gave in question 4.	[4]
6	Define what is meant by a central bank.	[2]
7	Explain how a central bank acts as banker to the government.	[2]
8	Define the term commercial bank.	[2]
9	Explain **two** ways in which a commercial bank benefits a producer.	[4]
10	(E) Discuss whether commercial banks are entirely beneficial for consumers.	[8]

Check your progress

Read the unit objectives below and reflect on your progress in each.

- Describe the different forms that money may take.
- Explain the functions of money.
- Explain the characteristics of money.
- Analyse the role and importance of central banks for government, producers and consumers.
- Discuss the role and importance of commercial banks for government, producers and consumers.

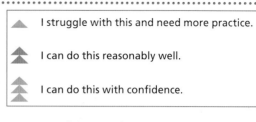

I struggle with this and need more practice.

I can do this reasonably well.

I can do this with confidence.

Households

Learning objectives

By the end of this unit, you should be able to:

- explain the factors that influence household spending, such as saving, borrowing, rate of interest and confidence
- explain how these factors may change over time
- analyse how these factors affect different types of households.

Starting point

Answer these questions in pairs:

1 You are given an extra $20. What will you do with it?

2 What factors will affect your decision about what to do with this extra money?

3 Do you save more money today than you did two years ago? Why is this?

4 Have you ever borrowed any money? If so, why did you borrow?

5 Which functions of money relate directly to spending, saving and borrowing?

Exploring

Discuss these questions in pairs:

1 As people get older what happens to the percentage of income they save?

2 You have been given $1000 to put into savings. Find out about the rates of interest that you could get. Where would you decide to save it and why?

3 How important is the idea of opportunity cost when deciding what to do with your money?

Developing

What influences the spending, saving and borrowing of households?

A **household** is a group of people who share the same living accommodation, pool at least some of their income and consume certain goods and services such as housing and food collectively. Someone living on their own could be considered a household.

Key term

Household – a group of people who share the same living accommodation, who pool at least some of their income and who consume certain goods and services such as housing and food collectively

Income is probably the major factor in determining the overall levels of **spending**, **saving** and **borrowing** by households. As income increases, households are able to do more of both spending and saving. This is certainly the case if a household's income rises faster than the **rate of inflation** so that their **real income** is greater – that is, they can buy more with their income. In general, the proportion of savings to income will rise as incomes increase. For example, someone on a low income might not save anything (0% of their income), those on a middle income might be able to save some money (5–10%) and those earning high incomes might be able to save quite a large proportion (20–25%).

In some countries the level of state welfare provision plays a major role in determining saving. One reason that there is a high level of savings in China is the relative lack of a welfare state, encouraging many people to save for the future. However, some countries with well-developed welfare provision have a culture of saving. Singapore, for instance, has an average 24% savings ratio.

It seems obvious that those with higher incomes will be able to borrow more. This is certainly true when it comes to expensive items such as housing, as lenders take into account the ability of the borrower to repay the money. However, it is not just wealthy households who borrow money. Very often poorer households need to borrow money in order to survive. In this case the money is required for necessities such as food and clothing.

Linked to income, the level of **direct taxes** and **indirect taxes** also affects levels of spending and saving. If direct taxes such as income tax are cut then consumers will see a rise in their **disposable income** and thus their ability to spend and save. On the other hand, an increase in indirect taxes, such as import duties or value added tax, lead to a rise in prices and a fall in real incomes.

Interest rates are another factor affecting spending and saving. If the rate of interest falls then it is cheaper for households to gain credit from banks, so borrowing increases, allowing them to spend more. Since the financial crisis of 2008, central banks have kept interest rates low in order to encourage consumer spending. In July 2017 the Japanese rate was 0%, the UK's 0.25% and Canada's 0.75%. Conversely, higher interest rates attract savers as they earn more money. In July 2017 the Argentine interest rate was 26.25%, Ghana's 21% and Ukraine's 12.5%.

Key terms

Income – the reward for the services provided by a factor of production, including labour

Spending – the use of money to purchase goods and services

Saving – that part of someone's income which is not spent on consumption

Borrowing – the act of taking out a loan with the requirement to pay the money back over an agreed period of time, very often with interest

Rate of inflation – the persistent rise in the general price level over time

Real income – income taking the effects of inflation into account (the purchasing power of income)

Direct tax – a tax on income or wealth

Indirect tax – a tax on spending that is initially charged to the producer, but may then be passed on to consumers through an increase in price

Disposable income – the income available to spend and save after direct taxes have been deducted and any state benefits added

 With the central bank's base rate being 0%, savers in Japan were offered negative interest rates. What effects might this have had on both saving and spending by Japanese households?

The increasing use of credit cards and mobile apps has also made credit more easily available to households and encouraged borrowing and spending. The Reserve Bank of India stated that, by the end of March 2017, 29.8 million credit cards had been issued, while spending on credit cards had risen by 275% since

2012. While many households pay off their credit card accounts each month and, thus, are using them instead of carrying cash, others do not. The average household credit card debt at the end of 2016 in the UK was £13 200.

In some parts of the world access to banking is very limited. The World Bank estimates that only 55% of Kenyans have bank accounts. On the other hand, 82% have mobile phones. The answer has been to develop mobile banking. Enabling people to have access to formal financial services is called financial inclusion.

CASE STUDY

Increasing financial inclusion in Africa

Increasing access to and use of financial services promotes economic development. The problem in many developing countries is that the majority of the population does not have a bank account. In countries such as the UK the main commercial banks have traditionally reached people by having branches in most towns. These cost money and time to set up, however, and so this is not easy to duplicate in developing countries.

In Kenya the number of people with access to financial services is more than double that in any other sub-Saharan African country – and this is due to the development of mobile banking. According to a research paper by Jay Rosengard of Harvard University's John F. Kennedy School of Government, 42% of adults had access to financial services in 2011. By 2014, this had increased to 75%. Financial inclusion of the poorest Kenyans was especially dramatic, increasing from 21% in 2011 to 63% in 2014.

This increase in financial inclusion improves the livelihood of families. It allows them, for instance, to deal with a poor harvest or temporary unemployment without having to drastically cut household consumption. It particularly benefits those people, such as many women, who have not been part of the formal economy. The overall effect is to boost development at local and national levels.

1 Explain why setting up a chain of commercial bank branches across a developing country might be difficult.

2 Calculate the percentage increase from 2011 to 2014 in the number of Kenyans who have access to a financial account.

3 Discuss whether mobile banking would be the best way to increase financial inclusion in your country.

Consumer confidence is the outlook that consumers have both towards the economy and their own personal financial situation. This is an important factor determining a household's decisions on spending, saving and borrowing. When confidence is low, households will save more because of fears about job security and future income. On the other hand, if people are confident about the future they are likely to spend more, and also borrow larger sums of money in order to buy expensive items such as housing and cars.

The total wealth of a household in terms of assets such as property, bank accounts or shares can be important, especially where spending and borrowing are concerned. Some assets can be turned into money to increase spending power. Others can be used to support applications for borrowing. Therefore, if house or share prices fall this is likely to lead to less spending and borrowing.

The availability of savings institutions and people's confidence in them is important for encouraging saving. As far as availability is concerned, internet and mobile banking may make it easier for more people to access banks, but could have a negative effect on people who do not have access to the internet. Confidence often depends on the actions of governments. In 2013 in Cyprus, savings deposits of €100 000 or more were hit by an unexpected tax as part of the emergency help for the country. On the other hand, the UK government guarantees deposits at UK banks up to £85 000. Another factor determining savings is that most governments have some form of compulsory savings scheme. In Singapore the Central Provident Fund covers pensions, housing and medical care.

CASE STUDY   ## Saving and spending variations

A global survey at the end of 2016 asked what people did with their income once they had paid for basic necessities. The survey showed that people in the Asia-Pacific area were most likely to spend money on holidays, new clothes, new technology and entertainment away from home. In South America, however, the greatest emphasis was on paying off debts. North Americans focused more on home improvements.

Not every household can save. In the Middle East/Africa this was the case for almost a quarter of those surveyed. In Europe and South America it was under 20% while in North America it was just over 10%. The lowest figure was for Asia, with only 5% saying they would not be able to save.

This links to the figures showing Asia and North America having the highest percentage saving for retirement.

1 Give one possible reason why households in Latin America might be using more of their income to pay off debt.

2 Give two possible reasons why people in Asia appear to have both greater spending and greater saving power.

3 Using the internet, carry out research on spending and saving patterns in your country. Analyse the extent to which they match those in the case study.

How do the influences on spending, saving and borrowing change over time?

Before starting this section you may wish to revisit your answers to some of the questions in the Starting point and Exploring sections at the beginning of this unit.

Over long periods of time, for example 100 years, there will be considerable changes in spending, saving and borrowing patterns. Everyday goods such as computers, telephones/smartphones and televisions did not exist 100 years ago. However, even over short periods, the relative importance of spending on different products changes. For example, between 2013 and 2017 there was an increase of over 3000% in the number of electric cars sold in the UK.

In addition, spending and saving patterns often change as people get older. Young people are likely to spend most of their income, and spend it on things they want. Your parents, in contrast, are likely to spend a large part of the household's income either on household goods and services, such as furniture or insurance, or on consumption that benefits everyone in the household, such as food and holidays. Your grandparents may well have another spending pattern.

2 Analyse how age influences the spending and saving patterns of households.

The need to provide for yourself once you have retired is another factor that may affect your spending and saving during your working life. In many countries there is currently a pension crisis. The International Longevity Centre in the UK found in 2017 that across 30 advanced economies young people needed to save about 20% of their income if they were to match the retirement income of their parents/grandparents. Instead they found that over 30% of people between the ages of 25 and 44 made no savings. Clearly, more saving would mean less consumption.

How do the influences differ across different households?

As mentioned earlier, the percentage of income a person saves increases as their income rises. Figure 3.2.1 shows the savings ratio for each decile (10%) in Portugal. This clearly illustrates that those households with higher incomes not only save more, but the proportion of savings to income rises rapidly.

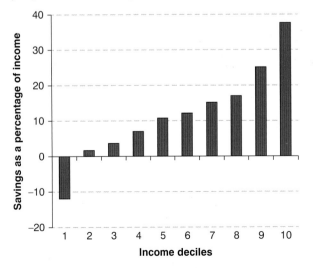

Figure 3.2.1 Saving rate, by income deciles

3 Using Figure 3.2.1, explain why the highest decile group (10) is able to save a much higher percentage of their income than those in the lower decile groups (1 and 2).

4 (E) With reference to Figure 3.2.1, construct a decile savings rate graph for your country.

As noted above, the rate of interest will affect households' decisions about spending and saving as well as borrowing. The basic rule is shown in Figure 3.2.2.

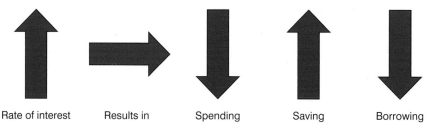

| Rate of interest | Results in | Spending | Saving | Borrowing |

Figure 3.2.2

5 Draw a flow diagram showing a fall in interest rates. Explain what it shows.

This may not always be the case. Households with high income levels may not need to reduce spending or borrowing as they can afford to pay the higher interest rates. On the other hand, poor households may not be able to save and so they do not benefit from the higher rates of interest. They may suffer, however, from paying the higher interest rates on the money they have borrowed.

Low rates of interest should lead to less saving. Lack of confidence may deter people from buying shares or houses. Evidence shows, however, that wealthier people turn to alternative ways to save their money by buying goods such as antiques, works of art or wine to hold and then sell at a profit.

Key knowledge

Summary of factors affecting household spending, saving and borrowing

Factors affecting spending	Factors affecting saving	Factors affecting borrowing
Income As income rises so does spending as a total, but as a percentage it declines	**Income** As income rises so does saving as a total, but it also increases as a percentage	**Income** Borrowing to cover basic needs is often a feature of the poorest groups, but higher income groups borrow to buy expensive items such as houses
Consumer confidence If confidence is high, spending increases	**Consumer confidence** Fall in confidence leads to more saving in case of, for example, loss of work	**Consumer confidence** Increase in confidence encourages borrowing as people expect to be able to pay back the loan as their income rises

Factors affecting spending	Factors affecting saving	Factors affecting borrowing
Interest rates Low interest rates encourage both borrowing and spending	**Interest rates** High interest rates encourage people to save as their money increases in value, while it is more expensive to borrow	**Interest rates** Low interest rates encourage borrowing; high interest rates discourage borrowing
Wealth If someone can fairly easily turn wealth into money, for example shares or bank accounts, then this increases their potential spending power	**Pension provision** Where there is no real state provision, or saving for a pension is compulsory, saving will increase	**Wealth** Greater wealth allows more borrowing as banks are more willing to lend if a person has wealth to back the loan
Age Young adults and those with children tend to spend more, as do the very elderly who may need to spend their savings	**Age** Saving tends to increase with age, at least up to retirement	**Age** Borrowing for many households peaks when they are buying expensive items such as houses and cars. This is usually between the ages of 25 and 55
Household type Spending will vary depending on factors such as number of children or number and age of adults	**Household type** Saving will vary according to whether there are many dependents, such as children and the elderly, or just adults	**Household type** Poorer households often have to borrow to afford essentials such as food or the rent for accommodation. Those with higher incomes may borrow for items such as houses and cars
Culture Examples of differences as a percentage of household income are: Japan 25% on housing, fuel and utilities; Russia 31% on food; USA 21% on health; South Korea 7% on education	**Culture** Examples of differences as a percentage of household income are: China 38%; Sweden 16%; Chile 9%; USA 6%; and New Zealand 1%	**Culture** Among the countries with the highest household debt (as a result of borrowing) are: Australia, Denmark and Switzerland
Taxation The higher the level of direct tax, the less people have to spend	**Availability of savings schemes** Savings depend on having organisations such as banks to save with	**Availability of credit schemes** The easier it is to borrow, the more likely it is that borrowing will increase

Applying

Project work

Research answers to the following questions:

1. How do your spending and saving patterns differ from those of your parents, or adults, and grandparents or the elderly? You might like to share this with the rest of your class so you build up a bigger picture.

2. Using the internet, find out how changes in the rate of interest over the last 15 years have affected spending, saving and borrowing of households in your country. Discuss the findings with the class.

3. How do spending patterns change for households? Choose a suitable time period of perhaps 20 or even 100 years. Discuss why these changes have taken place in your country.

Knowledge check questions

1 Define income.   [2]

2 Define real income.   [2]

3 Explain **two** reasons why households might save money.   [4]

4 Explain **two** reasons why people borrow money.   [4]

5 Define disposable income.   [2]

6 Explain the effects that a rise in direct tax might have on a household's spending and saving.   [4]

7 Analyse how an increase in consumer confidence could cause an increase in spending.   [6]

8 (E) Discuss the effects of people failing to save enough for their retirement.   [8]

Check your progress

Read the unit objectives below and reflect on your progress in each.

- Explain the factors that influence household spending, such as saving, borrowing, rate of interest and confidence.

- Explain how these factors may change over time.

- Analyse how these factors affect different types of households.

▲	I struggle with this and need more practice.
▲▲	I can do this reasonably well.
▲▲▲	I can do this with confidence.

Workers

Learning objectives

By the end of this unit, you should be able to:

* define what is meant by wages and non-wages
* explain how wages and non-wage factors affect choice of occupation
* analyse the determination of wages through supply and demand
* explain how relative bargaining power can determine wages
* analyse how the minimum wage influences wage determination
* explain how else government policy can help determine wages
* define earnings
* analyse the effects of changes in demand and supply on the labour market
* explain how changes in relative bargaining strengths, discrimination and government policy can all influence differences in earnings
* explain the advantages and disadvantages for workers, firms and the economy of the division of labour/specialisation.

Starting point

Answer these questions in pairs:

1 What factors might influence you in your choice of which occupation to have?

2 Would you prefer to know all there is about one part of an occupation (specialist) or would you rather have general knowledge about all aspects of the occupation?

3 Should all workers be paid the same?

Exploring

Discuss these questions in pairs:

1 Why do you think someone becomes a teacher? Once you have decided on one or more reasons, put your ideas to your teacher.

2 If there was an increase in demand for teachers what would happen to the quantity of teachers and their pay? (Hint: use your knowledge of demand and supply from Chapter 2.)

3 Why do you think some people are paid more than others?

Developing

How do wages and non-wage factors affect the choice of an occupation?

A **wage** is a payment to a worker for units of time or units of product (piecework). The most common unit is the hour. Workers are paid a **wage rate**, which is the amount of money paid to a worker per unit of time. This may be hourly, daily or weekly.

On the other hand, a **salary** is an annual sum of money paid to a worker, usually in 12 equal monthly amounts. For example, a salary of $60 000 would be paid in 12 amounts of $5000 each month.

The amount they will earn is an important factor for many people in choosing an occupation. Doctors, for example, normally earn more than nurses. Highly paid jobs normally require a high level of education and training, which limits the supply of workers in these professions. Dangerous jobs, such as working on offshore oil rigs, have to offer high pay in order to attract workers.

Basic pay is the amount guaranteed for the number of hours advertised in the job. If a job is for 40 hours per week at a wage rate of $20 an hour then the basic pay is $20 × 40 = $800 a week. In addition, you might work overtime (extra hours) or receive a bonus for reaching a production target, or receive a commission (a percentage of the value of sales made). Your wage rate plus any of these will give you your **earnings**. Earnings are the total amount of pay received including bonuses, commissions and overtime. It is sometimes called gross pay.

Non-wage factors are very important for many people when choosing an occupation. These are factors other than wage which influence an individual's choice of job, some of which are shown in the table below.

Non-wage factors in job choice

Factor	Example
Job satisfaction	Enjoying one's work and/or the people you work with may be more important than earning more money.
Career prospects	To some people it is important that there are good prospects of promotion.
Job security	Many people want a job which does not carry fears of being made unemployed.
Fringe benefits	Non-financial benefits of the occupation such as free healthcare or subsidised transport.

Key terms

Wage – a payment for labour based on units of time worked or units of a product produced

Wage rate – the amount of money paid to a worker per unit of time in exchange for their labour

Salary – an annual sum of money paid to a worker in exchange for their labour – usually paid in twelve equal monthly amounts

Key terms

Basic pay – the amount of money received before any additional payments are added or any deductions, such as income tax, are made

Earnings – the total amount received including additional payments

Non-wage factor – something other than pay that influences choice of occupation

Factor	Example
Working conditions	Having good working conditions is a legal requirement in most countries. This includes: suitable amenities, control of stress and noise levels, safe working environment and control of danger.
Travelling distance	Some workers prefer a short journey to work so they do not have to spend time travelling.

1 To what extent is pay more important than non-wage factors for teachers?

How does supply and demand determine wages?

Wages are the price of labour. Except where wages are fixed by a government, the wage will be determined mainly by the market forces of supply and demand (see Chapter 2, Units 2, 3, 5, 7 and 8).

The demand for labour slopes downwards because an employer will demand a greater number of workers at lower wage rates. On the other hand, the supply curve slopes upwards. This is because workers are usually willing to give up more of their leisure time in order to supply more of their labour in return for higher pay. In addition, as pay rises, some people who were not looking for work may be tempted to do so.

If the demand for labour should increase, due perhaps to the economy growing, then the demand curve for labour will shift to the right from D to D_1 in Figure 3.3.1. As a result, wages rise from W to W_1 and quantity of labour supplied and demanded increases from Q to Q_1, giving a new equilibrium position of $W_1 Q_1$.

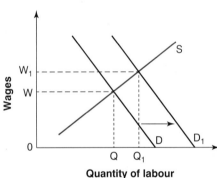

Figure 3.3.1 An increase in the demand for labour

Other factors that can cause the demand curve to shift outwards include an increase in the following:

- **Demand for the product**. Demand for labour is a **derived demand** as it is the increase in demand for the product which increases the demand for the labour used to make the product. Owners of smartphones and tablets demand apps. This then increases the demand for app programmers.

- **The productivity of labour** (see Unit 3.6). Labour becomes more cost-efficient and can be used in place of capital.

- **The profits of firms**. Firms with higher profits are likely to expand and demand more labour.

- **The cost of capital equipment**. If the cost of capital increases it could be cheaper to employ more labour.

The reverse will be the case for a fall in the demand for labour.

In a similar manner, if the supply of workers for a job falls due to lack of suitable education and training then the supply curve will shift to the left, from S to S_1 in Figure 3.3.2. As a result, wages rise from W to W_1 while quantity of labour supplied and demanded fall from Q to Q_1, giving a new equilibrium position of W_1 Q_1.

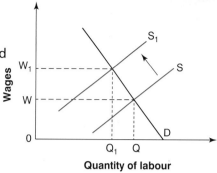

Other factors that can cause the supply curve to shift inwards include a decrease in:

- **the wage rate** and other monetary payments relative to those offered in other industries

- **the size of the working population** (see Unit 5.3) as there would be fewer people available to work

- **the number of qualified people**, due to an increase in the level of qualifications required to do a particular job, for example doctors, or an increase in the time needed for training

- **non-wage factors**, for example a deterioration in working conditions or job security.

Figure 3.3.2 A decrease in the supply of labour

The reverse will be the case for a rise in the supply for labour.

2 Using supply and demand analysis, explain what would happen to the pay of workers in a factory if the firm decided to use more capital-intensive methods of production such as automation.

How can relative bargaining power determine wages?

Bargaining power is the relative ability of parties in any situation to exert influence. Normally wages are set through a process of bargaining between workers and their employers. The level of wages will depend, therefore, on the relative bargaining power of the two sides. If the employers are in a stronger position, for example there are a lot of people out of work, then the wage level on offer is likely to be low. It is recognised that it is, however, very difficult to force actual wages down. At the present wage level the supply of labour tends to be perfectly elastic. Equally, if the demand for a product increases and employers need to increase output then the relative bargaining power of the workers increases and wages will rise. This is shown in Figure 3.3.1. The stronger the relative bargaining power of one side, the more likely it is that they will achieve most of what they want.

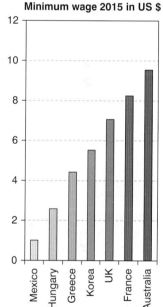

Figure 3.3.3 Minimum wage in selected countries, 2015 (US$)

How can government policy help determine wages?

One way a government can determine wages is by setting a **minimum wage**. A minimum wage is the lowest wage level that an employer may legally pay their workers. This varies greatly between countries, as can be seen in Figure 3.3.3, with a range from $9.54 to $1.01 per hour. Some countries are starting to adopt the idea of a **living wage**, which is a level required to enable workers to reach a minimum acceptable living standard.

Key terms

Minimum wage – the lowest wage level that an employer may legally pay their workers

Living wage – a wage set at a level to enable workers to reach a minimum acceptable living standard

Other ways in which a government can affect wages include equal pay and anti-discrimination legislation. While it is relatively straightforward to bring this about in the public sector, it is more difficult to do so in other organisations. A government can also affect wages through taxation. Raising top tax rates will reduce the amount of money available to the higher paid workers.

3 How does the government of your country try to affect the level of wages?

How can the minimum wage influence wage determination?

Before the minimum wage (W_1 in Figure 3.3.4) was introduced, the market was in equilibrium at WQ. If the government set the minimum wage at, or below, this level it would have no effect (see Unit 2.11). But if the minimum wage was set at W_1, the quantity of labour supplied would increase from Q to Q_S. More people would be willing to work. The quantity of labour demanded by employers, however, would fall from Q to Q_D. As the minimum wage increases a firm's costs, employers no longer wish to use as many workers. This leads to an excess of supply over demand (a surplus) of Q_S–Q_D. The extent to which there is an excess will depend on the level of the minimum wage, the price elasticity of demand for labour and the ability of employers/employees to increase productivity (see Unit 3.6). Evidence points to demand for labour being inelastic in the short run as employers cannot immediately substitute capital for labour.

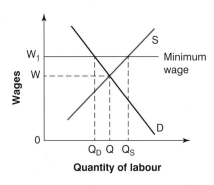

Figure 3.3.4 The effect of the imposition of a minimum wage

CASE STUDY   ## Guatemala increases minimum wage for agricultural workers

The Guatemalan government introduced an increase in the minimum wage of agricultural and non-agricultural workers starting from 1 January 2017. The minimum wage was increased from 81.87 Quetzales per day to 86.90 Quetzales per day. This promises to have a massive effect on the unskilled workers in the important agricultural sector. Unskilled workers account for as much as 31% of the labour force in important export products such as sugar, coffee, bananas and vegetables. With 76% of the rural population at the poverty line and the country having the lowest literacy rate in Central America, the Guatemalan government hopes the higher minimum wage will improve the situation for the workers. Employers, however, are less happy as they fear that higher wages may lead to lower demand for their products.

1 What is meant by the minimum wage?

2 Calculate the percentage increase in the minimum wage per hour in Guatemala.

3 Explain two possible effects that the increased minimum wage might have on agricultural workers.

4 Analyse why employers may be 'less happy' about the increased minimum wage.

5 (E) Discuss the extent to which an increase in the minimum wage would benefit the economy of your country.

What are the effects of changes in demand and supply on the labour market?

The basic effects were analysed above, where an increase in demand led to higher wages and quantity of labour employed, while a fall in supply led to higher wages and a fall in the quantity of labour employed.

In this section we investigate how price elasticity of demand (PED) and supply (PES) can influence what happens to the wage and quantity of labour when demand and supply change.

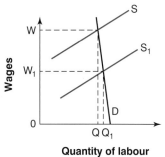

Figure 3.3.5 The effect of an increase in the supply of labour when demand is inelastic

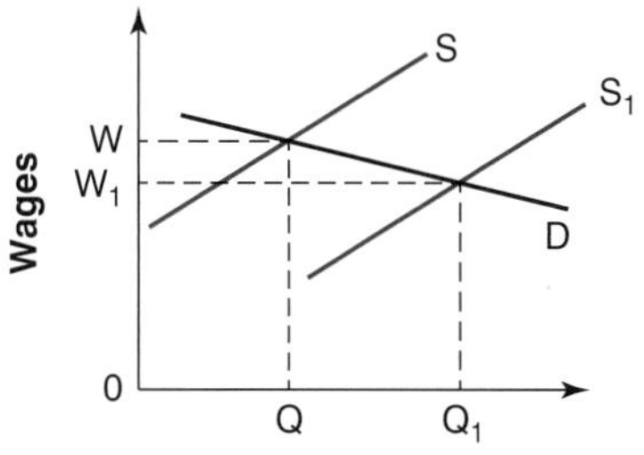

Figure 3.3.6 The effect of an increase in the supply of labour when demand is elastic

In Figure 3.3.5 the demand curve is inelastic. An increase in the supply of workers from S to S_1 leads to a fall in the wage rate from W to W_1 and a proportionately smaller increase in quantity from Q to Q_1.

In Figure 3.3.6 the demand curve is elastic. An increase in the supply of workers from S to S_1 in Figure 3.3.6 leads to a fall in wages from W to W_1 and a proportionately larger increase in quantity from Q to Q_1.

In the case of PES, Figure 3.3.7 shows an inelastic supply, while Figure 3.3.8 shows an elastic supply.

In Figure 3.3.7 an increase in demand from D to D_1 leads to a rise in wages from W to W_1 and a proportionately smaller rise in quantity. This is because it is more difficult to find people who are able to do the job.

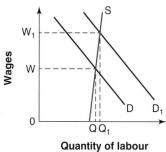
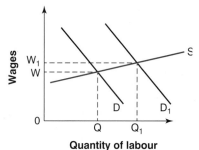

Figure 3.3.7 The effect of a decrease in demand for labour when supply is inelastic

Figure 3.3.8 The effect of a decrease in demand for labour when supply is elastic

On the other hand, in the case of elastic supply (Figure 3.3.8), an increase in demand from D to D_1 leads to a rise in wages from

W to W$_1$ and a proportionately larger increase in quantity from Q to Q$_1$. This could be the case in relatively unskilled professions, such as shop assistants, where there are a lot of people able to do the job.

In some cases the supply may be almost perfectly inelastic, leading to potentially very high wages. This will be the case if employers see the person as having a unique talent, for example Neymar Jr., the footballer, or Taylor Swift the pop star.

In Figure 3.3.9 supply is perfectly inelastic. The wage is determined entirely by demand. If demand is high, D$_1$, then the wage will be very high at W$_1$, but if the skill or talent is not required or unrecognised then the wage will be much lower at W.

All of the above, together with changes in relative bargaining strengths, discrimination and government policy, can influence differences in earnings between: skilled and unskilled; primary, secondary and tertiary; male and female; and private sector and public sector workers.

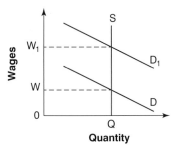

Figure 3.3.9

Groups of workers	Effect on earnings of changes in:				
	Relative bargaining strength	**Discrimination**	**Government policy**	**Price elasticity of demand**	**Price elasticity of supply**
Skilled and unskilled	Normally highly skilled workers will gain while unskilled workers will lose. Skilled workers may lose if they can be replaced by capital.	Removal of discrimination, e.g. between genders, may be more beneficial to skilled workers as the gap between the genders may be very large.	The introduction of a minimum wage or a living wage will mostly benefit the unskilled as they are likely to be paid less than the level set.	Demand for skilled workers is likely to be inelastic. Demand for unskilled workers is likely to be elastic, leading to higher wages.	Supply of skilled workers is likely to be inelastic, unless far more can be trained. While these workers are in demand this will result in high wages.
Primary, secondary and tertiary	If an economy moves from mainly primary to secondary or tertiary then so does the relative bargaining strengths of the workers.	While removing discrimination will benefit all, it is likely to be more beneficial in the tertiary sector where large numbers of women are often employed.	Workers in all sectors will benefit, but low pay is often found in primary and tertiary, especially retailing.	With the shift in demand from primary to secondary to tertiary it is likely that more tertiary jobs will have an inelastic demand than in the other sectors.	Increasingly more tertiary sector jobs need high levels of skill/education. This will result in a more inelastic supply.

	Relative bargaining strength	Discrimination	Government policy	Price elasticity of demand	Price elasticity of supply
Private and public sectors	Trade unions are often stronger in the public sector. Many tertiary occupations are either not unionised or have weak unions.	Enforcement has been easier in the public sector due to governments carrying out their own policies.	Governments can directly affect public sector pay, which may result in it being held down as has happened in many advanced economies since 2008.	The growth industries in both the public and the private sector will have an inelastic demand as they need specific workers.	In some economies supply is large and elastic, as public sector jobs are seen as safer/more desirable. It usually depends on the skills required.

4 Choose two individuals, or groups of people, whose wages are very different. Analyse why one individual/group is paid far more than the other individual/group.

What are the advantages and disadvantages for workers, firms and the economy of the division of labour and of specialisation?

The **division of labour** is the process by which workers specialise in, or concentrate on, one particular task. **Specialisation**, however, is the process by which individuals, firms, regions and whole economies concentrate on producing those products in which they have an advantage. As can be seen, these are very similar when we are talking about workers.

Specialisation can refer to an expert in a particular type of work, such as an economics teacher, a computer programmer or a hospital consultant. In these cases the person involved covers all the knowledge within, for example, the teaching of economics. On the other hand, a worker may only do one part of a production process, such as fitting the wings to an aeroplane on the production line or working in the bakery department of a supermarket. This is called division of labour. If you are taught by two or more economics teachers who divide up the specification between them so that Teacher A covers Units 1–3 and Teacher B covers Units 4–6 then this is division of labour.

Key terms

Division of labour – the process by which workers specialise in, or concentrate on, one particular task

Specialisation – the process by which individuals, firms, regions and whole economies concentrate on producing those products in which they have an advantage

The costs and benefits of specialisation for workers

Benefits	Costs
Increased skill – by specialising, workers become more skilful and knowledgeable about their work. This can result in them earning more money.	**Boredom** – doing the same job every day may become boring and lead to demotivation.

Benefits	Costs
Natural strengths – workers are able to do what they are best at and not have to do work they might not be so good at. This should again allow them to earn more.	**Deskilling** – by specialising, workers lose the skills to do other types of work and are less able to respond to changes in demand.
Increased job satisfaction – doing what workers are good at is likely to improve their motivation and satisfaction from work.	**Lack of job security** – if there is a fall in demand for a particular product, workers may find it difficult to get another job because they do not have the necessary skills or experience. This may also occur because their work can be replaced by machines.
Increased standard of living – by earning more money workers can buy more goods to satisfy not only their needs but also some of their wants.	

World output has increased by firms specialising in different types of products. Manufacturers may concentrate on the end product and buy in most, or all, of the components from other producers. Michelin specialises in tyres. Some of these are then sold to car producers who specialise in car manufacturing and buy in products like tyres and seats from other specialists.

The costs and benefits of specialisation for producers

Benefits	Costs
Higher output – total production of goods and services is increased. In some areas it is possible to use automated systems or specialist equipment.	**Increased costs** – as output increases, costs may eventually rise. This is because resources may become limited in supply or it may take more people to organise the workforce.
Higher productivity – workers who specialise in one task become as skilled as they possibly can in that area, which increases the productivity (see Unit 3.6).	**Dependency** – production of the goods and services depends on all parts working well. Problems such as a technical failure or a strike can lead to the whole production process stopping.
Higher quality – the best and most suitable factors of production can be employed to produce the output. Firms can buy the best components from specialists instead of having to make them themselves.	**Movement of workers** – workers may become bored and leave (called labour turnover), which will mean that new workers have to be recruited and trained. This can particularly affect low-skilled and low-paid work.
Economies of scale – larger output will enable the producer to gain economies of scale (see Unit 3.5).	
Time saving – it takes time to stop producing one product and to start another, so specialisation saves time and money.	

CASE STUDY **Specialisation and the car factory**

Henry Ford (1863–1947) was the first to use the automated assembly line and division of labour when he produced the Model T car in 1913, the first mass-produced car in the world. Before Ford developed this process, car manufacturers built cars by hand, one at a time, in a process which was extremely time consuming, labour intensive and required the use of highly skilled workers.

Ford produced his cars by placing them on a moving conveyor belt. As each car moved down the production line one person fitted the doors, another fitted the windows, another fitted the tyres, and so on. Each part of the car was the specialism of a different worker. While modern-day car manufacturing is highly automated, involving advanced robotics, the basic moving assembly line is still an important component of the car production process.

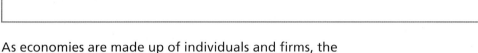

The advantages for Ford were clear: greater output, faster production and more productive workers. The problem was that the workers could sometimes become bored doing the same job every day. To overcome this problem in modern-day car manufacturing, some car makers such as Nissan group workers in teams so individuals can rotate between jobs, providing them with some variety in what they do.

1 What is meant by the division of labour?

2 Why might workers become bored?

3 Explain one other disadvantage to workers of specialisation.

4 Discuss whether the advantages of specialisation for the car manufacturer outweigh the disadvantages.

As economies are made up of individuals and firms, the advantages and disadvantages outlined above also apply to the economy as a whole (see Unit 6.1).

The main advantage to an economy of specialisation is that it can focus on what it is good at or has natural advantages in, and can import those products it is unable to produce as well. This should increase its income and growth and benefit its population. Ghana, for example, specialises in products such as gold and cocoa beans and brings in goods such as cars.

Project work

Research answers to the following questions:

1. How has the minimum wage changed since 2015 in either your country or another one?

2. Interview an adult (for example, a teacher or a parent) who works. What factors were important to them in choosing their present job?

3. Research the pay of skilled as against unskilled workers in your country. Explain why the gap exists.

4. (E) To what extent are men paid more than women in your country? You might want to use your answer as the basis of a discussion on gender pay with others in your class.

Knowledge check questions

1	Define wages.	[2]
2	Define salary.	[2]
3	Explain **two** non-wage factors which influence choice of occupation.	[4]
4	Using a diagram, explain what would happen to wages if demand fell.	[4]
5	Define earnings.	[2]
6	Define specialisation.	[2]
7	Explain **two** advantages to a worker of division of labour.	[4]
8	(E) Discuss whether workers always benefit from specialisation.	[8]

Check your progress

Read the unit objectives below and reflect on your progress in each.

▲ I struggle with this and need more practice.

▲ I can do this reasonably well.

▲ I can do this with confidence.

• Define what is meant by wages and non-wages.

• Explain how wages and non-wage factors affect choice of occupation.

• Analyse the determination of wages through supply and demand.

• Explain how relative bargaining power can determine wages.

• Analyse how the minimum wage influences wage determination.

• Explain how else government policy can help determine wages.

• Define earnings.

• Analyse the effects of changes in demand and supply on the labour market.

• Explain how changes in relative bargaining strengths, discrimination and government policy can all influence differences in earnings.

• Explain the advantages and disadvantages for workers, firms and the economy of the division of labour/specialisation.

Trade unions

Learning objectives

By the end of this unit, you should be able to:

- define what is a trade union
- explain the role of trade unions in the economy, including collective bargaining, employment protection and influencing government policy
- explain the factors influencing the strength of trade unions
- analyse the advantages and disadvantages of trade union membership for workers, firms and the government.

Starting point

Answer these questions in pairs.

1. Why would you join a club or society?

2. Do you have any power or influence in your school?

3. How could the students in your school try to play a more powerful role in the life of the school?

4. Why can your teachers not do exactly as they like?

Exploring

Discuss these questions in pairs:

1. Who influences what the rules are in your school?

2. How could you try to improve your working conditions?

3. Ask your teacher what is meant by a win–win situation. Do you think both sides in a negotiation should aim for this idea?

Developing

What is a trade union?

Workers can join a **trade union**, which is an organisation that looks after its members' interests. A trade union can help and support its members in various ways. It will negotiate better wages and working conditions by **collective bargaining**. It may also organise **industrial action** or political campaigns.

While we often think of unions being for manual workers, this is not the case. Organisations which call themselves professional bodies may be unions – for example, the Danish Medical Association, which represents doctors in Denmark.

Key terms

Trade union – an organisation of workers that actively supports its members in a variety of ways, such as increasing wages and improving working conditions

Collective bargaining – a process of negotiation over pay and conditions between a trade union, representing a group of workers, and employers

Industrial action – any measure taken by a trade union (or other organised labour) to try to enforce their demands or to address their complaints; this may take the form of strikes, overtime bans, go-slows, work-to-rules or sit-ins

What is the role of trade unions in the economy?

When it comes to pay, working hours, working conditions and protecting job security, not all workers are equal even if they do similar jobs. Individual workers normally have only weak power compared to employers, but collectively they may have far more power. Trade unions help to provide employees with equal bargaining power when negotiating with their employers, who traditionally have set the terms and conditions of work and pay. Unions represent workers within a given industry in negotiations with their employers. Since the union is made up of a group of workers, it has a greater voice than if employees were dealing with employers individually. This is called collective bargaining.

1 What would happen if one worker asked for a pay rise and threatened to go on strike if their demand was not met?

2 What would happen if all the workers asked for the same pay rise and all threatened to go on strike if their demand was not met?

Trade unions exist to protect their members and to advance their interests, including the following:

- Negotiating wage agreements and ensuring that workers are paid fairly. Overall, workers who belong to trade unions have better levels of wages (see below).

- Protecting jobs, including representing workers in disputes with employers. Unions try both to protect jobs in general, for example all the workers in the car industry in the USA, and to support individual employees in cases such as unfair dismissal.

- Ensuring that workers have satisfactory working conditions (see Unit 3.3), including **health and safety** and **equal opportunities**.

As mentioned above, in many countries trade unions also work to improve the quality of public services, undertake political campaigning or try to influence government thinking. In Mongolia, the trade unions pushed the government into adopting new employment policies based on the International Labour Organization's model. In Ghana, trade union activity helped to influence the government into taking back into state ownership the distribution of water.

Key terms

Health and safety – the laws and rules for identifying potential dangers and health problems at work and, also, the ways of preventing these issues and keeping people safe

Equal opportunities – the policies and practices in employment that prevent discrimination against someone on the grounds of race, age, gender, religion, disability or any other individual or group characteristic unrelated to ability, performance and qualification

The role of trade unions in the Costa Rican banana industry

The Costa Rican banana industry plays an important role in the economy. In 2016 it accounted for 2% of the value of output and directly employed 43 000 people, with the vast majority working in the plantation fields. However, only 10% of banana plantation workers are members of a trade union.

Although Costa Rica has adopted the International Labour Organization's 'decent work policy', a report by the International Trade Union Congress has stated: "In Costa Rica trade unionists are dismissed, intimidated and harassed and workers are strongly discouraged from even joining a trade union". In 2017 there was an increase in strikes and protests as unskilled workers strived for the opportunity to negotiate collective wages, working hours, working conditions and essential legal protection.

1 Why might only 10% of banana workers belong to a trade union?

2 Discuss ways in which trade unions in Costa Rica could try to improve the working condition of workers.

If workers belong to a strong trade union they will usually be paid more, and enjoy better conditions. This is achieved through the union restricting the supply of workers (see Figure 3.3.2). The ability of trade unions to win higher pay will depend, among other factors, on how important the workers are to the economy or to the firm. When the union is weak an employer may be able to bring in non-union workers to take the place of striking workers and thus undermine job security. If the union is strong it is likely to be able to prevent this. This strength can be enhanced if the demand for labour in the economy or a particular occupation is high. In this case, trade unions can try to restrict the supply of labour (see above and Unit 3.3).

 3 Explain why individual workers are often less able to improve their pay and working conditions than those who belong to trade unions.

Trade unions in Indonesia

Originally trade unions in Indonesia were controlled by the government, but in recent years many new unions have been set up. The older unions seek to settle disagreements through negotiation, but the new unions often use direct action such as strikes from the start.

In the 2014 presidential elections some unions backed Joko Widodo while others backed Prabowo Subianto. The latter lost, but the real loser was the divided trade union movement.

Since 2014 the unions have failed to make inroads into improving the pay and working conditions of the very large number of poorly paid workers. Indeed in 2016 the government changed how the minimum wage in Indonesia was set and excluded trade union participation.

Valter Sanches, a prominent trade union leader, said in March 2017: "The lack of participation of unions in setting the minimum wage has had an adverse effect on the minimum wage at the regional level, thus keeping wages far behind in relation to the rate of growth of the economy."

1 State two examples of the trade unions in Indonesia becoming less powerful.

2 Explain two reasons why "new unions often use direct action".

3 What is meant by a minimum wage?

4 Analyse how being excluded from minimum wage setting arrangements would affect the wages paid to workers.

What are the factors influencing the strength of trade unions?

The strength of trade unions depends on the level of control they have over the supply of labour and their ability to influence governments. As we have seen in the case study, the Indonesian government was able to ignore the unions when it came to setting minimum wage. On the other hand, trade unions in France have traditionally been able to exercise considerable influence.

The main economic factors leading to stronger trade unions include the following:

1. **High level of economic activity**. In periods of high economic activity there is a shortage of workers. Firms are more willing to grant union requests in order to retain their workers, especially if they are skilled.

2. **High membership**. Where the large majority of workers are members of unions this increases union control over the supply of workers. Economic decline, growth of new jobs (especially in technology) and the increase in self-employed workers have contributed to a decline in union membership in economies such as the UK and the USA.

3. **High bargaining power**. Workers in key industries such as the docks or power generation are in a stronger position than shop workers.

4. **High level of skill**. Skilled workers have a more inelastic supply curve than unskilled workers (see Unit 3.3). Training unskilled workers can be costly so firms are more inclined to grant union requests to retain these workers.

5. **High and consistent demand for the product.** If the product workers produce is in high demand, firms tend to make higher profits. A strong trade union will be in a better position to negotiate that some of this money is used to benefit the workers through higher wages and better conditions.

4 Explain why unions representing skilled workers have often been more successful in improving their members' situation than those with unskilled workers.

CASE STUDY   ## Teachers' strike in Argentina

The rate of inflation in Argentina in 2016 reached 40%. In June 2017 it was 21.9%.

Thousands of Argentine teachers hit the streets of Buenos Aires on Wednesday 14 June 2017 to protest for better salaries. The strike was called by the Front for the Teachers Unit of Bonaerense and brought together six of the city's largest teachers' unions. This was the 16th day of the strike in the Buenos Aires school district, which serves some 4.5 million students.

The government, who employs the teachers, claims there have been 13 meetings and nine sets of proposals between the teachers and the government with the most recent offer being a 21% pay rise in two instalments, but the two sides have not yet reached an agreement. Indeed the teachers have vowed to continue fighting for better wages.

1 Explain how the dispute between teachers and the government is an example of collective bargaining.

2 Using the information above, explain why teachers might be unwilling to accept a 21% pay rise.

3 Discuss whether the teachers' unions have a strong or weak bargaining position.

What are the advantages and disadvantages of trade union membership for workers, firms and the government?

The advantages and disadvantages of trade unions for the three groups are outlined in the table below.

	Advantages	Disadvantages
Workers	• Higher pay • Better working conditions/ensure legislation is adhered to • Increased job security • Protection against unfair employer action • Better fringe benefits	• Cost of membership • May not agree with political position taken by the union • Reduced job opportunities for those not in work • Employers encouraged to substitute capital for labour
Firms	• Easier to negotiate with one or few representatives than with each individual worker • Increase productivity by agreeing deals with the unions • Greater sales and revenue	• Workers may take industrial action, leading to a fall in production and productivity • As a result firms could go out of business • Increased costs to firms of pay rises, improving conditions
Government	• Can find out more easily what workers in general would like • Gets advice on work-related legislation • Receives help to implement work-related legislation	• Fewer people in work • Wage rises leading to higher prices making exports uncompetitive • Unions can become an opposing political force

Looking at the table of advantages and disadvantages you will notice that some of the points appear in both columns. One example is productivity from the point of view of firms. This is because unions are an advantage if they help a firm to change work practices in order to increase productivity. However, they are a disadvantage if they oppose changes to working practices.

Firms that have good relationships with their workers and make sure that workers' views are heard by the management generally have fewer industrial actions such as strikes and work-to-rules.

5　Analyse the advantages and disadvantages of trade unions for workers and employers.

Applying

Project work

Use the internet to research answers to the following questions:

1. What are the main trade unions in your country? How do they help their members?

2. How effective are trade unions in your country? Give reasons for your answer.

3. Find out about the amount of industrial action by unions in your country. If you are in a class you could all find out about different countries and then exchange information. What conclusions can you draw from your research?

4. (E) BP is one international firm that has traditionally worked hard to establish and maintain good industrial relations with its unions and workers. Using information available online, do you consider that unions and workers would agree?

Knowledge check questions

1 Define trade union. [2]

2 Define collective bargaining. [2]

3 Explain **two** roles that trade unions have in the economy. [4]

4 Define industrial action. [2]

5 Give **two** examples of industrial action. [2]

6 Explain **two** advantages to workers of trade union membership. [4]

7 Explain **two** disadvantages to governments of trade unions. [4]

8 Discuss whether workers always benefit from the actions of trade unions. [8]

9 (E) Analyse how in many Western industrial countries trade union membership has declined in the last 30 years. [6]

Check your progress

Read the unit objectives below and reflect on your progress in each.

- Define what is a trade union.

- Explain the role of trade unions in the economy, including collective bargaining, employment protection and influencing government policy.

- Explain the factors influencing the strength of trade unions.

- Analyse the advantages and disadvantages of trade union membership for workers, firms and the government.

▲	I struggle with this and need more practice.
▲	I can do this reasonably well.
▲	I can do this with confidence.

Firms

Learning objectives

By the end of this unit, you should be able to:

- define primary, secondary and tertiary sectors
- define private and public sectors
- explain how firms are classified by relative size
- analyse the advantages and disadvantages of small firms
- explain the challenges facing small firms and the reasons for their existence
- explain the reason for the existence of small firms
- explain the causes of the growth of firms
- explain the advantages and disadvantages of different types of mergers
- analyse how internal and external economies and diseconomies of scale can affect a firm/industry as the scale of production changes.

Starting point

Answer these questions in pairs:

1   Is your school owned by the government or by private individuals? How do you know?

2   Car manufacturers, shipbuilders and oil refiners can be thought of together. What do they have in common?

3   Think about your school. Would you prefer a larger school or a smaller school?

4   Would you prefer to be taught in a smaller or a larger class?

Exploring

Discuss these questions in pairs:

1   What are the economic differences between a car manufacturer and a garage that sells petrol and repairs cars?

2   Think about a small business owner you know, for example a small farmer or a hairdresser. What challenges do you think they face when competing with larger firms? What can they do to stay competitive?

3   How could your school become larger?

4   Why is your school larger than the school you attended when you were 8 years old?

Developing

What is the difference between the primary, secondary and tertiary sectors?

Firms are often classified as being either primary, secondary or tertiary. Farmers, for example, are part of the **primary sector**. The primary sector is concerned with all work that involves the direct use of natural resources or extraction. This includes agriculture, fishing, forestry, mining, oil and gas extraction and quarrying. All of these goods are either consumed directly, such as fish and vegetables, or form the raw materials used to produce other goods.

The **secondary sector** includes all manufacturing and construction activities. They involve using the products of the primary sector either directly, such as when raw materials are converted into manufactured goods, for example wood into furniture; or indirectly, for example making component parts for a mobile phone. Construction is the process of making a building or infrastructure. This could be the house, bungalow or apartment you live in or it could be an airport runway or a road.

The **tertiary sector** refers to all activities in the economy where a service is provided. This could be a service to another firm, such as supplying it with electricity, or to a consumer, such as servicing their car, or to a government, such as communications. Services involve a very wide range of different activities, including transport, retailing, entertainment, tourism and finance.

Key terms

Primary sector – the direct use of natural resources; it is the extraction of basic materials and goods from the land and sea

Secondary sector – all activities in an economy that are concerned with either manufacturing or construction

Tertiary sector – all activities in the economy that involve the idea of a service

 Explain why education is part of the tertiary sector.

 (E) Explain why oil extraction is in the primary sector, oil refining is in the secondary sector and a petrol/gas station is in the tertiary sector.

What is the difference between the private and public sectors?

Another way of grouping firms is through their ownership. If a firm is owned by private individuals then it is in the private sector. These firms may be very large international firms such as the Tata Group or Toyota or one-person businesses such as a hairdresser.

The public sector is owned by the government, either central or local. This can include services such as education, the French rail firm SNCF or primary and secondary producers such as the Sinopec Group in China.

How are firms classified by relative size?

We have already met two ways in which firms can be classified: by type of activity – primary, secondary and tertiary; and by ownership – private and public. The last way we are looking at is classifying firms by their size. Unfortunately, countries do not agree on what makes a firm small, medium or large, and individual countries often do not have a consistent definition themselves. Within the UK, for example, different government departments use different definitions.

One example of how the size of firms can be classified is that used by the European Union (EU). This is shown in the table below.

Classification of firms by size

Size	Description	
Micro	Less than 10 employees and turnover under £2 million	These two are often put together under 'small'.
Small	Less than 50 employees and turnover under £10 million	
Medium	Less than 250 employees and turnover under £50 million	
Large	More than 250 employees and turnover of more than £50 million	

Definitions, however, do depend on what industry is being considered. A general definition of a small business is an independently owned and operated company that is limited in size and in revenue depending on the industry. A local bakery that employs 10 people is an example of a small business. A manufacturing firm that employs fewer than 500 people is also an example of a small business.

3 Why would a local bakery that employs 10 people be an example of a small business?

4 Would you agree that a manufacturing facility that employs fewer than 500 people is an example of a small business? Give reasons for your answer.

What are the advantages and disadvantages of small firms?

The main advantages of small firms are their flexibility in the face of changing demand and their closer relationships with customers, leading to customer loyalty and knowledge of the customer's needs.

One of the main disadvantages is the difficulty of getting sufficient finance both to survive and to expand. Another disadvantage is that small firms often have to sell the same products at higher prices than large firms, due to lack of buying power.

The advantages and disadvantages of small firms

Advantages	Disadvantages
• **Greater flexibility** – can adapt to change more quickly • **Personal service** – more direct contact between the owner of the firm and consumers • **Better communication** – owner and staff in close contact leading to greater motivation • **Innovation** – more willing to innovate due to greater competition	• **Lack of finance** – it is difficult to raise large sums of money as banks are often less willing to lend. This limits ability to grow and to hire the best people. It may mean a small firm finds it more difficult to survive. • **Lack of highly qualified and experienced staff** – small firms cannot afford to pay the higher wages given by larger firms or the high-quality training and education workers require.

Advantages	Disadvantages
• **Niche markets** – can focus on small markets with specialist products where it would not be profitable for a large firm • **Lower costs** – small firms, especially in the tertiary sector, do not have the high costs associated with prestige buildings and locations • **Community support** – especially in smaller towns, people often prefer to support local small businesses	• **Higher costs** – small firms do not have the buying power as they only want small amounts. This means the cost of purchases is higher and so the firms have to sell at higher prices • **Recognition** – less ability to spend on advertising so may be less well known than a larger rival

5 Using examples from businesses you know of, to what extent do the advantages of being a small business outweigh the disadvantages?

What are the challenges facing small firms and the reasons for their existence?

The challenges facing small firms partly stem from their disadvantages. These include the following:

1. **Managing the flow of money in and out of the business (cash flow).** Suppliers demand payment on time; otherwise the firm gets a bad credit rating, which makes it more difficult to borrow money. However buyers, especially large firms, often do not pay on time, thus leading to a cash crisis. Failure to manage cash flow is a major cause of small firms failing.

2. **Leadership.** Owners are often too concerned about the day-to-day running of the business and fail to plan effectively. This is often the result of not recruiting well-qualified managers and skilled staff.

3. **Using information technology to enhance their business.** Smartphones (and cell phones) enable sales people who are out visiting customers to keep in touch with their office. The internet can enable firms to keep customers informed of products and new offers as well as online orders. Technology can increase the productivity of workers (see Unit 3.6), helping to make small firms more competitive.

4. **Lack of brand image.** Well-known brands, such as Kellogg's (breakfast cereals) or Wesfarmers (Australian supermarket) may be more trusted. Small firms may need to rely on the quality of the product or on personal service to develop a local reputation and sales.

Some challenges are common to almost every economy, but others are country or regionally specific. In all economies, firms face the problem of how to remain competitive. In Kazakhstan, however, firms often have to deal with the incorrect implementation at local level of new laws governing businesses; while Ecuador ranks 166 out of 190 countries according to the World Bank in terms of ease of starting a new business.

What are the causes of the growth of firms?

One of the aims of firms is to develop and grow in size through revenue and/or sales. There are two main sources of growth: internal and external.

Internal growth

Internal growth is based on expanding the capabilities of the business by using the firm's own resources. This is described in more detail in the table below.

Causes of internal growth

Cause	Explanation
Greater market share	Firms seek greater sales and share of the market in order to increase their ability to control the prices they charge customers. Greater sales will mean they will be able to get their supplies at a lower cost per unit and thus achieve lower input costs. In addition, managers often see greater sales as a measurable objective, which, if achieved, could lead to higher pay and/or promotion.
Increased profits	**Profit maximisation** is often seen as a major objective of firms. More sales can lead to higher profits, which can finance further growth and also give better returns to owners/shareholders.
Lower costs	By growing, firms may be able to reduce the cost per unit of their product resulting in greater profit. It could also allow firms to reduce the selling price. Overall, lower costs would enable a firm to gain market share.
Reduced risk	Through growing, a firm can produce a range of products by having the finances to fund the development and marketing of more than one product line. If the demand for one product falls, the firm can still survive by receiving revenue from its other products.
More effective marketing	If a firm can reach more customers through better advertising this can lead to greater sales.

External growth

External growth usually involves **mergers** with, or takeovers of, other firms (see the next section for greater detail). A merger is when two independent firms come together to form a new firm. Mergers take place by agreement. A takeover is the process by which one firm buys another firm either by buying out the owner or by purchasing more than 50% of its shares. Takeovers can be by agreement or can be hostile. An example of a hostile takeover was Westlake Chemicals' takeover of Axiall in the summer of 2016.

Unlike internal growth where money is put back into the business to expand output or demand, external growth uses the firm's money to purchase other firms. While this is a faster way to grow than the internal methods it also carries more risk due to the possibility of the merger being unsuccessful.

What are the advantages and disadvantages of different types of mergers?

A merger can come about in different ways.

- A **horizontal merger** is when two firms at the same stage of production, for example both in the secondary sector, in the same industry, join together. An example would be that of Westlake and Axiall, which both manufacture chemicals and plastic products.

- A **vertical merger** is when two firms at different stages of production in the same industry join together, for example Apple buying Faceshift. A vertical merger can take two forms: backward or forward. A backward vertical merger involves a firm merging with another firm at a previous stage of production, for example an olive oil bottler buys a producer of olive oil. A forward vertical merger includes a manufacturer buying a retailer, for example a car producer buying a car seller.

- A **conglomerate merger** (sometimes called a lateral merger) is where two firms with unrelated business activities join together. Samsung is a good example of such a firm. It is best known for its electronics and technology, but it also builds ships and buildings, sells life insurance, operates an advertising agency and runs a theme park.

Key terms

Horizontal merger – two firms at the same stage of production in the same industry join together

Vertical merger – two firms at different stages in the same industry join together; this may be forward or backward

Conglomerate merger – two firms with unrelated business activities join together

Horizontal merger

Advantages	Disadvantages
Reduces the competition by cutting the number of companies in the industry, which leads to more sales and greater profits. May open new markets if the firms are in different countries.	Lack of diversification so could be more open to problems if demand falls or government policy changes.
Increases the new firm's purchasing power with suppliers, leading to a fall in the cost per unit allowing prices to be reduced or profits to increase.	Each firm will have its own management style and information technology system so it may be difficult to bring these approaches together. Failure to integrate these successfully can lead to the merger failing.
Cost saving as the new firm does not need two marketing or accountancy departments or to spend as much on advertising.	Consumers can lose as the new firm has a greater share of the market, leading to higher prices and less choice.

Vertical merger

Advantages	Disadvantages
Reduces the reliance on suppliers (backward) or outlets (forward)	Reduced efficiency can lead to higher costs due to lack of competition. The supplier no longer has to seek business. Alternatively, the firm no longer has to find outlets for the products.
Reduces costs as there is no barrier between one stage and the next thus increasing co-ordination in terms of the supply chain	Competition between the different stages of production of the firm may lead to a situation where money spent on the earlier stage may limit the amount available to spend on the next stage. An example could be installing a new information technology system in a supermarket to order products when the supply stage is not ready to use this new system.
Increased profits due to the lower costs and the advantage this gives over non-integrated rivals	Firms may feel it necessary to increase potential output at the supply stage of the firm in order to ensure sufficient supplies if demand at the second stage suddenly increases. If the increase in demand does not eventuate the money will have been wasted.

Conglomerate merger

Advantages	Disadvantages
Diversification of interests so the firm is less vulnerable to losses due to decline in sales in one sector or industry	The managers from the different firms brought together may not fully understand the other parts of the business. This can lead to poor decision making.
Increases the customer base of the firm, leading to a potential increase in sales of both parts of the new business, resulting in higher profits	Loss of profits as the need to understand how the other industry works leads to rising costs
Better use of finance in that this can be used in the area where there is likely to be most growth	Problems in bringing entirely different work practices and values together, which are even greater if the firms are in different countries

CASE STUDY **The Flipkart–Myntra merger**

A massive consolidation of Indian e-commerce took place in May 2014 when the domestic e-retailer Flipkart acquired the Indian online fashion retailer Myntra.

Flipkart started as an electronics retailer and the majority of its revenue both before and after the merger comes from that sector. However, since its founding in 2007 it has diversified and it added a fashion category to its site in 2012.

By adding Myntra's 30 per cent share of the online fashion market, the two companies are expected to attract around half of India's online fashion sales after the merger.

E-commerce has grown rapidly in India in the last decade and the global market leader Amazon commenced operations there in 2013. Flipkart hopes that the merger will strengthen its position against Amazon and other local rivals such as Snapdeal.

1 What type of integration does the merger between Flipkart and Myntra represent?

2 Analyse the possible advantages and disadvantages of the merger.

3 (E) Discuss whether this merger is likely to be beneficial for the consumer.

How can internal and external economies and diseconomies of scale affect a firm/industry as the scale of production changes?

Economies of scale are the cost advantages a firm can gain by increasing its scale of production. As a result of these economies of scale the **average cost** of production falls as output rises.

The opposite are **diseconomies of scale**, which are the disadvantages to a firm of increasing production, leading to a rise in the average cost of production.

Figure 3.5.1 shows the average cost curve for a firm. As the output of the firm increases from X to A, its average cost initially falls (economies of scale). However, as the output of the firm continues to increase from A to Y, average cost rises (diseconomies of scale).

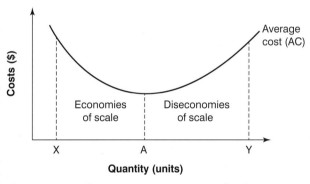

Figure 3.5.1 The average cost curve of a firm

Economies and diseconomies of scale are usually divided into **internal** and **external**. Internal economies of scale is the fall in average cost resulting from growth in the size of the firm itself. External economies of scale, on the other hand, is the fall in average cost which arises from growth in the size of the industry (which consists of many firms). Similarly, internal diseconomies of scale results from the increase in the size of the firm while external diseconomies of scale results from the increase in the size of the industry.

Key terms

Economies of scale – where an increase in the level of production results in a fall in the average cost of production

Average cost – the cost of producing a unit (unit cost of production). It is calculated by dividing total cost by output or quantity

Diseconomies of scale – where an increase in the level of production results in a rise in the average cost of production

Internal economies – come from the growth of the firm itself, resulting in a fall in average cost (economies) or rise in average cost (diseconomies)

External economies – arise from factors outside the control of a firm and result in changes in the average costs of all firms in the industry regardless of size

Internal and external economies of scale

Internal	External
Technical economies – large firms purchase expensive specialist equipment as costs can be spread across a very large output	**Education and training facilities** – a local university's research and development facilities can provide help to all firms
Economies of increased dimensions – if you double the dimensions of a lorry the volume increases eight times, thus reducing the transport cost of each item	**Concentration of firms** – if suppliers of parts locate near the main producer this cuts transport costs and time taken
Purchasing economies (or bulk buying) – buying in large quantities will enable a firm to negotiate bulk discounts with suppliers leading to a lower cost per unit	**Transport** – if transport links are improved such as better roads, faster rail travel and deeper ports, then the costs of transport fall
Financial economies – larger firms are able to borrow money from banks more easily and at lower rates of interest and have a greater range of sources for new capital such as the issuing of shares	**Finance** – if there is a concentration of an industry in an area then banks will develop specialist facilities for these firms
Managerial economies – larger firms can afford to employ specialist staff in areas such as finance, marketing and production.	**Location** – certain areas get a reputation for an industry, for example Silicon Valley in California. This attracts support firms, which benefits all firms in the industry
Marketing economies – larger firms are able to use more expensive marketing methods as the cost can be spread across more units of output thereby lowering cost per unit	
Risk-bearing economies – larger firms are able to spread risk by offering a range of products. If one product loses sales then it can still rely on the others to remain profitable thereby minimising losses.	
Division of labour – larger firms can divide work into separate tasks so their workers become specialised	

6   Explain why a technology firm would want to locate in an area with good educational and finance facilities.

Diseconomies of scale occur when average costs rise (see Figure 3.5.1).

Internal diseconomies include:

- Managerial – managers find it more difficult to coordinate production.

- Communication – may become more difficult and time consuming thus leading to inefficiencies, such as miscommunication and delays in decision making.

- Motivation – workers may feel cut off from decision making and become alienated and demotivated.

External diseconomies tend to arise due to the overconcentration of firms in an area. This causes the costs of the factors of production to increase. An example would be where the demand by the firms for skilled labour exceeds the supply available, causing the wage rates for all the firms to rise. Another effect is that roads become congested. In this case it will take longer to receive raw materials and to deliver finished products, thereby increasing the costs of transport.

Applying

Project work

Use the internet or research local firms to answer the following questions:

1. How does your government classify the size of firms?

2. Find out what are the challenges facing small firms in your country. You could try to talk to owners of small firms and/or use the internet to research this.

3. Find recent examples of horizontal, vertical and conglomerate mergers, if possible in your country. Taking one of these mergers, analyse the advantages and disadvantages to the new firm of this merger.

4. Identify an area of your country where there is a concentration of firms. What advantages and disadvantages do you think these firms gain from this concentration?

5. (E) Investigate one firm in your area. What economies of scale does this firm benefit from? If it increased output would it be able to gain more economies or would it suffer from diseconomies? Make a presentation to the class.

6. (E) How easy is it to conduct business in your country? You could use the World Bank's 'doing business' website to help you.

Knowledge check questions

1 Define primary sector. [2]

2 Define tertiary sector. [2]

3 Explain how a firm operating in the secondary sector uses suppliers in the primary sector and is itself a supplier to firms in the tertiary sector. [4]

4 Explain **two** advantages that small firms may enjoy. [4]

5 Define merger. [2]

6 Explain **two** types of merger. [4]

7 Define economies of scale. [2]

8 Explain **two** types of economies of scale. [4]

9 (E) Analyse the effects of a forward vertical merger on the economies of scale a firm could achieve. [6]

Check your progress

Read the unit objectives below and reflect on your progress in each.

- Define primary, secondary and tertiary sectors.

- Define private and public sectors.

- Explain how firms are classified by relative size.

- Analyse the advantages and disadvantages of small firms.

- Explain the challenges facing small firms and the reasons for their existence.

- Explain the reason for the existence of small firms.

- Explain the causes of the growth of firms.

- Explain the advantages and disadvantages of different types of mergers.

- Analyse how internal and external economies and diseconomies of scale can affect a firm/industry as the scale of production changes.

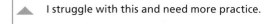 I struggle with this and need more practice.

 I can do this reasonably well.

 I can do this with confidence.

Firms and production

Learning objectives
By the end of this unit, you should be able to:
- define production
- define productivity
- explain what influences the demand for factors of production
- define labour intensive production
- define capital intensive production
- explain the reasons for adopting the different forms of production
- analyse the advantages and disadvantages of different forms of production
- explain what influences the levels of production and productivity.

Starting point

Answer these questions in pairs:

1. Give two examples each of land, labour, capital and enterprise.

2. Which does your school employ more of: labour or capital?

3. Using a PPC diagram, show the effect of the substitution of more computers for teachers in your school.

Exploring

Discuss these questions in pairs:

1. How would you measure the output of your school?

2. Would it make any difference to your performance if there were two more or two fewer people in your class?

3. Would it make any difference to your performance if there were either 10 more or 10 fewer people in your class?

What is the difference between production and productivity?

Production is the total output of the goods and services produced by a firm or industry in a period of time. It records the total level of output produced regardless of the number of workers or machines employed to produce it. For example, a firm with 100 workers and an output of 1000 units has the same production as a firm with 50 workers and an output of 1000 units.

Productivity is a measure of output that takes into account the factors of production used to create the output. The productivity of labour can be measured by dividing the total output by the number of workers employed. It is measured in terms of output per unit of input:

$$\text{productivity} = \frac{\text{total output}}{\text{total input}}$$

Productivity is one measure of the degree of **efficiency** in the use of factors of production in the production process.

Using the example above:

- the productivity of the 100 workers is $\frac{1000}{100}$ = 10 units per worker

- while that of the 50 workers is $\frac{1000}{50}$ = 20 units per worker

Although the production is the same, the firm with 50 workers has twice the **labour productivity**.

What is meant by labour intensive production and capital intensive production?

Labour intensive production is where the production of a good or service depends more heavily on labour than the other factors of production. Traditional farming is labour intensive, but nowadays in many economies the tertiary sector is often more labour intensive than the primary or secondary sectors. For example, a hotel will employ many different people including managers, receptionists, chefs, waiters and cleaners.

Capital intensive production is where a high level of investment is required, such as in machinery, equipment and vehicles, compared to the other factors of production. For example, in oil refining the process is largely automated with lots of equipment and relatively few people involved.

Key terms

Production – the total output of the goods and services produced by a firm or industry in a period of time

Productivity – measures the contribution to production (total output) by each factor of production employed. It is one measure of the degree of efficiency in the use of factors of production in the production process. It is measured in terms of output per unit of input.

Labour productivity – output per worker per time period

Efficiency – how effective the firm is in using factors of production to generate its output

Labour intensive production – where the production of a good or service depends more heavily on labour than the other factors of production

Capital intensive production – where a high level of investment in capital is required, such as in machinery, equipment and vehicles compared to the other factors of production

Reasons for adopting the different forms of production

Labour intensive	Capital intensive
Availability and cost – if labour is plentiful then it is likely to be relatively inexpensive, which will keep production costs down	**Lack of labour/skills shortage** – capital intensive production is not dependent on finding enough workers or workers with the necessary skills
Flexible – easier to meet changing levels of consumer demand	**Uniformity** – able to produce exactly the same product every time
Meet consumer needs – able to provide specific products for different customers	**Greater output** – more can be produced in a set time period, which will increase labour productivity
Personal service – can interact with customers; a lot of services cannot be provided by machinery	**Technical economies of scale** – greater efficiency with lower average costs

 Analyse why, as countries become wealthier, farming has become more capital intensive.

How do the advantages and disadvantages of different forms of production compare?

A firm's choice of whether to use capital intensive or labour intensive methods is usually driven by profit in that the firm will choose whichever method is more profitable. The advantages of the two methods are given above. There are disadvantages, however, of using each method. These are given in the table below.

Disadvantages of the different forms of production

Labour intensive	Capital intensive
Cost – in the long run labour can be more expensive than machinery due to lower productivity and need for training	**Cost** – the initial cost can be very high, which can make it unaffordable
Low supply – in some areas there can be a shortage of the right type of labour (skills shortage), which can lead to high costs if demand exceeds supply	**Inflexible** – machines can often only perform one task and cannot easily be changed in line with changes in consumer demand
Less efficient – labour will not produce the same every time and its effort will vary, for example it can be affected by personal issues	**Small versus large scale** – to be efficient machinery often needs to operate on a large scale, which may not be relevant for all production
Labour relations – workers can go on strike or take other industrial action	**Lack of initiative** – unlike labour, machinery cannot come up with new ideas or take on new responsibilities

Worked example

Discuss whether a television manufacturer should adopt a capital intensive production process.

Capital intensive production is where a high level of investment is required compared to the other factors of production.

It is important for a television manufacturer to be capital intensive. This is because it is vital that each television is the same to ensure they work and meet the required standards. Machines are much more likely than people to be able to do this as people can lose concentration or become bored. In addition, the producer is not dependent on finding a large supply of labour with suitable skills. If labour was in short supply workers could demand higher wages, pushing up costs. Having efficient machinery could lead to large-scale production, leading to greater economies of scale and resulting in lower average costs. This would allow the producer to gain more profit. Alternatively, they could sell their products at a lower price, which may lead to them gaining market share and higher profits in the long run.

There are some problems with using a lot of capital. Machines are inflexible and do not think. This means they cannot take responsibility if there is a problem, nor can they develop new ideas to improve production. The initial cost of purchasing the capital equipment can be very high so the producer must have large sums of money or be able to borrow it. The producer will have to employ some people, for example supervisors, repair workers and sales people.

Overall, the television manufacturer would be advised to adopt capital intensive production. The main aim is to produce identical products on a large scale and only machines can do this.

Commentary

The key points are as follows:

1. The response starts with a clear definition as the whole question depends on an understanding of capital intensive production. The reader knows you understand the concept and it gives you a basis for writing the rest of the answer.

2. The second paragraph analyses the advantages of using capital intensive production for television production. There is no need to cover every possible point, but the response should be sufficient to show sound understanding.

3. The third paragraph points out some of the problems with capital intensive methods. The question says 'discuss' so both sides are needed.

4. Finally you bring it together and offer a short evaluation of why you agree with the idea in the question.

CASE STUDY   ## The advantages to India of labour intensive production

The unemployment rate in India at the start of 2017 was about 6%.

In some areas of India labour intensive industries such as handicrafts and small-scale production have been increased to try to reduce the number of people who are unemployed. It has been suggested that these industries could be set up anywhere in the country because they are not dependent on expensive, and often foreign, machinery. This would then increase output in other areas.

Increased output would lead to more money for these workers, allowing them to purchase more goods. This would then lead to a reduction in poverty.

1 What is meant by labour intensive production?

2 Other than the advantages in the text, explain two other advantages for India of using labour intensive methods.

3 Discuss whether your country should make greater use of labour intensive production methods.

What influences the demand for factors of production?

In Unit 3.3 we discovered that factors of production are not demanded for themselves, but are needed in response to the demand for a good or service (derived demand).

Which factors are employed depends on what is being produced. Anything that is mass produced such as baked beans, motor tyres or washing powder is likely to require a lot of capital, whereas a craft product such as handmade pottery or a face-to-face service such as a hairdresser is likely to be labour intensive.

If it is possible to substitute one factor for another then a rise in the productivity, or a fall in the cost of one of the factors, may result in a change in the combination of resources being employed. A fall in the price of capital goods, for example, might lead to the replacement of some workers by machines.

For example, a potter who makes pots by hand decides to add more capital, in the form of a hand-controlled wheel, to increase output. The potter then realises that by substituting more capital for labour, such as mechanised wheels and machines to shape the clay, the pots can be mass produced, thus increasing the total output.

On the other hand, if factors are complementary to each other, a fall in the price of one or a rise in its productivity may increase the employment of all the factors in a firm. A fall in the price of aircraft could lead an airline to order more planes (capital) to fly to more destinations, increasing the demand for pilots and cabin staff (labour) and more take-off and landing slots at airports (land).

Equally, as the demand for factors of production is derived demand, any change in demand for the product will lead to a change in demand for the factors of production used to make that product. This is true between industries and within an industry. In many countries manufacturing industries are declining while tertiary sector industries continue to grow. As a result people move from working in manufacturing to working in areas such as finance, entertainment and tourism. At the same time, capital and land use also move to these industries. A good example of derived demand within an industry is the fashion industry. As one fashion declines and another takes its place workers move from making one type of garment to producing its replacement.

Other influences can be more complex. The use of more advanced technology can lead to a fall in demand for less skilled workers (capital replaces labour) but an increase in demand for those with relevant skills. The availability of the factors is also important. If labour is both plentiful and cheap a firm may employ more labour than capital. However, if there is a shortage of labour and it is expensive then a firm will substitute capital for labour.

Productivity can also be important. If capital has a higher productivity than labour it would make sense for a firm to try to employ more capital and less labour. Agriculture is a good example. Capital such as tractors can do far more work in a day than labour can. This is why in countries where labour is in relatively short supply or is expensive, capital equipment has replaced people. A second related point is the relative price of the factors of production. In developed countries labour is expensive so firms seek, where possible, to replace labour with machines. This helps to explain what has happened in agriculture. However, if labour is cheap then a firm will use more labour than capital.

 Many towns and cities have high-rise buildings (for example, apartment blocks and office skyscrapers). Explain the economic factors that cause buildings to be built upwards rather than outwards in towns and cities.

What are the influences on production and productivity?

Production can be increased by employing more factors of production or by increasing the productivity of the factors. Productivity can be increased by improving one or more of the factors of production.

Influences on production include the following:

- **Natural factors** such as climate and soil. These are especially important for agriculture, with climate change already starting to affect the growing of some crops. Finding new sources of metals, oil and gas is also important for industries such as oil and gas extraction and refining.

- **Technology** can lead to better and faster production as well as new methods.

- **Infrastructure** such as better transport facilities can lead to greater output of both goods and services.

- **Government policies** can be very important. Changes in taxation can encourage or discourage production. Equally, improvements to education and healthcare can lead to a more skilled and healthier workforce, thus leading to greater output.

Influences on productivity include:

- **Technology** can increase the productivity of workers; workers with new technology are likely to be more productive than those using older technology. Technology can also increase the productivity of land, by increasing the amount that can be produced.

- **Education** is not only important in improving the skills of the workers, but can also lead to better technology. People with higher skills are more likely to be able to improve the productivity of capital.

- **Quality and quantity of raw materials available** can affect both labour and capital. For example, if it becomes more difficult to extract resources, such as coal, then the amount produced per worker per day is likely to fall.

- **Effective management** can improve the productivity of land, labour and capital. If resources are well organised then output per input should rise.

- **The culture of the firm** can influence productivity. Japanese manufacturers, such as Nissan, practise what is called 'kaizen', which means continuous small improvements. This does not depend on expensive investment or training, but on workers coming up with simple small ways to make their work better.

Project work

Use the internet or research local firms to answer the following questions:

1. By searching online or by making a visit, gather information about one producer that is labour intensive and one that is capital intensive. If possible, use producers in your country. Find out why they use this method and whether there are any disadvantages as well as advantages.

2. Make a presentation of your findings to the class.

3. How could the productivity of your class/year/other pupils be increased? Try to make a presentation to your class and also to others who would be interested: teachers, governors, parents, etc.

4. (E) Either investigate how the output of your school could be improved, or investigate a local firm and how its output could be improved. Write a report or make a presentation to an appropriate person.

Knowledge check questions

1 Define production. [2]

2 Define productivity. [2]

3 Calculate the productivity of the workforce if there are 25 workers and the output each week is 250 units. By how much would productivity have increased if the number of workers increased to 30 and output to 360 units? Show your working. [4]

4 Define derived demand. [2]

5 Explain **two** ways in which the demand for a factor of production could increase. [4]

6 Explain **two** disadvantages of labour intensive production. [4]

7 Explain **two** disadvantages of capital intensive production. [4]

8 Explain **two** ways in which a farmer could increase the productivity of the land. [4]

9 (E) Discuss whether a car producer should seek to first improve productivity or increase production. [8]

Check your progress

Read the unit objectives below and reflect on your progress in each.

- Define production.

- Define productivity.

- Explain what influences the demand for factors of production.

- Define labour intensive production.

- Define capital intensive production.

- Explain the reasons for adopting the different forms of production.

- Analyse the advantages and disadvantages of different forms of production.

- Explain what influences the levels of production and productivity.

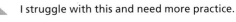 I struggle with this and need more practice.

 I can do this reasonably well.

 I can do this with confidence.

Firms' costs, revenue and objectives

Learning objectives
By the end of this unit, you should be able to:
* define the costs of production
* calculate total cost, average cost, fixed cost, average fixed cost, variable cost and average variable cost
* analyse how change in output affects the costs of production
* define revenue
* calculate total and average revenue
* analyse the influence of sales on revenue
* explain the objectives of firms.

....

Starting point

Answer these questions in pairs:

1. Do you think it is cheaper to feed just one person or to feed several at the same time?

2. Think of your favourite sweet or snack. How much does it cost? What difference might it make to the price if you could buy a month's worth of this sweet or snack in one go? Why is this?

3. Have you ever sold anything? How much did you get for it? What influenced the amount you got?

4. What are the four factors of production?

Exploring

Discuss these questions in pairs:

1. How much does it cost to feed your household each week? If you had a younger brother or sister, how much extra would that cost?

2. If you were in charge of the finances of your school, how could you try to reduce the costs per pupil? What might be the results of your cost reductions?

3. What influences the amount of money your school receives each year?

4. If you were in charge of the finances of your school, how could you try to increase the revenue of the school?

Developing

What are the costs of production and how are they calculated?

Producing goods and services costs money as the factors of production have to be paid. A producer, such as a car manufacturer, can analyse these costs by answering questions such as these:

* How much does it cost to produce 100 cars?

* How much does it cost to produce each car?

* What would our costs be if we did not produce any cars?

In this section you will learn what the costs are, how to calculate each of them and why knowing them is useful for the entrepreneur.

Total costs (TC) are all the costs of the firm added together. These costs can be divided into fixed costs and variable costs.

Fixed costs (FC) are those costs that do not vary with output. These are the costs which a firm would incur even if it produced nothing. If a firm shuts down for a holiday period it will still have to pay, for example, salaries, interest on loans and rent.

Variable costs (VC) are those costs that change as output changes. If output increases so do the variable costs. This is because to produce more you will need, for example, more raw materials, labour and capital equipment.

Total cost is calculated by:

total cost = fixed cost + variable cost **or** TC = FC + VC

If at 20 units FC = $100 and VC = $40 then TC = $(100 + 40) = $140

Average cost (AC) is the cost of producing a unit. It is calculated by dividing total cost by output or quantity (Q):

$$\text{average cost} = \frac{\text{total cost}}{\text{quantity}} \quad \textbf{or} \quad AC = \frac{TC}{Q}$$

If TC is $140 and Q is 20 then $AC = \dfrac{140}{20} = \$7$

A fall in average costs shows that a firm is becoming more efficient (gaining greater economies of scale – see Unit 3.5). A rise in average costs due to an increase in output shows that the firm is becoming less efficient (suffering from diseconomies of scale – see Unit 3.5).

Average fixed costs (AFC) are the fixed costs per unit. AFC is calculated by dividing fixed costs by output or quantity:

$$\text{average fixed cost} = \frac{\text{fixed cost}}{\text{quantity}} \quad \textbf{or} \quad AFC = \frac{FC}{Q}$$

If FC = $100 and Q = 20 then $AFC = \dfrac{100}{20} = \$5$

Average variable costs (AVC) are the variable costs per unit. AVC is calculated by dividing the variable costs by the output or quantity:

$$\text{average variable cost} = \frac{\text{variable cost}}{\text{quantity}} \quad \textbf{or} \quad AVC = \frac{FC}{Q}$$

If VC = $40 and Q = 20 then $AVC = \dfrac{40}{20} = \$2$

Application task

Farah's costs

Farah has taken over a shop previously owned by a relative. The relative has left her some information, but it is incomplete.

Output	Fixed cost	Variable cost	Total cost	Average cost
0	100	0	100	
5		40		
10			170	
15		110		

Make a copy of Farah's information.

1. Using the information provided, calculate fixed cost, total variable cost, total cost and average cost for each level of output.

2. Using the information you have calculated, would you advise Farah to increase or decrease output?

How does a change in output affect the costs of production?

As output increases, total costs will rise. This is because the variable costs increase, as more labour and raw materials are required. The fixed costs, however, will remain the same. For example, the rent for the offices does not change. In the Application task, Farah's fixed costs were 100 when output was zero, but were also 100 when output was 15.

Figure 3.7.1 shows that as output increases so do the total and variable costs. When output is zero there are no variable costs (because nothing is being produced) so total cost equals fixed cost. Fixed costs, as we saw above, do not vary with output so they are shown by a straight horizontal line which is above zero (this is because there are some fixed costs to pay even if output is zero). On the other hand, as output rises so do the variable costs. As we already know, this is because the amount of inputs such as labour, raw materials and capital equipment increase. This was shown in the Application task above, where VC rose from 15 to 110 and TC started equal to FC, but then increased in line with VC.

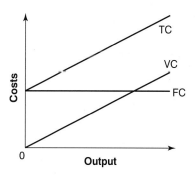

Figure 3.7.1 Total costs

The three average costs all behave in different ways.

- As fixed costs do not vary with output, average fixed costs must fall at each level of output.

- Average variable costs, however, will fall at first but then rise. This is because, for example, existing workers can do more work, but as production expands it becomes necessary either to employ more people or to pay workers overtime to work longer hours.

- Average total costs will continue to fall even though AVC starts to rise as AFC is falling by a higher amount. As output continues to increase it becomes more and more costly to obtain the variable factors of production. AVC rises by more than AFC falls, causing average total costs to increase. If you are unsure about this, you might want to go back to the Application task and calculate AFC and AVC and then compare them to your AC column.

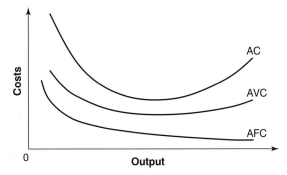

Figure 3.7.2 Average costs

Figure 3.7.2 shows that as output increases: AFC falls while AVC and AC fall at first but then rise.

 With the help of examples, explain why, as output increases, average fixed costs fall at a decreasing rate.

How can revenue be defined and calculated?

A cost is money spent by a firm or individual on buying, for example, a good, a service or a factor of production. For example, a cost for an individual could be the purchase of a new book. An example of a firm's cost would be the purchase of new machinery. Revenue is money that a firm, or individual, earns by selling something. It is the firm's income. Your teacher sells their labour and in return receives a salary (income). A clothes shop receives income (revenue) by selling its clothes.

A producer, such as a clothes shop, can analyse the revenue it receives by answering questions such as these:

- How much revenue will it receive by selling 100 coats?
- How much revenue does each coat bring in to the shop?

Total revenue (TR) is the total amount of money a firm receives from the sale of its goods or services. Total revenue is often called sales revenue or sales turnover. The value of total revenue is found by multiplying the price of the product by the quantity sold.

total revenue = price × quantity **or** $TR = P \times Q$

A computer store that sells 10 laptops in a week at $400 each will make $4000 in revenue ($400 × 10 = $4000).

Average revenue (AR) is the revenue per unit sold. It is calculated by dividing total revenue by the quantity sold.

$$\text{average revenue} = \frac{\text{total revenue}}{\text{quantity}} \ \textbf{or} \ AR = \frac{TR}{Q}$$

Key terms

Total revenue (TR) – the total income of a firm from the sale of its goods and services

Average revenue (AR) – the revenue per unit sold

Average revenue is the same, therefore, as the price of the product: AR = P. The calculation above for total revenue shows why this is the case. If TR = $4000 but Q = 10, then AR = $400, which is the price of the laptops.

What is the influence of sales on revenue?

In the example above, 10 laptops were sold at $400 each, giving a total revenue of $4000. Assuming the price of the laptops does not change, an increase in the number of laptops sold will lead to an increase in total revenue. For example, if 20 were sold, total revenue would increase to $8000. This positive relationship between total revenue and the quantity sold is shown in Figure 3.7.3.

As price remains unchanged at $400, the average revenue also remains unchanged at $400 as more laptops are sold. As can be seen in Figure 3.7.4, average revenue (or price) remains constant at $400 regardless of the number of laptops sold. The average revenue curve is also the demand curve as it shows quantity demand at a price (average revenue) of $400. In this example, the price elasticity of demand for laptops is infinite (perfectly elastic) as any number of laptops could be demanded at a price of $400.

However, in reality, most firms face demand curves which are downward sloping (see Units 2.3, 2.5 and 2.6) as shown in Figure 3.7.5. This means that they are able to influence the quantity sold (quantity demanded) by raising or lowering price. For example, an increase in price from P to P_1 leads to a fall in quantity demanded from Q to Q_1 in Figure 3.7.5. As discussed in Unit 2.7, if the demand for a firm's product is price inelastic, it will be able to increase total revenue by raising its price. On the other hand, if demand for its product is price elastic, it will be able to increase total revenue by lowering price.

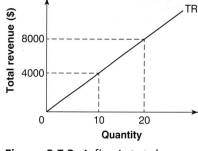

Figure 3.7.3 A firm's total revenue curve

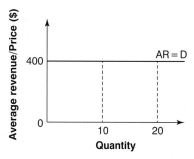

Figure 3.7.4 A firm's average revenue curve when demand is perfectly elastic

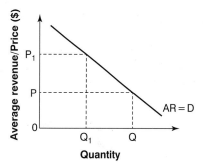

Figure 3.7.5 A firm's average revenue curve when its demand curve is downward sloping

 Explain the relationship between price and average revenue.

Application task

José's garden centre

José owns a small garden centre selling plants and also a whole range of garden tools, fertilisers and other garden-related products. He is short of time so has asked you to calculate his total and average revenue and to tell him whether he should reduce his prices in order to both sell more plants and increase his revenue.

Price ($)	Sales (no. of plants per week)
10	50
8	72
6	90
4	110
2	125

1. Using the information above, calculate total and average revenue for each price.

2. From the information provided, explain to José why aiming to sell more plants might conflict with his aim to earn more revenue.

What are the objectives of firms?

Profit occurs when a firm's total revenue is greater than its total costs. Profit, or at least not making a loss, is needed by all firms that are in the private sector if they are to survive. It also provides financing (money) for firms to expand and buy new capital equipment. As was seen in Unit 1.2, profit is the reward to entrepreneurs for taking risk. It is calculated by:

profit = total revenue − total cost **or** profit = TR − TC

If, for example, a small business such as a shop has a total revenue of $100 000, but has to spend $50 000 on costs such as labour, products to sell and rent, then the profit would be:

profit = TR − TC

$\quad$ = $100 000 − $50 000

$\quad$ = $50 000

As noted above, firms cannot survive and grow unless they make a profit. Economists therefore generally assume that firms aim to maximise profits.

Key terms

Profit – the income a firm receives after expenses have been deducted (total revenue – total costs). Profit is the factor reward for enterprise.

Worked example

Firm A has the following total costs and total revenue for a range of output:

Quantity	Total revenue ($)	Total cost ($)
100	200	300
200	400	480
300	600	600
400	800	700
500	1000	950
600	1200	1400

At which level of output is the firm maximising its profits?

Quantity	Total revenue ($)	Total cost ($)	Profit ($)
100	200	300	−100
200	400	480	−80
300	600	600	0
400	800	700	100
500	1000	950	50
600	1200	1400	−200

The firm is maximising its profit where TR − TC is the greatest positive number, which is at output 400 and profit of $100.

While it is probably true that firms aim to earn high levels of profit, it is unlikely that all their decisions are motivated by the desire to make maximum profits. For example, some firms aim to expand and take a larger share of the market. Many firms also find it difficult to pursue profit maximisation and opt for alternatives. Some of these are explained below.

One possibility is to try and grow the size of the firm, which is likely to lead to a larger market share. This may be through mergers and takeovers. This could lead not only to an increase in size, but also greater economies of scale with lower average cost and so higher profits.

A firm might also try to grow by **sales (revenue) maximisation**. In Unit 3.5 we noted that managers often see greater sales as a measurable objective which, if achieved, could lead to higher pay or promotion. This is linked to the idea of increasing total revenue as much as possible. It is easy to measure, but may conflict with the need for profit as average costs rise with output.

For many small firms the main objective may be **survival**. This will certainly be the case for a new firm, or for one entering a new market or in an economic crisis. The objective is to make sure you are around next year and the year after and to try to avoid making a loss.

Key terms

Sales (revenue) maximisation – where a firm increases market share and/or increases total revenue

Survival – the objective of remaining in business

Greta and Lorenzo

Greta and Lorenzo took over the running of Greta's family business in 2010. Greta's father, who had previously run the business, had survival as his main objective and concentrated on making enough total revenue to survive. Greta and Lorenzo, however, were more ambitious. They wanted to grow the business.

To do so they had offered to take over Lorenzo's uncle's business. To Greta and Lorenzo this made a lot of sense as their business supplied products to the uncle's business. By becoming larger they hoped to move towards maximising their profits.

Lorenzo's uncle, however, was not so sure. He pointed out that their business was in the secondary sector while his provided a service. While Greta and Lorenzo's business had high fixed costs, his had high variable costs.

1 Explain how making 'enough total revenue' would have enabled Greta's father's business to survive.

2 Discuss the advantages and disadvantages of Greta and Lorenzo's proposed takeover.

3 (E) Why might a secondary sector business have high fixed costs while a service sector one has high variable costs?

Another possible objective is **social welfare**. Owners and managers of firms may be concerned with both the welfare of their workers and also of society as a whole. This has become more prominent with concerns over the environment and climate change. Firms may also be involved with the local community or charitable concerns. Public sector firms may have this as their main objective as governments can subsidise them if they make a loss.

While these objectives may be in conflict this is not necessarily the case. Concern for the environment, for example, could lead to more people being in favour of the firm, leading to greater sales, revenue, market share and economies of scale. In turn this could lead to profit maximisation.

Key term

Social welfare – a firm being concerned about the welfare of its workers, society as a whole or local community

Applying

Project work

Research answers to the following questions:

1. Costs and revenue of your school. If this is not possible, try to find out the information about a local business.

   a. Divide costs into fixed and variable; if possible discuss this as a class.

   b. Work out the average revenue.

   c. What would happen to costs and revenue if the school/firm grew in size, but the size of the buildings/rooms did not?

   d. If possible make a presentation of your findings.

2. Think of a firm that you are familiar with. It could be one whose products you use or one that a family member works for. Based on its recent activities, what do you think its objectives are? Why is this?

Knowledge check questions

1 Define total cost. [2]

2 Define average cost. [2]

3 Give **two** examples each of fixed and variable costs. [4]

4 Explain why average fixed costs continually fall, but average variable costs fall and then rise. [4]

5 Define total revenue. [2]

6 Explain why average revenue for most firms falls as sales rise. [4]

7 Explain **two** objectives that a firm may have. [4]

8 Analyse the effects on average costs of the growth of a firm. [8]

9 (E) Discuss whether firms should always aim to maximise profits. [8]

Check your progress

Read the unit objectives below and reflect on your progress in each.

- Define the costs of production.

- Calculate total cost, average cost, fixed cost, average fixed cost, variable cost and average variable cost.

- Analyse how change in output affects the costs of production.

- Define revenue.

- Calculate total and average revenue.

- Analyse the influence of sales on revenue.

- Explain the objectives of firms.

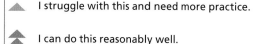

    I struggle with this and need more practice.

    I can do this reasonably well.

    I can do this with confidence.

Market structure

Learning objectives

By the end of this unit, you should be able to:

- define what is meant by a competitive market
- define what is meant by a monopoly
- analyse the effects of competition on price, quality, choice and profit
- describe the characteristics of monopoly markets
- discuss the advantages and disadvantages of monopolies.

Starting point

Answer these questions in pairs:

1. Have you ever taken part in a competition? How many other people took part?

2. If you wanted to buy a new pair of shoes would you prefer to have just one shop to go to or several? Why?

3. Think of a type of business, for example shoe shops or supermarkets, of which there are several near where you live. How could one of these firms become the only business selling the product in the area?

Exploring

Discuss these questions in pairs:

1. How can firms compete with each other? Try to think of three different ways.

2. How do you think a small firm might try to compete with a large firm?

3. Why might governments want to limit the size of firms?

Developing

What is a competitive market?

Competition is where different firms are trying to sell a similar product to a consumer.

In a **competitive market** a large number of firms are in competition with each other to satisfy the wants and needs of a large number of consumers. No single firm or consumer, or group of firms or consumers, can decide on the price or quantity of the goods and services in the market. A competitive market should lead to better prices, products and choice for consumers.

In addition, competition ensures that firms are both efficient and innovative, or else they will go out of business. To be efficient,

Key terms

Competition – where different firms are trying to sell a similar product to a customer

Competitive market – where a large number of firms compete with each other to satisfy the wants and needs of a large number of consumers

firms must minimise their costs in order to keep prices low and remain competitive. To be innovative, firms must find new ways both to reduce costs and to develop new products. Competition also forces businesses to meet consumer demands by providing the right products at the right price and quality.

The key features of a competitive market are as follows:

- There are many firms and many buyers.
- Firms and consumers must accept the market price.
- New firms can enter the market easily: there are no **barriers to entry**.
- Products are very similar or identical.
- Consumers have full information about the product.

Firms can compete in many different ways:

- price
- advertising
- quality
- customer service
- specialist products.

These can be divided into price and non-price competition.

1 Why do many firms use advertising to compete with their rivals?

2 Using the internet, other media, local research or your own knowledge, try to find a range of both local and national competition between businesses. Look for a variety of methods of competition. Share your findings with the rest of the group.

Price competition

To many people a competitive market means price competition. This is where firms lower their prices to gain customers and so increase their share of the market. In order to do this, firms have to be more efficient. The effect is shown in Figure 3.8.1 where greater efficiency leads to the supply curve shifting to the right, from S to S_1, leading to a lower price, P_1.

The extent of the fall in the price and the increase in the quantity sold will depend on the price elasticity of demand for the product. In Figure 3.8.2, the demand curve, D, is price inelastic. As a result, price falls sharply from P to P_1, with little effect on the quantity, Q to Q_1. This would be typical of products that are necessities. The increase in competition means that the sellers are fighting to take each other's customers.

Key term

Barriers to entry – ways in which new firms are prevented from entering a particular industry

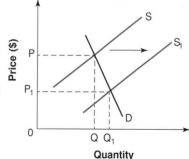

Figure 3.8.1 The effect of an increase in efficiency in a market

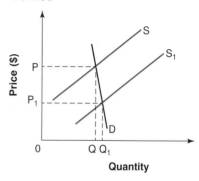

Figure 3.8.2 The effect of an increase in efficiency in a market (PED inelastic)

On the other hand, if demand is price elastic, as shown by the demand curve, D, in Figure 3.8.3, then price only falls by a small amount, from P to P$_1$, but there is a proportionately larger effect on quantity, from Q to Q$_1$. This would be typical of non-essential goods. Here the fall in price is creating new quantity demanded.

Firms that cannot cut their prices will start to lose customers. It is not possible, however, to continue to cut prices for ever. Firms cannot sell at less than the cost of producing the item for any length of time as this policy results in a loss and the firm eventually going out of business. This would lead to a much smaller number of larger firms. Price competition, therefore, is limited. This form of competition is more likely to take place where there are a number of larger firms, for example between supermarkets.

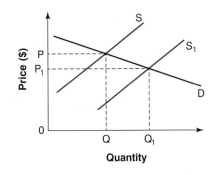

Figure 3.8.3 The effect of an increase in efficiency in a market (PED elastic)

 Why do small firms often not engage in price competition?

Competition can, however, lead to higher prices. One way in which this can happen is through extensive marketing, for example advertising. These costs have to be paid by someone. Producers will try to pass the costs on to consumers by charging more. This is one of the reasons why branded and heavily advertised goods often cost more than those that are not heavily advertised, for example Kellogg's breakfast cereals compared with a supermarket's own brand cereals.

The effects of a high number of firms on quality, choice and profit

	Advantages	Disadvantages
Quality	**For consumers:** producers need to maintain quality or else consumers switch to rivals. Some producers may choose to compete through quality and not price.	**For consumers:** with prices falling, producers may reduce the quality in order to cut costs and still make a profit.
Choice	**For consumers:** firms may compete in different ways, offering customers a range of choices (i) through price, so customers can buy cheaper products, (ii) by increasing the range of products or (iii) by focusing on quality or better customer service.	**For consumers:** falling prices lead to some sellers going out of business, thereby reducing choice. Increased choice may also lead to greater confusion, with consumers unable to compare all the choices.
Profit	**For firms:** price competition forces some rivals out of business, increasing market share of the remaining firms and leading to higher profits.	**For firms:** falling prices will lead to lower revenue and profit. If competition is high then firms are likely to end up making the minimum profit needed to survive.

CASE STUDY — Problems for traditional clothing manufacturers in the UK

Low-cost clothing producers in countries such as China have forced traditional producers in the UK to find ways of competing. Those who have tried to cut their prices have usually failed due to higher costs.

Another response has been to move production to these lower-cost countries. This has led consumers to accuse firms of having lower prices, but also lower quality. In order to maintain quality, Marks and Spencer plc sends all the basic materials such as cloth, buttons, zips, etc. required to make their clothes to countries such as Thailand. Here the materials are made into clothes which are then sent back to the UK.

1 Explain how low-cost clothing producers have forced traditional producers to cut prices.

2 Explain why low-priced products are often claimed to be of low quality when compared to similar higher-priced rival products.

3 Analyse the effect of the competition in the clothing industry on consumers.

Non-price competition

Non-price competition can take many different forms. German and Japanese car manufacturers over the last 70 years have focused on quality. The results can be seen in the growth of companies such as Volkswagen and Toyota. Consumers seemed to prefer to pay slightly more to buy a car that was reliable. Smaller producers can often compete by offering a specialist product, or better and more personalised consumer service. Small shops continue to exist not only because they offer either one or both of the above, but also because they may be more conveniently located.

Many producers use marketing as the main way to compete. This lets people know that they exist, what they sell and what they can offer in the way of services. Advertising is probably the best known method. One of the aims of advertising is to make consumers loyal to a certain brand through **product differentiation** by emphasising small differences between products. Buyers are often prepared to pay higher prices for a brand they know, and that has been heavily advertised, rather than an unknown brand or a shop's own make, even when they are basically the same.

Key terms

Product differentiation – setting one product apart from another by emphasising a particular aspect or aspects; it is used to increase consumer interest

Monopoly – the sole producer or seller of a good or service

What is meant by a monopoly?

In economics a **monopoly** is a sole producer of a good or service. This means that there is no competition. A monopoly could be in a country as a whole or in a region or even in a village or town of the country. If someone wants to go direct to Luxor, in Egypt, by air from Cairo the only provider of flights is EgyptAir. In this situation it is a monopoly supplier of aeroplane flights.

In most countries, either the government or a regulator – in the case of Egypt, for example, the regulator is the Egyptian Competition Authority – will try to prevent monopolies from taking advantage of their consumers. Without any type of control, monopolies are able to set either the price or the quantity of their products. If a monopoly sets the price then consumers will decide how much they wish to buy at that price and, therefore, how much will be supplied. Equally, if a monopoly decides to sell a particular amount of its product then the price will be determined by consumer demand.

 4 What would happen to price and to quantity if there was an increase in demand for the products of a monopolist?

Characteristics of a monopoly

Characteristic	Description
Sole supplier	A (pure) monopoly is one firm so there is no competition.
Price setter	Monopolists can determine the price they wish to sell at as there is no competition. They cannot set both the price and the quantity.
Barriers to entry	Monopolists can prevent firms entering the market either by building barriers such as massive advertising campaigns or by controlling supplies of materials; or they can be protected by government legislation or by patents and copyrights that cannot be used without permission.
Profit	Private monopolists are usually driven by the wish to make as much profit as possible (profit maximisation). Government-owned monopolies may have other motives.
Imperfect information	Consumers will suffer from having imperfect information so may not be able to discover alternative suppliers.

> **Key knowledge**
>
> A monopoly is able to set either the price of its product or the quantity it wishes to sell, but not both.

Advantages and disadvantages of a monopoly

Advantages	Disadvantages
Economies of scale: increased output will lead to a decrease in average costs of production. This allows firms to increase their profits and/or to charge consumers lower prices.	**Inefficiency**: with no competition, monopolists have no incentive to become efficient by cutting average costs. This leads to consumers paying higher prices.
Avoiding wastage of resources: having only one firm prevents duplication of products and thus avoids wastage of resources. For example, it would be a waste of resources to build a second Channel Tunnel linking the UK with France.	**Lower wages**: as the only employer for certain types of workers/skills, the monopolist may be able to get away with paying lower wages.
International competitiveness: as markets become increasingly global, it may be necessary for a firm to have a domestic monopoly in order to be competitive internationally.	**Exploitation of suppliers**: similarly, as the only buyer of supplies/raw materials, the monopolist can force suppliers to accept lower prices.

Advantages	Disadvantages
Research and development: monopoly profits can be used to invent and develop new and improved products and to invest in new technology. Firms can benefit from keeping ahead of potential rivals and in lowering costs. This is especially important in industries such as telecommunications, aeroplane manufacture and pharmaceuticals. Consumers benefit from new products and from a variety of choices.	**Lower incentive**: with no competition, monopolists have less incentive to develop new products leading not only to less choice, but also to lower quality. This is because there is no **consumer sovereignty** in that consumers lack the power to decide what is produced and for whom.

In many countries, in addition to pure monopoly, as described above, there is also a legal definition of what constitutes a monopoly. In the UK this is set at 25% of the market. In this case, a firm with more than 25% of the market is said to have monopoly power.

Key term

Consumer sovereignty – the power of consumers over how the market allocates resources through determining what is produced and for whom

---

CASE STUDY The European Union (EU) takes on Google

In June 2017 the EU declared that Google had acted illegally using its power in the market.

"What Google has done is illegal under EU antitrust rules", said Margrethe Vestager, the bloc's top antitrust official. [Anti-trust is very similar to anti-monopoly.] "It denied other companies the chance to compete on the merits and to innovate. And most importantly, it denied European consumers a genuine choice of services and the full benefits of innovation."

The EU said that Google acted illegally by giving preference in search results to its own shopping service, while relegating results from rivals to areas where potential buyers were much less likely to click. A Google search for, say, handbags or televisions will produce a picture-filled box showing deals for different retailers. This is run by Google who take a percentage of the value of the sales. Previously other comparison sites were given greater prominence.

In response a Google spokesperson said that "When you shop online you want to find the products quickly and easily and advertisers want to promote those same products. That is why Google shows shopping ads, connecting our users with thousands of advertisers, large and small, in ways which are useful for both."

1 Explain why the EU considers that Google is behaving like a monopolist.

2 Discuss the advantages and disadvantages to the consumer of Google's method of listing advertisers.

Project work

Use the internet or research local firms to answer the following questions.

1. Visit a supermarket or another large shop selling several brands of the same product. Compare the prices of heavily advertised brands with those of less well-known ones. Discuss your findings in class.

2. Choose a firm in your country, or region or town, that is a monopoly. What advantages and disadvantages are there for you from it being a monopoly?

3. (E) Select a local firm that is in competition with a larger national firm. Analyse the non-price methods of competition that both use.

Knowledge check questions

1 Define competition.   [2]

2 Define competitive market.   [2]

3 Explain **two** advantages of competition to the consumer.   [4]

4 Explain **two** effects of competition for the profits of a firm.   [4]

5 Define monopoly.   [2]

6 Define barrier to entry.   [2]

7 Explain **two** advantages to a firm of becoming a monopoly.   [4]

8 Explain **two** disadvantages to the consumer of a monopoly.   [4]

9 (E) Discuss whether monopoly firms are always harmful for consumers.   [8]

Check your progress

Read the unit objectives below and reflect on your progress in each.

- Define what is meant by a competitive market.

- Define what is meant by a monopoly.

- Analyse the effects of competition on price, quality, choice and profit.

- Describe the characteristics of monopoly markets.

- Discuss the advantages and disadvantages of monopolies.

I struggle with this and need more practice.

I can do this reasonably well.

I can do this with confidence.

Chapter review

Multiple-choice questions

1 Which of the following correctly describes money as a medium of exchange?

    A   Money enables goods and services to be bought now and paid for later.

    B   Money is normally found in most economies to be in the form of notes and coins.

    C   Money is the common standard for measuring the relative worth of goods and services.

    D   Money takes the place of exchanging goods and services through bartering.

2 What would be the **most** likely outcome of a fall in consumer confidence?

    A   Households would borrow more.

    B   Households would save more.

    C   Households would spend more.

    D   Households would use credit cards more.

3 Chibundo is a marketing assistant. Her pay last week is shown in the table below.

Work contract	25 hour week
Pay	$25 an hour
Overtime worked	5 hours
Overtime pay	$35 per hour
Bonus for meeting targets	$100

What was her basic pay?

    A $625   **B** $725   **C** $800   **D** $900

4 If a government introduced a minimum wage, what level on the diagram would it **most** likely be set at?

    A   OK

    B   OL

    C   OM

    D   ON

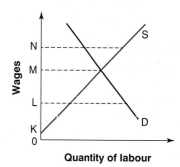

5 What is an advantage to a firm of its workers belonging to a trade union?

    A   advice on legislation

    B   easier to negotiate

    C   increase in job security

    D   substitution of capital for labour

6 Which of these is an example of a tertiary sector industry?

    A   construction   **B**   farming

    C   finance   **D**   oil refining

7 A ship builder is thinking of merging with a car manufacturer. What is the **most** likely benefit of such a merger?

A	better use of finance	**B**	increased purchasing power
C	less reliance on suppliers	**D**	reduction in competition

8 The table below shows the revenue and costs of a firm for the year 2017.

	$m
Total revenue	250
Average revenue	0.25
Average cost	0.2
Total fixed cost	5
Total variable cost	195

How much profit did the firm make?

A	$0.05m	**B**	$25m	**C**	$50m	**D**	$55m

9 If the demand for a good in a competitive market is price elastic, which policy would you **most** advise the firm to adopt?

A Increase the price, but improve the quality of the products.

B Keep the same price, but improve customer service.

C Lower the price and increase advertising of the product.

D Wait to see what competitors do and increase efficiency.

10 Which of the following is a disadvantage of a monopoly?

A Profits can be used for research and development.

B Suppliers may have to accept lower prices.

C There is no duplication of products.

D Trade increases due to international competitiveness.

Structured questions

1 Production and productivity

Since the financial crises of 2008 both world production and world productivity have increased. The increase in production has not been consistent either in terms of countries or size of firms. Japan, for example, has had both rises and falls in production. Not all countries have managed to raise the production levels for the secondary sector above the 2010 level.

Source: https://data.oecd.org/industry/industrial-production.htm] Base Year 2010 = 100

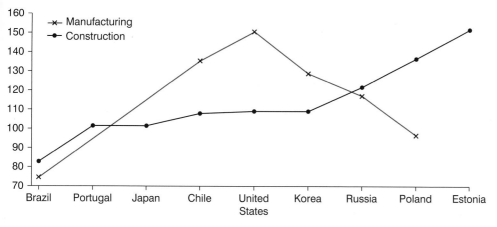

Figure 1 Secondary sector production, 2017

Equally, productivity in many developed countries has seen only slow growth since 2008, with countries such as Finland seeing negative labour productivity growth in some years. In many economies, growth in labour productivity in manufacturing has been the same in small and large firms. In business services, however, small and medium size firms have often done better than large firms.

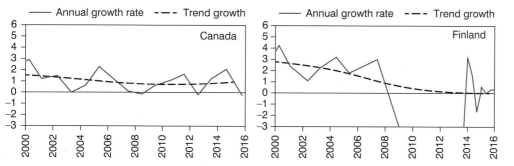

Figure 2 Yearly change in productivity for Canada and Finland, 2000–2016

The slow growth in productivity has limited employers' ability to pay higher average real wages. Despite this the pay gap between unskilled and skilled workers has widened.

Nevertheless, although the growth in production and productivity has been slow in some countries, others have seen more rapid growth in both, often due to specialisation.

(a) According to Figure 1, which country has failed to raise its production level? [1]

(b) Explain why Japan has seen both positive and negative growth in production levels. [2]

(c) Explain the difference between production and productivity. [3]

(d) Compare the growth in productivity between Canada and Finland. [3]

(e) Analyse why productivity growth in many developed countries has been slow. [6]

(f) Explain how slow growth in productivity can limit the ability of employers to pay higher wages. [4]

(g) Analyse how the pay gap between unskilled and skilled workers can widen. [5]

(h) Discuss whether producers will always benefit from specialisation. [6]

2 One of the functions of money is 'standard for deferred payment', which allows someone to borrow money and pay it back at a later date. To be called money, something needs to be both acceptable and divisible. In Ghana, the Bank of Ghana is the central bank. Commercial banks, such as Capital Bank Limited, can then lend money to customers who wish to borrow.

   (a) State **two** functions of money other than standard for deferred payment. [2]

   (b) In addition to acceptable and divisible, explain **two** other characteristics of money. [4]

   (c) Analyse the role a central bank plays in an economy. [6]

   (d) Discuss whether an increase in bank lending is always good for an economy. [8]

3 Pakistan has the tenth largest labour force in the world. There are 945 active trade unions, but they only represent 3% of the workers and most of these are in the public sector. Only workers on permanent contracts can form unions, but these are heavily restricted in their ability to collectively bargain for their members. Nevertheless, Pakistan is in the top 34% of all countries based on the yearly minimum wage rate with only 67 countries having a higher minimum wage rate. Most workers, however, are on very short-term contracts, which means that with many out of work they are more concerned with ensuring contracts are renewed than in organising effectively or campaigning for better pay and conditions. Many workers are unaware of labour rights provided by the law.

   (a) Define public sector. [2]

   (b) Explain **two** advantages to members, other than collective bargaining, of belonging to a trade union. [4]

   (c) Analyse the effects of setting a minimum wage above the equilibrium price. [6]

   (d) Discuss whether trade unions are always of benefits to workers. [8]

4 América Móvil (AM) claims that it is the leading provider of telecommunications services in Latin America. AM can offer, by being a conglomerate, a world-class integrated telecommunications system giving consumers a wide range of communications solutions.

   In April 2017 a report stated that AM controlled over 60% of the Mexican telecommunications market. This is seen as a monopoly. There have been claims that the actions of AM have led to an inefficient telecommunications market that has led to many disadvantages for the Mexican economy, while overcharging its customers. AM's control has hardly declined since 2013 when Mexico introduced new measures to increase competition in the market. There is some evidence, however, that competition may increase, helped by the US firm AT&T entering the market and already gaining over 13%.

   (a) Define a monopoly. [2]

   (b) Explain **two** advantages to consumers of a conglomerate merger. [4]

   (c) Analyse how increased competition could lead to lower prices for the consumer. [6]

   (d) Discuss the extent to which large firms are better for the consumer than small firms. [8]

Government and the macro economy

4

The government plays an important role in the growth, development and economic prosperity of a country at a local, national and international level. In this chapter, you will begin by looking at the broader role of government before focusing on the macroeconomic aims of economic growth, low unemployment, low inflation, balance of payments stability and redistribution of income. You will then look in detail at the key policies (fiscal policy, monetary policy and supply-side policy) a government can use to achieve these aims and how it may choose between conflicting aims. Finally, you will examine the macroeconomic indicators of economic growth, employment and inflation in terms of how they are measured and what changes in them might tell us about an economy.

4.1   The role of government

4.2   The macroeconomic aims of government

4.3   Fiscal policy

4.4   Monetary policy

4.5   Supply-side policy

4.6   Economic growth

4.7   Employment and unemployment

4.8   Inflation and deflation

The role of government

Learning objectives

By the end of this unit, you should be able to:

- identify and describe the types of goods and services provided by government
- describe the role of government locally, nationally and internationally.

Starting point

Answer these questions in pairs:

1 What services are shown in each of the pictures below?

2 Which of these services would be provided by local government and which would be provided by national government in your country?

3 Why are these services generally provided by the government and not the private sector?

Exploring

Discuss these questions in pairs:

1 How does a government help an economy to function effectively?

2 How does this differ at local, national and international levels?

3 What jobs are available for people in the public sector?

Developing

The role of government

One of the main roles of government is to manage the economy at a local, national and international level. An important part of this is providing goods and services that will ensure the sustainable (continued over a long period) wellbeing of a population.

Which goods and services does a government provide?

Goods and services provided by the government

Key terms

Welfare services – financial support provided by the government to those most in need, including the elderly, children and the unemployed

Infrastructure – facilities that are essential for an economy to function, including roads, a transport network, a communication network, electricity supply, etc.

Type of good or service	Description	Examples
Merit goods	**Merit goods** are goods and services that have both private benefits for the user and external benefits to third parties (see Unit 2.10). Merit goods tend to be underprovided by the market. Governments therefore seek to produce merit goods in order to make them affordable and accessible for everyone.	Education, vaccinations, health services
Public goods	**Public goods** are non-excludable and non-rival (see Unit 2.10). As nobody can be excluded from benefiting from public goods once they are provided, private firms are unable to profit from producing them. It is therefore left to the government to provide public goods that are essential to the growth and development of a country.	Street lighting, national defence, city flood defences
Welfare services	In many countries, the government provides **welfare services** to financially support individuals who are unable to earn enough income to cover their daily living expenses. This could be for reasons including sickness, unemployment or old age.	Unemployment benefit, sickness benefit, child benefit, pensions
Public services	**Public services** are services that are considered to be essential for a modern society to function effectively. They are provided by the government for the general public.	Police force, fire service, rubbish collection
Infrastructure	Governments spend money on the development of **infrastructure** (essential facilities such as roads and a reliable power supply) in order to facilitate economic activity within the country.	Roads, sanitation, communication networks, power grids, transport links

1 Identify three goods or services which fall under more than one of the above classifications.

Role of government at a local level

The role of a local government is to ensure the sustainable wellbeing of the local population, for example, in a village, district, town or city. This includes:

- providing local infrastructure, including sewerage, water management and roads
- providing local public services, such as a fire service and refuse (rubbish) collection
- enforcing laws and regulations, such as restrictions on building, noise levels and the disposal of waste
- managing public transport services in the local area, for example bus and train services
- providing public goods, such as street lighting and defences against flooding
- collecting taxes and fees, including parking fees and rates paid by land owners.

Role of government at a national level

At a national level, the government is responsible for managing the domestic economy. This includes:

- providing public services, such as a police force
- providing public goods, such as national defence
- providing merit goods, such as education and healthcare
- providing welfare services, for example, unemployment benefits, sickness benefits and old age pensions
- developing and maintaining infrastructure, such as state highways, electricity supply and communications at a national level
- imposing taxes and collecting tax revenue
- printing notes and coins and controlling the money supply of the economy
- using policy measures to achieve macroeconomic aims, such as **economic growth** and low unemployment
- gathering data to measure economic indicators, including growth, employment and the price level in the economy
- creating and enforcing laws and regulations to protect consumers, workers, businesses, local communities and the environment
- financing and implementing educational campaigns to raise awareness of social problems, such as drink driving and the harmful effects of smoking.

Key term

....

Economic growth – the change in the value of the goods and services produced within a country over time

Role of government internationally

At an international level, governments engage in negotiations and form agreements with other countries. This includes:

- using diplomacy to maintain good relations and settle disagreements with other countries, such as disputes over trade

- negotiating trade agreements so domestic firms have greater access to international markets and consumers benefit from more choice and lower prices

- imposing trade restrictions to protect domestic businesses, workers and consumers

- providing aid to other countries, when needed.

 1 Identify three other ways, not mentioned above, in which the government could influence the economy.

CASE STUDY **Government-funded mega projects in Thailand**

In 2014, the Thai government announced a plan to spend 2.4 trillion baht (US$69 billion) on developing infrastructure in the country. The plan involved investment in transportation, including the construction of a high speed rail network to link Thailand with neighbouring countries and southern China. An extensive metropolitan rail system for Bangkok was also envisaged. In addition to this, the plan allocated funds to the development of ICT and the building of fibre-optic networks to link up with other countries.

1 Why do you think the Thai government decided to spend money on the provision of the goods and services mentioned in the text?

2 What jobs will be created from the provision of these goods and services?

Applying

Project work

Find an article in a newspaper or online about a good or service provided by a government at local, national or international level. Read the article and produce written answers to the following questions.

1. What is the good or service being provided?

2. What type of good or service is it and why?

3. How does the provision of the good or service benefit society?

Print a copy of the article and bring it to your next lesson. You will be asked to share your article and your responses to the above questions with your peers.

4. (E) Summarise the main ideas in the article in no more than 100 words.

Knowledge check questions

1 Give **three** examples of goods and services provided by the government.   [3]

2 Define merit good and give an example.   [2]

3 Using examples, explain the difference between a public good and a public service.   [4]

4   Discuss whether healthcare should be provided by the government or by private firms.   [8]

Check your progress

Read the unit objectives below and reflect on your progress in each.

- Identify and describe the types of goods and services provided by government.

- Describe the role of government locally, nationally and internationally.

 I struggle with this and need more practice.

 I can do this reasonably well.

I can do this with confidence.

The macroeconomic aims of government

Learning objectives

By the end of this unit, you should be able to:

- describe the aims of government policies, such as economic growth, full employment/low unemployment, stable prices/low inflation, balance of payments stability, redistribution of income
- explain the reasons behind the choice of aims and the criteria that governments set for each aim
- analyse the possible conflicts between aims, including:
  - o full employment versus stable prices
  - o economic growth versus balance of payments stability
  - o full employment versus balance of payments stability.

Starting point

Answer these questions in pairs:

1. What are the features of a strong economy?

2. What factors might help an economy to grow?

3. What factors might prevent an economy from growing?

Exploring

Discuss these questions in pairs:

1. What are some of the economic issues your country faces?

2. Are these issues typical of those faced by other countries? Why or why not?

3. Which economic issues do you think are most important for governments to solve? Why?

Developing

The macroeconomic aims of government

Macro economics is the study of economies at a national and international level (see Unit 2.1). **Macroeconomic aims** are the goals that a government seeks to achieve for the economy as a whole. There are five main macroeconomic aims of government. These are shown in the following table.

Key term

Macroeconomic aims – the goals a government wishes to achieve for the economy as a whole at a national and international level

Macroeconomic aims of government

What is the macroeconomic aim?	Why does a government want to achieve it?	How does a government know when it is achieved?
Economic growth Economic growth **refers to the increase in the value of goods and services produced in an economy over time.**	Economic growth is likely to lead to lower unemployment as jobs are created when firms increase their production. This generally leads to higher incomes and increased consumer spending. If this is sustained over a long period of time the **living standards** of the population should rise.	Governments aim for *positive* and *sustainable* economic growth – *positive* because they want the economy to be producing more goods and services each year and *sustainable* because they want the growth to be maintained over a long period of time. Economic growth and how it is measured is discussed in more detail in Unit 4.6.
Full employment (low unemployment) In theory, **full employment** means that all individuals in the economy who are willing and able to work have jobs. However, at any point in time there is likely to be a small amount of unemployment as there will always be some individuals who are in the process of finding work or moving between jobs. Economists therefore accept that an economy is at 'full employment' when *almost all* individuals who are willing and able to work have jobs.	Full employment (low unemployment) is likely to result in higher incomes, leading to an increase in consumer spending and rising standards of living within the population of the economy. Higher consumer spending may also benefit producers, who are likely to experience an increase in sales and receive higher profits.	Governments aim to keep unemployment as low as possible. An **unemployment rate** of about 4% of the total labour force is acceptable for most governments. Unemployment and how it is measured is discussed in more detail in Unit 4.7.
Stable prices (low inflation) In an economy, the prices of goods and services tend to rise over time. Even in your lifetime, you are likely to have noticed an increase in the prices of some of the goods and services you buy. Economists refer to this sustained rise in the general level of prices as **inflation**.	Low and stable inflation is important as it creates a degree of certainty for consumers and producers. They can be reasonably confident that the money they earn today will buy about the same amount of goods and services in the future. This encourages consumers to spend more. It also encourages businesses to invest in capital equipment to expand production, leading to higher economic growth.	Governments aim to keep inflation low and stable. An average increase in the general level of prices in an economy of between 1% and 3% is acceptable for most governments. Inflation and how it is measured is discussed in more detail in Unit 4.8.

What is the macroeconomic aim?	Why does a government want to achieve it?	How does a government know when it is achieved?
Balance of payments stability The **balance of payments** refers to flows of money into and out of a country. An important component of the balance of payments is the **current account**. The net flow of money from international trade is recorded in the current account of the balance of payments. Money flows into the country from the sale of **exports** (locally-made goods sold abroad). Money flows out of the country from spending on **imports** (foreign-made goods purchased locally).	While small differences between a country's export revenue and import expenditure are not normally of concern, large differences which persist over a long period of time can become unsustainable for an economy. For example, too high a demand for exports can cause inflation (see Unit 4.8). Too high a spending on imports, on the other hand, must be financed by borrowing from abroad (see Unit 6.4).	Governments aim to maintain a stable balance of payments. One way they can do this is by avoiding large differences between the value of exports and the value of imports over time. A **trade deficit** occurs when spending on imports is greater than revenue from exports. A **trade surplus**, on the other hand, is when export revenue is greater than import expenditure. The balance of payments and the current account are discussed in more detail in Unit 6.4.
Redistribution of income **Redistribution of income** refers to the transfer of income and wealth (ownership of property) between individuals within an economy.	Creating a more equal distribution of income and wealth within the population helps to reduce poverty in an economy. Poverty is undesirable due to the hardship and suffering it creates for individuals and their families. It is also a waste of resources as it prevents individuals from contributing to the economy to their full potential.	Governments aim to create a more equal distribution of income and wealth between individuals through the use of taxation, welfare payments and the provision of public services, such as education and healthcare. Poverty is discussed in more detail in Unit 5.2.

Key terms

Living standards – the economic wellbeing and quality of life of members of a population

Full employment – also referred to as **low unemployment**, this is a situation in which the vast majority of the labour force in an economy are in paid work

Unemployment rate – the percentage of a country's labour force which is without paid employment but actively seeking work

Inflation – the sustained rise in the general level of prices in an economy over time

Balance of payments – a record of the flows of money into and out of a country

Current account – a component of a country's balance of payments in which inflows and outflows of money from international trade and income flows are recorded

Exports – locally-made goods and services sold abroad

Imports – foreign-made goods and services purchased locally

Trade deficit – a situation where the value of imports of a country is greater than the value of exports

Trade surplus – a situation where the value of exports is greater than the value of imports

1 Which of these aims is most important to your country? Why?

CASE STUDY ## Export-led growth in China

Throughout the 1990s and early 2000s, China's abundance of relatively cheap labour enabled it to sell exports to advanced economies at highly competitive prices. As a result, the Chinese government was able to achieve one of its main aims of increasing economic growth, which peaked at 14.2% in 2007. This rapid growth led to higher wages, particularly for factory workers employed in export industries. Consequently, consumer spending in China increased and the overall living standards of the population improved significantly.

However, demand for Chinese exports began to fall after the financial crisis of 2008, which resulted in a large fall in the **economic growth rates** and incomes of countries worldwide. This, combined with increased competition from goods produced by other low-cost countries, such as Vietnam, led to a slowdown in China's economic growth. In 2017, China's growth rate dropped to 6.5%, the lowest since 1990. Economic growth has also resulted in dangerously high levels of air pollution from China's numerous coal-fired power stations.

1 What are the advantages and disadvantages of China's higher economic growth mentioned in the case study?

2 Other than increasing its exports, explain one other way in which China could increase economic growth.

Possible conflicts between macroeconomic aims

 How might consumer spending affect producers in an economy?

Full employment (low unemployment) versus stable prices (low inflation)

Government policies aimed at achieving low unemployment are likely to result in higher inflation.

In order to reduce unemployment, the government may seek to increase consumer spending in the economy. Higher consumer spending should lead to an increase in the demand for goods and services in an economy. As a result, firms are likely to increase production, creating more jobs and lowering unemployment. However, increased demand from consumers is also likely to put upward pressure on prices, leading to higher inflation.

Low unemployment may also mean that firms have to pay higher wages in order to attract the workers they need. This will result in an increase in firms' production costs, which may be passed on to consumers in the form of higher prices, also contributing to higher inflation.

Key term

Economic growth rate – the percentage increase in the value of goods and services produced in an economy over time (usually a year)

Governments aiming to lower inflation, on the other hand, may seek to reduce consumer spending in the economy, which is likely to result in falling demand for goods and services and higher unemployment.

3 Why might a fall in consumer spending lead to higher unemployment?

Economic growth versus balance of payments stability

Government policies aimed at creating economic growth may result in balance of payments instability.

Economic growth resulting from higher domestic consumption (the purchase of goods and services within the country) may lead to a *trade deficit* on the current account of the balance of payments. Higher consumer demand within the domestic economy is likely to result in increased spending on imported goods and services, such as brand name products and overseas holidays. Over time, this may result in a large trade deficit on the current account of the balance of payments as the money leaving the country from spending on imports is likely to far exceed the money entering the country from the sale of exports abroad.

Economic growth due to the sale of exports abroad (export-led growth), on the other hand, may result in a large *trade surplus* on the current account of the balance of payments over time. That is, the money flowing into the country from the sale of exports may exceed the outflow of money from spending on imports. In May 2017, China had a trade surplus of US$40.81 billion.

Full employment (low unemployment) versus balance of payments stability

Government policies aimed at achieving low unemployment may lead to balance of payments instability due to increased consumer spending on imports.

When unemployment is low, most people have jobs and consumer incomes are generally higher. As a result, consumers tend to spend more on goods and services, including imports. Over time, increased spending on imports could result in a large trade deficit on the current account of the balance of payments.

Conversely, government policy aimed at correcting a trade deficit on the current account of the balance of payments may result in falling economic growth and higher unemployment. In order to correct a trade deficit, a government may seek to reduce consumer spending in the economy. This is likely to result in a fall in consumer spending on imports, thus improving the trade deficit. However, reduced consumer spending in the economy will also decrease spending on domestic goods and services, leading to a fall in production and higher unemployment.

4 How might a slowdown in economic growth affect unemployment?

Key term

Inflation rate – the percentage increase in the general price level in an economy over time (usually a year)

CASE STUDY — Inflation target set for India's central bank

One of the roles of India's central bank, the Reserve Bank of India (RBI), is to use monetary policy (see Unit 4.4) to control inflation. In 2016, India's government set the RBI the target of maintaining an **inflation rate** of between 2% and 6%. The Indian government hoped that by maintaining a relatively low and stable inflation rate, sustainable economic growth would be achieved in the longer run.

Setting an inflation target also enabled the RBI to prioritise the aim of low inflation over other aims, such as higher economic growth and lower unemployment. For example, if inflation was approaching the upper limit of 6%, the RBI would respond by raising interest rates in order to control inflation, despite the unfavourable effects it might have on economic growth and unemployment.

1 What policy conflicts are mentioned in the case study?

2 An upper inflation limit of 6% might be considered high by some economists. Why do you think the Indian government set an upper inflation limit at 6% rather than making it lower?

Applying

Project work

Using the internet, research the economy of a country of your choice.

1. Identify three macroeconomic aims that might be relevant to the government of the country you investigated.

2. Explain why each aim might be important.

Present your findings to your classmates in the form of a poster or PowerPoint presentation.

Knowledge check questions

1 Identify **five** macroeconomic aims of governments. [5]

2 Explain why full employment (low unemployment) is desirable for a country. [4]

3 Explain how high inflation might affect consumers. [4]

4 Analyse why the government aim of low inflation might lead to higher unemployment. [6]

5 Analyse why the government aim of low unemployment may lead to a trade deficit on the current account of the balance of payments. [6]

6 (E) Discuss whether economic growth should be a government's main economic aim. [8]

Check your progress

Read the unit objectives below and reflect on your progress in each.

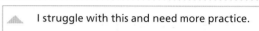 I struggle with this and need more practice.

 I can do this reasonably well.

- Describe the aims of government policies, such as economic growth, full employment/low unemployment, stable prices/low inflation, balance of payments stability, redistribution of income.

  I can do this with confidence.

- Explain the reasons behind the choice of aims and the criteria that governments set for each aim.

- Analyse the possible conflicts between aims, including:

  – full employment versus stable prices

  – economic growth versus balance of payments stability

  – full employment versus balance of payments stability.

Fiscal policy

Learning objectives

By the end of this unit, you should be able to:

- define government budget
- describe the main areas of government spending and explain the reasons for and the effects of spending in these areas
- explain what is meant by taxation and describe the reasons for governments levying (collecting) taxes
- describe the different ways in which taxes can be classified, such as direct or indirect, progressive, regressive or proportional
- describe the qualities of a good tax
- analyse the impact of taxation on consumers, producers, government and the economy as a whole
- define fiscal policy
- explain tax and spending changes, in the form of fiscal policy, that cause budget balance or imbalance
- calculate the size of a budget deficit or surplus
- analyse how fiscal policy measures may enable the government to achieve its macroeconomic aims.

Starting point

Answer these questions in pairs:

1. Explain the difference between the following terms:

   a) private sector and public sector

   b) a good and a service

   c) a consumer good and a producer good

   d) a merit good and a demerit good

   e) a private good and a public good

   f) positive externality (external benefit) and negative externality (external cost)

2. Provide an example of each of the above.

Exploring

Discuss these questions in pairs:

1. What are the areas of government spending in each of the pictures below?

2. How does a government finance its spending?

3. How does a government decide what to spend money on?

Developing

Government spending

What is a government budget?

A **government budget** is a plan of a government's future income and expected spending over a period of time (usually a year). The government's main source of income is from **tax revenue**, which it uses to finance expenditure on operating expenses, including the payment of salaries to public sector workers, as well as the provision of public services, welfare benefits and the development of infrastructure.

Why do governments spend?

As discussed in Unit 4.1, governments spend for a variety of reasons. These are summarised in the table below.

Key terms

Government budget – a plan of a government's future income and expected spending over a period of time (usually a year)

Tax revenue – the money a government receives from direct and indirect taxes

Reasons for government expenditure

Reason	Description
To provide essential public services	Governments spend in order to make public services, such as a police force and fire service, available to the population. Public services are essential to the functioning of a modern society.
To provide merit goods	Governments seek to make merit goods, such as healthcare and education, affordable and accessible to everyone in the country (see Unit 2.10). This helps to reduce inequality and improves the living standards of the population.
To provide public goods	Governments seek to provide public goods, such as street lighting and national defence. Without government provision, public goods would not be provided at all due to the **free rider problem** (see Unit 2.10).
To facilitate economic activity	Governments spend on maintaining and improving the infrastructure of the economy. Infrastructure refers to essential facilities a country needs to develop, such as roads, a reliable power supply, sanitation and access to clean water. Well-developed infrastructure is necessary to facilitate economic activity, such as the production of goods and services within an economy.
To redistribute income more equally	In many countries, governments spend on the provision of welfare services, such as unemployment benefits. This helps to redistribute income within the economy to increase equality and reduce poverty (see Unit 5.2).
To achieve macroeconomic objectives	Governments often use spending as a policy tool to achieve macroeconomic aims. For example, increasing spending on building new roads will create jobs, thereby helping to lower unemployment. Decreasing spending, on the other hand, may help to control inflation by reducing demand in the economy.

1 Which reason for government spending do you think is most important for your country? Why?

Taxation

Why do governments impose taxes?

Reasons for taxation

Reason	Description
To raise tax revenue	One of the main reasons a government imposes taxes is to raise revenue to cover its operating expenses and to finance spending on merit goods and public goods, such as healthcare, education and street lighting.
To discourage consumption of demerit goods	Governments often impose taxes on demerit goods, which are potentially harmful to consumers and those around them (third parties), such as cigarettes and alcohol. The imposition of a tax on a demerit good should lead to an increase in its price and a fall in consumption.
To redistribute income	Governments tend to tax workers on higher incomes at higher tax rates and workers on lower incomes at lower tax rates, which helps to redistribute income within the economy and improve equality. They may also use the revenue they raise from taxes to provide welfare services to the poor, such as pensions and unemployment benefits.
To protect domestic producers	Governments may impose taxes (**tariffs**) on imported goods. The effect of a tariff is to increase the price of imports, thus increasing the competitiveness of domestic producers.

 Identify three types of goods which are taxed in your country. Why might the government impose taxes on these goods?

Classification of taxes

Direct and indirect taxation

Direct taxation is a tax on income. **Income tax** and **corporation tax** are two types of direct taxation. Income tax is paid by individuals from their earnings (wages and salaries). Corporation tax is paid by businesses from their profits. Direct taxes are calculated as a proportion of income; for example, in the UK the top income tax rate is 45% and the corporation tax rate is 20% (2017 figures).

Indirect taxation is a tax on expenditure. When individuals and firms spend, a portion of the price they pay goes to the government in the form of indirect tax. **Value added tax (VAT)**, (called a **goods and services tax (GST)** in some countries) and **excise duties** are examples of indirect taxes. The VAT on most goods and services in the UK in 2017 was 20%. Taxes on imported goods (tariffs) are also a form of indirect taxation.

Key terms

Tariff – a tax imposed on imported goods

Income tax – a tax levied on a person's earnings from employment

Corporation tax – a tax levied on a firm's profits

Value added tax (VAT) – a tax levied on goods and services sold in a country calculated as a percentage of the sales price (also called a goods and services tax (GST) in some countries)

Excise duty – a tax levied on goods that are manufactured in a country

Progressive, regressive and proportional taxation

Progressive taxation takes a higher proportion of income from the rich than the poor. It is therefore based on 'ability to pay'. Those who have the ability to do so (high income earners), pay a higher proportion of their income in tax. Those who are less able (low income earners) pay a lower proportion of their income in tax. Income tax is progressive in most countries. In New Zealand, individuals earning up to NZ$14 000 (US$9800) per year are taxed at a rate of 10.5%, while those earning over NZ$70 000 (US$49 300) a year are taxed at the higher rate of 33% on a portion of their income.

Regressive taxation takes a higher proportion of income from the poor than the rich. The impact of the tax is therefore felt more heavily by those on lower incomes. Indirect taxes tend to be regressive. For example, if VAT is 20%, $20 would be paid in tax on a $100 grocery bill from a supermarket. That $20 would make up 10% of the income of a person earning $200 per week but only 2% of the income of a person earning $1000 per week. Thus, indirect taxes tend to take a higher proportion of a poor person's income than a rich person's income. For this reason, governments often make some necessities and merit goods, such as basic food items, medicine and educational books, exempt from VAT.

Proportional taxation takes an equal proportion of income, regardless of whether the taxpayer is rich or poor. Some countries have proportional taxes on income. For example, a proportional tax of 20% on income would mean that an individual earning $10 000 a year would pay $2000 in tax, while someone earning $100 000 a year would pay $20 000 in tax.

3 Which classification (progressive, regressive or proportional) best describes the income tax system in your country? Why?

Principles of taxation

The qualities of a 'good' tax include the following:

- **Fairness**. A tax should be based on ability to pay. The rich should pay a higher proportion of their income in taxes than the poor.

- **Certainty**. The requirements of the tax should be clear and certain. The taxpayer should know exactly how much they need to pay in tax and when it needs to be paid by.

- **Convenience**. The payment of the tax should be convenient for the taxpayer. For example, the payment of a tax on farmers' income could be timed to coincide with the sale of their crops as this is when they have the money available to pay the tax. A government may also provide a number of payment methods, such as internet banking or cheque, to make it more convenient for the taxpayer.

- **Efficiency**. The cost of collecting the tax should be relatively low. High administration and enforcement costs may make some taxes too costly to collect. There is little point in imposing a tax that will cost more to collect than it generates in revenue.

Impact of taxation

Impact of an increase in direct taxation

An increase in direct taxation affects different parts of the economy in different ways. These are outlined in the table below.

Impact of an increase in direct taxation

Individuals (consumers and workers)	• **Reduced consumer spending**. An increase in income tax would reduce consumers' disposable income. As a result, consumers will have less money to spend, which may result in lower standards of living. • **Reduced incentives to work**. An increase in income tax would increase the proportion of a worker's income that is taken by the government, leaving the worker with less financial reward for their labour. People's incentive to work is therefore reduced. Some individuals may therefore choose to work fewer hours or not work at all. • **Increase in tax evasion**. If income tax rates rise, some individuals may try to evade taxes illegally by not declaring their income to the government.
Producers	• **Lower profits**. An increase in corporation tax would have the effect of lowering the after-tax profit received by business owners. • **Reduced incentives for entrepreneurs**. Lower profit (the factor reward for enterprise) may reduce the incentive for entrepreneurs to start up new businesses. This may decrease the number of new businesses starting up. • **Relocation**. Higher corporation tax rates in one country may result in large **multinational companies** relocating to other countries with lower tax rates. • **Tax evasion**. Some businesses may try to evade taxes illegally by not declaring some of their earnings to the government, for example, accepting cash payment for some jobs. • **Tax avoidance**. Other businesses may hire professional accountants to find legal ways to reduce the amount of tax they pay.

Key terms

Multinational company (MNC) – a company that produces in more than one country

Tax evasion – illegal non-payment of taxes to the government

Tax avoidance – the process of finding legal ways to minimise the amount of tax paid to the government

Government	• **Tax revenue**. Direct taxation is the largest source of revenue for most governments. It can be used to finance public expenditure in a range of areas (see Unit 4.1).
	• **Achievement of government aims**. The government can use the income tax rate as a policy tool to achieve its macroeconomic aims. For example, the government could increase income tax rates in order to achieve the aim of low inflation (see Unit 4.3).
Economy	• **Lower inflation**. As higher income tax rates reduce consumers' disposable income, spending in the economy is likely to fall, leading to lower inflation. 
	• **A fall in economic growth and higher unemployment**. Lower consumer spending is likely to lead to a fall in production in the economy, resulting in a slowdown in economic growth. As firms cut back their production, workers are made **redundant** (they lose their jobs because they are no longer needed), which increases unemployment. 
	• **A more equal distribution of income**. As income taxes are usually progressive in nature, it is possible for the government to make the distribution of income in the economy more equal by taxing individuals on higher incomes at higher rates than those on lower incomes. The government can further improve the distribution of income by using the revenue gained from income tax to pay welfare benefits to the poor, thus reducing poverty.
	• **Reduced incentives**. Higher direct taxes on individuals and firms may act as a disincentive to work and start up new businesses, thereby reducing production in the economy.

 Who is likely to benefit from a decrease in direct taxation?

Impact of an increase in indirect taxation

An increase in indirect taxation affects different parts of the economy in different ways. These are outlined in the table on the next page.

Key term

Redundant – a worker is made redundant when they lose their job because their skills are no longer needed by the business

Impact of an increase in indirect taxation

Individuals (consumers and workers)	• **Higher prices**. Producers may pass the cost of an indirect tax on to consumers in the form of higher prices. The extent to which they are able to do this will depend on the price elasticity of demand for the product (see Unit 2.7). The more inelastic the demand for the product, the more the burden of the tax falls on consumers (see Unit 2.11).
	• **Reduced consumption**. Higher prices may result in some consumers, particularly those on low incomes, reducing their consumption of goods and services.
	• **Reduced consumption of demerit goods**. Consumption of demerit goods, such as cigarettes, may fall as a result of higher indirect taxes which cause them to become more expensive.
Producers	• **An increase in costs of production**. It is the responsibility of the producer to pay the indirect tax to the government. The money paid to the government is therefore an expense to the producer. A rise in indirect taxes will therefore have the effect of increasing the costs of production of producers.
	• **An increase in the price of the product**. Businesses are likely to raise their prices in order to cover the cost of an indirect tax. As a result, they may suffer a fall in sales.
Government	• **An increase in tax revenue**. Higher indirect taxation should generate more tax revenue for the government, which it can use to finance public expenditure on areas including education and the development of infrastructure.
	• **An increase in government expenditure**. Revenue raised from the imposition of indirect taxes can be used to improve public services such as healthcare, leading to higher living standards for the population (see Unit 5.1).
Economy	• **Higher inflation**. Higher indirect taxes are likely to raise the general price level in the economy. This is because higher indirect taxes will increase firms' production costs, some of which will be passed on to consumers in the form of higher prices.
	• **A fall in the living standards of poor households**. As indirect taxes are regressive in nature, they tend to fall more heavily on the poor. Some very poor households may not be able to afford the higher prices brought about by higher indirect taxes. They may therefore be forced to reduce their consumption of certain goods and services, lowering their living standards and worsening poverty.
	• **An increase in tax evasion**. Some individuals may try to evade taxes by bringing goods into the country illegally and selling them to consumers at lower prices on the **black market** in the informal economy. This will result in lost tax revenue for the government and may also lead to increased costs if the government is forced to spend more money on policing the country's borders.

Key term

Black market – an illegal market in which goods and services are traded without any government controls

5　Who is likely to benefit from a decrease in indirect taxation?

'Fat tax' introduced in India

In 2016, the government of the Indian state of Kerala introduced a 'fat tax' of 14.5% on burgers, pizzas, doughnuts and other junk food served in branded fast food restaurant chains, including McDonald's, Pizza Hut and Dunkin' Donuts. The government hoped that the tax would help reduce the growing problem of obesity in India as well as increase people's awareness of the food they eat.

Other countries to have imposed fat taxes include Denmark and Hungary. Denmark, however, removed its tax on high-fat foods after it found consumers were shopping internationally in Germany and Sweden to avoid the tax or switching to less expensive alternatives that were equally as unhealthy. Mexico also taxes drinks and foods high in sugar, while Philadelphia became the first major US city to impose a tax on sugary soda drinks.

1 Discuss the benefits and drawbacks of the imposition of the 'fat tax' in India.

2 Discuss whether a 'fat tax' is the best way for the government to tackle the problem of obesity.

Fiscal policy

What is fiscal policy?

Fiscal policy is when the government seeks to influence total demand in the economy by changing either government spending or income tax rates.

Fiscal policy – the use of government spending and income tax rates to achieve certain macroeconomic objectives

Extension topic

Aggregate demand

Aggregate demand refers to the total demand for all goods and services in an economy as a whole. It is different from individual demand and market demand (see Unit 2.3), which refer to demand by an individual and demand within a market, respectively. Aggregate demand is made up of four components:

- **Consumption (C)**: the purchase of goods and services by households (also referred to as **consumer spending**). For example, if households purchase more cars, TVs and smartphones, consumption in the economy will increase and aggregate demand will rise.

The economic term used to talk about the total demand in an economy is **aggregate demand**. While the IGCSE Economics specification does not require you to use the term aggregate demand, an understanding of the concept is expected. From this point forward, we will use the term aggregate demand to refer to total demand in the economy.

- **Investment (I)**: the purchase of capital goods by firms to expand production. For example, the purchase of capital equipment and machinery by firms will lead to an increase in investment in the economy and a rise in aggregate demand.

- **Government spending (G)**: expenditure (spending) by government in the economy. For example, if a government decides to build more schools and hospitals, government spending in the economy will increase, leading to a rise in aggregate demand.

- **Net exports (X – M)**: the difference between the value of exports (X) and the value of imports (M). A rise in the revenue earned from exports will increase aggregate demand. A rise in spending on imports, on the other hand, will decrease aggregate demand.

The components of aggregate demand can be summarised as:

$$AD = C + I + G + (X - M)$$

6 How would a decrease in income tax rates affect aggregate demand in an economy?

Fiscal policy measures

Changing government spending

Part of the government's role is to provide certain goods and services, such as infrastructure and education (see Unit 4.1). Increasing government spending on these types of goods is one way in which a government can increase aggregate demand in an economy. This **expansionary fiscal policy** enables a government to achieve certain macroeconomic objectives, such as economic growth and low unemployment. A government wishing to reduce aggregate demand in the economy will decrease spending. A government may use **contractionary fiscal policy** to maintain low inflation and balance of payments stability as it leads to a decrease in aggregate demand in the economy. Government spending is usually financed using tax revenue.

Key terms

Aggregate demand (AD) – the total demand for all goods and services in an economy from consumption (C), investment (I), government spending (G) and net exports (X – M)

Consumption (C) – the purchase of goods and services by households; also referred to as consumer spending

Investment (I) – the purchase of capital goods by firms to expand production

Government spending (G) – expenditure by the government

Net exports (X – M) – the difference between the value of exports and the value of imports

Expansionary fiscal policy – an increase in government spending and/or a reduction in income tax rates in order to increase aggregate demand in the economy

Contractionary fiscal policy – a reduction in government spending and/or an increase in income tax rates in order to reduce aggregate demand in the economy

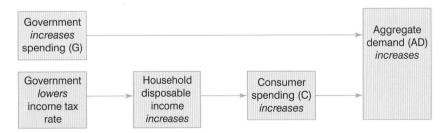

Figure 4.3.1 Expansionary fiscal policy

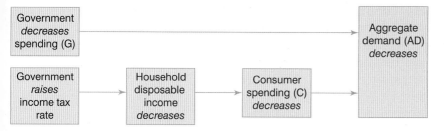

Figure 4.3.2 Contractionary fiscal policy

Changing income tax rates

Another fiscal policy measure is when the government changes income tax rates in order to influence aggregate demand in the economy. Expansionary fiscal policy, for example, would involve lowering income tax rates. As a result, workers will have higher disposable income, which is likely to lead to higher consumer spending, thus increasing aggregate demand. Conversely, the use of contractionary fiscal policy by increasing income tax rates will have the effect of reducing disposable income, leading to a fall in consumer spending and lower aggregate demand in the economy.

The effect of fiscal policy on the government budget

If you had $10 and wanted to buy a book costing $12, how would you go about finding the additional funds? You'd probably borrow the extra $2 from your parents or a friend and pay it back later. The same principle applies to a government. As we have seen, government earns most of its revenue from taxes, which it spends on operating costs and on goods and services for the population of a country. In order to do this effectively, it must plan future spending and how this will be financed by preparing a **budget**. If a government spends more than it earns in tax revenue, it will need to borrow in order to make up the difference.

A government is said to operate a **balanced budget** if the revenue it earns from taxes is enough to cover its planned expenditure. If revenue exceeds planned expenditure, the government is said to run a **budget surplus**. If, on the other hand, planned government expenditure exceeds revenue from taxes, it is said to be running a **budget deficit**. Budget deficits usually need to be financed by borrowing. Borrowed funds in the form of a **loan** must be paid back with interest in the future.

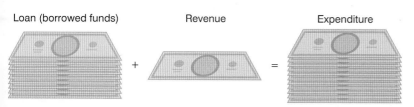

Figure 4.3.3 Balancing the government budget

Key terms

Balanced budget – revenue = spending

Budget surplus – revenue > spending

Budget deficit – spending > revenue

Loan – a sum of money that is given to a person or entity on the promise that it will be repaid at an agreed time in the future with interest

A government generally runs a budget deficit in times of economic recession when it increases its spending in order to increase aggregate demand and stimulate growth in the economy. For example, the US government ran a large budget deficit of almost 10% of the country's total GDP in 2009 after it was plunged into recession as a result of the global financial crisis of 2008. A budget surplus is more common in an economic boom period when the tax revenue earned from rising incomes is increasing and the government is cutting back spending in order to control inflation. Prior to the global financial crisis of 2008, Norway's budget surplus was as high as 18.7% of the country's total GDP.

A budget deficit or surplus can be calculated using the following formula:

$$\text{budget deficit/surplus} = \frac{\text{total government}}{\text{revenue}} - \frac{\text{total government}}{\text{spending}}$$

The overall effect of fiscal policy on a government budget depends on:

- the fiscal policy measure being used (for example, if the government is increasing spending, there is a greater likelihood the budget will be in deficit)
- whether the budget is in deficit, surplus or in balance when the fiscal policy measure is used.

The possible effects of fiscal policy on a government budget are summarised in the table below.

The effects of fiscal policy on a government budget

Fiscal policy measure		Overall effect on government budget
Increase in government spending	Spending rises	• A budget deficit will worsen • A budget surplus will decrease.
Decrease in income tax rates	Revenue falls	• A balanced budget will be pushed into deficit.
Decrease in government spending	Spending falls	• A budget deficit will improve. • A budget surplus will increase.
Increase in income tax rates	Revenue rises	• A balanced budget will be pushed into surplus.

Calculating the size of a budget deficit or surplus

Worked example

Using the information below, calculate the size of the government budget imbalance.

Government revenue (income)	Billions ($)	Government spending	Billions ($)
Tax revenue	74	Operating expenses (including salaries paid to public sector employees, electricity, etc.)	12
Non-tax revenue (interest on loans, fines, dividends paid on state-owned enterprises)	14		
Sale of state assets	7	Subsidies	11
		Law and order	8
		National defence	10
		Welfare payments	18
		Education	9
		Healthcare	8
		Infrastructure	23
		Interest on loans	1

Commentary

In order to calculate whether the government budget is in balance, surplus or deficit, the following formula must be used.

government budget surplus/deficit = total government revenue – total government spending

From the above information:

total government revenue = $74bn + $14bn + $7bn = $95bn

total government spending = $12bn + $11bn + $8bn + $10bn + $15bn + $9bn + $8bn + $23bn + $1bn = $100bn

government budget = $95bn – $100bn = –$5bn

NOTE

The minus sign indicates that the government budget is in *deficit* by $5bn.

This government budget deficit of $5 billion will need to be financed, either by borrowing or some other method such as sales of state-owned assets. If financed by borrowing, the government will be required to repay the funds over a fixed period of time with interest.

Effects of fiscal policy on government macroeconomic aims

The fiscal policy measure that the government uses depends on the macroeconomic aims it is trying to achieve. For example, if a government is aiming for higher economic growth and lower unemployment, it may choose to use expansionary fiscal policy, such as increasing government spending, by building a new hospital, for instance.

By spending money on a new hospital, the government will create jobs for people, including construction workers, cleaners, doctors and nurses, thereby lowering unemployment. Materials and equipment must also be purchased from local businesses to build and run the hospital, contributing to increased production and higher economic growth.

Those employed in the construction and running of the hospital will likely increase spending as a result of their higher incomes, leading to an increase in aggregate demand in the economy.

While this increase in consumer spending is likely to help further reduce unemployment and increase economic growth, it may also result in higher inflation and increased spending on imports. Increased spending on imports may result in more money leaving the country, which may lead to a trade deficit on the current account of the balance of payments.

The effects of expansionary and contractionary fiscal policy measures on the different government aims are summarised in the following table.

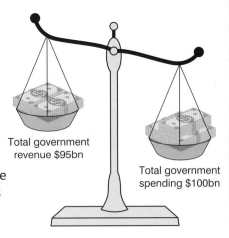

Total government revenue $95bn

Total government spending $100bn

Figure 4.3.4 Government budget deficit of $5bn

The effects of fiscal policy measures on the macroeconomic aims of government

Fiscal policy measure	Effects of fiscal policy measure on the government aim of:			
	Low unemployment	High economic growth	Low and stable inflation	Balance of payments stability
An increase in government spending	✓ – More jobs created as a result of the rise in government spending	✓ – Increased production resulting from the rise in government spending	✗ – Higher aggregate demand in the economy puts upward pressure on prices	✗ – Rising incomes result in increased spending on imports
A decrease in income tax rates, raising household disposable income	✓ – More jobs created as a result of higher consumer spending	✓ – Increased production resulting from higher consumer spending	✗ – Higher aggregate demand in the economy puts upward pressure on prices	✗ – Rising incomes result in increased spending on imports

Fiscal policy measure	Effects of fiscal policy measure on the government aim of:			
	Low unemployment	**High economic growth**	**Low and stable inflation**	**Balance of payments stability**
A decrease in government spending	✗ – A fall in government spending results in fewer jobs available	✗ – Decreased production resulting from a decrease in government spending	✓ – Reduced aggregate demand in the economy puts downward pressure on prices	✓ – Falling incomes result in reduced spending on imports
An increase in income tax rates, reducing household disposable income	✗ – Reduced consumer spending leads to a decrease in production and fewer jobs available	✗ – Decreased production resulting from the fall in consumer spending	✓ – Reduced aggregate demand in the economy puts downward pressure on prices	✓ – Falling incomes result in reduced spending on imports

7 Explain a fiscal policy measure a government could use to lower inflation.

How might fiscal policy affect the government aim of redistributing income more equally?

Expansionary fiscal policy measures have the potential to improve the distribution of income and wealth within an economy:

- **Increased employment opportunities**. Increased government spending and lower income tax rates increase aggregate demand in the economy, leading to higher production. As a result, firms are likely to employ more workers, enabling them to earn higher incomes.

- **Spending on education**. Improving education within a country could improve the skills and productivity of workers so they are able to earn a higher wage. In the longer run, this may help to raise the incomes of the poor, thus lifting them out of poverty.

- **Spending on healthcare**. The provision of quality healthcare may improve the health and productivity of the poor, thus enabling them to receive higher incomes throughout their lifetimes.

- **Spending on welfare benefits**. The provision of welfare benefits to the most vulnerable members of society, including the old, unemployed, sick and disabled, can help to reduce poverty and narrow the income gap between rich and poor.

- **Higher income tax rates for the rich**. A government may be able to make the distribution of income more equal by making the tax system more progressive. For example, it may increase the income tax rates for the rich but not the poor.

- **Lower indirect taxes on necessities**. A government could help the poor by making the tax system less regressive. For example, it could impose high indirect taxes on luxury items but lower (or remove) indirect taxes on basic necessities, such as bread, rice and fresh vegetables.

8 Identify three goods which are not taxed (exempt from VAT) in your country. Why might the government choose not to tax these goods?

Obama's fiscal stimulus package

Following the 2008/9 global financial crisis, President Barack Obama approved a $831 billion fiscal stimulus package aimed at boosting consumer spending and saving up to 2.3 million jobs in the US economy.

The package consisted of tax cuts worth $288 billion and involved spending $224 billion on education, healthcare and unemployment benefits. An additional $275 billion was allocated to government contracts, grants and loans.

Government contracts awarded to private sector firms to build roads and public buildings were desperately needed to save jobs in the construction industry. Small businesses, in particular, benefited from increased access to grants, loans and lower corporate tax rates.

1 How might Obama's fiscal stimulus package have helped the US economy to lower unemployment and increase economic growth?

2 How do you think Obama's fiscal stimulus package affected the US government's budget?

Applying

Project work

Working in pairs, create a one-minute media report for a TV or radio news programme about a government-funded project in your local area. Use the internet to research the project. In your media report, say what the project is, give its estimated cost and outline the benefits it will bring to the local and national economy.

Knowledge check questions

1 Define government budget.   [2]

2 State **three** reasons why governments spend money.   [3]

3 Using examples, explain the difference between direct taxation and indirect taxation. [4]

4 Using examples, explain the difference between progressive taxation and regressive taxation. [4]

5 Define fiscal policy.   [2]

6 Identify the **four** components of aggregate demand.   [4]

7 Distinguish between expansionary and contractionary fiscal policy.   [2]

8 Analyse the impact of a reduction in income tax rates on economic growth in an economy. [6]

9 Explain **two** reasons why a government may choose to reduce government spending. [4]

10 Analyse how a reduction in government spending might affect employment in an economy. [6]

11 (E) Discuss whether healthcare should be provided by the government or by the
      private sector.   [8]

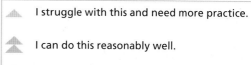

Check your progress

Read the unit objectives below and reflect on your progress in each.

🔺	I struggle with this and need more practice.
🔺	I can do this reasonably well.
🔺	I can do this with confidence.

• Define government budget.

• Describe the main areas of government spending and explain the reasons for and the effects of spending in these areas.

• Explain what is meant by taxation and describe the reasons for governments levying (collecting) taxes.

• Describe the different ways in which taxes can be classified, such as direct or indirect, progressive, regressive or proportional.

• Describe the qualities of a good tax.

• Analyse the impact of taxation on consumers, producers, government and the economy as a whole.

• Define fiscal policy.

• Explain tax and spending changes, in the form of fiscal policy, that cause budget balance or imbalance.

• Calculate the size of a budget deficit or surplus.

• Analyse how fiscal policy measures may enable the government to achieve its macroeconomic aims.

Monetary policy

Learning objectives
- By the end of this unit, you should be able to:
- define money supply
- define monetary policy
- explain monetary policy measures: changes in interest rates, money supply and foreign exchange rates
- analyse how monetary policy measures may enable the government to achieve its macroeconomic aims.

Starting point

Answer these questions in pairs:

1. What are the functions and characteristics of money?

2. How does money facilitate trade and exchange?

3. What are the different forms that money takes?

Exploring

1. What things do you and your family spend money on?

2. How does your spending help businesses and other individuals?

3. How would a fall in consumer spending affect businesses and individuals?

Developing

What is the money supply and monetary policy?

When you spend $1 on a cup of freshly squeezed orange juice from a drinks stall, where does the money go? It becomes the income of the drinks vendor. He or she may then spend it, perhaps on supplies of fresh oranges. The $1 then becomes the income of the fruit vendor, and so on. Your $1 is 'in circulation' (being

passed from buyer to seller) and forms part of the **money supply** of the economy.

The money supply is the quantity of money in circulation in the economy. The government is able to increase or decrease the money supply through the use of **monetary policy** in order to achieve its macroeconomic aims. An increase in the money supply tends to increase aggregate demand in the economy as there is more money available for consumers and businesses to spend. Conversely, a decrease in the money supply tends to reduce aggregate demand in the economy.

There are a number of monetary policy measures the government can use to influence the money supply.

Monetary policy measures

Changing interest rates

One way in which governments control the money supply is by changing **interest rates**. The interest rate is the price of money (the cost of borrowing money). If interest rates rise, the cost of borrowing money rises, so consumers borrow less and spend less. Firms similarly reduce their borrowing and investment in capital equipment. This decrease in consumption and investment reduces the quantity of money in circulation, resulting in a fall in aggregate demand.

If interest rates fall, on the other hand, the cost of borrowing money falls, so consumers and firms borrow more. As a result, consumption and investment increase, leading to an increase in the quantity of money in circulation and an increase in aggregate demand.

Thus, by changing interest rates, governments are able to influence the money supply and the level of aggregate demand in the economy to achieve certain macroeconomic aims.

In many countries, interest rates are controlled by the central bank – the banker to the government and the country's commercial banks (see Unit 3.1). When the central bank changes its interest rate, commercial banks tend to follow, by changing their interest rates in line with that of the central bank. In most countries the central bank is responsible for changing interest rates to control inflation. However, it is the government that sets the targets for inflation that the central bank has to achieve. For example, New Zealand's government has set the Reserve Bank of New Zealand (RBNZ), New Zealand's central bank, an inflation rate target of between 1% and 3%. Thus, one of the RBNZ's main functions is to change interest rates to maintain inflation within this target range (see Unit 3.1).

Key terms

Money supply – the quantity of money in circulation in the economy

Monetary policy – when the government controls the money supply (usually by changing interest rates) in order to achieve certain macroeconomic aims

Interest rate – the cost of borrowing money

Expansionary monetary policy raises aggregate demand in the economy by increasing the money supply. As discussed, the central bank can achieve this by lowering interest rates. Expansionary monetary policy is likely to result in lower unemployment and higher economic growth.

Contractionary monetary policy, on the other hand, decreases aggregate demand in the economy by reducing the money supply. The central bank can achieve this by raising interest rates. Contractionary monetary policy is likely to result in lower inflation and balance of payments stability. For example, higher interest rates will increase the cost of borrowing. The consequent reduction in consumption and investment will reduce the quantity of money in circulation. As a result, aggregate demand in the economy will fall, putting downward pressure on the general price level (lowering inflation) and reducing spending on imports (stabilising the balance of payments).

Higher interest rates may also increase the costs to those consumers and firms with existing loans as their interest payments on borrowed funds may increase. These consumers will have less money to spend, resulting in a fall in consumption. The higher costs incurred by firms with existing loans may lead to a fall in production, further reducing aggregate demand in the economy.

Key terms

Expansionary monetary policy – the increase in the money supply by the government, leading to a rise in aggregate demand

Contractionary monetary policy – the decrease in the money supply by the government, leading to a fall in aggregate demand

1 Find out the current interest rate set by the central bank in your country. Why do you think it is set at this rate?

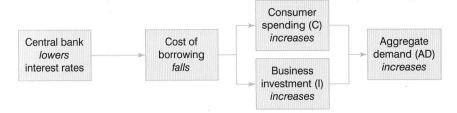

Figure 4.4.1 Expansionary monetary policy

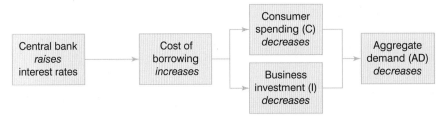

Figure 4.4.2 Contractionary monetary policy

Other monetary policy measures

Quantitative easing

Another way in which a government can increase the money supply is through a process known as quantitative easing (QE). As the sole provider of notes and coins in the economy, the government is able to create (print) new money, which it can inject into the economy in order to increase the money supply. It does this by lending the newly created money to commercial banks, which are then able to lend it on to consumers and business at very low interest rates (see the case study below). The increase in the availability of money should lead to an increase in spending by consumers and business, thereby stimulating aggregate demand. The money supply will decrease again when the commercial banks repay the money to the government at an agreed time in the future.

> **Key knowledge**
>
> **Quantitative easing (QE)** is the process by which the government increases the money supply by injecting money directly into the economy.

CASE STUDY   ## QE – an alternative form of monetary policy

In 2008, the world was hit by a financial crisis which plunged economies into deep recession. As a result, many countries faced rapidly decreasing economic growth and rising unemployment. Central banks like the US Federal Reserve (the Fed) and the Bank of England responded by cutting interest rates to near zero, but even this failed to boost consumer spending and investment. Central banks therefore looked for other ways to stimulate aggregate demand, one of which was quantitative easing (QE).

To carry out QE, central banks increase the money supply by printing money, which they inject into the economy by purchasing bond certificates (bonds) from commercial banks. As the holder of the bonds, the central bank is entitled to be repaid their full value with interest at a point in the future, for example, after 10 years. In return, commercial banks receive the newly created money which they can use to increase lending, thereby stimulating consumer spending and business investment in the economy.

In the years following the financial crisis, the US government carried out several rounds of QE, pumping over $3 trillion into the US economy. QE has also been undertaken by Japan, the UK, and the Eurozone.

1 How could QE lead to higher economic growth and lower unemployment?

2 Other than monetary policy, what are three other functions of a central bank?

Changing foreign exchange rates

Another way in which a government is able to influence the money supply in the economy is through changing the value of its currency on the foreign exchange market. If a government wishes to increase the domestic money supply, it may choose to devalue (reduce the value of) its currency. A **devaluation** is when a government increases

the supply of its currency in the foreign exchange market, causing its value to fall (see Unit 6.3). For example, in 2017, the Pakistani government devalued the Pakistani rupee, causing it to fall 3.1% against the US dollar, the lowest level since 2013.

A devaluation reduces the price of exports and increases the price of imports. As a result, sales of exports are likely to increase, leading to increased inflow of export revenue into the country from abroad. Furthermore, domestic consumers may switch away from purchasing higher priced imports towards relatively cheaper home-produced substitutes, thereby reducing the money flowing out of the country.

The reduction in the value of the currency would also make it cheaper for foreign multinational companies to set up operations in the country. This could lead to an inflow of investment capital into the country, thus increasing the quantity of money in circulation.

Key terms
....

Devaluation – a fall in the value of the domestic currency as a result of government intervention in the foreign exchange market

Revaluation – a rise in the value of the domestic currency as a result of government intervention in the foreign exchange market

 How might the devaluation of the Pakistani rupee in 2017 have affected domestic producers?

Effects of monetary policy on government macroeconomic aims

The monetary policy measure that a government uses will depend on the macroeconomic aims it is trying to achieve. If a government is aiming to achieve low unemployment and high economic growth, it will use expansionary monetary policy to increase the money supply and aggregate demand in the economy. If, on the other hand, it is aiming for low inflation and balance of payments stability, it will use contractionary monetary policy to decrease the money supply and reduce aggregate demand in the economy. These effects of the different monetary policy measures are summarised in the table below.

The effects of monetary policy measures on the macroeconomic aims of government

Monetary policy measure	Effects of monetary policy measure on the government aim of:			
	Low unemployment	High economic growth	Low and stable inflation	Balance of payments stability
A fall in interest rates, reducing the cost of borrowing	✓ – Businesses employ more workers to expand production in response to higher consumer spending	✓ – Businesses expand production due to higher consumer spending	✗ – Prices rise as a result of higher consumer spending and increased business investment (aggregate demand rises)	✗ – Higher consumer spending on imports worsens the trade balance on the current account of the balance of payments
A rise in interest rates, increasing the cost of borrowing	✗ – Businesses employ fewer workers as they cut back production due to the fall in consumer spending	✗ – Businesses produce fewer goods and services in response to the fall in consumer spending	✓ – Prices fall as a result of the fall in consumer spending and reduced business investment (aggregate demand falls)	✓ – Reduced consumer spending on imports improves the trade balance on the current account of the balance of payments

Monetary policy measure	Effects of monetary policy measure on the government aim of:			
	Low unemployment	High economic growth	Low and stable inflation	Balance of payments stability
An increase in the money supply using quantitative easing (QE)	✓ – Businesses employ more workers as they increase production in response to higher consumer spending	✓ – Businesses expand production in response to higher consumer spending	✗ – Prices rise as a result of higher consumer spending and increased business investment (aggregate demand rises)	✗ – Higher consumer spending on imports worsens the trade balance on the current account of the balance of payments
An exchange rate devaluation (value of the currency falls)	✓ – More workers are employed as businesses expand output in response to higher demand for both exports and home-produced goods	✓ – Production of exports and domestically produced goods and services increases	✗ – Prices rise due to increased demand for exports and home-produced goods (aggregate demand rises) and an increase in the cost of imported raw materials	✓ – Increased export revenue and reduced spending on imports improves the trade balance on the current account of the balance of payments
An exchange rate **revaluation** (value of the currency rises)	✗ – Fewer workers are employed as businesses cut back production in response to reduced demand for both exports and home-produced goods	✗ – Production of exports and domestically produced goods and services decreases	✓ – Prices fall due to reduced demand for exports and home-produced goods (aggregate demand falls) and a fall in the cost of imported raw materials	✗ – Decreased export revenue and increased spending on imports worsens the trade balance on the current account of the balance of payments

 3 What policy conflicts can you identify in the table?

How might monetary policy affect the government aim of redistributing income more equally?

Expansionary monetary policy has the potential to make the distribution of income within an economy more equal. By increasing the money supply, a government is able to increase aggregate demand in the economy, leading to an increase in the production of goods and services by firms. The resulting increase in economic growth and fall in unemployment may help to raise the incomes of the poor, thus improving the distribution of income and wealth within the economy.

However, there is evidence to suggest that the benefits of rising incomes resulting from higher economic growth are not spread evenly across a population, leading to a widening gap between rich and poor. Much depends on the government's commitment to implementing policies and regulations to redistribute income, including a progressive tax system, payment of state benefits, improved education and enforcement of labour laws, to prevent exploitation of workers. These are discussed in detail in Unit 5.2.

Applying

Project work

Using the internet, investigate the changes the central bank has made to interest rates in your country over the past year. Write a brief report answering the questions below.

- How have interest rates changed over the past year?
- Why did the central bank make these changes?
- How might these changes have affected domestic consumers and producers?

A good place to start your research might be the website of the central bank of the country you are investigating.

(E) How might these changes in interest rates have affected the country's exchange rate?

Knowledge check questions

1 Define money supply.   [2]

2 Define monetary policy.   [2]

3 Distinguish between expansionary and contractionary monetary policy.   [2]

4 Identify the monetary policy measures a government might use to lower inflation. [3]

5 Analyse how a decrease in interest rates may affect inflation.   [6]

6 Analyse how an increase in interest rates may affect unemployment.   [6]

7 (E) Discuss whether expansionary monetary policy or expansionary fiscal policy is more effective in lowering unemployment.   [8]

Check your progress

Read the unit objectives below and reflect on your progress in each.

- Define money supply.

- Define monetary policy.

- Explain monetary policy measures: changes in interest rates, money supply and foreign exchange rates.

- Analyse how monetary policy measures may enable the government to achieve its macroeconomic aims.

I struggle with this and need more practice.

I can do this reasonably well.

I can do this with confidence.

Supply-side policy

Learning objectives

By the end of this unit, you should be able to:

- define supply-side policy
- explain supply-side policy measures including education and training, labour market reforms, lower direct taxes, deregulation, improving incentives to work and invest, and privatisation
- analyse how supply-side policy measures may enable the government to achieve its macroeconomic aims.

Starting point

Answer these questions in pairs:

1. What are the four factors of production?

2. What is productivity?

3. What is the difference between productivity and production?

Exploring

Discuss these questions in pairs:

1. Using the pictures to help you, how might a government increase the *quantity* of each of the factors of production in an economy?

2. How might a government improve the *quality* of each of the factors of production in an economy?

Developing

What is supply-side policy?

A **supply-side policy** is a measure taken by a government to increase the **aggregate supply (AS)** of an economy. Aggregate supply is the total quantity of goods and services produced in an economy. An increase in aggregate supply increases the **productive capacity** (or **productive potential**) of the economy – the quantity of goods and services an economy is able to produce given its available resources.

Key terms

Supply-side policy – a government action which leads to an increase in aggregate supply in an economy by improving either the quality or the quantity of resources

Aggregate supply (AS) – the total supply of goods and services in an economy

Productive capacity (productive potential)

The productive capacity (or productive potential) of an economy refers to the quantity of goods and services that it is possible for an economy to produce given its available resources and technology. Productive capacity is represented by an economy's production possibility curve (PPC) (see Unit 1.4). An increase in the productive capacity of an economy will result in a shift of the PPC outwards from PPC to PPC_1 in Figure 4.5.1.

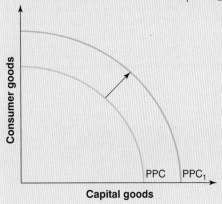

Figure 4.5.1 An improvement in the productive capacity of the economy

NOTE

The economic term used to talk about the total supply in an economy is **aggregate supply**. While the IGCSE Economics specification does not require you to use the term aggregate supply, an understanding of the concept is expected. From this point forward, we will use the term aggregate supply to refer to total supply in the economy.

Key terms

Productive capacity (or productive potential) – the ability of an economy to produce goods and services if all factors of production are fully employed

Supply-side policy measures

How will your education benefit you? How will it benefit the economy of the country in which you live? The benefits to you are obvious. An education will provide you with the knowledge and skills to gain a quality job in the future. However, your education is not only of benefit to you, but also to the economy of the country in which you work and reside. The knowledge and skills you learn will make you a more productive member of society, thus increasing the productive capacity of the economy as a whole.

A government can help to improve the productive capacity of an economy through the use of supply-side policy measures which aim to improve the *quality* and/or *quantity* of the resources in an economy. We look at each in turn below.

Education and training

Government spending on education and training should lead to an improvement in workers' knowledge and skills over time. This may lead to an increase in **labour productivity** (output per worker), thus increasing the productive potential of the economy.

Labour market reforms

A government may make changes to the labour market to increase the number of people employed, thus increasing the productive capacity of the economy. One labour market reform a government could make is reducing the power of trade unions (see Unit 3.4).

Policies designed to reduce the power of trade unions may lead to lower wages and higher levels of employment in the economy. It may also result in less time being lost to strikes and other forms of industrial action, thus increasing the number of people in work and the productive capacity of the economy.

Lower direct taxes

Reducing taxes on the incomes of workers and businesses can encourage individuals to work and firms to increase production.

- **Lower income tax**. The increase in disposable income from lower income tax rates may act as an incentive for more individuals to enter the workforce and/or for existing workers to work longer hours, thus increasing the quantity of labour in the economy.

- **Lower corporation tax**. A lower corporation tax rate will result in more profit for business owners. Higher profits may act as an incentive for entrepreneurs to increase production or invest in starting up new businesses, thus increasing the productive capacity of the economy.

Increasing competition

A government may seek to encourage competition within an economy. Increased competition will force domestic businesses to cut costs in order to remain profitable and survive. Businesses are able to cut costs by using their land, labour and capital more efficiently, thus leading to increased productivity. Policies to increase competition include:

- **Deregulation**. Deregulation is the removal of laws, rules and regulations by the government, making it easier for new business to enter or operate in an industry. By deregulating certain industries, the government is able to encourage increased competition, forcing firms to lower costs and increase productivity.

- **Privatisation**. Privatisation is when ownership of a public sector business is transferred to the private sector. Private owners are likely to run a business more efficiently and productively due to the profit motive. By lowering costs and becoming more competitive, business owners are able to maximise their profit.

Subsidies and grants

A government can encourage entrepreneurs to start up new businesses by providing them with subsidies or **grants**, thus improving the productive potential of the economy. Government agencies in the UK provide funding to thousands of small

Key terms

Deregulation – the removal of laws, rules and regulations, making it easier for a business to enter or operate in an industry

Grant – a sum of money that is given by the government which does not have to be repaid

businesses to help them get started. Subsidies can also be provided to existing businesses to encourage them to innovate.

- **Product innovation** – a subsidy on research and development may encourage firms to produce new and improved goods and services which better meet the needs and wants of consumers. This enables them to compete more effectively with foreign firms, thus increasing the productive capacity of the economy.

- **Process innovation** – subsidies may also encourage firms to develop new technology, which lowers costs by improving the efficiency of the production process. This improvement in the quality of capital increases productivity, thereby increasing aggregate supply in the economy.

Improving infrastructure

By improving and maintaining infrastructure in the economy, such as reliable transport links, communication networks and power grids, the government is able to facilitate the efficient production of goods and services throughout the economy and minimise waste. For example, an estimated 40% of India's fresh food, worth $8.3 billon, spoils before reaching consumers due to inadequate transport infrastructure, including poor roads and improper storage.

1 What is the difference between an improvement in the *quality* of labour and an improvement in the *quantity* of labour?

Effects of supply-side policy measures on government macroeconomic aims

By improving the quantity and quality of resources, supply-side policies make it possible for the government to increase the amount of goods and services that an economy is able to supply. Supply-side policies therefore increase aggregate supply and the productive potential of an economy, leading to lower inflation, higher economic growth and lower unemployment.

Spending on improving the quality of education in a country, for example, will create a more skilled and productive workforce over time. As a result, the capacity of the country to supply goods and services will increase, leading to lower inflation. The increase in the productivity of the population will also result in an increase in output and economic growth within the economy. With higher production, more jobs will be created, leading to lower unemployment.

It is worth noting here that supply-side policies, such as improving education, often take many years (possibly an entire generation) before the benefits are felt by an economy. Governments must therefore plan ahead, investing now to improve the productive capacities of their economies in the future.

Extension topic

Showing the effect of supply-side policy measures using an aggregate demand and aggregate supply diagram

The effect of a supply-side policy can be illustrated using an aggregate demand and aggregate supply diagram. The model of aggregate demand and supply shows the effects of changes in aggregate demand (AD) and aggregate supply (AS) on the general level of prices (P) and the **real output** (Y) of an economy. In Figure 4.5.2, the point at which the aggregate demand and aggregate supply curves intersect determines the equilibrium price level (P_E) and equilibrium real output (Y_E) of the economy as a whole.

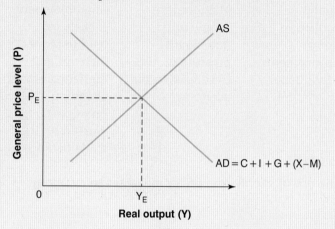

> **Key term**
>
> **Real output** – the total value of goods and services produced in an economy after inflation (rising prices) has been taken into account

Figure 4.5.2 Equilibrium price and real output in an economy

Supply-side policies have the effect of increasing the productive capacity of the economy, shifting the aggregate supply curve outwards to the right from AS to AS_1 in Figure 4.5.3. This helps to control inflation by reducing the general price level in the economy from P to P_1. It also leads to an increase in the real output of the economy from Y to Y_1, resulting in higher economic growth.

Increased production from higher economic growth is likely to lead to the creation of more jobs and lower unemployment. There is also likely to be an increase in spending on imports as a result of rising consumer incomes in the economy which, over time, may lead to a trade deficit on the balance of payments.

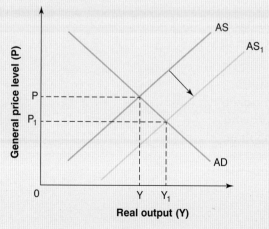

Figure 4.5.3 The effect of supply-side policy on the price level and real output of an economy

2   What similarities and differences are there between the model of aggregate demand and aggregate supply and the model of demand and supply presented in Chapter 2?

The effects of supply-side policy measures on government aims

Supply-side policy	Effects of supply-side policy measures on the government aim of:			
	Low unemployment	High economic growth	Low and stable inflation	Balance of payments stability
An improvement in the quality or quantity of resources in the economy, for example, education and training	✓ – By increasing the productive capacity of the economy, supply-side policies lead to greater production and more jobs	✓ – Businesses expand production due to improvements in productivity	✓ – The increase in aggregate supply puts downward pressure on the price level in the economy	✗ – Lower unemployment is likely to lead to higher incomes and higher consumer spending on imports, worsening the trade balance

3   What policy conflicts might arise from the use of supply-side policy measures to increase economic growth?

How might supply-side policy affect the government aim of redistributing income more equally?

Supply-side policy which leads to an increase in economic growth may create jobs and raise the incomes of low-skilled workers, thus reducing the gap between rich and poor. However, the effectiveness of this depends on the types of jobs (skilled or unskilled) that are created, as well as the laws and regulations in place to protect workers from exploitation, such as low pay and poor working conditions. High economic growth in some developing countries has in fact led to a widening distribution of income within the economy, as the benefits have failed to 'trickle down' to the poor.

Despite this, there are some supply-side policies which can have a more direct impact on improving the redistribution of income in an economy. These include the following:

- **Improved education and training**. Lack of education and training is one of the main reasons why the poor struggle to raise themselves out of poverty (see Unit 5.2). Improving the quality and accessibility of education and training in an economy can provide the poor with the skills they need to enhance their productivity and raise their earning potential in the longer run.
- **Lower income taxes**. Lower income taxes, particularly for workers earning low incomes, may encourage more people to work. As a result of lower income taxes, people's

disposable incomes will rise, providing them with an incentive to enter the labour force or work longer hours. This type of supply-side policy is likely to be more effective when unemployment is voluntary in nature (see Unit 4.7).

- **Subsidies on essential goods.** Government subsidies on the production of certain goods and services, such as housing and basic food items, can make them more available and affordable for low income households, thus improving living standards.

(see Unit 4.7)

CASE STUDY Investment in education in Finland

Finland, which consistently ranks among the top countries in the world for educational standards, has invested heavily in education and training over the past 50 years.

Finland's state-funded education system includes subsidised day care for babies and toddlers, pre-school, and nine years of comprehensive school education for every child. Between the ages of 16 and 19, students choose either to continue their upper secondary education or to go to vocational school where they receive training for various careers. In addition to funding education, the government also provides school lunches and free healthcare for all students; it also subsidises parents with around 150 euros a month for every child until the age of 17.

Sixty-five per cent of young people go on to pursue higher education in universities or other tertiary institutions in Finland – also provided free of charge by the government. For those already in work, the Finnish government has programmes in place to help them develop skills in areas including ICT. A state-funded network of public libraries also supports reading and literacy development throughout the population.

Finland's commitment to investing in education and training has created a high-wage, high-skill economy, which has enabled the country to remain competitive internationally, particularly with the low-cost economies of Asia.

1 What are three ways in which the Finnish government is investing in education and training?

2 How might investment in education and training benefit Finland's economy?

Applying

Project work

Using the internet, find one news article that provides evidence of a supply-side policy measure being used by a government. Read the article and answer the questions below:

1. What is the supply-side policy measure?

2. What will be the effect of the supply-side policy measure on the economy in the short run?

3. What will be the effect of the supply-side policy measure on the economy in the long run?

Knowledge check questions

1 Distinguish between a supply-side policy and a demand-side policy. [2]

2 Define privatisation. [2]

3 Define deregulation. [2]

4 Identify **three** supply-side policies and explain how each is likely to increase aggregate supply in an economy. [6]

5 Analyse how an improvement in education and training might affect unemployment. [6]

6 (E) Discuss whether supply-side policy or demand-side policy is more effective in achieving low inflation. [8]

Check your progress

Read the unit objectives below and reflect on your progress in each.

- Define supply-side policy.

- Explain supply-side policy measures including education and training, labour market reforms, lower direct taxes, deregulation, improving incentives to work and invest, and privatisation.

- Analyse how supply-side policy measures may enable the government to achieve its macroeconomic aims.

 I struggle with this and need more practice.

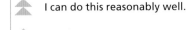 I can do this reasonably well.

I can do this with confidence.

Economic growth

Learning objectives

By the end of this unit, you should be able to:

- define economic growth
- explain real gross domestic product (GDP) and how it can be used to measure economic growth
- explain GDP per head and GDP per capita
- describe the different stages of the economic cycle
- define recession and explain how a recession moves the economy within its PPC
- explain how changes in aggregate (total) demand may increase the utilisation of resources and GDP – resulting in a movement from inside towards the PPC
- explain how economic growth shifts the economy's PPC to the right and is caused by changes in investment, technology, and the quantity and quality of the factors of production
- describe the costs and benefits of economic growth in the context of different economies
- analyse the range of policies available to promote economic growth and discuss how effective they might be.

Starting point

Answer these questions in pairs:

1. What is the difference between consumer goods and capital goods?

2. Why is spending on consumer goods important to an economy?

3. Why is business investment in capital goods important to an economy?

Exploring

Discuss these questions in pairs:

1. Why might China's economic growth rate be higher than the UK's?

2. Will China's growth rate always be higher than the UK's? Why or why not?

3. What can a government do to increase economic growth in an economy?

Key terms

What is economic growth and how is it measured?

Economic growth is the increase in the value of goods and services produced in an economy over time (usually a year). It is measured using **gross domestic product (GDP)**. GDP is the total value of all **final goods and services** produced within a country over a year.

Gross = total

Domestic = within a country

Product = goods and services produced/output

GDP is measured by adding up the total spending on final goods and services produced in a country over a one-year period. This includes **household spending** on **consumer goods**, **business spending** on **capital goods**, **government spending** and **net spending by foreigners** on exports. In many countries, the figure for net spending by foreigners on exports is negative as more money flows out of the country from spending on imports than flows in from spending on exports. As imports are produced abroad, purchasing them contributes to the GDP of another country rather than the country in which they are bought.

Gross domestic product (GDP) – the total value of all final goods and services produced within a country over a year

Final goods and services – goods and services that are ready to be used by the end consumer (both households and firms) when they are purchased, such as televisions, cars, pizza, etc.

Consumer goods – final goods and services purchased and used by consumers

Capital goods – equipment and machinery purchased and used by firms for the purpose of increasing production of goods and services

---

Extension topic

Total expenditure and aggregate demand

It is worth noting that the components of total expenditure (total spending) used to measure GDP correspond to the components of aggregate demand outlined Unit 4.3.
The components of aggregate demand are summarised in the formula:

$$AD = C + I + G + (X - M)$$

where consumption (C) is the same as household spending; investment (I) is the same as business spending; government spending (G) is the same as government spending, and net exports (X – M) corresponds to net spending by foreigners.

The equation for measuring GDP can therefore be summarised as:

$$\text{total expenditure} = C + I + G + (X - M) = GDP$$

---

1   In what ways does the economic activity in the photo contribute to the GDP of an economy?

Money GDP and real GDP

Money GDP is the dollar value of the GDP of a country. Money GDP can rise for two reasons:

1. Because the output of the economy increases. In other words, more goods and services are being produced and consumed.

2. Because the general level of prices of goods and services in the economy increases, which may be due to inflation.

Economists are interested in the rise in money GDP resulting from the rise in output (or production) rather than the rise in the general price level, as this gives a more accurate indication of the economic growth of the country. The total value of goods and services produced in a country which has been adjusted for rising prices (inflation) is called **real GDP**.

Key terms

Money GDP – the total money value of the goods and services produced in an economy, not accounting for inflation (may also be referred to as GDP or nominal GDP)

Real GDP – the total value of goods and services produced in an economy which has been adjusted to take inflation into account

Worked example

Measuring real GDP

Total output of Khaoland

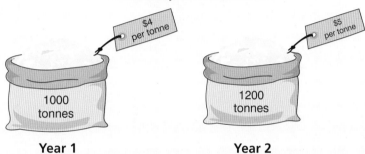

Khaoland is a country that produces one good – rice. In Year 1, Khaoland produces 1000 tonnes of rice, which it sells to households at a price of $4 per tonne. What is Khaoland's money GDP in Year 1?

Khaoland's money GDP in Year 1 is $4000. This is calculated as $4 per tonne × 1000 tonnes of rice.

In Year 2, Khaoland produces 1200 tonnes of rice, which it sells at the higher price of $5. What is Khaoland's money GDP in Year 2?

Khaoland's money GDP in Year 2 is $6000. This is calculated as $5 per tonne × 1200 tonnes of rice.

Khaoland's money GDP has therefore increased from $4000 in Year 1 to $6000 in Year 2, an increase of 50%. Does this mean that Khaoland has experienced an increase in actual rice production (an increase in real GDP) of 50%?

The answer is no, because a portion of that increase is due to the higher price level rather than increased output.

Real GDP, which takes into account rising prices (inflation), therefore provides a more accurate indication of the actual economic growth of a country.

Going back to our example of Khaoland, the actual output of the economy increased from 1000 tonnes to 1200 tonnes of rice. This is an increase *in real GDP* of 20%. The remaining difference between the money GDP and real GDP is accounted for by the rising price of rice rather than an increase in rice production. Thus, real GDP measures changes in the value of the actual output of the economy, which, in the case of Khaoland, is 200 tonnes of rice.

The table below shows figures for the countries with the highest growth rates (highest real GDP) and lowest growth rates (lowest real GDP) in the world in 2016.

Countries with the fastest and slowest growth rates in the world in 2016

Highest economic growth in 2016			Lowest economic growth in 2016		
	Country	Real GDP growth (annual %)		Country	Real GDP growth annual (%)
1	Iraq	11.0	1	Suriname	−10.4
2	Nauru	10.4	2	Yemen	−9.8
3	Côte d'Ivoire	8.8	3	Equatorial Guinea	−9.7
4	Uzbekistan	7.8	4	Chad	−7.0
5	Ethiopia	7.6	5	Trinidad and Tobago	−5.1
6	Iceland	7.2	6	Brazil	−3.6
7	Bangladesh	7.1	7	Azerbaijan	−3.1
8	India	7.1	8	Belarus	−2.6
9	Lao PDR	7.0	9	Brunei Darussalam	−2.5
10	Tanzania	7.0	10	Argentina	−2.3

Source: World Bank national accounts data, and OECD National Accounts data files

2 Why is real GDP a more accurate indicator of economic growth than money GDP?

Key knowledge

Real GDP as a measure of the income of a country

As we have discussed, real GDP is a measure of the total expenditure in an economy. We calculate total expenditure as:

$$\text{total expenditure in the economy} = \text{price level} \times \text{total output}$$

By definition, this is also the total income of a country as total income of a country (or total revenue) is also calculated as:

$$\text{total income (total revenue) of the economy} = \text{price level} \times \text{total output}$$

Thus, real GDP is a measure of the total expenditure and the total income of an economy.

Real GDP per head

In order to compare rates of economic growth between countries, it is useful to calculate **real GDP per head (real GDP per capita)**. Real GDP per head measures the average income of a population. Real GDP per head can be calculated as:

$$\text{real GDP per head} = \frac{\text{real GDP}}{\text{population}}$$

Real GDP per head also gives an indication of the change in living standards of a population over time. This is discussed in more detail in Unit 5.1.

The economic cycle

The real GDP of an economy tends to fluctuate over time, alternating between periods of rising income and periods of falling income. These variations are referred to as the **economic cycle** (also called the **business cycle** or **trade cycle**). Figure 4.6.1 shows the four main stages of the economic cycle that an economy moves through over time: **boom**, **recession**, **slump** and **recovery**. In the short run, the real GDP of an economy fluctuates between periods of rising and falling income; in the long run it generally follows an upward trend, as indicated by the **trend line** in Figure 4.6.1.

Key terms

Real GDP per head (real GDP per capita) – a measure of the average income of the population within a country

Economic cycle (also called the **business cycle** or **trade cycle**) – changes in the real GDP of an economy over time through periods of boom, recession, slump and recovery

Boom – a period of high and rising real GDP in the economy over time

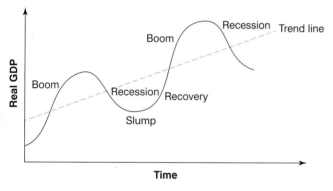

Figure 4.6.1 The economic cycle

- **Boom**. During a boom period, the real GDP (or output) of the economy is rising over time. As a result of increasing production of goods and services, unemployment is low. With most people employed, incomes are rising and consumer spending tends to be high. Firms therefore experience rising sales and profits and respond by expanding production, further increasing the output of the economy. However, rising aggregate demand for goods and services eventually leads to rising prices. Production costs may also rise as firms may need to pay higher prices for factor inputs, such as labour and raw materials, which are becoming increasingly scarce. This adds to the problem of inflation as firms increase their prices to cover their increased costs. The government may implement policies to lower inflation, such as increasing interest rates. Demand for exports may also fall as they become less competitive internationally due to the rising domestic price level.

- **Recession.** Aggregate demand eventually begins to fall as a result of government policies to control rising inflation and falling demand for exports. This causes real GDP to fall over time, resulting in rising unemployment and falling consumer incomes. Decreased consumer spending leads to falling sales and lower profits for firms. Firms respond by cutting production, further increasing unemployment. If the resulting fall in real GDP is sustained over time, it is likely to lead to a recession.

- **Slump.** During a slump, aggregate demand in the economy is low. As a result, firms' sales and profits are also low. There is high unemployment and real GDP may be negative as a result of falling production. The general level of prices in the economy is likely to be low and may even be falling (deflation). As a result of low inflation, export prices become more competitive. The government may reduce interest rates and increase spending in order to stimulate aggregate demand.

- **Recovery.** Aggregate demand eventually rises as government policies begin to take effect and the economy begins its recovery. More competitive exports resulting from low inflation also contribute to rising aggregate demand as sales of exports increase. Firms expand production, lowering unemployment. This causes the incomes of the population to rise, leading to a rise in consumer spending. Firms' sales and profits further increase, leading to higher production levels. As a result, more jobs are created, generating more consumer spending, and so on. The recovery stage eventually turns into an economic boom period, and so the economic cycle continues.

Key terms

Recession – a sustained period of negative GDP in the economy over time; also defined as two consecutive quarters (three-monthly periods) of negative economic growth

Slump – a period of negative real GDP characterised by low aggregate demand in the economy

Recovery – a period in which real GDP begins to rise as a result of rising aggregate demand in the economy

 What are the characteristics of a recession?

Causes and consequences of recession

A recession is when there is falling output (negative economic growth) in an economy over a sustained period of time, usually two consecutive quarters (a six-month period). A fall in output occurs when the percentage change in real GDP is negative. For example, a real GDP figure of –5% would indicate that the economy is producing 5% fewer goods and services than before and is therefore experiencing negative economic growth. A recession can be caused by either demand-side or supply-side factors.

Demand-side causes of a recession

A recession can be caused by a fall in aggregate demand (the demand side) in an economy. The possible causes of a fall in aggregate demand are summarised in the table below.

Demand-side causes of a recession

Factor	Possible causes
A fall in consumption – a decrease in consumer spending is likely to result in a fall in aggregate demand for goods and services	• Contractionary fiscal policy (reduced government spending and higher income tax rates) (see Unit 4.3) • Contractionary monetary policy (lower interest rates), leading to decreases in borrowing (see Unit 4.4) • High unemployment, resulting in lower consumer incomes • Low **consumer confidence**, leading to increased saving (and decreased spending)
A fall in investment – a decrease in business investment in capital equipment and machinery as firms seek to cut back production	• Contractionary monetary policy (higher interest rates), leading to an increase in the cost of borrowing • Lower consumer spending, leading to falling sales • Low **business confidence**, leading to a reduction in planned investment
A fall in government spending	• Decreased government spending on infrastructure and public services, for example • Loss of jobs, leading to lower consumer spending. For example, decreased spending on the building of new roads will reduce employment in the construction industry.
A fall in net exports (the difference between the value of exports and the value of imports) – a decrease in export revenue and/or a rise in spending on imports	• A recession in the economies of trading partners may lead to a decrease in demand for exports • Excessive spending on imported consumer goods may lead to an unsustainable deficit on the current account which has to be financed by borrowing from abroad. Economies may be required to increase taxes and cut spending in order to repay borrowed funds, which may lead to a recession (see Unit 6.4).

Key terms

Consumer confidence – the extent to which consumers feel optimistic about the future: if consumer confidence is high, consumers are likely to spend more and save less

Business confidence – the extent to which businesses feel optimistic about the future: if business confidence is high, producers are likely to invest more in capital equipment to expand output

Factor	Possible causes
	• An increase in the value of the currency, leading to an increase in the price of exports and a fall in the price of imports (see Unit 6.3).
	• High domestic inflation may make a country's exports less competitive and imports more competitive over time.
	• The imposition of trade barriers, such as a tariff, on a country's exports will make them more expensive in overseas markets (see Unit 6.2).
	• The removal of tariffs on imports will make imported goods cheaper, leading to increased spending on imports.

Picture A   Picture B

④ Picture A shows unemployed people in the USA in the 1930s. Picture B shows unemployed people in Ethiopia in 2012. How might unemployment such as this be shown on a PPC diagram for a country?

A recession caused by a fall in aggregate demand is likely to lead to unemployment of resources (land, labour and capital) in an economy. The deeper (worse) the recession, the greater is the level of unemployment. This can be shown on a production possibility curve (PPC) diagram as a movement from a position on the PPC at point A (a position of full employment) to a position under the PPC at point B (a position of unemployment) in Figure 4.6.2 (see Unit 1.4 to review points under, on and beyond the PPC). As a result, production of consumer goods decreases from W to Y and production of capital goods decreases from X to Z, which may lead to an overall fall in real GDP.

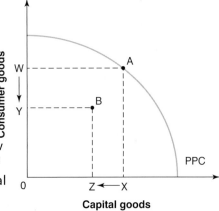

Figure 4.6.2 Unemployment of resources in an economy

Supply-side causes of a recession

A recession can also be caused by a fall in aggregate supply (supply-side factors) which reduces the quality or quantity of resources in an economy. These could include:

* the depletion (using up) of natural resources, such as oil reserves
* natural disasters, such as earthquakes or flooding
* a net outflow of skilled workers from the country
* rising costs of production.

5 The picture shows a factory that has been destroyed by a fire. Use a PPC diagram to show the effect of this on the country's economy.

Each of the above factors reducing aggregate supply has the effect of reducing the productive capacity of the economy, shifting the PPC curve inwards from PPC to PPC_1 in Figure 4.6.3. As a result, the economy's ability to produce goods and services falls, which could lead to a decrease in actual output and recession.

Causes of economic growth

Demand-side causes of economic growth

Economic growth can be caused by a rise in aggregate demand in an economy. The causes are summarised in the table below.

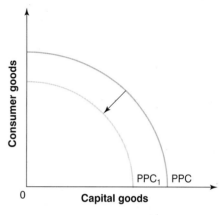

Figure 4.6.3 A fall in the productive capacity of the economy

Demand-side causes of economic growth

Factor	Possible causes
A rise in consumption – an increase in consumer spending, resulting in higher demand for goods and services	• Expansionary monetary policy (lower interest rates), leading to increased borrowing • Expansionary fiscal policy (increased government spending and income tax cuts) • Low unemployment, resulting in rising consumer incomes • Increased consumer confidence, leading to a reduction in saving (and increased spending)
A rise in investment – an increase in investment in capital equipment and machinery by firms as they seek to expand production	• Expansionary monetary policy (lower interest rates), leading to a fall in the cost of borrowing • Higher consumer spending, leading to increased sales • Increased business confidence, leading to an increase in planned investment
A rise in government spending	• Increased government spending on areas including education, healthcare and infrastructure • The creation of jobs as a result of government spending, leading to higher incomes and higher consumer spending

Factor	Possible causes
A rise in net exports (the difference between the value of exports and the value of imports) – an increase in export revenue and/or a fall in spending on imports	<ul><li>Economic boom and rising aggregate demand in the economies of trading partners, leading to increased demand for exports</li><li>A fall in the value of the currency, lowering the price of exports and increasing the price of imports</li><li>Lower inflation relative to other countries, making exports more competitive and imports less competitive over time</li><li>The removal of trade restrictions, such as tariffs, on exports, making exports more price competitive</li><li>The imposition of trade restrictions on imports, making imports more expensive and increasing demand for home-produced goods</li></ul>

6 How might the economic activity in the picture contribute to economic growth?

Economic growth puts unemployed resources (land, labour and capital) to work, thus minimising the wasteful use of resources in the economy and increasing output. This can be shown on a production possibility curve (PPC) as a movement from a position under the PPC at point C (a position of unemployment) to a position on the PPC at point D (a position of full employment) in Figure 4.6.4. As a result, production of consumer goods increases from Y to W and production of capital goods increases from Z to X, thus increasing the real GDP of the economy.

Supply-side causes of economic growth

Economic growth may also be caused by supply-side factors which increase the aggregate supply of the economy. An increase in aggregate supply may result from:

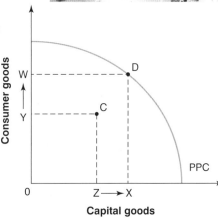

Figure 4.6.4 An increase in the utilisation of resources and GDP

- business investment in capital equipment and machinery, leading to an increase in productivity
- development of new technology used in the production process, increasing productivity and lowering unit costs
- immigration of skilled labour into the country
- the discovery of natural resources in a country, such as oil, coal or iron ore.

Each of these factors will have the effect of improving the quality and/or quantity of resources, thus increasing the productive capacity of the economy. This can be shown as a shift of the PPC outwards from PPC to PPC₁ in Figure 4.6.5. As a result, it is now possible for the economy to produce combinations of consumer and capital goods which were previously unattainable.

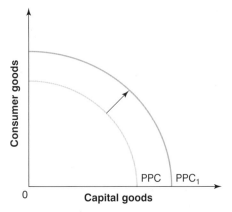

Figure 4.6.5 An improvement in the productive capacity of the economy

Consequences of economic growth

7 What are the benefits of economic growth for businesses and households?

Benefits of economic growth

Individuals	**Employment opportunities**. Economic growth leads to increased employment opportunities for individuals as firms expand production. This results in rising incomes and higher living standards for the population. Consequently, the distribution of income may be improved and poverty may be reduced.
Firms	**Rising sales and profits**. During periods of high economic growth when the incomes of the population are rising, firms' sales and profits tend to increase due to high consumer spending. As a result, many firms expand production by investing in capital equipment and machinery.
Government	**Higher tax revenue**. Economic growth generally results in higher income for individuals and businesses. Consequently, the revenue a government receives from direct taxes increases. Revenue from indirect taxes may also rise due to increased spending on goods and services. Tax revenue could be spent on improving public services and infrastructure in the economy. Alternatively, the government may run a budget surplus and use the surplus funds to repay government debt.
The economy	**Low unemployment**. Economic growth usually leads to lower unemployment as firms hire workers in order to expand production. With more people working, the incomes and living standards of the population generally rise.

Costs of economic growth

Individuals	**Exploitation of labour and reduced quality of life**. The benefits of economic growth are not shared equally throughout the population. Some individuals benefit a lot, while others may not benefit at all or may even become worse off. For example, in some developing countries, adults and children may be exploited for their labour in order to satisfy overseas demand for cheap products. Increased pollution from higher levels of production in the economy may also reduce the quality of life for some individuals living in affected areas.
Firms	**Rising production costs**. As the economy grows, resources such as labour and raw materials are likely to become increasingly scarce. Competition for these resources may mean that firms have to pay more for them. For example, firms may have to pay higher wages to attract the workers they need. This increases firms' costs of production. Some of this increase in costs may be passed on to consumers, thus contributing to higher inflation.

The economy

Rising inflation. Economic growth is likely to lead to higher inflation due to increasing aggregate demand in the economy and higher production costs. Higher inflation may reduce the competitiveness of exports and decrease consumer and business confidence (see Unit 4.8).

Distribution of income becomes more unequal. In times of economic growth, the gap between rich and poor widens in some countries. Private owners of factors of production, such as land and capital, tend to gain far more from economic growth than the poor and unskilled.

Depletion of non-renewable natural resources. Economic growth tends to result in the exploitation of a country's resources. Non-renewable resources such as fossil fuels and timber may be used up, leaving little for future generations.

Pollution and environmental damage. Economic growth tends to result in higher levels of air, water and soil pollution. Environmental damage, such as air pollution and deforestation, may contribute to global warming and climate change.

8 How do the pictures illustrate the potential benefits and problems of economic growth?

CASE STUDY   Economic growth in Ethiopia

According to the World Bank, Ethiopia had the fastest-growing economy in the world in 2017 with an economic growth rate of over 8%. Growth was driven largely by public investment in infrastructure and the development of industrial parks, which are expected to facilitate the future expansion of the secondary sector of the economy.

The government is hoping to transform Ethiopia into a manufacturing hub over the coming decade, with the goal of Ethiopia becoming a low to middle income status country by 2025.

Rising domestic consumption as a result of rising incomes has also been a key contributor to Ethiopia's rapid growth. Despite this, the country's real GDP per head is only $590 per year, substantially lower than the average in the region.

Ethiopia's strong growth in 2017 follows a decade in which the country's economy has grown at an average 10% a year.

Ethiopia's annual GDP growth rate 2007–17

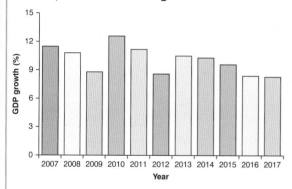

Source: World Bank

Economic growth in Ethiopia has been accompanied by a reduction in absolute poverty as measured by the international poverty line of less than $1.90 a day from 55.3% of the population in 2000 to 33.5% in 2011.

Source: Data from World Bank, The World Bank In Ethiopia, Oct 30, 2017

1 What is one benefit of economic growth for Ethiopia mentioned in the extract?

2 How is the Ethiopian government helping to facilitate economic growth?

Policies to promote economic growth

Monetary policy

Expansionary monetary policy can be used to increase economic growth. This would involve the central bank *lowering interest rates*, thus reducing the cost of borrowing. As a result, consumers and firms would borrow more (and save less), leading to an increase in consumer spending and business investment. The consequent increase in aggregate demand would lead to an increase in the number of jobs available as firms seek to expand production in response to higher consumer demand.

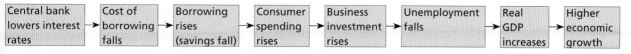

| Central bank lowers interest rates | → | Cost of borrowing falls | → | Borrowing rises (savings fall) | → | Consumer spending rises | → | Business investment rises | → | Unemployment falls | → | Real GDP increases | → | Higher economic growth |

The effectiveness of monetary policy depends on the current level of interest rates. If interest rates are already close to zero, it would only be possible for governments to lower them slightly, thus reducing the effectiveness of this form of monetary policy to increase economic growth. In this instance, a government may have to consider other monetary policy options, such as quantitative easing (see Unit 4.4) in order to stimulate economic growth.

Fiscal policy

Expansionary fiscal policy (see Unit 4.3) can also be used to raise economic growth. This would involve increasing government spending and/or lowering income tax rates. An increase in government spending would create jobs, helping to lower unemployment. Higher incomes from rising levels of employment are likely to lead to an increase in consumer spending, thus increasing aggregate demand in the economy. Firms are likely to respond to the increased demand for goods and services by expanding production, thus leading to higher real GDP and positive economic growth.

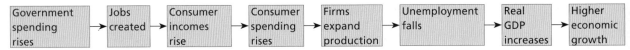

Government spending rises → Jobs created → Consumer incomes rise → Consumer spending rises → Firms expand production → Unemployment falls → Real GDP increases → Higher economic growth

A reduction in income tax rates increases consumers' disposable income. As a result, consumer spending is likely to increase, leading to a rise in aggregate demand and higher economic growth in the economy.

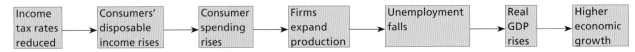

Income tax rates reduced → Consumers' disposable income rises → Consumer spending rises → Firms expand production → Unemployment falls → Real GDP rises → Higher economic growth

The effectiveness of fiscal policy will depend on the extent of the increase in government spending or reduction in income tax rates. The greater the spending increase or income tax cut, the greater is the impact on economic growth.

The effectiveness of monetary and fiscal policy in increasing the output (or real GDP) of an economy will also depend on aggregate supply. What is likely to happen to the output of an economy if aggregate supply is falling? The answer is that it is likely to decrease. Thus, it will limit the effectiveness of demand-side policies in raising output and increasing economic growth. Rising aggregate supply, on the other hand, will increase the effectiveness of demand-side policies in increasing economic growth as the productive capacity of the economy will be greater.

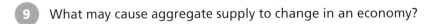 9   What may cause aggregate supply to change in an economy?

Supply-side policy

Supply-side policy seeks to increase aggregate supply and the productive capacity of an economy by improving the quantity and/or quality of its resources.

- **Subsidies on research and development**. By subsidising research and development, firms may be encouraged to innovate by developing new, more efficient production processes. This will make domestic firms more productive and so lead to lower prices and increased output. Lower prices may also make firms' exports more competitive abroad. An increase in the sale of exports will lead to higher economic growth in the domestic economy.

- **Privatisation and deregulation**. Some governments may seek to increase the level of competition through privatisation and deregulation of industries (see Unit 4.5). This will force domestic firms to find ways to lower costs through innovation in order to compete. In the long run, those firms that are able to survive will be more productive, thus increasing the quantity of goods and services the economy is able to produce and increasing economic growth.

- **Lowering corporation tax**. Reducing the tax rate businesses pay on their profits may provide an incentive for entrepreneurs to start up new businesses, thus increasing the productive potential of the economy.

Supply-side policies generally take time to implement and are therefore unlikely to be effective in increasing economic growth in the short run. In the long run, however, supply-side policies can make a significant contribution to achieving sustainable growth in an economy.

Protectionist policies

The government may impose restrictions, such as tariffs and **quotas**, on imports in order to protect domestic industries from foreign competition. This will increase the price of imports, leading to an increase in the demand for locally made substitutes that will now be relatively cheaper. As a result, domestic production should rise, leading to an increase in real GDP and higher economic growth.

However, the effectiveness of protectionist policies in raising economic growth may be reduced if trading partners respond by also imposing tariffs and quotas on a country's exports in retaliation for those imposed on their goods (see Unit 6.2).

Exchange rate devaluation

A government may choose to devalue their currency by intervening in the foreign exchange market (see Unit 6.3). By reducing the value of their currency, they are able to make their exports cheaper in overseas markets. The resulting increase in sales of exports may lead to higher real GDP and economic growth. A devaluation will also make the price of imports more expensive, leading consumers to switch away from higher-priced imports to the relatively cheaper locally produced goods. This also has the effect of raising real GDP and growth in the economy.

The effectiveness of this policy may be reduced if trading partners feel that it is unfair and respond by imposing trade restrictions on the exports of the country devaluing its currency. It may also result in higher inflation as aggregate demand in the domestic economy increases (see Unit 4.8).

Key term

Quota – a physical limit on the quantity of a good that is allowed into a country

Project work

Using information from the CIA World Factbook website, create a mini profile for a country of your choice. In your country profile, include:

- name of country
- population

- real GDP over the past three years
- real GDP per capita over the past three years.

Then, using this data and additional information from the internet, answer the questions below.

1. How has real GDP changed over the past three years?

2. What are some possible reasons for this change?

Knowledge check questions

1 Define economic growth.	[2]
2 Describe how economic growth is measured.	[4]
3 Explain the difference between money GDP and real GDP.	[3]
4 Define GDP per capita.	[2]
5 Define recession.	[2]
6 Using a PPC diagram, show the impact of a recession on an economy.	[4]
7 Explain **two** causes of economic growth.	[6]
8 Analyse the effect of lower interest rates on economic growth.	[6]
9 (E) Discuss whether economic growth is always good for an economy.	[8]

Check your progress

Read the unit objectives below and reflect on your progress in each.

- Define economic growth.
- Explain real gross domestic product (GDP) and how it can be used to measure economic growth.
- Explain GDP per head and GDP per capita.
- Describe the different stages of the economic cycle.
- Define recession and explain how a recession moves the economy within its PPC.
- Explain how changes in aggregate (total) demand may increase the utilisation of resources and GDP – resulting in a movement from inside towards the PPC.
- Explain how economic growth shifts the economy's PPC to the right and is caused by changes in investment, technology, and the quantity and quality of the factors of production.
- Describe the costs and benefits of economic growth in the context of different economies.
- Analyse the range of policies available to promote economic growth and discuss how effective they might be.

 I struggle with this and need more practice.

 I can do this reasonably well.

 I can do this with confidence.

Employment and unemployment

Learning objectives

By the end of this unit, you should be able to:

- define employment, unemployment and full employment
- describe the changing patterns and level of employment
- explain how unemployment is measured – claimant count and labour force survey
- state the formula for the unemployment rate
- describe the causes of unemployment
- describe the types of unemployment – frictional, structural and cyclical
- explain the consequences of unemployment for individuals, firms and the economy as a whole
- analyse the range of policies available to reduce unemployment and discuss how effective they might be.

Starting point

Answer these questions in pairs:

1. Why do people work?

2. What may stop people from working or finding work?

Exploring

Discuss these questions in pairs:

1. What might be the effects of unemployment on an individual?

2. What might be the effects of unemployment on society and the economy?

Developing

What is employment and unemployment?

Employment is when people are working for payment, for example for a wage or salary. **Unemployment** is when people are without paid work and are *willing* and *able* to work – 'willing' in the sense that they are actively looking for work and 'able' in the sense that they are available and have the ability to start working almost immediately. The sum of the people employed and the people unemployed is the total **labour force** of an economy.

The macroeconomic aim of full employment is achieved in an economy when *almost all* people who are willing and able to work are employed. Economists accept that even when an economy is at 'full employment', a small amount of

Key terms

Employment – the state of having paid work

Unemployment – the state of being without paid work but willing and able to work if a job becomes available

Labour force – all individuals of working age (between the ages of 15 and 65 in most countries) who are either employed or unemployed in a country

unemployment will exist. This is known as the **natural rate of unemployment**. It occurs because, at any point in time, there will be a small proportion of workers (about 4% of the labour force) who are unemployed either because they are in the process of finding work or because they are learning new skills due to the changing structure of the economy.

Changing patterns and levels of employment

Workers employed in the tertiary sector

The proportion of workers employed in the tertiary sector (services) tends to rise as a country develops, while employment in the primary sector (agriculture) and secondary sector (manufacturing) tends to fall. For example, in 2013, over 70% of Ethiopia's labour force was employed in the primary sector. In contrast, only about 1% of workers in the UK were employed in the primary sector in 2013, while the tertiary sector employed over 80% of the UK's labour force. This pattern results from:

- manufacturing industries relocating abroad in search of lower labour costs

- rising consumer incomes, leading to increased demand for services in industries such as retail, entertainment and tourism

- more educated workers seeking higher-paying jobs in the tertiary sector, for example as managers, accountants or lawyers

- advances in technology, which have reduced the need for labour in the primary industry.

1 What differences are there between the primary sectors of a developed country and a developing country?

Workers employed in the formal economy

The proportion of workers employed in the **formal economy**, rather than the **informal economy**, tends to rise as a country becomes more developed. Workers employed in the formal (official) economy are protected by labour laws, such as minimum wage legislation. They also have formal, written agreements with their employers and pay tax on their income. Those employed in the informal (unofficial) economy tend to be paid in cash and do not pay tax on their income. For example, a housekeeper working in an international hotel chain would be employed in the formal economy, whereas a housekeeper or maid employed by a private household may be employed in the informal economy.

Women in the labour force

Changing social attitudes have resulted in more women looking for work and undertaking higher level education and training. Consequently, women are making up an increasingly higher proportion of the total labour force in many countries.

Workers employed in the private and public sectors

There has been a movement away from government control towards market economies over recent decades. Through privatisation and deregulation (see Unit 4.5), governments have increased the size of the private sector in their economies. As a result, an increasing proportion of jobs are now found in the private sector in many countries, while the proportion of workers employed in the public sector has decreased.

Part-time workers

Firms in many countries prefer to employ workers on a part-time rather than full-time basis. This allows firms more flexibility. In periods when demand for their product is high, firms increase the hours available to part-time workers. In periods when demand is low, on the other hand, they reduce the hours of part-time workers. Employing workers part-time also lowers production costs for firms as the hourly wage for part-time workers may be lower than that paid to full-time workers; also, part-time workers may not be legally entitled to the same benefits, such as holiday pay and health insurance, which full-time workers receive.

Youth unemployment

Young people between the ages of 15 and 24 years are making up an increasingly high proportion of the unemployed in many countries. For example, the youth unemployment rate in Spain peaked at over 56% in 2013. The main reason for this is that young people often lack work experience. Employers tend to prefer to employ workers who already have the required skills and experience to do a job as it reduces training costs and results in higher labour productivity.

2 What could the government do to help young people to find work?

How is unemployment measured?

There are two ways in which unemployment can be measured in an economy.

- The **claimant count** method involves counting all individuals who register as unemployed. In most countries, this is done by counting the number of people claiming unemployment benefits.

- The **Labour Force Survey (LFS)** is a government survey of a sample of households in a country to determine who is employed and who is unemployed. From this information the government is able to calculate the unemployment rate for the country. The LFS is used by countries worldwide under the guidance of the International Labour Organization (ILO) and provides a standardised measure for unemployment which can be compared between countries. In the UK, the government

Key terms

Claimant count – a measure of unemployment that is calculated by counting all individuals who receive an unemployment benefit as being unemployed

Labour Force Survey (LFS) – a measure of unemployment that uses data gathered from a survey of a sample of households to calculate the unemployment rate

surveys around 40 000 households (approximately 90 000 individuals) every three months. An individual is counted as unemployed if they are:

o without a paid job

o willing and able to work

o actively seeking work

o available to start work within the next two weeks.

The unemployment rate

Unemployment is usually expressed as a percentage and is calculated as:

$$\text{unemployment rate} = \frac{\text{number of unemployed}}{\text{total labour force (number of unemployed + number of employed)}} \times 100$$

The unemployment rate shows the proportion of a country's workforce that is unemployed. The table below shows the countries with the highest and lowest levels of unemployment in the world in 2016 using the LFS measure.

Countries with the highest and lowest unemployment rates in 2016

Highest unemployment rates in 2016			Lowest unemployment rates in 2016		
	Country	LFS unemployment rate (%)		Country	LFS unemployment rate (%)
1	Solomon Islands	31.4	1	Qatar	0.2
2	Gambia	29.7	2	Cambodia	0.3
3	Lesotho	27.4	3	Belarus	0.5
4	Macedonia, FYR	26.7	4	Thailand	0.6
5	South Africa	25.9	5	Myanmar	0.8
6	Bosnia and Herzegovina	25.8	6	Benin	1.0
7	Namibia	25.6	7	Bahrain	1.3
8	Swaziland	25.3	8	Lao PDR	1.5
9	West Bank and Gaza	24.9	9	Burundi	1.6
10	Mozambique	24.4	10	Singapore	1.8

Source: International Labour Organization, ILOSTAT database

The LFS figure for unemployment is usually higher than the claimant count figure. This is because not all individuals who are unemployed claim the unemployment benefit. For example, a female unemployed worker may be actively looking for work but

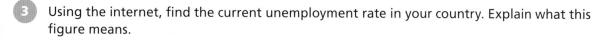

not entitled to an unemployment benefit because her husband earns too high a wage. The LFS figure is the official figure for unemployment and is generally considered to be more accurate, especially when comparing unemployment rates between countries.

Worked example

Calculating the unemployment rate

In New Zealand, 2 510 000 people were employed and 139 000 people were unemployed as at December 2016. Calculate the unemployment rate in New Zealand at this time.

The formula for the unemployment rate is:

$$\text{unemployment rate} = \frac{\text{number of unemployed}}{\text{total labour force}} \times 100$$

New Zealand's total labour force in December 2016 was:

   total labour force = employed + unemployed

   total labour force = 2 510 000 + 139 000 = 2 649 000 people

New Zealand's unemployment rate in December 2016 was therefore:

$$\text{unemployment rate} = \frac{139\ 000}{2\ 649\ 000} \times 100 = 5.2\%$$

In other words, 5.2% of New Zealand's labour force was unemployed in December 2016.

Suppose New Zealand's labour force increased to 3 000 000 people and the unemployment rate fell to 5%. Calculate the change in the number of unemployed people in New Zealand.

The number of people unemployed can be calculated as 5% of the total labour force of 3 000 000 people. The number of people unemployed is therefore:

   3 000 000 × 5/100 = 150 000 people

This is an increase in the number of unemployed of:

   150 000 – 139 000 = 11 000 people

3 Using the internet, find the current unemployment rate in your country. Explain what this figure means.

Types of unemployment

Frictional unemployment occurs when individuals move between jobs. People leave jobs for many reasons. They may be unhappy in their job, no longer needed by their employer, want to look for a better job elsewhere or simply want a change. Frictional unemployment is the period an individual is without paid work

Key term

Frictional unemployment – unemployment that exists when people are between jobs, moving from one job to another between leaving their old job and starting a new one. During this period, individuals spend time searching and applying for work opportunities. Frictional unemployment is unavoidable in an economy. It is usually temporary and is not considered to be a serious form of unemployment.

Seasonal unemployment occurs at certain times of the year as workers' skills in some industries are not needed all year round. For example, fruit pickers will be employed during the fruit harvest season, but may be unemployed at other times of the year. Seasonal unemployment also occurs in the tourism industry during off-peak seasons when demand is low. Seasonal unemployment is generally not considered serious in most countries as it affects a relatively small number of industries.

Technological unemployment occurs when workers are replaced by machinery. As technology becomes more advanced, capital equipment and machinery is developed, which reduces the need for human labour. In the tertiary sector, for example, self-checkout machines in supermarkets have resulted in fewer service staff being employed. In the secondary sector, advances in computer-aided manufacturing have replaced production workers in some industries. Technological unemployment is generally not considered to be a serious problem as, while it creates unemployment for some, it also tends to create employment opportunities in other industries, for example in the design and manufacture of machinery and computer software.

Structural unemployment results from changes in the structure of the economy. For example, as an economy develops and the incomes of the population rise, jobs in manufacturing tend to be lost to less developed countries which benefit from lower labour costs. This change in the structure of the economy away from manufacturing has the potential to cause wide-scale unemployment in some industries. The effects of structural unemployment can be highly localised, impacting regions that are particularly reliant on manufacturing for jobs, for example. Structural unemployment is a serious concern for most governments as it may result in a large number of job losses. It may also require retraining large numbers of workers so they have the necessary skills to re-enter the labour force, which can take many years.

Cyclical unemployment (also called **demand-deficient unemployment**) occurs when aggregate demand decreases and the economy enters a recession. During a recessionary period in the economic cycle, incomes are falling and consumer spending decreases. As a result, demand for goods and services falls, prompting businesses to cut back production and employ fewer workers. The greater the fall in aggregate demand, the more severe is the cyclical unemployment. Cyclical unemployment is generally considered to be a serious concern as it affects the whole economy and can last for a long period of time if a recession is bad enough.

Key terms

Seasonal unemployment – unemployment that exists because the workers are not needed all year round

Technological unemployment – unemployment that exists because people are replaced by machines

Structural unemployment – unemployment that exists due to a change in the structure of an economy, usually because it is becoming more developed

Cyclical unemployment (also called **demand-deficient unemployment**) – unemployment that exists due to falling aggregate demand, which occurs when an economy enters a recessionary period in its economic cycle

4 What are the most serious types of unemployment for an economy? Why?

Consequences of unemployment

The consequences of high unemployment are widespread, directly or indirectly affecting most members of the population of a country in some way.

Individuals

- **The unemployed**. Most affected by unemployment are the unemployed people themselves. Without paid work, their living standards fall dramatically – many unemployed individuals are not able to afford even basic necessities such as food, shelter and clothing for themselves or their families without financial support from the government. In addition to financial hardship, long-term unemployment can lead to depression and a loss of self-worth and can put significant stress on family relationships.

- **Tax payers**. In times of high unemployment, the government may increase taxes in order to raise revenue to fund the payment of unemployment benefits and job creation programmes.

Firms

- **Lower demand for goods and services**. When unemployment is high, consumer incomes tend to fall, resulting in reduced demand for goods and services. Consequently, many firms are likely to suffer a fall in sales and profits, which may force some producers to cut back production or close down. This is likely to result in further job losses, which may compound the problem as it leads to further reductions in consumer incomes and spending.

- **Increased availability of workers at lower wages**. When unemployment is high, competition for jobs is likely to be strong. Individuals, many desperate for paid work, may be willing to accept lower wages in return for their labour. This is good news for those firms in a position to expand production, as it will make it easier for them to find the workers they need at lower wages.

Government

- **Reduced tax revenue**. When unemployment is high, the revenue the government receives from income taxes decreases. As a result, the government has less money available to spend on areas such as infrastructure and the provision of public services.

- **Increased spending**. Despite having less tax revenue, governments are often forced to increase their spending on the provision of unemployment benefits and welfare benefits such as housing allowances, during periods of high unemployment. This has an opportunity cost as spending in other areas, such as the development of infrastructure and public services, has to be given up. It may also result in higher government debt as the government may have to borrow in order to finance its spending.

The whole economy

- **Reduced efficiency.** Unemployment is an inefficient use of an economy's resources as labour is not being fully utilised. This is wasteful and is likely to result in lost productivity and reduced economic growth.

- **Increased poverty.** Unemployment is one of the main causes of poverty in many countries and widens the gap between rich and poor (see Unit 5.2). Without jobs, the unemployed are unable to lift themselves out of poverty and provide themselves and their families with the same opportunities and living standards that are accessible to those on higher incomes.

- **Falling economic growth.** When unemployment is high, consumer spending is likely to decrease, leading to falling sales for many firms. In response, firms are likely to cut back production, slowing economic growth and worsening unemployment in the economy.

- **Lower inflation/deflation.** Falling aggregate demand from reduced consumer spending and business investment during a period of high unemployment is likely to result in lower inflation. If an economy is in recession for a prolonged period of time, it may enter a period of deflation, which can lead to worsening unemployment and negative economic growth (see Unit 4.8).

5. What might cause a factory to close? What types of unemployment might these different causes create?

Policies to reduce unemployment

Monetary policy

Expansionary monetary policy can be used to reduce unemployment. This would involve the central bank *lowering* interest rates, thus reducing the cost of borrowing. As a result, consumers and firms would borrow more (and save less), leading to an increase in consumer spending and business investment. The consequent increase in aggregate demand will lead to an increase in the number of jobs available as firms seek to expand production in response to higher consumer demand.

| Central bank lowers interest rates | → | Cost of borrowing falls | → | Borrowing increases (savings fall) | → | Consumer spending rises | → | Business investment rises | → | Aggregate demand increases | → | Unemployment falls |

Fiscal policy

Expansionary fiscal policy can also be used to reduce unemployment. This would involve increasing government spending and/or lowering income tax rates. An increase in government spending on training programmes or the construction of roads, for instance, will create jobs and so help to lower unemployment. Higher incomes from rising levels of employment are likely to lead to an increase in consumer spending, increasing aggregate demand in the economy. Firms are likely to employ more workers to expand production in response to the increased demand for goods and services.

| Government spending rises | → | Creation of jobs | → | Consumer incomes rise | → | Consumer spending rises | → | Aggregate demand rises | → | Firms expand production | → | Unemployment falls |

A reduction in income tax rates will mean that consumers' disposable income increases. As a result, consumer spending is likely to increase, leading to a rise in aggregate demand and a fall in unemployment.

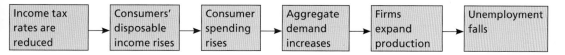

| Income tax rates are reduced | → | Consumers' disposable income rises | → | Consumer spending rises | → | Aggregate demand increases | → | Firms expand production | → | Unemployment falls |

The effectiveness of fiscal policy will depend on the extent of government involvement. The greater the spending increase or income tax cut, the greater will be the impact on aggregate demand and employment. However, in times of high unemployment it is likely that high levels of government spending will need to be financed by borrowing, resulting in an increase in government debt, which will need to be repaid in the future.

The effectiveness of monetary and fiscal policy in lowering unemployment also depends on aggregate supply in the economy. Falling aggregate supply will limit the effectiveness of monetary and fiscal policies in lowering unemployment. Rising aggregate supply, on the other hand, will increase their effectiveness as it means the economy is able to produce more goods and services over time.

 How might the building of a new bridge help to lower unemployment?

Supply-side policies

Supply-side policies increase the aggregate supply and productive capacity of the economy by improving the quantity and/or quality of its available resources.

- **Improvements in education and training**. Governments may provide education and training for unemployed workers to equip them with the knowledge and skills they need to find work. This would include retraining workers so that they have the skills needed to find jobs in other industries and sectors in response to structural unemployment.

- **A reduction in the power of trade unions**. The government could seek to reduce the power of trade unions, for example, by making it more difficult for them to take strike action. This will reduce the ability of trade unions to negotiate higher wages, thus keeping wages low in some industries. Lower wages should result in firms employing larger numbers of workers, thereby lowering unemployment.

- **Incentives for workers**. Governments can increase incentives for the unemployed to enter the workforce by lowering income tax rates, thereby increasing the disposable income they would receive from working. Similarly, structuring welfare benefits so that individuals are financially better off when taking up paid employment can also increase incentives to work. These policies are more likely to be effective when unemployment is **voluntary** rather than structural or cyclical in nature.

- **Incentives for firms**. Governments may offer subsidies or tax benefits to firms to encourage them to set up in regions suffering from high unemployment. This policy can be particularly effective if unemployment is high in a particular geographical area due to a change in the structure of the economy (**regional unemployment**). An example would be when manufacturing businesses relocate to lower-cost countries abroad.

Supply-side policies generally take time to implement and are therefore unlikely to be effective in the short term. In the long term, however, supply-side policies can have a significant impact in maintaining low unemployment.

Import restrictions

Some governments may impose trade restrictions, such as tariffs and quotas (see Unit 6.2), on goods imported from abroad. Trade restrictions have the effect of increasing the price of imports, thus making locally produced goods more competitive and helping to safeguard jobs in domestic industries.

CASE STUDY   Youth unemployment in South Africa

The youth unemployment rate is the number of unemployed 15–24-year-olds expressed as a percentage of the youth labour force. According to OECD data, in 2017 South Africa faced the highest youth unemployment in the world with a youth unemployment rate of 53.3%.

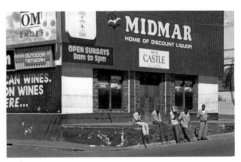

Unemployed youth miss out on a critical stage in their career development. Young people in employment gain various benefits including confidence, discipline, work ethics and the interpersonal communication skills needed throughout life.

Should South Africa's trend of high youth unemployment continue it could lead to increased social inequality, an underperforming economy, emigration of educated youth and eventually falling tax revenues for the government in the future.

1 Why do young people have difficulty finding employment?

2 What are two consequences of youth unemployment mentioned in the extract?

Applying

Project work

Using the internet, find evidence for one of the types of unemployment – frictional, seasonal, technological, structural or cyclical. This could be a newspaper article or supporting data in the form of a chart or table. Write a paragraph explaining the type of unemployment, with reference to the information in the newspaper article or supporting data.

Knowledge check questions

1 Define unemployment. [2]

2 Define full employment. [2]

3 Describe the **two** measures used to measure unemployment. [4]

4 Describe **three** different types of unemployment. [6]

5 Explain the effects of unemployment on an economy. [6]

6 Analyse how a government could use supply-side policy to reduce unemployment. [6]

7 (E) Discuss whether an increase in government spending will always reduce unemployment. [8]

Check your progress

Read the unit objectives below and reflect on your progress in each.

	I struggle with this and need more practice.
	I can do this reasonably well.
	I can do this with confidence.

- Define employment, unemployment and full employment.
- Describe the changing patterns and level of employment.
- Explain how unemployment is measured – claimant count and labour force survey.
- State the formula for the unemployment rate.
- Describe the causes of unemployment.
- Describe the types of unemployment – frictional, structural and cyclical.
- Explain the consequences of unemployment for individuals, firms and the economy as a whole.
- Analyse the range of policies available to reduce unemployment and discuss how effective they might be.

Inflation and deflation

Learning objectives

By the end of this unit, you should be able to:

- define inflation and deflation
- describe how inflation is measured using the consumer prices index (CPI)
- explain the causes of inflation: demand-pull and cost-push
- explain the causes of deflation: demand-side and supply-side
- describe the consequences of inflation and deflation for consumers, workers, savers, lenders, firms and the economy as a whole
- analyse the range of policies available to control inflation and deflation
- analyse policies to control inflation and deflation and discuss how effective they might be for different countries.

Starting point

Answer these questions in pairs:

1. If all consumers suddenly receive more money, what is likely to happen to their demand for goods and services?

2. How might firms respond to this change in demand for goods and services?

3. What might be the consequences for the level of prices in the economy?

Exploring

Discuss these questions in pairs:

1. What goods and services do you spend your money on?

2. How have the prices of these goods and services changed over time?

3. Why might businesses increase or decrease their prices?

Developing

What is inflation and deflation?

Inflation is the sustained rise in the general level of prices of goods and services in an economy over time. This does not mean that the prices of *all* goods and services are increasing. The prices of some goods, such as flat screen TVs, may in fact be falling. Inflation occurs when the prices of goods and services in an economy are rising *on average* over an extended period of time. **Deflation**, on the other hand, is the sustained fall in the general level of prices of goods and services in an economy over time.

How are inflation and deflation measured?

Changes in the general price level are measured using the **consumer prices index (CPI)**. From the CPI it is possible to calculate the inflation rate, the annual percentage change in the general price level of an economy. The CPI is a **weighted price index**. It is constructed using the process outlined in the table below.

Key terms

Deflation – the sustained fall in the general level of prices of goods and services in an economy over time

Consumer prices index (CPI) – a measure of the changes in the prices of a selection of goods and services normally purchased by a typical (ordinary) household

Weighted price index – an index (with a base year of 100) in which the prices of goods are weighted according to their importance

Measuring inflation	Description	Simplified example
Step 1: Household expenditure survey	Government officials randomly select a number of households from all over the country (12 000 households in the UK) to participate in a survey on their spending patterns. As part of this, all members in each household are asked to record their daily spending over a month.	The government of Country A conducts a household expenditure survey to determine how households spend their income.
Step 2: Basket of goods	From the survey results, the government is able to identify the goods and services normally purchased by a typical (ordinary) household. These items are referred to as the **basket of goods**. There are over 700 items in the basket of goods in the UK.	From the survey, the government of Country A determines that a typical household spends their income on a basket of four items: food, clothing, transport and furniture.
Step 3: Collection price data	Each month, price collectors gather data on the prices of each of the items in the basket of goods from different retail outlets throughout the country and online. In total, about 180 000 prices are collected each month in the UK.	Price collectors gather data on the prices of each of the items in the basket of goods. Their findings show the following price changes from the previous year:

Item	Price change
Food	+10% (rise)
Clothing	−20% (fall)
Transport	+10% (rise)
Furniture	+30% (rise)

Measuring inflation	Description	Simplified example
Step 4: Weights assigned to each item in the basket of goods	From the household expenditure survey, government officials are able to determine **weightings** for each of the items in the basket of goods. The more important the item, the higher the weighting. For example, households in the UK tend to spend more of their income on transport than on furniture. Transport therefore receives a higher weighting than furniture – a change in the price of transport will affect the typical household more than a change in the price of furniture.	From the household expenditure survey, the government of Country A determines the following weightings from analysing household spending patterns: **Item** — **Weighting** Food — 0.4 Clothing — 0.2 Transport — 0.3 Furniture — 0.1 Note that the sum of all of the weights in the basket of goods always equals 1.
Step 5: Weighted average calculated	Each month, government officials calculate the **weighted average** of the items in the basket of goods. The weighted average is the sum of the average price change for each item in the basket multiplied by its respective weighting. The final figure is the change in the general price level in the economy.	Government officials of Country A calculate the weighted average using the data above. Weighted average = Food — (+10% × 0.4)+ Clothing — (−20% × 0.2)+ Transport — (+10% × 0.3)+ Furniture — (+30% × 0.1) Weighted average = +6% The general level of prices in Country A rose by 6%.
Step 6: Convert to index form	Government officials then convert the change in the weighted average price level to index form to get the consumer prices index (CPI). To do this, they select a **base year** which is equal to 100 index points. From this, they are able to express the percentage change in the price level between two points in time as an index number.	The government of Country A converts the weighted average to index form to get the consumer prices index (CPI). They do this by making Year 1 the base year = 100. The current year is Year 2. **CPI** Year 1 — 100 Year 2 — 106 The change in prices between Year 1 and Year 2 was an increase of six index points or 6%.

1 A simple average weights all items equally. Calculate the simple average using the price changes given in Step 5 above and compare this figure to the weighted average. Why does the weighted average provide a more accurate indication of inflation?

Key terms

Basket of goods – a selection of goods and services normally purchased by a typical (ordinary) household which is used in the calculation of the consumer prices index to measure inflation

Weighting – an indication of the importance of a good when calculating a weighted average; the more important the good, the higher the weighting it receives

Weighted average – the calculation of an average by multiplying each item by a factor indicating its importance; the total sum of the weightings in a calculation equals 1

Base year – a year which is allocated a value of 100 index points against which other years are compared

What are the causes of inflation?

Demand-pull inflation is when an increase in the general price level in an economy is caused by an increase in aggregate demand. Aggregate demand may rise for a number of reasons, including an increase in consumer spending (household consumption), business investment (the purchase of capital equipment and machinery), government spending, export revenue or because of a decrease in spending on imports (see Unit 4.3). A rise in one or more of these components will cause aggregate demand in the economy to increase, thus leading to an increase in inflation.

Cost-push inflation is when the general price level in an economy rises due to an increase in firms' production costs. Production costs may rise for a number of reasons, including an increase in the cost of raw materials, higher wages for workers or the imposition of indirect taxes. An increase in production costs would make it more expensive for firms to produce their products. As a result, firms would decrease the quantity of goods and services they supply, leading to a fall in the aggregate supply of the economy. Fewer goods being supplied in the economy would lead to a rise in the general price level, thus causing inflation.

Key terms

Demand-pull inflation – an increase in the general price level in an economy caused by an increase in aggregate demand

Cost-push inflation – an increase in the general price level in an economy due to an increase in firms' production costs

 How might an increase in the price of oil lead to inflation?

Diagrams showing demand-pull and cost-push inflation

Both demand-pull and cost-push inflation can be illustrated using aggregate demand and aggregate supply diagrams.

Demand-pull inflation

An increase in aggregate demand would shift the AD curve from AD to AD_1 in Figure 4.8.1. This would increase real GDP (real output) in the economy from Y to Y_1 and result in demand-pull inflation, raising the general price level from P to P_1.

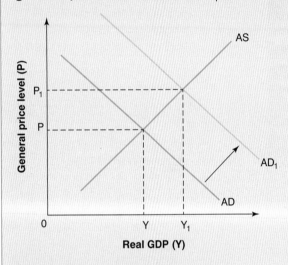

Figure 4.8.1 Demand-pull inflation

Cost-push inflation

An increase in firms' production costs due to an increase in the cost of labour, for example, would shift the AS curve from AS to AS_1 in Figure 4.8.2. This would result in cost-push inflation, increasing the general price level from P to P_1. The fall in aggregate supply would reduce the productive capacity of the economy, decreasing real GDP from Y to Y_1.

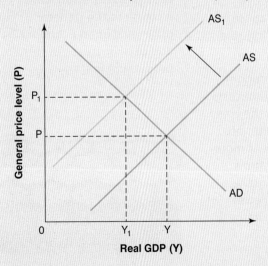

Figure 4.8.2 Cost-push inflation

What are the causes of deflation?

Deflation can be caused by either demand-side factors or supply-side factors in the economy.

On the demand side, deflation is most likely to occur in an economy during a recession when unemployment is high and incomes are falling. As a result, consumer spending and business investment are likely to decrease, causing aggregate demand in the economy to fall and putting downward pressure on prices.

On the supply side, a falling general price level can be the consequence of a decrease in costs of production. For example, the decrease in the price of a barrel of oil from $110 in 2014 to $60 in 2015 reduced raw material, transport and energy costs for producers, leading to cheaper prices for a range of goods, such as food, which tends to be costly to transport and requires a lot of plastic packaging. This is an example of a **positive supply shock**, which enables economies to supply more goods at lower prices.

As well as lowering the general price level, an increase in aggregate supply also results in lower unemployment and higher economic growth in an economy. Deflation resulting from an increase in aggregate supply, therefore, is unlikely to be a concern for a government. Deflation as a result of falling aggregate demand, on the other hand, can be highly damaging to an economy over time and can be very difficult to recover from (see consequences of deflation below).

Key term

Positive supply shock – a sudden increase in aggregate supply in an economy, such as a sudden fall in oil prices

3. What happens to the quantity of goods and services a consumer can buy with their income during periods of deflation?

Diagrams showing deflation

Deflation caused by a fall in aggregate demand

The fall in aggregate demand can be shown as a shift of the AD curve from AD to AD_1 in Figure 4.8.3, leading to a decrease in real GDP from Y to Y_1 and a fall in the general price level from P to P_1.

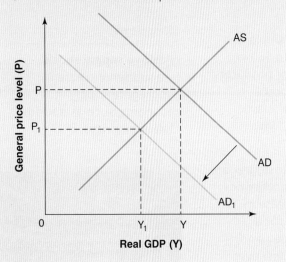

Figure 4.8.3 Deflation caused by a decrease in aggregate demand

Deflation caused by an increase in aggregate supply

An increase in aggregate supply shifts the AS curve from AS to AS_1 in Figure 4.8.4, resulting in an increase in real GDP from Y to Y_1 and a fall in the general price level from P to P_1.

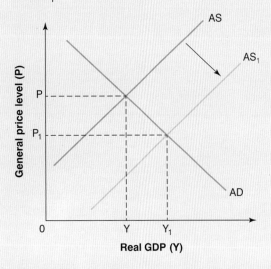

Figure 4.8.4 Deflation caused by an increase in aggregate supply

4   How will a fall in inflation from 5% to 1% affect the price level in an economy?

Consequences of inflation

Inflation is not always a problem for an economy. In fact, a low and stable inflation rate of around 2% or 3% per year can be an indication that aggregate demand is strong and an economy is growing at a sustainable rate. Low and stable inflation also creates certainty for businesses. As well as benefiting from gradually rising prices for their products, they are able to plan future production and investment with confidence. Knowing that the money in their wallets and bank accounts will hold its value, consumers and workers are able to plan future consumption, perhaps saving for a house or a new car. In the meantime, spending patterns tend to be relatively stable and firms benefit from steady demand for their goods and services.

However, problems can arise when inflation is high and prices are rising rapidly. At its worst, **hyperinflation** can see prices rising by hundreds, thousands or even millions of percentage points each year! High inflation creates uncertainty for consumers, workers and firms, reducing their confidence to make decisions about the future. The possible consequences of high inflation for individuals, firms and the economy as a whole are outlined below.

 5 What would happen to the value of the money in your pocket if all prices suddenly rose by 100%? Would it buy more or less?

Consequences of inflation

Consumers	In times of high inflation, consumers are likely to experience a fall in their **purchasing power**. In other words, as prices in the economy rise and the **cost of living** increases – the money that consumers have to spend buys less than it did before, as illustrated in Figure 4.8.5. Living standards of the population therefore tend to decline, particularly for low-income households, as consumers are unable to afford the same goods and services as previously.

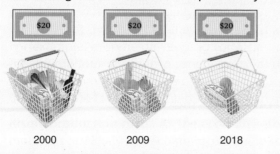

2000   2009   2018

Figure 4.8.5 The effect of inflation on consumers' purchasing power

Key terms

Purchasing power – the value of money in terms of the quantity of goods and services it can buy

Cost of living – the day-to-day living expenses incurred by an individual

| **Workers** | As prices in an economy rise, the income that workers earn buys fewer goods and services than before. That is, they suffer a fall in their real income. Some workers (usually those with skills) are able to negotiate wage increases with their employers. However, unskilled workers may find it more difficult to negotiate higher wages. As a result, they are likely to suffer a fall in their living standards as they will not be able to afford the same goods and services as previously. |

Key terms

Fixed income earners – individuals who receive a set amount of income at regular intervals (weekly or monthly), for example pensioners and those who receive welfare payments

Pensioners – individuals who are retired (no longer work) and receive a pension as their income

| **Fixed income earners** | **Fixed income earners** receive a set amount of income at regular intervals. For example, old-aged **pensioners** may receive a fixed portion of their savings to live off each month. High inflation increases the prices of basic necessities, such as food, clothing and electricity. Pensioners, in particular, spend a large proportion of their income on food and energy, so increases in the prices of these goods have a significant impact on their cost of living. As a result, they may be forced to reduce consumption of these goods. For example, a pensioner may have to cut back on heating in winter due to an increase in the price of energy, reducing their living standard. |

| **Savers** | Inflation causes the real value of savings to decrease over time. Some banks pay their customers interest, which can help to maintain the value of savings. However, interest rates are unlikely to keep pace with rising prices during periods of high inflation. Individuals and businesses may respond by reducing savings during periods of high inflation, instead holding their money in other forms such as gold, foreign currency or property, which store value more effectively. This reduces the money that is available for banks to lend out in the economy and may contribute to a fall in business investment in the economy. |

Lenders	Lenders tend to lose in times of high inflation as the money they lend out today is likely to buy fewer goods and services when it is repaid in the future.
Borrowers	Borrowers tend to gain in times of high inflation as the money they borrow buys more today than it will when they pay it back in the future.
Firms	High inflation may require firms to make frequent adjustments to the prices of the products they sell. The costs incurred by firms in changing their prices are called **menu costs**. Menu costs can be significant during periods of high inflation. They may include the costs involved in deciding what prices to charge, updating price lists, printing and replacing price tags, keeping up with competitors' prices, printing and distributing new catalogues (or menus) and advertising new prices.

During periods of high inflation, businesses try to hold as little cash as possible. Instead they may seek to hold money in other forms, such as interest-bearing bank accounts, which offer a better store of value. Rising prices of raw materials may also mean that businesses have to spend time searching for suppliers with the cheapest prices. The costs incurred by a business in 'shopping around' are called **shoe leather costs**, as the continual searching when inflation is high wears out the leather on their shoes!

Workers may demand higher wages in periods of high inflation when their living costs are rising. Higher wages increase firms' production costs. Some of this increase in costs may be passed on to consumers in the form of higher prices, thus contributing to higher cost-push inflation. This could lead to the **wage–price spiral** effect on inflation shown in Figure 4.8.6.

Key terms
....

Menu costs – the costs incurred by firms in changing their prices

Shoe leather costs – the costs incurred by a business in searching for the best prices from suppliers

Wage–price spiral – the inflationary cycle of higher wages, leading to higher production costs, which in turn leads to higher prices and living costs, which lead again to higher wages, and so on

Figure 4.8.6 The wage–price spiral of inflation

The economy   High inflation increases the general level of prices in a country, including the prices of its exports. As a result, exports become less competitive in overseas markets, leading to a fall in sales. In response to this, exporters may cut back production, which could result in unemployment in export industries and a slowdown in the economic growth of the country.

High inflation increases the prices of goods and services produced domestically, making imports more competitive. This may encourage some consumers to purchase fewer locally produced goods, instead turning to imports, which are now relatively cheaper. Some domestic producers may therefore experience a fall in sales, which may lead to reduced production, higher unemployment and a fall in economic growth.

High inflation creates uncertainty in an economy. Producers, unable to accurately predict future costs and revenues, may delay planned investment and expansion. Multinational companies may also be reluctant to set up operations in countries suffering from high inflation because of the economic uncertainty it creates. As a result, investment in the economy is likely to fall, resulting in a fall in aggregate demand and reduced economic growth.

6 Is it better for an individual to hold their money in the form of cash or gold during periods of high inflation? Why?

CASE STUDY   **Hyperinflation in Venezuela**

Venezuela's consumer price inflation rose to a staggering 254.9% in 2016. Problems started in 2014 when the price of oil fell sharply, significantly reducing Venezuela's export revenue, 95% of which came from oil exports. As a result of the decline in its oil revenue, the Venezuelan government turned to the printing of money to service debt obligations, cover operating expenses and fund its massive welfare schemes.

The increase in the money supply from the printing of money caused the general level of prices in the economy to rise. Rather than tighten monetary policy, the government continued printing money to finance its spending, placing more upward pressure on prices. As a result, consumers, expecting prices to rise, began stockpiling goods to avoid paying higher prices later. This led to demand-pull inflation which spiralled into hyperinflation. The stockpiling and hoarding of goods also created shortages of even perishable items, like bread and milk.

As prices continued to rise rapidly, people lost their life savings as cash became worthless. Banks and lenders went bankrupt as their loans lost value and people stopped making deposits. The value of the Bolivar plummeted in foreign exchange markets, sending importers out of business, as the cost of foreign goods skyrocketed. Unemployment rose as companies shut down. Government tax revenues also fell, preventing it from providing basic services.

IMF projects the inflation rate to touch 720.5% in 2017, leading to hyperinflation of 2068% in 2018 and 4684% by 2022.

1 How has the printing of money led to hyperinflation in Venezuela?

2 What are two consequences of inflation mentioned in the extract?

Consequences of deflation

Deflation resulting from decreasing costs of production is generally beneficial for an economy. Lower costs can help to make domestic firms more competitive, leading to an increase in sales of exports abroad. Consumers are also likely to purchase fewer imports, instead choosing to consume locally produced goods at relatively cheaper prices. Consumers will also experience an increase in their **purchasing power**, enabling them to increase consumption and improve their standards of living. With higher demand for products both domestically and abroad, firms are likely to expand production, leading to increased employment and stronger economic growth.

Deflation resulting from a fall in aggregate demand, on the other hand, can be a serious problem for an economy.

The consequences of deflation for different groups are shown in the table below.

Consequences of deflation caused by a fall in aggregate damand

Consumers	If consumers expect the prices of goods and services to be cheaper in the future, they may choose to delay their consumption of some goods and services until a future date. The effect of this would be a fall in consumer spending today, which would result in a fall in aggregate demand in the economy. This would lead to an increase in unemployment, reducing economic growth and worsening deflation.
Workers	When deflation is caused by falling aggregate demand, unemployment in the economy is likely to be high and job security for many of those still in work is likely to be low. Many workers, feeling uncertain about the future, may choose to save a higher proportion of their income. As a result, consumer spending in the economy may fall, leading to a further reduction in aggregate demand and worsening unemployment and deflation.
Savers	Deflation provides an incentive to save as the real value of money held in bank accounts will increase over time. In other words, if the general level of prices in an economy is falling, money saved today will buy more goods and services in the future. Individuals and firms may therefore save more and spend less in deflationary periods. The effect of this is a further reduction in consumption and business investment, resulting in higher unemployment, falling economic growth and worsening deflation.

Lenders	Lenders are likely to gain from deflation as the money they lend out today will buy more goods and services when it is repaid in the future.
Borrowers	Deflation provides a disincentive to borrow as money borrowed today will be worth more when it has to be repaid in the future. Individuals and firms are therefore likely to reduce borrowing, resulting in reduced consumer spending and business investment in the economy. Again, this will have the effect of lowering aggregate demand and worsening unemployment and deflation. If falling prices persist, existing debt will increase in real terms and become harder for households, firms and the government to repay.
Firms	Deflation provides an incentive for firms to increase their cash holdings when prices are falling as the value of cash increases over time. In times of deflation, therefore, firms tend to hold large sums of cash rather than invest it in the purchase of capital equipment and machinery, which is more risky. The resulting reduction in investment leads to a further decrease in aggregate demand in the economy, worsening unemployment and deflation.
The economy	Deflation makes exports cheaper relative to the goods and services of other countries. As a result, sales of exports are likely to increase, generating revenue for exporters, who are likely to respond by increasing production. The effect of this will be the creation of jobs in export industries, thereby lowering unemployment and increasing aggregate demand in the economy.
	Deflation reduces the price of locally produced goods relative to imports. Consequently, consumers are likely to switch away from consuming imports to the relatively cheaper home-produced goods. This will result in increased sales for some domestic firms, increasing aggregate demand in the economy and lowering unemployment.
	If the overall effect of deflation on the economy is falling aggregate demand, it is likely that it will result in prolonged periods of high unemployment and falling economic growth. This, in turn, is likely to put further downward pressure on the general price level in the economy, leading to a downward deflationary spiral that can be very difficult for an economy to recover from.

 7 How might consumers behave if they want to buy a new car but expect prices of cars to fall in the future because of deflation? How will this affect aggregate demand in the economy?

Policies to control inflation

Monetary policy

Contractionary monetary policy involves reducing the money supply to reduce aggregate demand in the economy. To do this, a central bank could raise interest rates, thus increasing the cost of borrowing. Consumers and firms are likely to respond by borrowing less (and saving more). Consequently, there is likely to be a reduction in consumer spending and business investment, leading to a fall in aggregate demand and a decrease in the general level of prices in the economy.

| Central bank raises interest rates | → | Cost of borrowing rises | → | Borrowing falls (savings rise) | → | Consumer spending falls | → | Business investment falls | → | Aggregate demand decreases | → | Lower inflation |

8   What effect are higher interest rates likely to have on sales of houses?

Fiscal policy

Contractionary fiscal policy can be used by governments to lower inflation. This could be achieved by either reducing government spending or increasing income tax rates. A reduction in government spending is likely to reduce the number of jobs available, thereby creating unemployment. As a result, consumer incomes will fall, leading to a reduction in consumer spending and a fall in aggregate demand. This fall in aggregate demand should have the effect of lowering inflation.

Government spending reduced	→	Fewer jobs created	→	Consumer incomes fall	→	Consumer spending falls	→	Aggregate demand falls	→	Inflation lower

An increase in income tax rates will reduce the disposable income consumers have to spend. As a result, consumer spending is likely to decrease, leading to a fall in aggregate demand, thus putting downward pressure on the general level of prices.

Income tax rates rise	→	Consumers' disposable income falls	→	Consumer spending falls	→	Aggregate demand falls	→	Lower inflation

The effectiveness of demand-side policies in lowering inflation

While monetary and fiscal policy measures may be effective in lowering inflation, the resulting fall in aggregate demand may also have undesirable consequences on an economy, including higher unemployment and reduced economic growth.

The effectiveness of demand-side policies in controlling inflation also depends on aggregate supply in the economy. As falling aggregate supply puts upward pressure on the price level, it will reduce the effectiveness of demand-side policies in controlling inflation. Rising aggregate supply, on the other hand, will increase the effectiveness of these policies in controlling inflation.

Supply-side policy

Supply-side policy seeks to increase aggregate supply by improving the quantity and/or quality of resources in the economy. Supply-side policies that may be effective in lowering inflation over the longer term include the following:

- **Investment in education and training**. A more educated and skilled labour force will increase the productivity of the economy, which may eventually lead to lower unit costs and lower prices.

- **Increased competition**. The government may choose to increase competition in domestic industries through deregulation and privatisation (see Unit 4.5). This will force domestic firms to lower their costs and prices in order to remain competitive, thus leading to an overall reduction in the general price level over time.

- **Improvements in the productivity of domestic firms**. By offering subsidies, governments can encourage firms to innovate and develop new production processes that increase productivity, leading to lower unit costs and lower prices.

Supply-side policies have the effect of increasing the productive capacity of an economy. The resulting increase in aggregate supply is likely to put downward pressure on prices, thereby helping to control inflation.

The effectiveness of supply-side policies in lowering inflation

The effects of supply-side policy tend to be seen over the longer term and are unlikely to be effective in lowering inflation in the short run. For example, there could be a **time lag** of many years before money spent on improving a country's education system results in a more highly educated and productive labour force. In the long run, however, supply-side policies can be very effective in achieving and maintaining a low and stable inflation rate. As well as helping to lower inflation, supply-side policies also lead to increased economic growth and lower unemployment, making them a particularly important policy tool for governments.

Key term

Time lag – the period of time between an economic action and when it starts to take effect

Policies to control deflation

Monetary policy

Expansionary monetary policy can be used to tackle the problem of deflation. This involves the central bank lowering interest rates in order to stimulate consumer spending and business investment in the economy. As a result, aggregate demand is likely to rise, putting upward pressure on the general level of prices.

Fiscal policy

Expansionary fiscal policy may also help to solve the problem of deflation. This involves increasing government spending and/or lowering income tax rates to increase aggregate demand and the general price level in the economy.

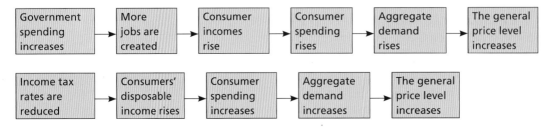

9 How might a restaurant be affected by a government's expansionary fiscal policy to tackle the problem of deflation?

Quantitative easing (QE)

The government could also combat deflation through the use of quantitative easing (QE). This involves the central bank increasing the money supply by printing new money and injecting it into the economy (see Unit 4.4). With money more accessible, consumer spending and business investment are likely to increase. Consequently, aggregate demand in the economy should rise, leading to increased economic growth, low unemployment and upward pressure on the general price level.

| Central bank creates (prints) new money and injects it into the economy | → | Money supply increases | → | Consumer spending rises | → | Business investment rises | → | Aggregate demand increases | → | The general price level increases |

The effectiveness of policies to control deflation

The effectiveness of policies to control deflation depends on levels of consumer confidence and business confidence in an economy. If confidence in the economy is low and consumers and businesses feel pessimistic about the future, they will be reluctant to borrow and spend, preferring instead to save. As a result, the effectiveness of policies to control deflation will be significantly reduced. However, if consumers and businesses feel relatively optimistic about the future, they are more likely to spend and invest in response to government policy measures, thus putting upward pressure on prices.

Applying

Project work

Using the internet, research a country that is experiencing high inflation or deflation and answer the questions below.

1. What is the name of the country?

2. What is its current inflation rate?

3. What is causing the general price level to rise/fall?

4. How has the inflation/deflation affected individuals and firms in the country?

Summarise your findings in the form of a one-page report. Be ready to share your research with your classmates in your next lesson.

Knowledge check questions

1 Define inflation.   [2]

2 Define deflation.   [2]

3 Explain how inflation is measured.   [4]

4 Explain **two** causes of inflation.   [4]

5 Explain **two** causes of deflation.   [4]

6 Analyse the impact of inflation on firms.   [6]

7 (E) Discuss whether deflation is always harmful to an economy.   [8]

Check your progress

Read the unit objectives below and reflect on your progress in each.

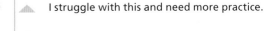 I struggle with this and need more practice.

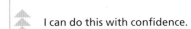 I can do this reasonably well.

I can do this with confidence.

• Define inflation and deflation.

• Describe how inflation is measured using the consumer prices index (CPI).

• Explain the causes of inflation: demand-pull and cost-push.

• Explain the causes of deflation: demand-side and supply-side.

• Describe the consequences of inflation and deflation for consumers, workers, savers, lenders, firms and the economy as a whole.

• Analyse the range of policies available to control inflation and deflation.

• Analyse policies to control inflation and deflation and discuss how effective they might be for different countries.

Chapter review

Multiple-choice questions

1   A government uses tax revenue to produce goods and services. Which types of goods and services is it **least** likely to produce?

   A   consumer goods   **B**   merit goods

   C   public goods   **D**   public services

2   A government wants to improve the economy. Which is **least** likely to be an aim of government policy?

   A   balance of payments deficit   **B**   economic growth

   C   full employment   **D**   price stability

3   A government decides to use expansionary fiscal policy to achieve higher economic growth. What is a **likely** disadvantage of this?

   A   a fall in the living standards of the population

   B   a more equal distribution of income

   C   an increase in the cost of living

   D   higher unemployment

4   A government decides to decrease spending and raise interest rates. Which aims might it be trying to achieve?

   A   balance of payments stability and price stability

   B   balance of payments surplus and full employment

   C   economic growth and redistribution of income

   D   price stability and full employment

5   A government wants to use a supply-side policy to increase the productive potential of the economy. Which policy might it use?

   A   decrease interest rates   **B**   impose higher taxes on imports

   C   increase income taxes   **D**   reduce the power of trade unions

6   A government decides to subsidise technological development in order to stimulate investment by firms. How might this be described?

   A   as fiscal and monetary policy   **B**   as fiscal and supply-side policy

   C   as fiscal, monetary and supply-side policy   **D**   as monetary and supply-side policy

7   A government uses a progressive system to tax workers' income. Which **best** describes a progressive tax?

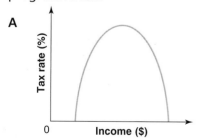

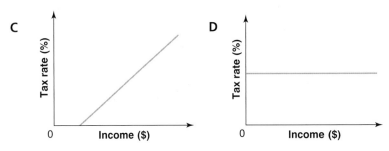

8 A government increases the highest rate of income tax from 38% to 40% and increases the tax on food. How do these changes affect the regressive nature of the tax system?

	Higher income tax	**Higher food tax**
A	less regressive	less regressive
B	less regressive	more regressive
C	more regressive	less regressive
D	more regressive	more regressive

9 A government subsidises the production of rice. What is **likely** to increase?

A the cost of producing rice   **B** the demand for rice at every price

C the price of rice   **D** the supply of rice at every price

10 The diagram shows the imposition of a tax of $U on a good. Which area represents the incidence of the tax on the consumer?

A RSTW

B RSVU

C RSXW

D WTUV

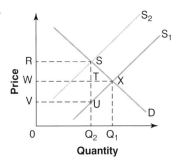

Structured questions

1 **The Australian economy**

One of the largest mixed economies in the world, Australia has experienced over two decades of positive economic growth, low inflation and low unemployment. This is largely due to two factors:

- **Structural reforms** – throughout the 1980s and 1990s the Australian government implemented a range of structural reforms, including the privatisation of the telecommunications, electricity, water, road and rail; the removal of tariffs (taxes on imports); the lowering of income tax rates and the deregulation of industries, including domestic aviation.

- **Strong demand for exports** – Australia has experienced strong demand for its mineral and energy resources, especially iron ore (used to make steel), coal and uranium. Demand was particularly high from China throughout much of the 2000s and early 2010s as it required a steady supply of mineral and energy resources to support its rapidly growing economy.

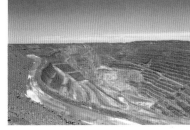

In 2012, the Australian government introduced a Minerals Resource Rent Tax (MRRT) of 30% on the profits generated by large mining firms from the production of iron ore and coal. The additional revenue raised from the MRRT enabled the government to reduce corporate tax rates paid by small businesses in other industries throughout the economy. The Australian government also has regulations in place to control the activities of mining firms, including restrictions on the dumping of waste and the location of mining sites.

(a) Identify **two** aims of the Australian government mentioned in the extract. [2]

(b) Using an example from the extract, explain what is meant by supply-side policy. [3]

(c) Using information from the extract, explain **two** possible reasons why inflation in Australia has remained relatively low. [4]

(d) Explain **two** possible reasons why the Australian government imposed the MRRT. [4]

(e) Define the term direct tax. [2]

(f) Analyse the effect of the imposition of the MRRT on producers. [5]

(g) Analyse how strong demand for minerals impacted Australia's economic growth. [4]

(h) Discuss whether government should always regulate producers. [6]

2   The macroeconomic aims of the New Zealand government include sustainable economic growth, full employment and price stability. Monetary policy is controlled by the central bank, the Reserve Bank of New Zealand (RBNZ), which aims to maintain inflation between 2% and 3%. By targeting low and stable inflation the RBNZ seeks to encourage sustainable long-run economic growth.

(a) Define monetary policy. [2]

(b) Explain **two** macroeconomic aims of government. [4]

(c) Analyse how a change in interest rates could lead to low inflation. [6]

(d) Discuss whether there is likely to be a conflict between the aims of low inflation and economic growth. [8]

3   In 2018, the government of the United Arab Emirates (UAE) introduced a 5% value added tax (VAT) on most goods and services. The VAT was introduced to provide the government with a new source of revenue to reduce its dependence on revenue earned from oil exports. The revenue generated from the VAT is being used to improve public services, such as education, for the population.

(a) Define indirect tax. [2]

(b) Using a demand and supply diagram, show how the imposition of an indirect tax impacts the equilibrium price and quantity of a good. [4]

(c) Analyse how an increase in VAT might affect the distribution of income within an economy. [6]

(d) Discuss whether education should be provided by the public or private sector. [8]

4   In 2014, the European Central Bank (ECB) cut interest rates and began a programme of quantitative easing (QE) to increase economic growth and avoid deflation.

(a) Define deflation. [2]

(b) Explain how inflation is measured. [4]

(c) Analyse how lower interest rates could lead to higher economic growth. [6]

(d) Discuss whether deflation is always harmful to an economy. [8]

5 Economic development

Economic development encompasses not only economic growth but also other factors affecting the wellbeing of a population. These factors include the quality of education, healthcare, the environment and the level of income equality. In this chapter, you will begin by looking at the various ways of comparing living standards between countries, before examining the problem of poverty in developing and developed economies and how it can be alleviated. You will go on to compare populations between countries in terms of growth, size and age, and gender distribution. By the end of this chapter, you should have a clear understanding of the characteristics of developing and developed countries and the key differences between them.

5.1 Living standards

5.2 Poverty

5.3 Population

5.4 Differences in economic development between countries

Living standards

Learning objectives

By the end of this unit, you should be able to:

- identify indicators of living standards, including real GDP per head and the human development index (HDI)
- describe the components of real GDP per head and HDI
- explain the advantages and disadvantages of real GDP per head and HDI
- analyse the reasons for differences in living standards and income distribution within and between countries.

Starting point

Answer these questions in pairs:

1 What is real GDP?

2 What does real GDP per head measure?

3 What are the differences between the primary, secondary and tertiary sectors in an economy?

Exploring

Discuss these questions in pairs:

1 What makes you happy?

2 What factors influence an individual's wellbeing and quality of life?

3 Which of these factors could the government help to provide?

Developing

Indicators of living standards

Living standards refer to the general economic wealth, wellbeing and quality of life of a country's population. Two economic indicators that are commonly used to measure living standards within a country are real GDP per head and the **human development index (HDI)**.

Key term

Human development index (HDI) – a measure of human development and wellbeing that takes into account the three dimensions of living standards, health and education

Real GDP per head

As discussed in Unit 4.6, real GDP per head (real GDP per capita) is the real GDP of the country averaged across its population. It can be calculated using the following formula:

$$\text{real GDP per head} = \frac{\text{real GDP}}{\text{population}}$$

In general, the higher the GDP per head, the higher are the living standards within a country. According to the data in the table below, Luxembourg was the richest country in 2015, with a real GDP per head of $107 036, while Burundi was the poorest, with a real GDP per head of only $207.

Real GDP per head by country in 2015

Country	Real GDP per head (US$)	Country	Real GDP per head (US$)	Country	Real GDP per head (US$)
Luxembourg	107 036	Brunei Darussalam	32 226	Sri Lanka	3 638
Norway	89 591	Korea, Rep.	25 023	Nigeria	2 535
Qatar	74 687	Malaysia	10 878	India	1 752
Australia	54 688	Argentina	10 502	Lesotho	1 370
Singapore	51 855	Mexico	9 511	Pakistan	1 143
USA	51 638	Mauritius	9 469	Kenya	1 134
Japan	47 150	South Africa	7 586	Bangladesh	973
UK	41 183	Maldives	7 222	Afghanistan	620
UAE	39 313	China	6 498	Ethiopia	486
New Zealand	36 801	Thailand	5 776	Liberia	367
Hong Kong	36 173	Indonesia	3 834	Burundi	207

Source: World Bank national accounts data, and OECD National Accounts data files

Real GDP per head is useful because it provides an indication of the economic wealth and living standards of a population in a country. Furthermore, the information used to calculate real GDP per head is available for all countries. However, it has a number of drawbacks that limit its accuracy as an indicator of living standards.

Limitations of real GDP per head as a measure of living standards

1. Real GDP per head ignores factors other than income that may contribute to improved living standards, such as access to healthcare, education and clean water, levels of environmental pollution and political freedom.

2. As the value for real GDP is an average, it gives no indication as to how the income of a country is distributed (spread) across the population. A large gap between rich and poor may mean a

significant number of people receive incomes well below the average. In such cases, there would be a large proportion of the population with much lower living standards than the value for real GDP per head indicates.

3. The living standards of a country will depend on the types of goods and services a country is producing. If a country is producing consumer goods such as cars and smartphones, healthcare or education, the living standards of the population are likely to be rising. The production of nuclear weapons and cigarettes, on the other hand, may not contribute to living standards in the same way despite a high figure for real GDP per head.

4. Some countries have large informal economies in which transactions are not officially recorded (see Unit 4.7). As goods and services produced in the informal economy will not be included in GDP, the calculation for real GDP per head in a country with a large informal economy may underestimate the average income of a population.

Key term

Gross national income (GNI) – total income earned by the residents of a country (individuals and businesses) at home and abroad

Gross national income per head – gross national income averaged across the population of a country (GNI per head = GNI/population)

Summary of the advantages and disadvantages of using real GDP per head as an indicator of living standards

Advantages	Disadvantages
It provides a useful indication of the living standards of people within a country.	It only measures average income and ignores other factors that may affect living standards.
It is calculated using income, which is a good indicator of living standards.	It gives no indication as to how income is distributed within a country.
It is calculated using data that is available and relatively easy to access.	It does not take into account the types of goods and services that are produced.
It can be used to compare living standards between countries as all countries record real GDP and population.	A large informal economy may affect the accuracy of the figure for a country's GDP.

Human development index (HDI)

An alternative measure of the living standards of the population of a country is provided by the human development index (HDI). Developed by the United Nations (UN), the HDI is a broader measure of human development than real GDP per head. It measures a country's performance in three key dimensions. These are shown in the following table.

HDI dimensions

Dimension	Economic indicator	Explanation	Example
Living standards	Gross national income per head	Measured by the average income per person	China's gross national income per head was estimated to be $13 345 in 2017 by the UNDP (based on 2011 data).
Health	Life expectancy	Measured by **life expectancy** at birth	According to UNDP data, China's life expectancy at birth was 76 years in 2017.

Dimension	Economic indicator	Explanation	Example
Education	Years in schooling	Measured by the average number of years an adult (aged 25 or over) has spent in schools and the number of years a child is expected to spend in schools from the age of 5 years	In China, the average number of years in schooling for individuals aged 25 years and over in 2015 was 7.6. According to UNDP data, the number of years of schooling a child could expect to receive at the age of 5 in 2017 was 13.5.

(Source: United Nations Development Programme (UNDP) Human Development Reports)

Each of the three dimensions are weighted according to their overall contribution to human development and combined into a single HDI value of between 0 and 1, with 0 being the lowest level of human development and 1 being the highest. According to the data provided in the table below, China had a HDI value of 0.738, giving it an overall ranking of 90th in the world in 2015. Norway topped the HDI rankings in 2015 with a value of 0.949, while the Central African Republic had the lowest HDI with a value of 0.352, placing it 188th in the world.

Key term

Life expectancy – the number of years a person in a country is expected to live

HDI rankings and values for selected countries in 2015

HDI rank	Country	HDI value	HDI rank	Country	HDI value
Very high human development			**Medium human development**		
1	Norway	0.949	115	Vietnam	0.683
5	Singapore	0.925	119	South Africa	0.666
13	New Zealand	0.915	131	India	0.624
18	Korea (Republic of)	0.901	139	Bangladesh	0.579
30	Brunei Darussalam	0.865	146	Kenya	0.555
High human development			**Low human development**		
59	Malaysia	0.789	152	Nigeria	0.527
73	Sri Lanka	0.766	160	Lesotho	0.497
79	Brazil	0.754	176	Congo (Democratic Republic of the)	0.435
87	Thailand	0.740	184	Burundi	0.404
90	China	0.738	188	Central African Republic	0.352

Source: UNDP

1 Research current HDI rankings on the internet. Which countries in the above table have improved their ranking?

It is important to remember that the HDI only measures a small part of what makes up human development and wellbeing. There are other important factors that contribute to people's overall living standards and quality of life, including the level of inequality, poverty, safety and political freedom within a country.

Summary of the advantages and disadvantages of using the HDI as an indicator of living standards

Advantages	Disadvantages
The HDI provides a wider measure of human development than real GDP per head, covering three dimensions: living standards, health and education.	The HDI does not take into account all factors affecting living standards. Factors such as the distribution of income, levels of pollution, water quality, security and internet access are ignored by the HDI.
As the HDI is produced by the UN, data is collected objectively and can be trusted to be accurate.	The weightings (importance) placed on each of the three dimensions may not accurately reflect their actual contribution to overall living standards in a country.

Extension topic

An alternative measure of living standards – the multidimensional poverty index (MPI)

The MPI measures the wellbeing of an individual across the three dimensions of health, education and living standards.

Dimension	Indicator
Health	Measured by adequate *nutrition* and *child mortality* (the death of a sibling under the age of 5 years)
Education	Measured by *years in school* and *attendance at school*
Living standards	Measured by access to *cooking fuel*, *sanitation*, *clean water*, *electricity*, adequate *housing* and *possessions*, such as a radio, TV, bicycle or motorcycle

An individual is considered to be multidimensionally poor if they are deprived (lacking) in more than one of the above indicators.

Why do living standards and income distribution differ *within* countries?

Economic growth unevenly spread

It is unlikely that the higher incomes and wealth that come with economic growth will reach all members of a country's population equally. Individuals with skills and the owners of the factors of production, such as land and capital, tend to gain a larger share of increased income and wealth than those who have limited skills and only their labour with which to generate income. In India, for example, the richest 1% of the country's population owned 53% of the country's wealth in 2016, up from 36.8% in 2000, despite significant economic growth over this period. In contrast, in 2016, the poorest half of India's population owned just 4.1% of national wealth.

Employment by sector

Individuals employed in agriculture (primary sector) tend to receive lower wages than those employed in manufacturing (secondary sector) and services (tertiary sector). This is because jobs in agriculture, particularly in developing countries, are generally lower skilled than those in manufacturing and services. Thus, there is a greater supply of people able to fill job vacancies, leading to lower wages and lower living standards. Rural communities that are dependent on the agricultural sector for employment and food are also vulnerable to drought, crop failure and exploitation, all of which may result in economic hardship and lower living standards.

Education and training

Limited access to quality education can also lead to differences in living standards and income distribution. Education for children, particularly in rural areas, may not be affordable or easily accessible in some countries. Those unable to afford or access quality education will have fewer opportunities to earn higher incomes and improve their living standards relative to others in society.

2 Compare photos A and B. What might explain the differences in living standards between these two groups of children now and in the future?

Photo A

Government policy

The extent of the difference in the distribution of wealth and living standards will depend on the tax and welfare system in place within a country. A progressive tax system (see Unit 4.3) will help to redistribute income more equally by taking money from the rich in the form of taxes and giving it to the poor in the form of welfare payments, such as pensions and unemployment benefits. Governments may also provide quality education and

Photo B

healthcare for all members for the population. A higher standard of education and healthcare should help the poor to access better quality jobs in the future, leading to higher incomes and improved living standards.

3 Which of these reasons explains why living standards differ within your country?

Why do living standards and income distribution differ *between* countries?

Level of economic development

Developed countries tend to have higher income, wealth and living standards than developing countries. Efficient progressive tax systems enable them to provide financial support to the poor in the form of welfare payments. Tax revenue is also allocated to the provision of quality education and healthcare for all members of the population and the development of infrastructure. A more skilled and healthier population is able to gain higher-paying jobs in services (the tertiary sector). In developing countries, on the other hand, a large proportion of the population is often employed in agriculture (the primary sector) where wages are lower.

Factor endowments

Some countries are able to generate income and wealth due to the factors of production they are endowed with (have available). For example, countries like Saudi Arabia and Brunei Darussalam are endowed with reserves of oil, much of which is exported, thus earning income for those countries. This can then be invested in improving infrastructure and essential public services.

The state of the economy

Countries suffering from unfavourable economic conditions, such as rapidly rising inflation and high unemployment, are likely to experience a fall in living standards relative to other countries. For example, in 2017, Venezuela, facing an annual inflation rate of over 400% and widespread unemployment, experienced a significant fall in real GDP and the living standards of the population. Many households were unable to access even basic necessities, including food and medicine.

The effectiveness of government

Government policies and decisions can greatly impact the economic wealth and living standards of a population. Responsible government policies that encourage trade, innovation and investment in education, healthcare and infrastructure are likely to result in higher economic growth and employment. Economic mismanagement and widespread corruption, on the other hand, are likely to lead to greater inequality and lower living standards within a population.

War and conflict

Countries engaged in war and violent conflict are unlikely to have the resources available to invest in improving the welfare of their citizens. For example, Burundi, the country with the world's lowest GDP per head ($207) and an HDI of only 0.404 in 2015, has a history of civil war, with devastating effects on the wellbeing of the country's population.

 4 What economic policies could a government use to improve living standards?

CASE STUDY   ## Sri Lanka's human development

In 2015, Sri Lanka's HDI value was 0.766, giving it a ranking of 73 out of 188 countries and placing it in the high human development category. The Maldives, with an HDI value of 0.701 and a ranking of 105, was the only other South Asian Association for Regional Development (SAARD) country to make it into this category. Sri Lanka's HDI value has increased an impressive 22.4% from 0.626 in 1990. Over this period, life expectancy at birth increased by 5.5 years and expected years in schooling increased by 2.7 years.

	2015	1990
HDI value	0.766	0.626
HDI rank	73	–
Life expectancy at birth	75	69.5
Expected years in schooling	14.0	11.3
Average years of schooling	10.9	8.4
Gross national income (GNI) per head	$10 789	$3 639

Several factors have contributed to Sri Lanka's position in the high human development category, despite it being a developing country. These include the end of civil war in 2009, the provision of free education and healthcare for all citizens, a welfare system, and development programmes that provide housing, electricity, clean water and sanitation to the poor.

1. What government policies have helped Sri Lanka to be placed in the high human development category?

2. Why might Sri Lanka's HDI value not be an accurate indicator of overall living standards in the country?

> ## Applying

Project work

Using the internet, research the living standards of two countries of your choice. Compare the two countries in terms of:

a. real GDP per head

b. HDI values

c. other factors affecting living standards, such as access to education, healthcare, clean water, environment and sanitation.

Which country has the higher standard of living? Write a paragraph explaining the reasons for your opinion.

(E) Create your own indicator of living standards that is designed to overcome some of the limitations of the HDI.

Knowledge check questions

1 Define GDP per capita. [2]

2 Explain **two** advantages of using the human development index (HDI) as a measure of living standards in a country. [4]

3 Explain **two** reasons why living standards might differ within a country. [4]

4 Explain **two** reasons why living standards might differ between countries. [4]

5 Analyse how investment in education could improve living standards within a country. [6]

6 (E) Discuss whether real GDP per head is the best measure of living standards. [8]

Check your progress

Read the unit objectives below and reflect on your progress in each.

- Identify indicators of living standards, including real GDP per head and the human development index (HDI).

- Describe the components of real GDP per head and HDI.

- Explain the advantages and disadvantages of real GDP per head and HDI.

- Analyse the reasons for differences in living standards and income distribution within and between countries.

▲	I struggle with this and need more practice.
▲	I can do this reasonably well.
▲	I can do this with confidence.

Poverty

Learning objectives

By the end of this unit, you should be able to:

- define absolute poverty and relative poverty
- explain the difference between absolute poverty and relative poverty
- describe the main causes of poverty, including unemployment, low wages, illness and age
- analyse the policies to alleviate poverty and redistribute income, including those promoting economic growth, improved education, more generous state benefits, progressive taxation, and national minimum wage.

Starting point

Answer these questions in pairs:

1. What are the disadvantages of a market economy?

2. What are the differences between progressive, regressive and proportional taxation?

3. What policies could a government use to lower unemployment?

Exploring

Discuss these questions in pairs:

1. Why might people find themselves without enough money for food or housing?

2. What can governments do to prevent hunger and inadequate housing?

3. To what extent is a large income and wealth gap between the rich and poor undesirable for an economy?

Developing

What is poverty?

What would you do if you did not have enough money for food or a place to sleep? You would probably ask your parents. Throughout your life, your parents, or perhaps your government, might provide you with a 'safety net' if you ever find yourself in this situation. However, not everyone in the world who is hungry and homeless is lucky enough to have a safety net.

Poverty is an obstacle which prevents individuals from enjoying opportunities – and thus a decent quality of life – that should be available to everyone. These opportunities include food, clothing, shelter, a quality education, healthcare, clean drinking water, sanitation and other basic services.

There are two broad types of poverty:

- **Absolute poverty** is a situation in which an individual does not have enough income to satisfy even their most basic needs, such as food, clothing, shelter, safe drinking water, sanitation, healthcare and education. For example, an individual who is hungry and malnourished because they cannot afford to buy food, or who is homeless, is said to be living in absolute poverty. The World Bank has set the global line for extreme (absolute) poverty at US$1.90 per day (revised up from US$1.25 in October 2015). In 2013, 10.7% of the world's population (approximately 767 million people) lived below the poverty line on less than US$1.90 per day.

- **Relative poverty** is a situation in which an individual does not have enough income to purchase the goods and services normally consumed by other members of the society in which they live. For example, an individual who cannot afford a mobile phone or internet access when other people in their country normally possess these products, would be considered to be living in relative poverty.

The causes of poverty

Unemployment

One of the main causes of both absolute and relative poverty is unemployment. Individuals who are unemployed receive no income from work. As a result, they may not have enough money for even their most basic needs, such as food and shelter. In some countries, governments pay welfare benefits to the unemployed, which may be enough to keep them out of absolute poverty. In other countries, unemployed people may rely on relatives or charities for the money they need to meet their basic needs.

Low wages

Unskilled workers may be forced to accept low wages, making it difficult for them to escape relative poverty. Opportunities for quality education and training are limited in many countries, so the poorer members of the population may be unable to develop the knowledge and skills they need to gain higher-paying jobs and raise themselves out of poverty.

Key terms

Absolute poverty – a situation in which an individual does not have enough income to satisfy their most basic needs of food, clean water, clothing, shelter, education and healthcare

Relative poverty – a situation in which an individual does not have enough income to buy the goods and services normally consumed by members of the society in which they live

Old age

The elderly are particularly vulnerable to poverty as they are often unable to work due to old age, disability, sickness or discrimination. In some countries, elderly people have traditionally relied on their children to look after and provide for them in their old age rather than saving for their retirements. However, as increasing numbers of young people travel to cities in search of work, their elderly parents are often left to look after themselves with little or no financial assistance from their children, who may also struggle economically. Ageing populations in many countries are contributing to the rise of poverty among the older members of the population.

Sickness and disability

Some people are unable to work due to long-term illness or disability. Without financial support from the government, relatives or charities, sick and disabled people may be unable to earn any income and may fall into poverty.

Increasing household debt

Increasing household debt due to excessive spending on consumer goods has led to an increase in relative poverty in many countries. Bombarded with advertisements for new cars, televisions and smartphones, many people are borrowing money to purchase goods they cannot afford. Burdened with debt and struggling to repay the money they owe, individuals have less to spend, leading to an increase in relative poverty.

Lack of opportunities in rural regions

The majority of people suffering from absolute poverty in the world live in rural areas and are employed in the agricultural sector. Farmers in developing countries, often burdened with large amounts of debt, are particularly vulnerable to drought, crop failure and natural disasters. In each of these situations, the income that farmers receive from their crops would be significantly reduced. As a result, farmers would face economic hardship, which may result in them (and those working for them) falling into poverty.

War and conflict

Individuals may be displaced (forced from their homes) due to war and violence. Fearing for their safety, some may flee to other countries as refugees in the hope of a better life. These people are often forced to leave all of their possessions behind and are reliant on governments, charities and organisations like the UN to provide them with basic necessities such as food, clothing and shelter. In 2017, after six years of conflict, an estimated

4.8 million Syrian refugees had fled civil war and violence in their home country, with over 3 million ending up in neighbouring Turkey. While Turkey provided Syrian refugees with free access to healthcare and education, many were poorly educated and vulnerable to exploitation.

 Which type of poverty is most applicable to your country? Why?

Policies to alleviate poverty and redistribute income

From an economic perspective, individuals in absolute poverty lack the opportunities they need to realise their full potential as productive members of society. Poverty therefore reduces the productive capacity of an economy. In extreme cases, people, including children, suffer from hunger, malnutrition and homelessness and have limited access to education, healthcare, sanitation and clean water because of their economic circumstances.

The reality is that the absolute poverty endured by over 700 million people worldwide is preventable. Through the use of appropriate policy measures, many governments have been successful in eliminating absolute poverty in their countries. Other governments, including those in sub-Saharan Africa, which has the highest rate of poverty in the world, are committed to eradicating absolute poverty in their countries by 2030 – a sustainable development goal set by the UN. Some of the policies governments use to alleviate both absolute and relative poverty are described below.

Progressive taxation

Progressive taxation is when the rich pay a higher proportion of their income in taxes than the poor (see Unit 4.3). By structuring tax systems so that they are more progressive, governments are able to redistribute income within an economy. Revenue generated from taxes imposed on the rich can also be given to the poor through the provision of welfare benefits and public services to raise their living standards and alleviate poverty.

Welfare benefits

Governments can use tax revenue to provide financial support through the payment of welfare benefits to those most at risk of falling into poverty, including the sick, disabled, elderly and the unemployed. Most developed countries including the UK have been able to eliminate absolute poverty through the provision of a welfare system. Relative poverty, however, is an ongoing problem and still very much a concern for the governments of these countries.

Education and training

Another way in which governments can combat poverty is by providing equal access to quality education, skills, training and opportunities to all members of society. With access to education and training, the poor are able to develop the knowledge and skills they need to gain higher-paying jobs, breaking the cycle of intergenerational poverty. As well as investing public funds in improving school education, governments may provide subsidies or scholarships to students from poor backgrounds to further their education.

Minimum wage legislation

Governments may impose minimum wage legislation on employers (see Unit 3.3). The legal minimum wage set by the regional government of Shanghai, China, was 19 yuan (US$2.80) per hour in 2016, while in Australia it was A$17.29 (US$13.30) per hour, the highest in the world. A legal minimum wage ensures that low-skilled workers are paid a fair wage that is enough to keep them out of absolute, but not necessarily relative, poverty.

 Why might a worker earning the legal minimum wage still suffer from relative poverty?

Job creation

Governments may seek to create jobs using demand-side policies aimed at increasing economic growth and lowering unemployment. For example, government spending on infrastructure (expansionary fiscal policy), such as the construction of new roads, may create jobs and provide incomes for workers who may otherwise be unemployed and at risk of falling into absolute or relative poverty (see Unit 4.3).

Alternatively, the government could lower interest rates (expansionary monetary policy) to alleviate poverty (see Unit 4.4). Lower interest rates reduce the cost of borrowing, encouraging increased consumption and business investment. The resulting higher economic growth and lower unemployment are likely to raise the incomes of workers in the economy, thus helping to alleviate both absolute and relative poverty.

However, the benefits of economic growth are not necessarily spread evenly throughout the economy. Some individuals may benefit from a substantial increase in their income and wealth, while the benefits to others, usually the poor, may be negligible.

Subsidies

Governments may choose to use tax revenue to subsidise basic necessities such as food and housing for the poor. As a result, these essential items are made cheaper and more affordable for the poor, preventing them from falling into absolute poverty.

In Thailand, the government subsidises school lunches at a rate of 20 baht (approximately US$0.60) per child, ensuring that all children receive at least one nutritious meal a day at school. Governments may also choose to subsidise producers, such as farmers. A subsidy to rice farmers, for example, would reduce their production costs and enable them to sell their harvested rice crops at more competitive prices. This would increase the income received by farmers, thereby helping to lift them out of poverty. It would also help farmers to continue operating, thus safeguarding jobs and the incomes of workers in the agricultural industry.

3 What would be a potential drawback of paying a subsidy to farmers?

Direct provision of essential goods and services

Many governments provide essential goods and services such as education, healthcare, sanitation, clean water and housing directly to the poor. The direct provision of education ensures that children from poor families have the opportunity to develop important skills, such as reading and writing. With improved knowledge and skills, children will have a better chance of finding well-paid employment when they become adults, raising them out of poverty. The provision of free healthcare and sanitation by the government is likely to reduce the incidence of illness and disease among the poor and increase life expectancy. With adequate healthcare, poor people are in a better position to work and earn an income, preventing them from falling into absolute poverty.

Encourage multinational companies (MNCs) to set up in a country

Governments may seek to attract MNCs into their country, for instance by offering them generous tax benefits (see Unit 6.2). This is likely to create jobs, thus lowering unemployment in the host country. As a result, incomes and living standards are likely to rise, which may lead to a reduction in absolute and relative poverty. Tax revenue generated from the operation of MNCs in the host country could also be used to fund programmes aimed at alleviating poverty, such as training and education for the poor and job creation schemes.

Educate people about how to manage their finances

Some governments introduce programmes that encourage people to live within their means (purchase only what they can afford) and save for their futures. Compulsory savings schemes may also be introduced in which a portion of an individual's income is set aside for their retirement. These initiatives may help some individuals to save, thus reducing the chance of them suffering from absolute poverty in their old age when they can no longer work.

Create new income-generating opportunities for the elderly

Unable to rely on their children or government for financial support in their old age, some elderly people in developing countries are coming up with new ways of generating income. In Thailand, for example, with encouragement from the government, enterprising elderly villagers in rural areas are earning additional income from growing mushrooms and orchids for sale in local markets.

4 Which two policies would be most effective in reducing poverty in your country? Why?

CASE STUDY **Child poverty**

A Unicef–World Bank report released in 2016 estimated that 385 million children lived in absolute poverty, surviving on less than US$1.90 per day. The majority of extremely poor children (49%) were living in sub-Saharan Africa, followed by South Asia (36%), despite strong economic growth in these regions over the previous decade.

Children living in absolute poverty suffer from hunger and malnutrition and have limited access to education and other basic services. The report found that extreme poverty restricted children's educational development and reduced their potential to work productively as adults.

The report urged governments to invest in childhood development programmes for the poor, quality schooling, clean water, good sanitation and universal healthcare. It was hoped that these policies would increase the likelihood of children accessing quality jobs as adults, breaking the widespread cycle of intergenerational poverty.

Investment in the agricultural industry was also needed in order to increase productivity and crop yields. Increased availability of food would enhance governments' ability to fight the problems of hunger and malnutrition in children.

1 What are three consequences of child poverty mentioned in the extract?

2 Describe two policies to alleviate child poverty suggested in the report. Which do you think would be most effective and why?

Applying

Project work

Imagine you are working for your country's government. Write a brief report outlining three policies the government could introduce to alleviate poverty in your country. In your report:

- identify the type(s) of poverty that exist in your country
- outline three policy actions the government could take to alleviate poverty
- say which policy you think would be best and why.

Knowledge check questions

1 Define absolute poverty.   [2]

2 Define relative poverty.   [2]

3 Explain **two** causes of poverty.   [4]

4 Analyse how lower interest rates could help to alleviate poverty.   [6]

5 (E) Discuss whether improving education is the best way to alleviate poverty.   [8]

Check your progress

Read the unit objectives below and reflect on your progress in each.

- Define absolute poverty and relative poverty.

- Explain the difference between absolute poverty and relative poverty.

- Describe the main causes of poverty, including unemployment, low wages, illness and age.

- Analyse the policies to alleviate poverty and redistribute income, including those promoting economic growth, improved education, more generous state benefits, progressive taxation, and national minimum wage.

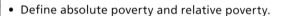 I struggle with this and need more practice.

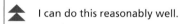 I can do this reasonably well.

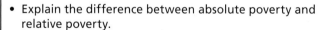 I can do this with confidence.

Population

Learning objectives

By the end of this unit, you should be able to:

- describe the factors that affect population growth, including birth rate, death rate, net migration, immigration and emigration
- analyse the reasons for different rates of population growth in different countries
- analyse how and why birth rates, death rates and net migration vary between countries
- explain the concept of an optimum population
- analyse the effects of increases and decreases in population size and changes in the age and gender distribution of a population
- describe a country's age and gender distribution from its population pyramid
- identify whether a country is developed or developing from its population pyramid.

Starting point

Answer these questions in pairs:

1 Do you know anyone who has migrated to live in another country – a friend, a relative, your teacher?

2 Why did they choose to live abroad?

3 What skills and abilities did they take with them to their new home?

4 What were the benefits and drawbacks of living abroad?

Exploring

Discuss these questions in pairs:

1 Using the pictures to help you, describe some of the reasons why people go to live in other countries.

2 What effects might this have on the economies of their home countries?

3 What effects might it have on the economies of the countries they are travelling to?

Developing

According to *World Population Prospects: The 2017 Revision* published by the United Nations (UN), the world population reached 7.6 billion in 2017 and is expected to reach 8.6 billion by 2030 and 9.8 billion by 2050. The world's population is growing by approximately 83 million people a year – over 227 000 people a day!

Factors affecting population growth

The factors that affect **population growth** are described in the following table.

Factors affecting population growth

Factor	Description
Birth rate	The **birth rate** is the number of live births for every 1000 people in a country in a year. An increase in the birth rate of a country will increase the rate of population growth, while a decrease in the birth rate will slow the rate of population growth.
Fertility rate	The **fertility rate** is the average number of live births per woman of childbearing age (between 15 and 44 years) in a country. As men cannot give birth, each woman in a country would need to have at least two children on average during their childbearing years in order to keep the population size constant. A fertility rate higher than two children per woman is likely to increase a country's population growth, while a fertility rate below two is likely to decrease it over time.
	According to UN data, the 47 poorest countries in the world had a fertility rate of 4.3 births per woman between 2010 and 2015, which corresponded to a 2.4% increase in population size each year. In contrast, the fertility rate in Europe was 1.6 births per woman during the same period.
Death rate	The **death rate** is the number of deaths for every 1000 people in a country in a year. An increase in the death rate will lead to a fall in the rate of population growth of a country, while a decrease in the death rate will raise it.

Key terms

Population growth – the change (increase or decrease) in the number of people living in a particular geographical area

Birth rate – the number of live births for every 1000 people in a country in a year

Fertility rate – the average number of children per woman of childbearing age in a country

Death rate – the number of deaths for every 1000 people in a country in a year

Factor	Description
Infant mortality rate	The **infant mortality rate** is the number of babies who die before their first birthday for every 1000 live births in a year.
Net migration	**Net migration** measures the difference between immigration and emigration. **Immigration** is the movement of people *into* a country to live permanently. **Emigration** is the movement of people *out of* a country to live permanently abroad. If the number of people emigrating from a country is greater than the number of people immigrating to a country, there is **net outward migration**, causing the country's population growth rate to decrease. **Net inward migration**, on the other hand, will cause the population growth rate of the country to increase.

Why do population growth rates differ between countries?

Population growth rates tend to increase more rapidly in developing countries (see Unit 5.4) and more slowly in developed countries. In some developed countries, the population growth rate may even be negative, meaning that its population is declining. There are a number of reasons for differences in population growth rates between countries.

Variations in birth rates

The cost of raising children

The high financial cost involved in raising and providing for children in developed countries discourages some couples from having large families. The relatively lower cost of raising children in developing countries, on the other hand, may mean that it is not a significant factor in people's decision to have children.

Subsistence farming

A **subsistence economy** is one in which people are self-sufficient, producing only enough to satisfy their own basic needs, including food, clothing and shelter, and those of their families. People in some of the poorest economies who still rely on subsistence farming may choose to have large numbers of children as they provide a valuable source of labour that can be used to provide food for the family. As countries develop and move away from subsistence farming, people may choose to have fewer children. Also, compulsory education for children, which is introduced as a country develops, may also contribute to smaller family sizes as it prevents people from using children for labour.

Key terms

Infant mortality rate – the number of babies who die before their first birthday for every 1000 live births in a year

Net migration – the difference between immigration into a country and emigration out of a country

Immigration – the movement of people into a country to reside there permanently

Emigration – the movement of people out of a country to reside permanently elsewhere

Population growth rate – the rate of change (expressed as a percentage) in the number of people residing in a country or a particular geographical area

Key knowledge

net inward migration = total immigration > total emigration

net outward migration = total immigration < total emigration

Key terms

Subsistence economy – an economy in which people are self-sufficient, producing only enough to satisfy their own basic needs, including food, clothing and shelter, and the basic needs of their families

Support for the old

In most developed countries governments provide pensions to elderly people when they reach retirement age. The pensions are usually enough to meet their basic living expenses, such as food, accommodation and electricity. However, many governments in developing countries provide little or no financial assistance to citizens who are too old to work. There is therefore no 'safety net' for people living in these countries in their old age. As a result, many choose to have large numbers of children to ensure there is someone to look after them and support them financially when they are old, thus avoiding absolute poverty.

Infant mortality rate

Due to inadequate healthcare, many of the poorest countries in the world have high infant mortality rates. According to the World Health Organization (WHO), children in developing countries are ten times more likely to die before the age of 5 years than children in developed countries. A significant number of these deaths could be prevented through the provision of safe drinking water, adequate sanitation and improved hygiene. Due to the high chance of one or more of their children dying before the age of 5 years, people in the poorest countries tend to have large families in the hope that some will live into adolescence and adulthood. At these ages, they will be old enough to work and earn an income to help provide for their families.

Social attitudes toward women in work

The proportion of women working varies depending on the culture and traditions of a country. In 2016, the United Arab Emirates had the lowest proportion of women in work, with females making up only 12.4% of the labour force. In Rwanda, on the other hand, women made up 54.4% of the country's labour force. The proportion of female workers in the labour force was 46.4% in the UK, 42.9% in Japan and 24.3% in India. An increasing number of women in a labour force may result in a lower birth rate as it may restrict their ability to take time off to have children. Some women may also choose not to have children, instead focusing on their careers.

Age of marriage

In developing countries, women and men tend to get married at a younger age, giving them more time to have children. In developed countries, on the other hand, men and women tend to be older when they marry, resulting in a lower birth rate. According to the WHO, more than 30% of girls in developing countries marry before the age of 18 and 14% before the age of 15. Once married, there is often social pressure on them to start having children.

A young population

The populations of developing countries tend to be made up of a high proportion of young people, resulting in more women of childbearing age. As a result, birth rates in developing countries tend to be higher than those of developed countries, which have an older median age. For example, many African countries including Burundi, the Central African Republic, Ethiopia, Kenya, Uganda and Zambia had median ages of under 20 years in 2016, with Niger's median age a mere 15.3 years. This contrasts with median ages of 40.5 in the UK, 37.9 in the USA, 46.9 years in Japan and 37.8 in New Zealand.

Awareness and availability of contraception

Sex education and greater awareness of contraception has led to declining birth rates in developed countries and some developing countries. However, in many poor countries, sex education and the practice of birth control is still very limited. Even where people do have knowledge of birth control, contraceptives may not be easily available or affordable or, due to social pressures, women may be too embarrassed or ashamed to access them. One of the consequences of this is a high number of teen pregnancies in these countries.

 What is the birth rate in your country? What does it indicate about the population of your country?

Variations in death rates

Age structure of the population

Developed countries are likely to have an **ageing population** with a higher proportion of people over the age of 65 years. As a result, more people are likely to die from illnesses related to old age. In developing countries with younger populations, on the other hand, death rates from old age are likely to be lower.

Access to healthcare

Advances in medical care are helping to reduce death rates and prolong people's lives, particularly in developed countries where a high standard of healthcare is available to most people. In many developing countries, however, there are still a significant number of people dying from treatable and preventable diseases due to inadequate healthcare. The leading cause of death in low-income countries in 2015 was lower respiratory infections, including bronchitis and pneumonia, which caused 84.9 deaths per 100 000 people. This contrasts with 38.2 deaths per 100 000 people in developed countries. In addition to this, HIV/AIDS, tuberculosis, malaria and birth complications were also leading causes of death in the poorest countries, despite many being treatable with modern medicine.

Safe drinking water and sanitation

Limited access to safe drinking water and inadequate sanitation can also lead to life-threatening waterborne illnesses and disease in the poorest developing countries. In 2015, diarrhoeal infection,

> **Key term**
>
> **Ageing population** – the increase in the median age of the population of a country over time

partly due to the consumption of contaminated water, was the second most common cause of death in low-income countries.

Lack of education and awareness

Lack of education and ignorance about nutrition, hygiene and harmful habits such as smoking contributes to poor health and higher death rates in some developing countries. A more highly educated population is more likely to lead to healthier lifestyle choices. For example, in Indonesia, 67.4% of males aged over 15 years were smokers in 2017, the highest rate in the world. This was partly due to lack of education and awareness about the harmful effects of smoking. About 200 000 people die in Indonesia each year from smoking-related illnesses.

Higher incomes

People in rich countries can afford to live healthier lifestyles than those in poor countries. The ability to purchase quality food, receive regular health check-ups and engage in fitness activities can prolong the lives of people in these countries. However, an abundance of cheap fatty foods and sugary drinks in developed countries has also led to a growing problem of obesity, which is linked to health problems including heart disease and diabetes. In 2015, heart disease was the leading cause of death in richer countries, killing 144.6 people per 100 000 population, compared to 48.6 per 100 000 in the poorest developing countries. Furthermore, office workers in some developed countries spend long hours at work, leaving little time for exercise and relaxation. In Japan, death by overwork or 'karoshi' was recorded as the official cause of death of over 2000 people in 2015.

Laws protecting people's safety

Many laws protecting the safety of consumers, workers and the public are not strictly enforced in many developing countries. Low food quality and hygiene standards may have a serious impact on the health of consumers, while lenient labour laws regarding safety in the workplace increase the chances of work-related deaths, particularly in the primary and secondary sectors, which employ a high proportion of workers in developing countries. Road accidents are also a leading cause of death in many developing countries, with laws on driving while drunk not strictly enforced by authorities. Thailand has some of the deadliest roads in the world, second only to war-torn Libya. The WHO estimates that 24 000 people die on Thailand's roads every year, with one in four deaths involving alcohol.

War and conflict

In 2014, approximately 180 000 people died in 42 armed conflicts in developing countries. This included violent fighting in Syria and Iraq, the Israeli–Palestinian conflict, and fighting in Libya, Yemen and the Central African Republic.

2 What is the death rate of your country? What does it indicate about the population of your country?

Variations in net migration between countries

Movement of migrants

Emigration from developing countries to developed countries slows the population growth of developing countries and increases the population growth of developed countries. About 3.2 million people migrated from developing to developed countries each year between 2010 and 2015 for reasons that included employment, education, being with family or to escape violence.

Movement of refugees

The movement of refugees fleeing persecution and violent conflict also has a significant impact on the population growth of some countries. For example, the Syrian refugee crisis involved net outward migration of approximately 4.2 million people from the Syrian Arab Republic between 2010 and 2015. Most of these refugees went to Syria's neighbouring countries, including Turkey, Lebanon and Jordan.

 3 Show the effect of emigration of skilled workers from a developing country using a production possibility curve (PPC).

Advantages and disadvantages for developing countries as a result of net outward migration

Advantages	Disadvantages
• Emigrants may send money back to relatives in their home countries, increasing living standards. In 2016, over US$420 billion in **remittances** was sent from developed to developing countries, making them an important source of income for these countries. • Emigrants may return to their home country in the future, bringing new knowledge and skills that may help to increase the productivity of the labour force. • Emigration will slow population growth and may help to ease pressure on the country's resources if it is suffering from **overpopulation**.	• Highly skilled workers emigrating to developed countries reduces the productive capacity of a developing economy, making it difficult for the country to achieve long-term economic growth and development. • Emigration may decrease the working population, meaning that there are fewer workers to provide the goods and services the dependent population needs. The **dependent population** is made up of citizens who do not work and who therefore rely on the working population to provide for them. It includes young children, old people, the sick, disabled, housewives and the unemployed.

Key terms

Remittance – a sum of money sent by a worker in a foreign country to relatives in their home country

Dependent population – the dependent population of a country consists of people who do not earn an income themselves and rely on others to provide them with the goods and services they need. It includes young children, the elderly, people who cannot work due to illness or disability, as well as those in full-time education.

Overpopulation – a situation where there are not enough resources to sustain the population of a country

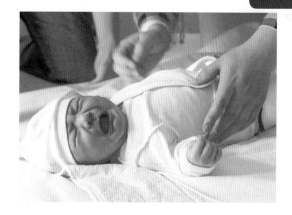

4 What problems might a large dependent population create for an economy?

What is the optimum population of a country?

Overpopulation is when a country's available resources are not enough to sustain and provide for the country's inhabitants because there are too many people. This situation is inefficient as overpopulation leads to a shortage (excess demand) of resources such as food and housing, meaning that some people may not receive all of the goods and services they need.

There are two ways in which efficiency could be improved in this situation. The first method would be to reduce the size of the country's population by restricting the population growth rate. For example, China's one-child policy between 1979 and 2015 restricted couples to having only one child to tackle the problem of overpopulation. The second method involves increasing either the quantity or the quality of resources so that there is enough for everyone. For example, food could be imported from abroad (increasing the quantity of resources) or farmland could be used more productively (increasing the quality of resources) in order to increase crop yields so that there is enough food for the whole population.

Underpopulation is when the resources of a country are so abundant that there are not enough people to make full use of them, leading to a surplus (excess supply) of resources. This may lead to some resources being wasted. For example, a country may have fertile land available, but not enough people to farm it to grow food crops. In this situation, the country would benefit from increasing the size of its population so that it could make more efficient use of its resources.

The **optimum population** is when there are enough people in a country to fully use all of the available resources, thereby maximising output. Thus, there is no shortage or surplus of resources and efficiency is maximised. As the quality and quantity of resources in a country change over time due to innovation, technology and a more skilled labour force, its optimum population also changes.

Key terms

Underpopulation – a situation where some of the resources of a country are left unused or wasted because there are not enough people to fully exploit them

Optimum population – a situation where a population is sufficient to ensure that all resources in a country are fully utilised and output is maximised

The effects of an increase in population size

- **Competition for the country's resources**. An increase in the size of a country's population is likely to result in increased competition for the country's resources, including water, food, housing and medical services. If a country is already overpopulated, this will spread resources more thinly across the population. Some goods, such as food, may need to be imported from overseas in order to make up the shortage, potentially leading to a current account deficit on the balance of payments, which may need to be financed by borrowing from abroad (see Unit 6.4). In the long run, the government may need to use supply-side policy to increase the productivity of the economy and/or take measures to reduce the size of the population to the optimal level. If a country is underpopulated, an increase in the size of the population may help the country to use its resources more efficiently, especially if the increase is due to net inward migration of skilled workers. This should increase the size and productivity of the labour force, leading to an increase in output and economic growth.

- **Overcrowding**. Population growth may lead to overcrowding in some countries, especially in the urban slums where poor people live. A **slum** is characterised by lack of durable housing, limited access to safe drinking water and inadequate sanitation and living space. In 2014, about 55% of sub-Saharan Africa's urban population lived in slum conditions. **Overcrowding** in these areas (three or more people living to a room) may put pressure on water supply and sanitation facilities and potentially lead to the spread of life-threatening diseases.

- **Increased demand for goods and services**. An increase in population size is likely to increase the demand for a wide variety of goods and services in an economy, including housing, education and healthcare. This increased aggregate demand will result in more goods and services being produced, thus creating jobs and lowering unemployment. For example, an increase in the demand for housing will provide jobs for builders in the construction of houses. However, it is also likely to lead to rising inflation as higher aggregate demand in the economy puts upward pressure on the general price level.

- **Competition for jobs**. An increase in the size of the **working-age population** may create increased competition for jobs, causing higher unemployment, particularly in low-skilled occupations. Higher unemployment will lead to falling incomes and reduced consumer spending. As a result, production and economic growth in the economy may fall.

Key terms

Slum – an area in a city in which people live in poor conditions characterised by non-durable housing, unpaved paths, and a lack of space, sanitation facilities and access to safe drinking water

Overcrowding – an increase in the number of people to beyond what is comfortable due to lack of living space

Key terms

Working-age population – the proportion of a country's population that is of working age, usually between the ages of 15 and 64

- **Increase in the dependent population**. An increase in population size due to higher birth rates or falling death rates may lead to an increase in the dependent population of the country. This will increase the burden on the working population to provide the goods and services the dependent population needs. For example, the government may need to increase income taxes on the working population in order to provide public services, such as healthcare and education, and welfare benefits to the dependent population.

- **Depletion of natural resources and higher pollution levels**. Increased population size is likely to result in increased use of non-renewable resources and higher levels of pollution and environmental damage. For example, an increase in energy consumption is likely to deplete the world's reserves of non-renewable resources, such as oil and coal. Higher energy consumption is also likely to lead to the burning of more fossil fuels, resulting in worsening air quality and environmental damage.

5 When is an increase in the size of a population not a problem for a country?

The effects of a decrease in population size

- **Lower demand in the economy**. A declining population is likely to result in falling demand for goods and services in the economy. As a result, firms are likely to cut production, leading to higher unemployment and slower economic growth. However, the reduced demand for goods and services may also reduce environmental problems in some countries, such as air pollution and traffic congestion.

- **Lower productive capacity of the economy**. A decrease in population size due to a fall in the number of people of working age will decrease the labour force and the productive capacity of the economy. For example, the emigration of skilled labour from developing countries would reduce the productivity of the labour force, making it difficult for the country to achieve long-term economic growth and development. The emigration of skilled labour would also reduce the number of workers to dependants, increasing the burden on the working population.

- **Inefficient use of resources**. If a country is underpopulated or at its optimum population, a decrease in population size will mean that the country may not have enough workers to use its resources fully. Thus, resources may be wasted, which would be inefficient for the economy. As a result, production would fall, leading to a slowdown in economic growth.

- **Reduction in overcrowding**. A decrease in the size of a country's population may ease overcrowding in some areas.

As a result, people would have more space so the pressure on the supply of clean water and sanitation facilities would reduce, thus decreasing the likelihood of disease and illness.

- **A change in government spending**. A significant fall in the size of a country's population due to an increase in the death rate may be a result of a serious health epidemic or a natural disaster. In these situations, a government would have to increase spending, which may lead to a budget deficit and increased government debt. However, a decrease in the size of a population due to a falling birth rate or rising death rate may lead to reduced demand for public services, such as education and healthcare. As a result, a government may be able to cut spending in these areas, which may lead to a budget surplus.

6 How might immigration help to solve some of the problems of a declining population?

Changes in the age distribution of a population

The **age distribution** of a country is the proportion of people within a population who fall into certain age groups. Figure 5.3.1 provides an overview of the proportion of people in three age groups (0–14 years, 15–64 years and 65+ years) in different countries in 2016. As can be seen from Figure 5.3.1, developing countries generally have a higher proportion of people in the 0–14 age group, while developed countries have a higher proportion of their populations aged 65 and above. This is mainly due to higher incomes, better healthcare and healthier lifestyles of people in developed countries, which result in them living longer. These countries are said to have ageing populations. Many developing countries, in contrast, have a high proportion of young people due to higher birth rates and relatively lower life expectancies.

Key term

Age distribution – the proportion of people within a population who fall into certain age groups, for example, young (0–14 years), of working age (15–65 years) and old (65 years and above)

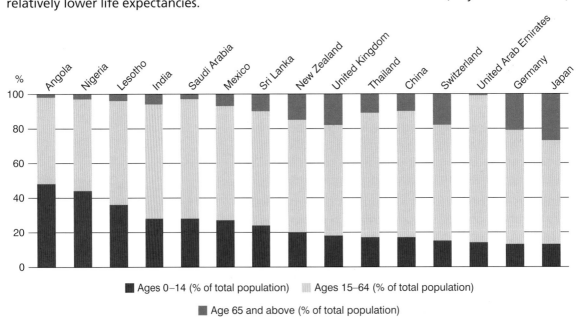

Figure 5.3.1 The proportion of people in different age groups in different countries in 2016 (as a percentage of total population)

The effects of an ageing population

An ageing population is when the median age of a country's population is increasing over time. This has a number of potential consequences, especially for those countries with a growing proportion of their populations aged 65 years and older.

Increase in the dependent population

An ageing population, which increases the proportion of people aged 65 years and over, will increase the dependent population of a country. As a result, there will be an increased burden on the working population to provide goods and services for a rising number of senior citizens who are too old to work.

Higher income taxes

In order to cover the higher costs of healthcare and pensions that come with an increasing number of old people, the government may have to raise more tax revenue by increasing income taxes on the working population. This reduces the disposable incomes of those in work, which may lead to a fall in their standards of living. Higher income taxes may also act as a disincentive to work, thus reducing the productivity and output of the labour force.

Increased government spending

A higher proportion of old people in a country is likely to result in an increase in government spending on healthcare and the provision of pensions. This will have an opportunity cost for society as investment in the economy, such as spending on infrastructure, may have to be given up in order to fund healthcare and the payment of pensions to the elderly.

Shortage of workers

The labour force may decrease in size as the population ages and an increasing number of workers retire from their professions. If not replaced by younger workers, the quantity of labour in the country will fall, reducing the productive potential of the economy. As a result, the output and economic growth of the country may decrease.

Reduced labour mobility

Younger workers tend to be more flexible, willing to retrain, try out new occupations and move to other geographical locations in search of work. As a country's population ages, older workers, who are often tied to a particular profession or geographical area for financial and family reasons, will be reluctant to change occupations or relocate for work purposes. As a result, the **occupational mobility** and **geographical mobility** of the population will be reduced.

Key terms

Occupational mobility – the ease with which an individual can change from one job in a particular field or industry to one in another field or industry

Geographical mobility – the ease with which an individual can change from one location to another for work purposes

Increase in productivity

One of the advantages of a higher proportion of older workers is the high level of knowledge, skills and experience they bring to a job. As a result, older workers are likely to be more productive than their younger counterparts, thus contributing to increased output and higher economic growth. They may also be able to pass some of their knowledge and expertise on to the next generation of workers, helping to further increase productivity.

Indicator of high living standards

An ageing population is an indication of a quality healthcare system and healthier lifestyles, which lead to longer lives and an improved living standard within the population.

What can governments do?

Governments can use a number of policies to alleviate the potentially harmful effects of an ageing population. One thing they can do is to encourage couples to have more children. For example, the Japanese government pays couples a 'baby bonus' – a financial incentive to encourage them to have babies. In one part of Japan, parents were paid 100 000 yen (about US$940) for the first baby and 1 million yen (about US$9400) for the fourth.

The government could also tackle the problem of an ageing population by raising the retirement age. For example, in 2017 the government of the UK announced a plan to raise the age at which people would receive a state pension from 67 to 68 from 2037. This change meant that 34 million people would have to work an additional year before receiving their pension from the government. This would have the effect of increasing the productive capacity of the UK economy and also delay government spending on the provision of state pensions.

A government may also choose to encourage the immigration of skilled workers into its country from abroad. Attracting skilled workers from other countries would increase the productive capacity of the economy as well as increase the working population so it is better able to provide for the dependent population.

 Who is likely to benefit most from an ageing population in an economy?

Changes in the gender distribution of a population

Gender distribution is the proportion of people in a country who are male and female. The table below provides data on males and females as a proportion of total population for selected countries in 2016. If left entirely to nature, the number of boys born is slightly higher than the number of girls. However, this ratio evens out over time as women live longer than men, on average. This is due to riskier behaviour in males and a higher likelihood of them suffering from serious health problems or dying in violent conflict.

Key term
....

Gender distribution – the proportions of people in a country who are male and female

Males and females as a proportion of total population in different countries in 2016

Country	Males (% of total population)	Females (% of total population)
United Arab Emirates	72.9	27.1
Bahrain	61.9	38.1
Saudi Arabia	56.5	43.5
India	51.8	48.2
China	51.5	48.5
Nigeria	50.9	49.1
Bangladesh	50.5	49.5
Norway	50.4	49.6
Maldives	50.1	49.9
Kenya	50.0	50.0
Lesotho	49.6	50.4
Mexico	49.7	50.3
Burundi	49.4	50.6
United Kingdom	49.3	50.7
Brazil	49.2	50.8
New Zealand	48.9	51.1
Japan	48.6	51.4
Portugal	47.3	52.7
Russian Federation	46.5	53.5
Latvia	45.9	54.1

 8 Are you surprised by any of the data in this table? Why or why not?

One of the largest gender imbalances in the world is in Asia and the Middle East where, according to the UN, there were an estimated 100 million more males than females in 2017. In India, there were 107.6 men for every 100 women in 2015, while in China there were 106.2 men for every 100 women, according to UN estimates. Vietnam also had an imbalance of 112.8 boys for every 100 girls at birth. In contrast, Europe had a surplus of 26 million females in 2015. Thailand also had more females than males, with 96.2 men for every 100 women, according to the country's 2010 census.

There are a number of reasons for the high overall proportion of males to females in Asia:

- **A preference for sons**. In countries such as India, China and Vietnam, there is a strong preference for sons as males are traditionally responsible for looking after their parents in old age. Daughters, on the other hand, tend to live with their husband's family after marriage in some countries, including India.

- **Immigration of male workers**. Some countries have significantly more males than females due to the immigration of male workers. The main reason why the United Arab Emirates and Qatar have the lowest proportion of females in the world (just 27.1% and 27.8% of their total populations, respectively) is the immigration of workers in the gas, oil and construction industries, which are heavily male dominated.

A significant gender imbalance can have serious economic and social consequences for a country:

- **Lower economic growth**. Having fewer female workers may limit the potential growth of an economy. Some jobs, especially those that require a high level of concentration and consistency, tend to be performed much more productively by women than men. With fewer women to do these jobs, the productive capacity of the economy may be reduced, thus resulting in lower economic growth.

- **Fewer marriages**. In countries such as India and China, some men are struggling to marry due to the shortage of women. Those most affected are men who are poor, uneducated and living in rural areas as they are less able to attract a bride.

- **Rising crime rates**. Some studies have found a slight correlation between a high proportion of males in a country and an increase in the rate of violent crime.

- **Increase in human trafficking**. Increasing numbers of unmarried men have resulted in a rise in the incidence of **human trafficking**. There has been an increase in the number of complaints to human rights organisations about women being trafficked from countries including Cambodia and Vietnam for marriage purposes.

Key term

Human trafficking – the forced and illegal transport of human beings from one country to another

Extension topic

Changes in occupational and geographical distribution of a population

Occupational distribution refers to the proportion of people working in the primary, secondary and tertiary sectors of an economy. In the early stages of development, a large proportion of a country's population is employed in farming and agriculture in the primary sector. As the country develops, the proportion of workers in the primary sector declines as people find work in manufacturing and construction in the secondary sector. At the later stages of development, a more educated labour force seeks higher wages and improved working conditions in service industries in the tertiary sector. As a result, the proportion of people employed in the primary and secondary sectors declines. Figure 5.3.2 shows a comparison of employment in the primary, secondary and tertiary sectors between two countries, Tanzania (a developing country) and Sweden (a developed country).

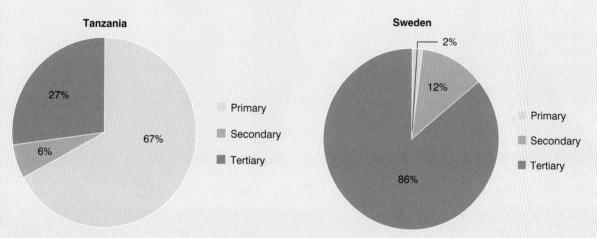

Figure 5.3.2 A comparison of employment by sector between Tanzania and Sweden

Source: World Bank/International Labour Organization

Geographical distribution refers to where people live and the way they are spread across a country or region. As an economy develops, there tends to be migration away from rural areas towards cities as people search for better employment and education opportunities. While this may lead to higher incomes and improved living standards for some, it is also likely to increase the **population density** in urban areas, which may result in overcrowding. According to UN-Habitat data, the most crowded city in the world in 2017 was Dhaka in Bangladesh, with a population density of 44 500 people per square kilometre. Mumbai in India was the second most densely populated city, followed by Medellin in South Africa in third place. Manila in the Philippines had the fourth highest population density in the world.

The population pyramid

A **population pyramid** shows the age and gender distribution of the population of a country. Figure 5.3.3 shows a population pyramid for a typical low-income developing country, and Figure 5.3.4 shows a population pyramid for a typical high-income developed country. Take a minute to examine the diagrams. What information indicates that these are developing and developed countries?

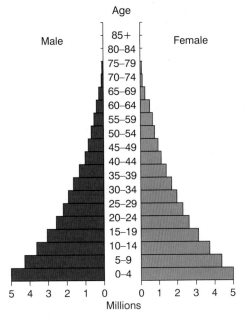

Figure 5.3.3 Population pyramid for a developing country

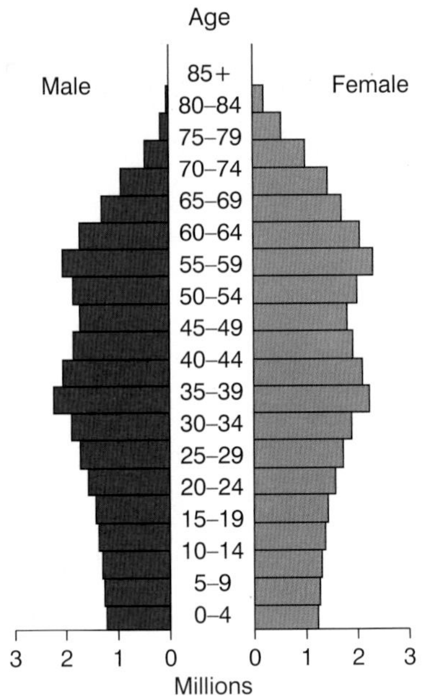

Figure 5.3.4 Population pyramid for a developed country

You may have noticed that a high proportion of the population in Figure 5.3.3 falls in the 0–4 age group, indicating that the country has a high birth rate. Furthermore, a low proportion of its population are aged 65 years and over, indicating low life expectancy. Both of these features are characteristics of a typical developing country. Figure 5.3.4, on the other hand, shows a much lower proportion of the population falling within the 0–4 age group, indicating a comparatively lower birth rate. Also, a high proportion of the population in Figure 5.3.4 is aged 65 years and above, indicating a high life expectancy and an ageing population. A low birth rate and ageing population are characteristics of a developed country.

Key terms

Occupational distribution – the proportion of people working in each of the primary, secondary and tertiary sectors of an economy

Geographical distribution – the way people are spread across a country or region, for example, the proportion of the population living in urban and rural areas

Population density – the number of people living in a certain area, usually one square kilometre

CASE STUDY | **Population growth in Malawi**

In 2017, Malawi had one of the highest population growth rates in the world. According to the CIA *World Factbook*, the rate was 3.32%, caused by a birth rate of 41.3 births per 1000 people compared with a death rate of only 8.1 deaths per 1000 people. In addition, the net migration rate was zero.

The main cause of the high birth rate in Malawi was improvements in maternal and child healthcare. In both rural and urban areas expectant mothers received improved prenatal care and skilled birth assistance. In addition, most children were vaccinated. These developments led to a lower infant mortality rate and fewer mothers dying during childbirth. Despite the lower infant mortality rate, Malawi's fertility rate remained high at 5.5 children per woman.

Rapid population growth and the high population density put pressure on the land, water and forest resources of Malawi. As Malawi's economy is mainly based on agriculture, the increased population reduced plot sizes per family. In addition, the increasing vulnerability to climate change further threatens the sustainability of Malawi's economy and could worsen the food shortages.

1 Give two reasons for Malawi's rapid population growth.

2 Using examples from the extract, give two problems created by Malawi's rapid population growth.

Applying

Project work

With the help of the internet, research the populations of two countries of your choice, one a developing country and the other a developed country. What are the differences between the populations of the two countries?

1. Identify three differences between the populations of the two countries.

2. Explain the reason for each difference.

3. Explain one way in which each difference might affect the economy of the country.

Write your research up in the form of a table, poster or mind map. Be ready to share your findings with your classmates.

Knowledge check questions

1 Define birth rate. [2]

2 Define death rate. [2]

3 Explain **two** reasons why population growth increases more rapidly in developing countries than developed countries. [4]

4 Define optimum population. [2]

5 Analyse the effect of an ageing population on the economic growth of a country. [6]

6 (E) Discuss whether an increase in population size will always increase unemployment. [8]

Check your progress

Read the unit objectives below and reflect on your progress in each.

	I struggle with this and need more practice.
	I can do this reasonably well.
	I can do this with confidence.

- Describe the factors that affect population growth, including birth rate, death rate, net migration, immigration and emigration.

- Analyse the reasons for different rates of population growth in different countries.

- Analyse how and why birth rates, death rates and net migration vary between countries.

- Explain the concept of an optimum population.

- Analyse the effects of increases and decreases in population size and changes in the age and gender distribution of a population.

- Describe a country's age and gender distribution from its population pyramid.

- Identify whether a country is developed or developing from its population pyramid.

Differences in economic development between countries

Learning objectives

By the end of this unit, you should be able to:

- define economic development
- explain the characteristics of developed and developing countries
- analyse the causes of differences in income; productivity; population growth; size of primary, secondary and tertiary sectors; saving and investment; education; and healthcare between developed and developing countries
- analyse the impact of these differences on the economic performance of developed and developing countries.

· ·

Starting point

Answer these questions in pairs:

1 What is economic growth?

2 Other than economic growth, what factors influence the living standards of a population?

3 What can governments do to improve these factors?

Exploring

Discuss these questions in pairs:

1 Using the pictures below, what three differences can you identify between developed and developing countries?

2 Why might these differences exist?

3 What impact might these differences have on the lives of the people in these countries?

What is economic development?

Economic development refers to the economic, social and political wellbeing of the people in a country. It includes the ability of a nation to provide its population with basic needs such as food, safe water, electricity, education and healthcare. The quality of the environment, people's ability to afford consumer goods, such as mobile phones and televisions, and the distribution of income within the country are also important indicators of its economic development. Political stability, the enforcement of laws protecting property rights, the level of corruption, as well as political freedom, free speech and self-esteem are also important factors.

 1 What might be the common characteristics of a country with a low level of economic development?

Developing and developed countries

A **developing country** is a country that has a low level of economic development. Such a country is characterised by low GDP per head and may have a low HDI ranking, indicating low living standards across the population. Life expectancy and access to education may be limited. Absolute poverty is likely to exist, particularly in rural parts of the country. The population growth rate is likely to be high and a large proportion of the labour force will be employed in low-skilled and low-paid jobs in agriculture (the primary sector). The farming methods are likely to be labour intensive and the infrastructure of the economy, including roads, communications and power supply, may be underdeveloped.

A **developed country**, on the other hand, is a country with a high level of economic development. It is likely to have high GDP per head and a high HDI ranking. In most developed countries, absolute poverty has been eradicated due to an efficient progressive tax system and the provision of welfare benefits to those most in need, such as the unemployed and pensioners. Infrastructure is highly developed and all members of the population have access to healthcare and education. As a result, life expectancy is high and a high proportion of the labour force have the skills to work in services (the tertiary sector). Only a small proportion of the labour force is employed in agriculture (the primary sector), in which farming methods are highly mechanised and capital intensive.

In practice, many nations share some of the characteristics of both developed and developing countries. Sri Lanka, for example, has many of the characteristics of a developed country but needs to

Key terms

Economic development – an improvement in the living standards and quality of life of the population of a country as it transitions from being reliant on the primary sector for employment and output towards the secondary and tertiary sectors

Developing country – a country that has a low income and is generally reliant on the agricultural industry for its employment and output

make further progress in areas including education, healthcare and productivity to reach a higher level of economic development. The Central African Republic, in contrast, which had the lowest HDI ranking in 2015, has many of the characteristics of a developing country. In order to be considered a 'developed country', a nation must satisfy almost all of the characteristics of a developed country outlined above. Countries including the USA, Canada, the UK, Germany, Japan, South Korea, Singapore, Australia and New Zealand are considered to be developed countries.

 Is your country classified as a developed or developing country? Why?

Differences between developed and developing countries

There are various differences between developed and developing countries. Some of these are outlined below, followed by a discussion of the impact that each difference might have on the economic performance of a country.

GDP per head (income)

Developed countries generate income from the production of a wide range of high-value goods and services. A highly skilled labour force and capital-intensive production methods increase productivity and output. Developing countries, on the other hand, generate much of their income from the production of agricultural goods. Prices of agricultural goods may be low, leading to low incomes. Protection policies, such as tariffs, are imposed on agricultural goods by some countries, reducing export revenue for developing countries. In 2015, Luxembourg had an annual GDP per head of $107 036, while Burundi's was a mere $207.

Impact on economic performance

The poorest countries struggle to earn the income they need to improve their level of economic development. They may therefore be forced to borrow money from abroad to invest in their economies, resulting in increased foreign debt. In countries like Burundi, a large proportion of the population lives below the (absolute) poverty line of $1.90 per day.

Distribution of income and wealth

Developed countries generally have efficient progressive tax systems in place and provide welfare benefits to the poor. Developing countries, in contrast, tend to have relatively large informal economies, making the imposition and collection of taxes difficult. They therefore may not have the tax revenue to provide welfare benefits or to invest in public services, such as education and healthcare. **Corruption** may also prevent public money from reaching the poorest sections of the population.

Key term

Developed country – a country that has high income and living standards with most of its economic activity based in the tertiary sector

Key term

Corruption – the dishonest behaviour of people in power for their own personal gain

Impact on economic performance

A large proportion of the population of some developing countries may suffer from absolute poverty, particularly in rural areas. Those developing countries that have managed to minimise extreme poverty may still have a relatively large proportion of the population living just above the poverty line of $1.90 per day. Absolute poverty has been eradicated in most developed countries, but relative poverty is still a concern.

Productivity

Developed countries tend to have a high productivity level due to a skilled labour force and investment in modern technology. Many developing countries, on the other hand, have a comparatively unskilled labour force due to a poor education system and limited training opportunities. Furthermore, poor countries may not have the funds to invest in capital equipment and machinery. Each of these factors is likely to contribute to low productivity.

Impact on economic performance

Low productivity in developing countries is likely to lead to fewer goods and services being produced and lower income (GDP). As a result, these countries are unlikely to have the income they need to invest in improving their economies and their levels of economic development.

Population growth

Developed countries tend to have relatively slow population growth rates (see Unit 5.3). This is partly due to some women choosing to focus on their careers, marrying later and having fewer children. The high cost of raising children is another reason for lower birth rates in developed countries. Many developing countries, in contrast, have rapidly growing populations due to high birth rates (see Unit 5.3). In 2016, the population growth rate in sub-Saharan Africa, the poorest region in the world, was 2.7%, compared with 0.4% in the European Union and −0.3% in Central Europe and the Baltics.

Impact

Rapid population growth in developing countries puts a strain on resources, which have to be shared across a growing number of people. Absolute poverty may rise if there are not enough resources, such as food, for everyone. The poorest developing countries tend to have large dependent populations, putting pressure on the working population and government to provide for them. For example, over half of Niger's population (51%) were aged under 14 in 2016.

Size of primary, secondary and tertiary sectors

The majority of the labour force of a developed country has jobs in the tertiary sector, which generally requires a higher level of education and skill. Developing countries, on the other hand, have a high proportion of workers employed in the primary sector in agriculture. As a country develops, an increasing proportion of its labour force is employed in the secondary sector in manufacturing. Figure 5.4.1 shows employment by sector in a range of countries.

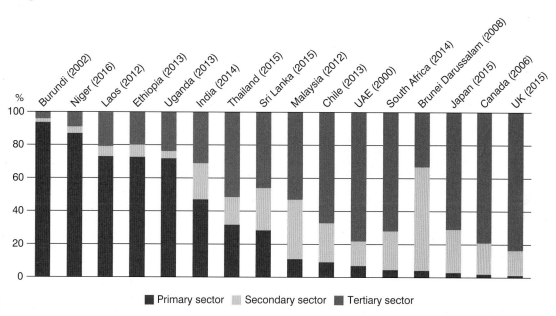

Figure 5.4.1 Estimated levels of employment by sector in a range of developed and developing countries

Source: Data from the CIA *World Fact Book*

3 Which countries in Figure 5.4.1 would you expect to be developed and which would you expect to be developing? Why?

Impact on economic performance

Farming practices in developing countries tend to be labour intensive. Workers are unskilled and receive low wages. Drought, crop failure and fluctuations in the prices of agricultural goods may result in higher absolute poverty. As an economy develops and the secondary sector expands, pollution levels may rise, reducing the quality of life of the population.

Saving and investment

The high incomes of developed countries enable them to save and invest in the purchase of capital equipment and the development of new technology to increase productivity and expand production. The poorest developing countries with the lowest incomes, on the other hand, find it difficult to save. Without savings, domestic investment in capital equipment remains low, leading to low productivity and low economic growth.

Impact on economic performance

The poorest developing countries may become trapped in a **poverty cycle** of low income, low saving, low investment, low productivity and low economic growth (illustrated in Figure 5.4.2). These countries may therefore have to borrow money from foreign countries to invest in their economies, leading to high levels of foreign debt. Debt repayments are likely to be large and countries may not be able to meet them. For these countries, further borrowing – which could improve their economic development – is difficult and interest rates on loans are likely to be high.

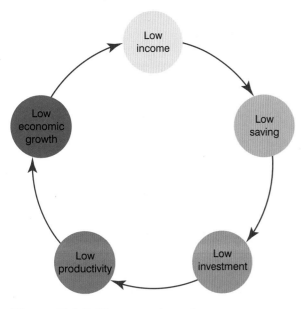

Figure 5.4.2 The poverty cycle

Education

In developed countries, a high quality of school education is accessible to all members of the population, with many going on to study at universities and vocational institutions. This results in a knowledgeable and skilled labour force, increasing the productivity of the country. Poor developing countries, on the other hand, lack the income to invest in providing a high standard of education to their people. As a result, the skill level and productivity of the labour force is likely to be low. A poor education system makes it difficult for people to raise themselves out of poverty.

Impact on economic performance

Without access to quality education, the poor are unable to improve their knowledge and skills and thus become trapped in a cycle of **intergenerational poverty** – poor people born into poverty have children who also suffer from poverty due to lack of education. Poor education also limits the productivity of the labour force, resulting in low economic growth for a country.

Healthcare

A high standard of medical care tends to be accessible to all citizens in most developed countries. People also have access to healthier food and a cleaner and safer environment. In the poorest developing countries, a large proportion of populations may lack access to even basic medical care, such as vaccinations against preventable diseases, including cholera and tuberculosis. Safe water and sanitation may also be unavailable, increasing the spread of potentially life-threatening disease and illness.

Impact on economic performance

Life expectancy tends to be high in developed countries, many of which have ageing populations. This may result in higher taxes, as governments seek revenue to provide the growing number of old people with pensions and health services. The number of elderly people living in relative poverty may also rise. Life expectancy in many developing countries, in contrast, is significantly lower. Poor health and shorter lifespans will reduce the productive capacity of developing economies. In 2015, Swaziland had the lowest life expectancy at birth in the world at just 49 years, while Japan had one of the highest at 84 years.

Infrastructure

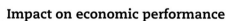

Developed countries have the money to invest in modern infrastructure, including roads, transport links and communication networks. Many developing countries, on the other hand, lack the funds to invest in infrastructure, which may result in problems such as poor roads and an unreliable power supply.

Impact on economic performance

Poor infrastructure reduces the productivity and productive capacity of an economy. For example, poor roads and transport links may result in goods being spoiled or damaged while being transported.

South Korea's economic development

After the Korean war ended in 1953, South Korea was one of the poorest countries in the world with a real GDP per head of only $64 – about the same as the poorest countries in Africa at the time. In 2016, South Korea was the fifteenth largest economy in the world with a real GDP per head of $35 751, not far behind Spain ($36 310) and New Zealand ($39 059).

Grants and loans of $60 billion from the USA between 1946 and 1978, along with policies which encouraged private enterprise and exports, have driven South Korea's economy, which grew an average of 7% per year for the 50 years leading up until 2014. This economic success corresponded with the eradication of absolute poverty, the modernisation of infrastructure and improvements in public services that have dramatically improved the living standards of the country's population.

With South Korean schools regularly topping international league tables and high household spending on university education, South Korean workers are among the most highly educated in the world. The high cost of educating children partly explains South Korea's low fertility rate, which was only 1.2 births per woman in 2015. A low birth rate combined with life expectancy at birth of 82 years in 2015 mean that South Korea has a rapidly ageing population and faces increasing relative poverty among the elderly.

1 What characteristics mentioned in the extract make South Korea a developed country?

2 What impact might an ageing population have on South Korea's future economic growth?

Applying

Project work

Investigate a developing country of your choice.

- Identify and explain five characteristics that make it a developing country.

- Explain the impact of each characteristic on the country's economy.

Present your findings in the form of a spider diagram, with the name of the country at the centre and information about each of the five characteristics branching off from it. Use pictures to support your analysis.

Knowledge check questions

1 Define economic development. [2]

2 Identify **three** characteristics of a developed country. [3]

3 Identify **three** characteristics of a developing country. [3]

4 Analyse how investment in education may lead to an improvement in the economic development of a country. [6]

5 (E) Discuss whether economic development is always going to benefit the population of a country. [8]

Check your progress

Read the unit objectives below and reflect on your progress in each.

- Define economic development.

- Explain the characteristics of developed and developing countries.

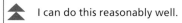

I struggle with this and need more practice.

I can do this reasonably well.

I can do this with confidence.

- Analyse the causes of differences in income; productivity; population growth; size of primary, secondary and tertiary sectors; saving and investment; education; and healthcare between developed and developing countries.

- Analyse the impact of these differences on the economic performance of developed and developing countries.

Chapter review

Multiple-choice questions

1   What is the problem with using real GDP per head as a measure of living standards?
  - **A**   It considers only the production of goods and services.
  - **B**   It considers the health and education of the population.
  - **C**   It does not take into account the effects of inflation.
  - **D**   It does not take into account the effects of population growth.

2   Which of the following is a possible reason why income distribution within a country might be unequal?
  - **A**   The government imposes high income taxes on the rich.
  - **B**   The government pays welfare benefits to the poor.
  - **C**   Some workers are employed in the primary sector.
  - **D**   Some workers emigrate to other countries in search of higher-paying jobs.

3   Which statement about poverty is correct?
  - **A**   Absolute poverty causes the production possibility curve of an economy to shift outwards.
  - **B**   Both relative and absolute poverty deny people access to clean water.
  - **C**   Both relative and absolute poverty limit people's access to opportunities.
  - **D**   Relative poverty occurs only in developed countries.

4   What is a potential cause of absolute poverty?
  - **A**   A fall in employment
  - **B**   A fall in inflation
  - **C**   An increase in government spending
  - **D**   An increase in the minimum wage

5   What is **most** likely to cause the population of a country to increase?
  - **A**   Net inward migration / a falling birth rate / a rising death rate
  - **B**   Net inward migration / a rising birth rate / a falling death rate
  - **C**   Net outward migration / a falling birth rate / a falling death rate
  - **D**   Net outward migration / a rising birth rate / a rising death rate

6   Which is **not** a characteristic of a typical developed country?
  - **A**   A high proportion of employment in the tertiary sector
  - **B**   A large informal economy
  - **C**   A low birth rate and a low death rate
  - **D**   Capital-intensive farming methods

7 The table shows the percentage change in the age structure of the population of a country.

Age group	Change (as a % of total population)
0–14	−5%
15–64	−8%
65 and above	+12%

Which statement **must** be correct?

A The country is becoming more developed.

B The population of the country has increased.

C The population of the country is getting older.

D The population of the country is getting younger.

8 What is **most** likely to improve the economic development of a poor country?

	Savings	Investment	Economic growth
A	Decrease	Decrease	Increase
B	Decrease	Increase	Decrease
C	Increase	Decrease	Decrease
D	Increase	Increase	Increase

9 In 2016, an estimated 2.2 million Filipinos (the native inhabitants of the Philippines) had emigrated abroad to work. What impact is this **likely** to have had on the Philippine economy?

A A decrease in cash transfers to the Philippines

B A decrease in the productive potential of the Philippine economy

C An increase in the Philippine labour force

D An increase in the productivity of the Philippine labour force

10 Which is **most** likely to be a developed country?

	Life expectancy	Expected years in school	Real GDP per head (US$)	Annual population growth rate (%)
A	56	10	12,122	4.2
B	65	16	13,551	2.7
C	48	8.5	4,337	8.3
D	68	15.5	16,879	1.4

Structured questions

1 Mongolia

Mongolia is a landlocked country in East Asia which borders China to the south and Russia to the north. It is endowed with agricultural resources and vast reserves of minerals, including copper, gold and coal, which are mostly unexploited. The country's economy is heavily dependent on the extraction and export of natural resources for its income and economic growth.

Mongolia's economy experienced an economic boom period from 2010, recording double-digit growth in 2011, 2012 and 2013. However, the country's growth slowed to 1% in 2016 due to falling export prices for its minerals and a slowdown in the Chinese economy, which purchases approximately 90% of Mongolia's exports.

	2010	2011	2012	2013	2014	2015	2016
GDP growth rate	6.4%	17.3%	12.3%	11.6%	7.9%	2.4%	1.0%
Real GDP per head	$2,650	$3,770	$4,368	$4,385	$4,182	$3,944	$3,686
Population (000)	2,713	2,762	2,814	2,869	2,924	2,977	3,027
Population below the poverty line	38.8%	33.7%	27.4%	–	21.6%	–	–
HDI*	0.695	0.706	0.714	0.722	0.727	0.735	–

Source: The World Bank
*Source: UNDP

Employment by sector in Mongolia, 2015	
Sector	% of total employment
Primary	28.4
Secondary	20.3
Tertiary	51.3

Age structure of Mongolia's population, 2016	
Age group	% of total population
0–14	28.6
15–64	67.3
65 and above	4.1

Source: The World Bank

Mongolia's poverty rate has declined steadily with the rise in economic growth. However, in 2014, over one-fifth of the country's population still lived in absolute poverty, with many people living only marginally above the poverty line of $1.90 per day. In 2015, Mongolia's HDI value was 0.735, ranking it 92 out of 187 countries.

Slums called Ger districts on the outskirts of Ulaanbaatar, the coldest capital city on earth, are home to about 700,000 people, most of whom live in absolute poverty. These districts lack water supply systems, forcing people to buy well water from nearby stations. Essential infrastructure including plumbing, sewage and paved roads are also not in place. These districts also lack schools and adequate medical facilities.

(a)   Using information from the extract, identify **three** characteristics which make Mongolia a developing country.   [3]

(b)   Calculate Mongolia's population growth rate from 2015 to 2016.   [3]

(c)   Using information from the extract, explain **two** reasons why Mongolia's economic growth slowed in 2016.   [4]

(d)   Explain **two** ways in which Mongolia could increase its HDI value.   [4]

(e)   Discuss whether GDP per head is a good indicator of living standards in Mongolia.   [8]

(f)   Analyse how increased investment in education might lead to a reduction in absolute poverty in Mongolia.   [4]

(g)   Discuss whether Mongolia will benefit from immigration.   [8]

2   In 2016, the number of births in Japan fell below one million for the first time since records began. With the country's death rate higher than its birth rate, Japan is facing a decline in the size of its population. This is having an effect on the job and housing markets, consumer spending and business investment, all of which are likely to worsen as Japan's population ages.

(a)   Define birth rate.   [2]

(b)   Explain **two** causes of a declining population.   [4]

(c)   Analyse how a falling population can result in a reduction in economic growth.   [6]

(d)   Discuss whether an ageing population is always a problem for a country.   [8]

3   With an estimated population of 50 million, Tanzania's economy grew by 7% in 2016. Tanzania had an HDI value of 0.531 in 2015, placing it 151 out of 188 countries in terms of human development. Life expectancy was 65.5 years and expected years in schooling at the age of 5 was 8.9. An estimated 47% of Tanzania's population lived in absolute poverty in 2016.

(a)   Define absolute poverty.   [2]

(b)   Explain **two** causes of absolute poverty.   [4]

(c)   Analyse how higher savings in an economy can result in increased economic development.   [6]

(d)   Discuss whether an increase in HDI always indicates an increase in a country's living standards.   [8]

4   In 2015, China began the process of phasing out its one-child policy, which it first implemented in 1979 to prevent overpopulation. The policy restricted couples to having only one child. As well as slowing population growth, the policy created a gender imbalance. In 2016, there were approximately 42 million more males in China than females.

(a)   Define optimum population.   [2]

(b)   Explain **two** economic consequences of a gender imbalance.   [4]

(c)   Analyse how overpopulation may result a more unequal distribution of income within an economy.   [6]

(d)   Discuss whether net outward migration will reduce the economic growth of a country.   [8]

6 International trade and globalisation

International trade and globalisation have the potential to increase economic growth and prosperity, but they also present significant challenges for many countries. In this chapter, you will learn about specialisation at national level before going on to analyse the potential benefits and drawbacks of multinational companies, free trade, and protection for consumers, producers and economies. Next, you will examine how exchange rates work and how fluctuations in the value of currencies can impact trade between countries. Finally, the causes and consequences of changes in a country's balance of payments are examined, along with policies a government can use to correct large imbalances in the current account.

6.1 International specialisation

6.2 Free trade and protection

6.3 Foreign exchange rates

6.4 Current account of balance of payments

International specialisation

Learning objectives

By the end of this unit, you should be able to:

• understand why specialisation at a national level is important

• discuss the advantages and disadvantages of specialisation at a national level.

Starting point

Answer these questions in pairs:

1 What is specialisation?

2 What is productivity?

3 Why is specialisation good for individuals and businesses?

Exploring

Discuss these questions in pairs:

1 What factors of production can you see in the pictures below?

2 How might these factors of production be used to increase the GDP of a country?

Developing

Specialisation at a national level

Specialisation is the process of developing expertise in a particular area. At an individual level, people specialise in developing particular skills (see Unit 3.3). At the level of a firm, businesses specialise in producing particular products. At a national level, countries specialise in producing goods and services in particular industries.

Key term

Specialisation – the process of developing expertise in a particular area

The main benefit of specialisation at national level is that it enables countries to become very good at producing goods and services in certain industries. As a result, productivity in these industries increases, leading to more efficient use of a country's resources and greater output. For example, Vietnam specialises in the production of rice, a large proportion of which is exported abroad, earning revenue for the country. Increased productivity and efficiency also reduces unit cost, leading to more competitive prices.

The goods and services a country specialises in depend on the country's **factor endowments**. Factor endowments are the factors of production a country has available. For example, Vietnam is endowed with fertile land and a climate suitable for growing rice. China is endowed with a large, skilled and relatively cheap labour force that is suitable for making manufactured goods. The Maldives is endowed with beautiful beaches and so specialises in tourism.

Specialisation therefore enables countries to concentrate on producing the goods and services they are best at, given their factor endowments. Countries can then export the goods they produce most efficiently and import the goods other countries produce most efficiently. If all countries specialise and trade with each other, total world output is likely to increase, potentially leading to higher living standards for the populations of all countries.

Key terms

Factor endowments – the factors of production a country has available to produce goods and services

Absolute advantage – a situation in which a country is able to produce a particular good or service at a lower cost (using fewer resources) relative to other countries

Extension topic

Absolute and comparative advantage

The theory of absolute and comparative advantage can be used to explain why specialisation and international trade increase efficiency and benefit all countries.

Absolute advantage is when a country is able to produce certain goods at a lower cost (using fewer resources) than other countries. **Comparative advantage** is when a country can produce a good at a lower opportunity cost (giving up fewer resources) than other countries. The law of comparative advantage states that all countries will be better off if they specialise in producing those goods and services in which they have comparative advantage and trade with other nations.

Key terms

Comparative advantage – a situation in which a country is able to produce a particular good or service at a lower opportunity cost (giving up fewer resources) relative to other countries

For example, Thailand has the ideal tropical climate and human and capital resources with which to produce rice. The opportunity cost to Thailand of producing another crop, such as wheat, would be very high, as the country is not endowed with the resources to grow wheat efficiently. In other words, by switching resources (land, labour and capital) away from rice production to wheat production, Thailand would give up (or forego) a large quantity of rice in order to produce a small quantity of wheat. It would be much more efficient for Thailand to specialise in producing rice (in which it has comparative advantage) and exchange it for wheat from a country that has comparative advantage in wheat production, such as China, India or the USA. If it does this, Thailand's total output and the output of its trading partner would be higher, leading to higher economic growth and living standards for the populations of both countries.

1 How might the factor endowments of a country change over time?

Advantages and disadvantages of specialisation at a national level

Specialisation at a national level has advantages and disadvantages for different sections of the economy. These are described in the following table.

Advantages and disadvantages of specialisation at a national level

	Advantages	Disadvantages
Consumers	**Increased choice**. Specialisation and trade between countries can increase the choice of products available to consumers, leading to higher living standards. **Lower prices**. Prices are likely to be lower for consumers as goods and services are being produced by the most efficient countries.	**External influences**. The price and availability of imported goods may be affected by external influences, such as exchange rate fluctuations or problems with supply in another country, such as crop failure due to flooding.
Producers	**Lower costs**. Due to the high volume of goods produced when countries specialise, firms are likely to benefit from economies of scale, thus lowering unit cost (see Unit 3.5). **Increased productivity**. Firms and industries are likely to develop faster and cheaper production methods as a result of concentrating their efforts on the production of a narrow range of goods.	**Reliance on imported raw materials**. As a result of specialisation, firms may be reliant on suppliers in other countries for their raw materials. Problems such as natural disasters may therefore disrupt supply chains, affecting production in other countries. **Exchange rate uncertainty**. Changes in exchange rates may affect the costs of imported raw materials and the prices firms receive for their products in overseas markets, making it difficult for them to plan future production.

	Advantages	Disadvantages
Economy	**Increased output**. An economy's GDP is likely to rise due to sales of its exports abroad. **Increased efficiency**. Specialisation means that countries concentrate on producing those goods and services they are best at, given their factor endowments. As a result, resources within the economy are put to their most productive use, leading to a more efficient allocation of resources.	**Overdependence**. A country that specialises may become overly dependent on the production of a particular product for its income. An unexpected fall in world demand for this product could therefore result in wide-scale unemployment and negative economic growth in the economy.

Key term

Overdependence – excessive reliance by a country on the production of a narrow range of products for income and jobs

2 How might the goods and services produced by a developing country differ from those produced by a developed country?

CASE STUDY — **Sri Lanka's tea industry**

Sri Lanka is one of the world's largest producers and exporters of tea. Famous for its Ceylon tea, the Sri Lankan tea industry has been in operation for over 150 years. Sri Lanka is able to produce tea more efficiently than many other countries due to the geographical and climatic conditions of its Central Highlands region, which are suitable for growing tea of the highest quality. The skill and expertise of workers in the industry also help Sri Lanka to produce tea efficiently.

Sri Lanka produces around 340 million kilograms of tea per year, over 90% of which is exported. Tea exports generate around 65% of export revenue from agricultural products. Tea production contributes about 2% to Sri Lanka's GDP. An estimated two million workers are directly or indirectly employed in the tea industry, around 10% of the country's population.

In recent years, Sri Lankan tea producers have lost market share to emerging producers from Kenya and other African countries, which are able to produce tea more cheaply.

1 Using information from the extract, what enables Sri Lanka to specialise in tea production?

2 Name one disadvantage for Sri Lanka of specialising in tea production?

Applying

Project work

Using the internet, prepare a poster for a country of your choice with the following information:

- the name of the country
- the main factor endowments of the country
- the goods and services the country specialises in producing
- the advantages that specialisation brings to the country
- the potential drawbacks of specialisation for the country.

Be ready to present your poster to your classmates in the next lesson.

Knowledge check questions

1 Define specialisation. [2]

2 Explain the benefits of specialisation for consumers. [4]

3 Explain **two** possible disadvantages of specialisation at a national level for a country. [4]

4 (E) Discuss whether all countries benefit from specialisation at a national level. [8]

Check your progress

Read the unit objectives below and reflect on your progress in each.

- Understand why specialisation at a national level is important.

- Discuss the advantages and disadvantages of specialisation at a national level.

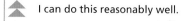   I struggle with this and need more practice.

I can do this reasonably well.

I can do this with confidence.

Free trade and protection

Learning objectives

By the end of this unit, you should be able to:

- define globalisation
- define multinational company (MNC)
- describe the costs and benefits of MNCs to their host countries and home countries
- explain the benefits and drawbacks of free trade for consumers, producers and the economy in a variety of countries
- describe methods of protection, including tariffs, import quotas, subsidies and embargoes
- explain the reasons for protection, including infant industry, declining industry, strategic industry and avoidance of dumping
- analyse the consequences and effectiveness of protection for the home country and its trading partners.

Starting point

Answer these questions in pairs:

1 What is an indirect tax?

2 What effect does an indirect tax have on the price and output of a product?

3 What is meant by internal economies of scale?

Exploring

Discuss these questions in pairs:

1 Identify three global brands that are produced in more than one country.

2 How might people benefit from consuming these brands?

3 How might businesses benefit from producing and selling their products in more than one country?

Developing

What is globalisation?

If you wanted to buy a book, where would you go to buy it? You might try your local bookstore. Alternatively, you could purchase it online through a website such as Amazon or Alibaba and have it sent to you, most likely from another country. If you choose the latter method, you are a consumer in a global marketplace. Due to the internet, improved communication and growing transport links between countries, it is possible for individuals and businesses to buy and sell products from almost anywhere in the world. This is **globalisation**, the integration of local markets into a single global marketplace.

Key term

Globalisation – the integration of local markets into a single global market

The role of multinational companies (MNCs)

The rise of multinational companies (MNCs) is also a feature of globalisation. A MNC is a business that produces in more than one country. Coca-Cola, Starbucks and Toyota are all multinational companies as they produce their products in many countries. As a consumer, you are able to purchase a bottle of Coca-Cola in almost any country in the world. Coca-Cola is a global brand and it is available in a global market.

1 What is the difference between a multinational company and an exporter?

The costs and benefits of MNCs to home countries

The **home country** of a MNC is the country in which the company was originally established. For example, Tata Motor's home country is India. It was first set up in India and has its headquarters in Mumbai. Tata Motors owns Jaguar Land Rover, the largest producer of cars in the UK.

Key term

Home country – the country in which a multinational company was originally established and where its headquarters are based

Benefits and costs of MNCs to their home country

Benefits	Costs
Inflow of profits. Profits flow into the home country from the overseas operations of the MNC.	**Loss of jobs**. MNCs moving production abroad to countries with cheaper labour may create job losses in their home countries, increasing unemployment.

Benefits	Costs
Improved reputation overseas. MNCs may help to enhance the reputation of the home country as a producer of high-quality products. Other businesses from the home country may then benefit from this, leading to an increase in sales. For example, the success of global brands such as Mercedes and BMW enhances the reputation of German manufacturers for quality engineering.	**Outflow of capital**. MNCs may have to invest large amounts of capital overseas in order to set up production facilities and retail outlets in other countries. There may therefore be an outflow of money from the home country.

Key term
....

Host country – any country in which a multinational company produces that is not its home country

The costs and benefits of MNCs to host countries

A **host country** is any country in which an MNC produces that is not its home country. For example, Thailand is a host country to the British retailer Tesco.

Benefits and costs of MNCs to the host country

Benefits	Costs
Lower unemployment. A MNC setting up operations in a host country will often create jobs for local workers, helping to lower unemployment.	**Low-skilled jobs**. Many of the jobs created by MNCs may be low skilled. Highly skilled jobs may go to foreign nationals from the MNC's home country.
Increased profits for local businesses. Local businesses, such as suppliers of raw materials and component parts, may receive higher sales and profits from selling to MNCs.	**Closure of local businesses**. Increased competition from MNCs may force local businesses to close, leading to higher unemployment.
Lower prices. Consumers may benefit from the increased availability of goods and lower prices due to increased competition.	**Depletion of natural resources**. MNCs may deplete (use up) the non-renewable natural resources of the host country, such as oil. Once natural resources are exhausted, the MNC may relocate to another country.
Inflow of investment capital. There will be an initial inflow of capital into the host country when the MNC sets up operations, for example, to purchase the land and equipment.	**Exploitation of labour**. Ineffective labour laws in developing countries may result in low wages and poor working conditions, particularly for unskilled workers in manufacturing industries.
Increased economic growth. The production of goods and services by MNCs contributes to the GDP and economic growth of the host country.	**Outflow of profits**. Profits made by MNCs may be sent out of the host county to the MNC's home country.

Benefits	Costs
Transfer of knowledge and skills. Technology, knowledge and skills may be transferred from the MNC to local workers and businesses. This may lead to an increase in the productivity of domestic firms in the longer run. 	**Increased pollution**. Production by MNCs may lead to higher levels of air, water and soil pollution, damaging the environment and reducing the quality of life of the local population. 
Increase in tax revenue. Taxes paid by the MNC will increase tax revenue for the government, which could be used to improve the infrastructure of the host country.	**Loss of tax revenue**. A government may offer MNCs generous tax benefits to set up in the host country, reducing the tax revenue it receives.
Improved trade balance. Goods produced by the MNC for export may improve the host country's balance of trade on its current account.	

2 Identify two ways in which the government can reduce the problems caused by MNCs to a host country.

CASE STUDY **Food retail in India**

In 2016, the Indian government announced plans to allow foreign multinational companies (MNCs) to open processed food retail stores in India on the condition that all products were sourced from Indian suppliers. With the food retail business in India worth an estimated $70 billion, MNCs were quick to respond, with US-based Walmart revealing plans to open 50 stores across India, a move that would bring much-needed foreign direct investment into the country.

The opening up of the food retail market to foreign MNCs would provide competition for large domestic firms including Reliance Fresh, Big Bazaar and Spencer's, leading to lower prices and greater choice of food products for Indian consumers. Farmers may also benefit from selling directly to foreign-owned retail stores. However, small traders including corner shops and traditional 'kirana' stores, were opposed to the move, fearing they may be forced out of business.

1 What are the advantages of opening up India's retail food industry to foreign MNCs?

2 How is the Indian government planning to control foreign food retailers? Do you think these controls will be effective?

Free trade

Free trade is when goods and services can be exchanged for money between countries without any limits or restrictions – for example, the import of Chinese-made electronic goods into a country without any government-imposed restrictions on volume or price. Two or more countries may negotiate a **free trade agreement (FTA)**, in which they agree to remove restrictions (also known as **barriers to trade**) such as tariffs and import quotas on all or some of the products traded between the countries concerned.

Free trade has both benefits and drawbacks for consumers, producers and economies.

Key terms

Free trade – the exchange of goods and services between countries without any government-imposed restrictions on volume or price

Free trade agreement (FTA) – an agreement between two or more countries to reduce restrictions on some or all products traded between them

Barriers to trade – restrictions imposed by a government that prevent the free trade of exports and imports between countries

Benefits of free trade

The benefits of free trade for consumers, producers and a country's economy are outlined in the table below.

The benefits of free trade

Consumers	• **Increased choice**. Free trade is likely to result in a greater variety of goods and services being made available to consumers, leading to higher living standards. • **Lower prices**. Prices are likely to fall due to increased competition from imports.
Producers	• **Access to overseas markets**. Firms are able to sell their products in overseas markets, which may lead to an increase in sales revenue and higher profits. • **Economies of scale**. Increasing output to satisfy demand in overseas markets should enable firms to benefit from economies of scale (see Unit 3.5). As a result of lower unit costs, they will be able to decrease prices and increase their competitiveness internationally. • **Improved innovation and efficiency**. Domestic firms will be forced to innovate due to strong competition from imported goods. This may include developing new and improved products for consumers (product innovation) or more efficient production processes that enable them to lower costs and charge cheaper prices (process innovation). • **Import of capital equipment and technology**. Free trade enables domestic firms to import capital equipment and technology at lower prices. This should help to increase their productivity, making them more competitive internationally.

Economy	• **Lower unemployment**. Sales of exports abroad may create employment opportunities as domestic firms increase output to satisfy demand in overseas markets. This may lead to higher incomes for the local population, helping to alleviate poverty in developing countries.
	• **Lower inflation**. Increased competition from imports may put downward pressure on the domestic price level. Producers may also be able to import raw materials more cheaply from other countries, lowering their production costs and enabling them to reduce their prices. 

Drawbacks of free trade

The disadvantages of free trade for consumers, producers and a country's economy are outlined in the table below.

The disadvantages of free trade

Consumers	• **Unequal distribution of the benefits of free trade**. Not all consumers benefit equally from free trade. Those on higher incomes will be able to enjoy the higher living standards that come from the consumption of imports such as luxury brand name products. Those on low incomes, however, are unlikely to be able to afford these products and may experience little or no change in their standards of living.
Producers	• **Falling sales and profits**. Some domestic producers may experience a decrease in sales and profits as a result of increased competition from cheaper imports. This may lead to some businesses closing down.
Economy	• **Higher unemployment**. Increased competition from cheaper imports may result in job losses as domestic firms lay off workers due to falling sales. 
	• **Environmental damage**. The use of fossil fuels to transport goods across vast distances and the depletion of non-renewable resources such as the world's rainforests may result in irreversible environmental damage in some countries and contribute to problems such as global warming.
	• **Unequal distribution of gains from trade.** Not all countries experience the gains from free trade equally. Richer countries tend to benefit from greater choice and cheaper imports, while some poorer countries may be exploited for their natural resources and cheap labour. 
	• **Current account instability**. Free trade may result in a growing imbalance between export revenue and import expenditure. This could lead to a large and persistent deficit or surplus on a country's current account of its balance of payments (see Unit 6.4).

3 Identify two ways in which a government could reduce the disadvantages of free trade.

Protection

Protection (or **protectionism**) is when a government imposes trade barriers that restrict free trade between countries. This could include restrictions placed on foreign imports sold in a country or restrictions placed on domestically produced exports to other countries. A government may impose protection policies on imports in order to safeguard jobs and industries in its home country.

Methods of protection

Tariffs

A tariff is a tax on imports. The imposition of a tariff by a government will raise the price of imports, making home-produced goods more competitive. As a result, demand for home-produced goods will increase, leading to higher sales and profits for domestic firms. A tariff also generates tax revenue for the government, which can be used to finance spending on areas including infrastructure, education and healthcare.

Import quotas

An **import quota** is a limit on the volume of imports allowed into a country. Restricting the supply of imports is likely to lead to an increase in their price, increasing the competitiveness of domestic firms. As a result, domestic firms are likely to experience increased sales and profits. Unlike a tariff, the government does not receive any tax revenue from the imposition of import quotas.

The imposition of an import quota would shift the supply curve for imports from S to S_1 in Figure 6.2.1. This would reduce the quantity of imports traded domestically from Q to Q_1 and raise their price from P to P_1. The import quota therefore restricts the quantity of imports supplied to Q_1. Foreign producers are willing to supply Q_1 imports at any price (supply is perfectly inelastic at Q_1). Due to the higher-priced imports, demand for domestically produced substitute goods is likely to increase.

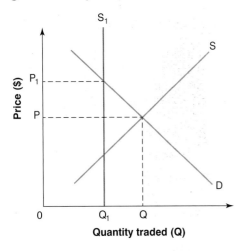

Figure 6.2.1 The effect of an import quota on the market for a good

Subsidies

A subsidy is a grant (a sum of money) paid to producers by the government; it does not need to be repaid (see Unit 2.11). The government finances subsidies from tax revenue. Subsidies paid to domestic producers help to reduce their costs of production. This enables them to lower their prices, making them more competitive with imports. The government may also pay an **export subsidy** to protect exporters. This reduces the production costs of exporters, enabling them to charge lower prices for their exports in overseas markets. The resulting increase in sales of exports also helps to safeguard jobs in the export industries of the home country.

A subsidy paid to domestic producers by the government would reduce their costs of production, leading to an increase in supply from S to S_1 in Figure 6.2.2. As result, the price of home-produced goods would fall from P to P_1, making them more competitive against imports and in international markets. The quantity of home-produced goods traded would therefore increase from Q to Q_1.

Key terms

Export subsidy – a financial grant given to exporters by the government that does not need to be repaid

Embargo – a complete ban on the import of a certain product or all products from a particular country

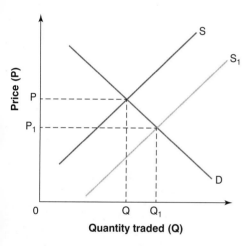

Embargoes

An **embargo** is a ban on imports and exports with another country. This could include a complete ban on all trade with a particular country. For example, the USA has had an embargo in place on all trade with the Republic of Cuba since 1962. An embargo could also refer to a complete ban on the import of certain products that may be harmful to consumers. For example, the EU has a ban in place on the import of chicken washed in chlorine from the USA due to concerns about the effects it might have on consumer health.

Reasons for protection

There are several reasons why a government may want to restrict trade with other countries.

Infant industry

An **infant industry** (or **sunrise industry**) is an industry that is emerging (newly established) in a country. Domestic firms operating in an infant industry may struggle to compete with large foreign competitors, who benefit from significant economies of scale (see Unit 3.5). Economies of scale enable foreign firms to charge lower prices, which makes it difficult for smaller domestic firms in infant industries to compete and become established. A government may use this as justification for protection. By restricting imports in these industries, domestic firms are better able to compete and grow. Once domestic firms are large enough to compete on their own, governments may remove the protection policies.

Declining industry

A **declining industry** (or **sunset industry**) is an industry that is experiencing falling sales, usually due to a structural change in the economy. For example, the garment manufacturing industry in the USA has been in decline for a number of years due to competition from cheap imported clothing produced in countries with lower labour costs. Governments may therefore impose protection policies in order to ease the impact that a declining industry may have on the economy, particularly in terms of unemployment. Protecting a declining industry could allow time for some workers to retrain and find new jobs.

Strategic industry

Some industries may be protected by a government because they are of strategic importance to the country. For example, farming is strategically important to an economy as governments want to ensure that they are able to produce enough food to sustain their population, if necessary. It would be risky to be entirely reliant on other countries for food production. As a result, some governments may choose to protect farmers in agricultural industries to ensure food continues to be produced domestically. Other **strategic industries** include telecommunications and energy.

Prevention of dumping

Dumping is when products are sold in overseas markets at prices below what it cost to produce them. Dumping can have a damaging effect on domestic producers, who are unable to compete with the extremely low-priced imports. In 2017, the Indian government imposed protection policies on imported steel, arguing that foreign steel manufacturers were dumping their products in the country. Dumping may be a deliberate attempt by foreign firms to force the closure of local competitors or a way

Key terms

Infant industry (or **sunrise industry**) – an emerging or newly established industry that is still too small to benefit from internal economies of scale and is therefore unable to compete with large foreign rivals

Declining industry (or **sunset industry**) – an industry that is experiencing falling sales due to a change in the structure of the economy

Strategic industry – an industry that is important to the long-term wellbeing of a country

Dumping – the sale of imported goods at a price below what it cost to produce them

for them to dispose of unwanted surplus stock. Regardless of the reason, governments may decide to impose measures to protect domestic producers if dumping is suspected.

Safeguarding of jobs

A government may decide to impose protection policies to protect jobs in domestic industries. Policies that increase the price of imports will make domestic industries more competitive. Increased sales of home-produced goods will lead to higher production and higher levels of employment.

Correction of a current account deficit

A government may impose protection policies to correct a deficit on the current account. Policies that increase the price of imports are likely to result in consumers switching away from buying imports to purchasing locally produced goods. As a result, spending on imports is likely to fall, thus improving a current account deficit (see Unit 6.4).

 4 Which reason do you think provides the best justification for protection? Why?

Consequences of protection

Impact of protection on the home country

Protection is likely to increase the price of imported goods for consumers, resulting in fewer imports entering the country. Consumer choice is therefore likely to be reduced and the living standards of the population may fall.

If protection policies are effective, producers in the home country will experience higher sales and profits. However, the effectiveness of these policies may be reduced if trading partners choose to retaliate. **Retaliation** is when a country imposes trade restrictions on the imports of a country in response to trade restrictions already imposed on its products. For example, in 2013, China retaliated to tariffs imposed on Chinese-made solar panels sold in the USA by imposing tariffs on certain US goods imported into China. This resulted in a reduction in export revenue and job losses in some American industries.

Protection policies can also benefit the economy by lowering levels of unemployment and increasing economic growth in the home country. However, as explained above, these benefits may be reduced if trading partners choose to retaliate.

A potential drawback of protection is that it may decrease the efficiency with which resources are allocated within the home country. Protected domestic industries, reliant on protection from the government, may become less efficient at producing their

Key term

Retaliation – the imposition of protection policies by a government on imports from another country in response to protection policies imposed on exports from its country

goods, leading to rising production costs and higher prices for consumers. Protected firms also have less incentive to innovate to remain competitive. As a result, prices are likely to rise and the quality of goods produced may decrease.

Inflation in the home country may also rise due to the increased cost of importing raw materials resulting from the protection in place. Higher domestic demand for the relatively cheaper home-produced goods may also cause demand-pull inflation.

Impact of protection on trading partners

Protection policies placed on imports are likely to have a negative impact on the economies of trading partners.

- Exporters of trading partners are likely to experience a fall in sales, resulting in lower profits and reduced production.
- The economies of trading partners may experience higher unemployment and a slowdown in economic growth resulting from reduced demand for their exports.

For example, it was estimated that US tariffs imposed on tyres imported from China cost the Chinese tyre industry $1 billion in lost revenue and resulted in approximately 100 000 job losses.

The extent of the impact on trading partners will depend on the importance of the country imposing the protection as a market for their exporters. The bigger the market, the more damaging the impact on trading partners.

Applying

Project work

Using the internet, find a newspaper article about a protection policy imposed by a government on imports from another country.

1. What are the countries involved?

2. What was the method of protection?

3. What products were affected?

4. Why were protection policies imposed?

5. What was the response of the country affected by the protection?

Be ready to share your article and your responses to the above questions with your classmates in your next lesson.

Knowledge check questions

1 Define globalisation. [2]

2 Define multinational company. [2]

3 Explain **two** potential drawbacks to a host country from allowing multinationals to set up. [4]

4 Explain **two** potential benefits of free trade to domestic producers in a country. [4]

5 Define tariff. [2]

6 Define import quota. [2]

7 Explain the impact of a tariff on domestic producers. [4]

8 Explain the infant industry argument as justification for protection. [4]

9 (E) Discuss whether free trade is always beneficial to an economy. [8]

Check your progress

Read the unit objectives below and reflect on your progress in each.

	I struggle with this and need more practice.
	I can do this reasonably well.
	I can do this with confidence.

- Define globalisation.

- Define multinational company (MNC).

- Describe the costs and benefits of MNCs to their host countries and home countries.

- Explain the benefits and drawbacks of free trade for consumers, producers and the economy in a variety of countries.

- Describe methods of protection, including tariffs, import quotas, subsidies and embargoes.

- Explain the reasons for protection, including infant industry, declining industry, strategic industry and avoidance of dumping.

- Analyse the consequences and effectiveness of protection for the home country and its trading partners.

Foreign exchange rates

Learning objectives

By the end of this unit, you should be able to:

- define foreign exchange rate
- identify the equilibrium foreign exchange rate
- explain the factors affecting the demand for and the supply of a currency in the foreign exchange market
- explain the effects of foreign exchange rate fluctuations on export and import prices
- analyse how price elasticity of demand (PED) for exports and imports affects export revenue and import expenditure
- distinguish between floating and fixed exchange rate systems
- describe the advantages and disadvantages of a floating and a fixed exchange rate system.

Starting point

Answer these questions in pairs:

1. What are the characteristics of a market?

2. What is price elasticity of demand?

3. What are the determinants of price elasticity of demand?

Exploring

Discuss these questions in pairs:

1. What is your local currency?

2. Where would you go to exchange your local currency into foreign currency?

3. How much would it cost to buy one US dollar in your local currency today?

Developing

What is a foreign exchange rate?

A **foreign exchange rate** (or **exchange rate**) is the price of one currency in terms of another currency. For example, in 2017 the exchange rate for Chinese yuan (CN¥) in terms of US dollars (US$)

Key term

Foreign exchange rate (or **exchange rate**) – the price of one currency in terms of another currency

was about CN¥6.9 to US$1. In other words, the price of US$1 was CN¥6.9.

Different countries operate different exchange rate systems to determine the value of their currencies. Under a **floating system** the exchange rate is determined by the market forces of demand and supply. Under a **fixed system** the exchange rate is controlled by the government and maintained at a certain (fixed) value.

Exchange rate determination in the foreign exchange market

Every time you buy foreign currency, to spend on an overseas holiday for instance, you are engaging in a transaction in the foreign exchange market. The **foreign exchange market** is where foreign currencies are traded (bought and sold).

 Why do consumers, businesses and governments need foreign currency?

The exchange rate of a currency is determined by demand and supply in the foreign exchange market. The **equilibrium foreign exchange rate**, ER_E in Figure 6.3.1, is where the quantity of the currency demanded equals the quantity of the currency supplied.

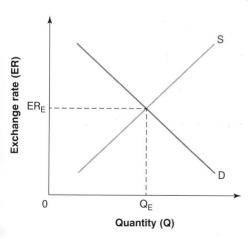

Figure 6.3.1 Equilibrium foreign exchange rate

An increase in the equilibrium exchange rate due to market forces is called an **appreciation**, while a fall in the equilibrium exchange rate is called a **depreciation**.

Key terms

Floating system – the value of a currency determined by the market forces of demand and supply in the foreign exchange market

Fixed system – the value of a currency maintained at a certain level by the government

Foreign exchange market – the place where buyers and sellers meet to trade foreign currencies

Appreciation – a rise in the value of a currency due to market forces

Depreciation – a fall in the value of a currency due to market forces

Key knowledge

Another way to say a currency has appreciated is to say that it *is stronger/has strengthened* against other currencies.

Another way to say a currency has depreciated is to say that it *is weaker/has weakened* against other currencies.

An increase in the demand for a currency will shift the demand curve up to the right from D to D₁ in Figure 6.3.2. As a result, the exchange rate will appreciate from ER to ER₁ and the quantity traded will rise from Q to Q₁.

A fall in the demand for a currency from D to D₂, on the other hand, will lead to a depreciation in the currency's value from ER to ER₂ and a decrease in quantity traded from Q to Q₂.

An increase in the supply of a currency will shift the supply curve down to the right, from S to S₁ in Figure 6.3.3. As a result, the exchange rate will depreciate from ER to ER₁ and quantity traded will rise from Q to Q₁.

Conversely, a fall in the supply of a currency from S to S₂ will result in an appreciation from ER to ER₂ and a fall in quantity traded from Q to Q₂.

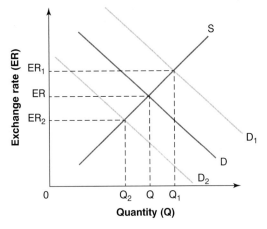

Figure 6.3.2 Changes in the demand for a currency

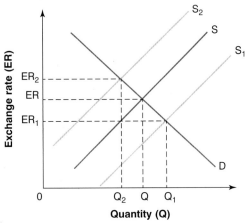

Figure 6.3.3 Changes in the supply of a currency

2 What similarities and differences are there between the market for a currency and the market for a product?

Key knowledge

Exchange rate changes explained

In 2012, £1 Great British Pound (GBP) bought $1.6 US dollars (USD). Five years later in 2017, £1 GBP bought $1.3 USD. What happened to the value of the pound against the dollar over this period? The answer is the pound depreciated (weakened) against the dollar. We know this because in 2017 it took more pounds to buy the same dollars as in 2012. The dollar, on the other hand, appreciated (strengthened) against the pound. It took fewer dollars in 2017 to buy the same amount of pounds as in 2012.

Causes of foreign exchange rate fluctuations

Fluctuations (changes) in the value of a currency result from changes in either demand or supply.

Changes in the demand for a currency

- **A change in the demand for exports.** In order to buy a country's exports, foreigners must use the currency of that country. For example, a British retailer purchasing clothing from Bangladesh will have to pay for those items in the local currency, Bangladeshi taka. The demand for a country's currency is therefore directly related to the demand for its exports. If more Bangladeshi exports are demanded, more Bangladeshi taka will be needed to pay for them and demand for the currency will rise. Conversely, if fewer Bangladeshi exports are demanded, less Bangladeshi taka will be needed to pay for them and demand for the currency will fall.

- **A change in a country's interest rate**. A change in interest rates will affect the return (interest income) that foreign investors receive on the capital (money) they are holding in a country. If a central bank raises interest rates, the return that foreign investors receive will increase. This will encourage more foreign investors to bring money into the country, leading **to short-term capital inflows ('hot money')**. As capital can only be invested in the local currency of the country, demand for the country's currency will rise. Similarly, a reduction in interest rates by the central bank will make the country less appealing to foreign investors. As a result, fewer foreigners will invest, resulting in a reduction of short-term capital inflows and a fall in the demand for the currency.

- **Speculation on the value of the domestic currency**. Speculation involves buying, holding and selling a foreign currency in order to make a profit when its price changes. For example, if speculators think the Thai baht will appreciate in value in the future, they will buy baht now while the price is low. When the baht appreciates, speculators will sell their holdings at the higher price and make a profit. Demand for a currency increases if speculators think there is a good chance the currency will appreciate in the future. Demand for the currency falls if they think there is little chance of it rising in value.

- **Entry of multinational companies (MNCs) into a country**. When MNCs enter a new host country, they often invest large sums of capital to purchase the resources they need to set up operations. For example, if IKEA sets up a new retail outlet in Malaysia, it must bring capital (called **foreign direct investment (FDI)**) into the country to purchase the resources, such as land, buildings and

Key terms

Short-term capital flows ('hot money') – the flow of money from one country to another on a temporary basis in order to earn income from changes in interest rates

Foreign direct investment (FDI) – money (capital) that flows into a country for the purpose of setting up business operations

equipment, that it needs. In order to purchase these resources it must first convert its funds into Malaysian ringgit, increasing the demand for ringgit. MNCs entering a country therefore increase the demand for the host country's currency. A reduction in the number of MNCs setting up in a country, on the other hand, will result in a fall in FDI, thereby decreasing the demand for the currency.

Changes in the supply of a currency

- **A change in spending on imports**. A change in spending on imported goods and services in a country will change the supply of that country's currency in the foreign exchange market. For example, a Malaysian resident paying for hotel accommodation in Singapore via an online website will increase the supply of Malaysian ringgit in the foreign exchange market. This is because ringgit (entering the foreign exchange market) will have to be exchanged for Singapore dollars (exiting the foreign exchange market) in order to pay the hotel in Singapore. Thus, increased spending on imported goods and services by Malaysian residents will result in an increase in the supply of ringgit in the foreign exchange market and a depreciation in the value of the currency. A decrease in spending on imports, on the other hand, will result in a fall in supply and an appreciation of the currency.

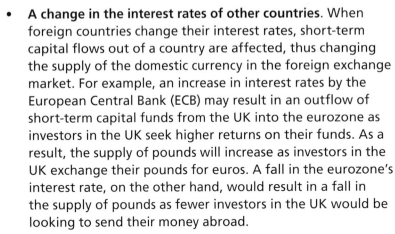

- **A change in the interest rates of other countries**. When foreign countries change their interest rates, short-term capital flows out of a country are affected, thus changing the supply of the domestic currency in the foreign exchange market. For example, an increase in interest rates by the European Central Bank (ECB) may result in an outflow of short-term capital funds from the UK into the eurozone as investors in the UK seek higher returns on their funds. As a result, the supply of pounds will increase as investors in the UK exchange their pounds for euros. A fall in the eurozone's interest rate, on the other hand, would result in a fall in the supply of pounds as fewer investors in the UK would be looking to send their money abroad.

- **Speculation on the values of foreign currencies**. The supply of a currency is affected by the actions of domestic speculators. For example, if speculators in India expect the Sri Lankan rupee to rise in value in the future, they will look to increase their holdings of Sri Lankan rupees. As speculators exchange their Indian rupees for Sri Lankan rupees in the foreign exchange market, the supply of Indian rupees rises.

- **Departure of MNCs from the country**. The departure of an MNC from a host country will influence the supply of the host country's currency in the foreign exchange market. For example, an MNC departing from Nigeria will lead to an outflow of capital from the country. This will result in an increase in the supply of Nigerian naira as the MNC exchanges naira for another currency in the foreign exchange market.

Consequences of a foreign exchange rate appreciation

An appreciation of a country's currency increases the price of exports and decreases the price of imports. As a result, foreigners will purchase fewer exports, and domestic consumers and producers will purchase more imports. The overall effect of this on the economy depends on the price elasticity of demand (PED) of both exports and imports.

 3   Why does an exchange rate appreciation make a country's exports more expensive?

Effect of an exchange rate appreciation on exports and imports when PED is inelastic

In the short run, the elasticity of demand for exports and imports is likely to be price inelastic. That is, a change in price will lead to a proportionately smaller change in the quantity of exports and imports demanded. Thus, the rise in the price of exports resulting from the exchange rate appreciation will lead to an increase in total export revenue for the country. The fall in the price of imports, on the other hand, will lead to a decrease in total import expenditure. The overall effect, therefore, is an improvement in a country's trade balance on its current account (see Unit 6.4).

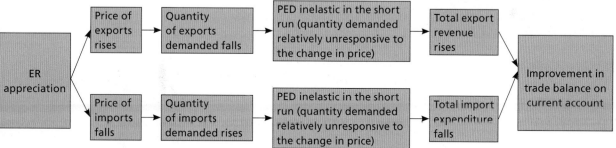

Effect of an exchange rate appreciation on exports and imports when PED is elastic

In the long run, however, elasticity of demand for exports and imports is likely to be price elastic. This is because foreign buyers of exports will have time to source cheaper alternatives from other countries, resulting in a proportionately larger fall in export sales over time in response to the higher price. Similarly, an increasing number of domestic producers and consumers will switch away from purchasing locally produced goods towards the relatively cheaper imports over time. The overall effect is a fall in export revenue and a rise in spending on imports, leading to a worsening of a country's trade balance on its current account.

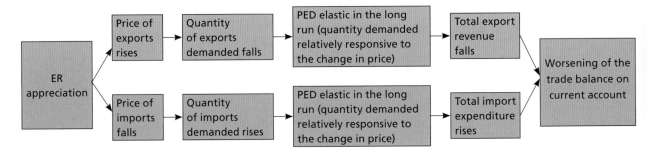

The fall in export revenue in the long run may also lead to unemployment as exporters lay off workers due to falling sales and revenue. However, the fall in the price of imports may lead to lower inflation as it will lower the cost of imported raw materials for domestic firms. Some of this cost saving will be passed on to consumers in the form of lower prices.

Consequences of a foreign exchange rate depreciation

A depreciation of a country's currency will lower the price of exports and raise the price of imports, leading to an increase in sales of exports and a fall in purchases of imports. Again, the overall effect on the economy depends on price elasticity of demand for both exports and imports.

In the short run, when demand for exports and imports is price inelastic, export revenue will fall and spending on imports will rise, leading to a worsening of the balance of trade on the current account. However, as demand for exports and imports becomes more price elastic over time, export revenue increases and import expenditure falls, improving the balance of trade on the current account.

The rise in export revenue is likely to lead to a fall in unemployment as exporters employ more workers to cope with the increase in the sales of exports. However, inflation may rise due to the increase in the cost of importing raw materials to domestic firms, some of which will be passed on to consumers in the form of higher prices. Higher demand for exports may also result in demand-pull inflation.

Floating exchange rate

A **floating exchange rate** is when the value of a country's currency is determined by the forces of demand and supply in the foreign exchange market. A government does not intervene in the foreign exchange market to influence the currency's value.

Key term

Floating exchange rate – a system where the value of a country's currency is determined by demand and supply

Advantages of a floating exchange rate

- **Adjusts automatically to stabilise the current account**. A floating exchange rate automatically adjusts to correct for a deficit or surplus on the current account (see Unit 6.4). For example, a country is likely to have a current account deficit when its spending on imports exceeds its revenue from exports. High demand for imports will lead to an increase in the supply of the currency, causing it to depreciate. Low demand for exports will lead to a fall in demand for the currency, also causing it to depreciate. Thus, the forces of demand and supply automatically adjust to cause a depreciation. As a result, the price of exports falls and the price of imports rises, leading to more exports and fewer imports being demanded and an improvement in the deficit on the current account.

- **Allows governments to focus on other aims**. Allowing the exchange rate to be determined by market forces enables a government to focus its attention on other aims that are important to the economy, such as low unemployment and low inflation. For example, a central bank can raise interest rates to lower inflation without being too concerned about the consequent effect this will have on the exchange rate – an inflow of short-term capital and an appreciation of the currency.

- **No need to maintain foreign currency reserves**. Reserves of foreign currency are used by the central bank to intervene in the foreign exchange market in order to influence the value of the country's currency. As there is no government intervention under a floating exchange rate system, there is no need for the central bank to store large reserves of foreign currency. Instead, these funds can be invested overseas in order to generate income for the country.

Disadvantages of a floating exchange rate

- **Uncertainty created by fluctuations in the value of the currency**. Floating exchange rates tend to be relatively volatile, regularly increasing and decreasing in value over time. This can create uncertainty for firms, making it difficult for them to plan future production and investment. Exchange rate fluctuations may therefore create uncertainty for exporters, importers and foreign investors.

  o Exporters may face uncertainty about how much revenue they will receive from sales of their goods abroad.

  o Importers may face uncertainty about the cost of imported raw materials.

  o Foreign MNCs may face uncertainty about how much capital they will need to invest in order to set up in a country.

Consequently, there may be a reduction in international trade and investment in a country, leading to higher unemployment and a slowdown in economic growth.

- **Speculators may influence the value of a currency**. Foreign currency speculators can influence the value of a currency under a floating system. This may have a destabilising effect on the current account of the balance of payments of a country. For example, if speculators expect the value of a currency to rise, they will buy up large quantities of the currency in the foreign exchange market, causing it to appreciate. This will increase the price of exports and decrease the price of imports, potentially worsening a current account deficit.

Fixed exchange rate

A **fixed exchange rate** is when the value of a currency is maintained at a particular level by a country's government (or central bank). The central bank intervenes in the foreign exchange market by buying and selling its own currency in order to maintain the exchange rate at a certain (fixed) value. An increase in the value of a currency due to direct intervention from the central bank is called a **revaluation**. A decrease in the value of a currency due to direct intervention from the central bank is called a **devaluation**.

Suppose the fixed exchange rate for a country is ER* in Figure 6.3.4. If, due to market forces, the exchange rate falls below ER* to ER_1, the central bank will intervene by buying up its own currency in the foreign exchange market using foreign currency reserves. This will increase demand for the currency from D_1 to D_2, revaluing the exchange rate from ER_1 to its fixed value of ER*. If, on the other hand, the exchange rate rises above ER* as in Figure 6.3.5, the central bank will respond by selling its own currency in the foreign exchange market, increasing supply from S_1 to S_2 and devaluing the exchange rate from ER_2 to its fixed value, ER*.

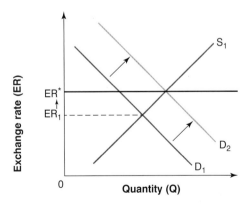

Figure 6.3.4 Revaluation of the currency to maintain a fixed exchange rate at ER*

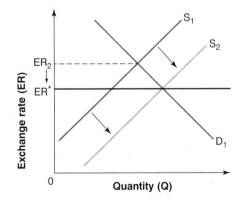

Figure 6.3.5 Devaluation of the currency to maintain a fixed exchange rate at ER*

In addition to buying and selling its own currency in the foreign exchange market, a central bank can also use monetary policy (see Unit 4.4) to influence the value of the exchange rate. If a central bank wanted to increase the value of its currency, it would raise interest rates. This will attract an inflow of short-term capital (hot money) into the country, increasing the demand for the currency and leading to a rise in its value. If, on the other hand, the central bank wanted to reduce the value of its currency, it will lower interest rates. This will result in an outflow of short-term capital from the country, increasing the supply of the currency in the foreign exchange market and reducing its value.

Advantages of a fixed exchange rate

- **More certainty for firms and investors**. A fixed exchange rate will create a greater degree of certainty for exporters, importers and foreign investors. Exporters will know how much revenue they will earn from the sale of their products abroad, while the cost of imported raw materials and finished goods will remain relatively stable for importers. MNCs will be able to effectively plan future investment in a country with a fixed exchange rate as they will be able to more accurately forecast (predict) future costs and revenues. As a result of increased certainly, international trade and investment in the country may increase.

- **Speculators less likely to influence the value of the currency**. As the exchange rate is fixed at a particular level, there is little opportunity for speculators to profit from fluctuations in the value of the currency. Thus, speculative movements in the exchange rate are less likely.

- **Increased demand for exports**. A country dependent on the sale of exports for growth can choose to set the value of its currency low. This will make the country's exports more competitive on the world market and will help to maintain low unemployment, particularly in export industries.

- **Lower inflation**. By setting the value of the currency high, a government is able to control inflation in the country. A strong exchange rate will reduce the price of imports, lowering the cost of imported raw materials for domestic firms. Some of these cost savings will be passed on to consumers in the form of lower prices, putting downward pressure on the domestic price level. Furthermore, higher-priced exports as a result of the stronger currency may reduce the demand for exports, thus also putting downward pressure on the general level of prices.

Disadvantages of a fixed exchange rate

- **The central bank must hold sufficient reserves of foreign currency**. The foreign currency reserves that the central bank uses to influence the value of its currency in the foreign exchange market must be sufficient to maintain the exchange rate at a particular value. This involves an opportunity cost, as foreign currency reserves held to maintain a fixed exchange rate cannot be used for other purposes, such as investment abroad.

- **Policies to maintain a fixed exchange rate may conflict with other macroeconomic aims**. A government may have to use monetary policy to influence the exchange rate even though it may affect the achievement of other important aims, such as low unemployment and low inflation. For example, lowering interest rates will result in an outflow of short-term capital from the country, increasing the supply of the currency in the foreign exchange market and lowering its value. However, this will conflict with the aim of low inflation, as the lower exchange rate will increase the cost of imported raw materials, putting upward pressure on the general price level.

- **The exchange rate may not be fixed at an appropriate level**. If the exchange rate is set too high, it may make exports uncompetitive, leading to higher unemployment and a slowdown in economic growth. On the other hand, if it is set too low, imports would be too expensive, increasing the cost of imported raw materials and contributing to higher inflation. An exchange rate that is fixed significantly low may also be considered unfair by trading partners unable to compete with the low price of the country's exports. A form of protection, this may lead to trade disputes and retaliation from trading partners.

4 Which type of exchange rate might be best for a country that is dependent on exports for its growth? Why?

Hong Kong's linked exchange rate system

An international trade and financial centre, Hong Kong operates a fixed exchange rate system in which the value of its currency is 'linked' to the value of the US dollar at a rate of HK$7.80 = US$1.

Why a fixed system? As an international hub for commerce, trade and finance, Hong Kong experiences large inflows and outflows of money on a daily basis. A fixed exchange rate avoids large fluctuations in the price of its exports, providing a degree of certainty for Hong Kong's exporters, particularly in trade with the USA, Hong Kong's second most important trading partner after Mainland China. A fixed system also helps to discourage 'predatory' speculation on the Hong Kong dollar from those aiming to profit from an appreciation of the currency or higher interest rates.

Why the US dollar? The US dollar is the most commonly used currency in international trade and financial transactions between countries. Also, America's central bank, the Federal Reserve, has a good track record of maintaining a low and stable inflation rate.

1 What are the benefits of a fixed exchange rate system for Hong Kong?

2 Why is it important for Hong Kong exporters that the Federal Reserve maintain a low and stable inflation rate?

Applying

Project work

Using the internet, investigate the exchange rate of a country of your choice.

1. What is the currency?

2. What has happened to the value of the currency against *one* other currency over the past 10 years?

3. What does this mean for consumers, firms and the economy as a whole?

Be ready to share your findings with your classmates in the next lesson.

Knowledge check questions

1 Define foreign exchange rate.   [2]

2 Explain **two** factors that affect the demand for a currency.   [4]

3 Explain **two** factors that affect the supply of a currency.   [4]

4 Using a diagram, show the equilibrium exchange rate for a currency.   [3]

5 Explain the difference between a floating exchange rate and a fixed exchange rate.   [4]

6 Explain **two** advantages of a floating exchange rate.   [4]

7 Explain **two** advantages of a fixed exchange rate.   [4]

8 Analyse how an appreciation of the exchange rate could lead to a lower rate of inflation.   [6]

9 (E) Discuss how an exchange rate depreciation might affect spending on exports and imports.   [8]

Check your progress

Read the unit objectives below and reflect on your progress in each.

▲	I struggle with this and need more practice.
▲	I can do this reasonably well.
▲	I can do this with confidence.

- Define foreign exchange rate.

- Identify the equilibrium foreign exchange rate.

- Explain the factors affecting the demand for and the supply of a currency in the foreign exchange market.

- Explain the effects of foreign exchange rate fluctuations on export and import prices.

- Analyse how price elasticity of demand (PED) for exports and imports affects export revenue and import expenditure.

- Distinguish between floating and fixed exchange rate systems.

- Describe the advantages and disadvantages of a floating and a fixed exchange rate system.

Current account of balance of payments

Learning objectives

By the end of this unit, you should be able to:

- identify and describe the components of the current account of the balance of payments – trade in goods, trade in services, primary income and secondary income
- calculate deficits and surpluses on the current account of the balance of payments and its component sections
- explain the reasons for current account deficits and surpluses
- analyse the consequences of a current account deficit and surplus – impact on GDP, employment, inflation and foreign exchange rate
- analyse the range of policies available to achieve balance of payments stability
- discuss the effectiveness of policies to achieve balance of payments stability.

Starting point

Answer these questions in pairs:

1 What is the difference between revenue and expenditure?

2 What effect might price elasticity of demand have on export revenue when prices change?

3 What effect might price elasticity of demand have on import expenditure when prices change?

Exploring

Discuss these questions in pairs:

1 Why is it important for firms to keep a record of their revenue and expenditure?

2 What problems may a firm face if its expenditure exceeds its revenue?

3 Why is it important for economies to keep a record of their export revenue and import expenditure?

Developing

The balance of payments

Just as individuals, households and firms need to keep track of their income (or revenue) and expenditure, so too a country needs to maintain a record of the money flowing in and flowing out of its borders over time. This record of financial transactions between one country and all other countries is called the balance of payments. The balance of payments enables a government to monitor flows of money into and out of the country so that serious imbalances can be avoided.

The balance of payments is made up of two components: the current account and the **capital account** (also called the **financial account**).

Structure of the current account of the balance of payments

The current account consists of four component sections.

1. **Trade in goods** (also known as the **balance of trade**). The trade in goods component of the current account records the value of visible exports and the value of visible imports. **Visibles** are goods that are tangible (they exist in physical form), such as cars, electronic goods and oil. If the value of visible exports is greater than the value of visible imports, there is a net inflow of money into the country and the balance of trade is said to be in surplus. However, if the value of visible imports is greater than the value of visible exports, there is a net outflow of money from the country and the balance of trade is said to be in deficit.

NOTE

While you should be aware of the existence of the capital account, the Cambridge ® IGCSE Economics specification only requires you to have a detailed understanding of the current account.

Key terms

Capital account (also called the **financial account**) – a record of the money flowing into and out of a country from investments, savings and foreign currency transactions to stabilise the exchange rate

Trade in goods (also known as the **balance of trade**) – this is the difference between the value of visible exports and the value of visible imports

Visibles – goods that are tangible (they exist in a physical form)

$$\text{balance of trade} = \begin{matrix} \text{value of visible exports} \\ \text{(revenue from visible} \\ \text{exports)} \end{matrix} - \begin{matrix} \text{value of visible imports} \\ \text{(expenditure on visible} \\ \text{imports)} \end{matrix}$$

surplus: value of visible exports > value of visible imports

deficit: value of visible exports < value of visible imports

2. **Trade in services** (also known as the **balance of trade in services**). The trade in services component of the current account records the value of invisible exports and the value of invisible imports. **Invisibles** are services that are intangible (they do not exist in physical form), for example a stay in a hotel, a flight on an airline or health insurance. If the revenue a country earns from invisible exports is greater than its spending on invisible imports, it is said to be in surplus. On the other hand, if a country's spending on invisible imports is greater than revenue from invisible exports, it is said to be in deficit.

balance of trade in services = value of invisible exports (revenue from invisible exports) − value of invisible imports (expenditure on invisible imports)

surplus: value of invisible exports > value of invisible imports

deficit: value of invisible exports < value of invisible imports

1 Name two visibles and two invisibles not mentioned in the text.

3. **Primary income.** Primary income is earnings that come from a factor of production (land, labour, capital or enterprise). The primary income component of the current account includes **wages** paid to individuals for their labour and **interest**, **profit** and **dividends** earned on investments. If the primary income flowing into a country is greater than the primary income flowing out, there is said to be a net inflow of primary income. However, if the primary income flowing out of a country is greater than the primary income flowing in, there is said to be a net outflow of primary income.

primary income = inflow of primary income − outflow of primary income

net inflow: inflow of primary income > outflow of primary income

net outflow: inflow of primary income < outflow of primary income

4. **Secondary income.** Secondary income is income received through current transfers. A **current transfer** is a sum of money that is given to an individual, firm or government in another country. It can be thought of as a gift because nothing of economic value is received by the sender in return for the money. Government aid and charitable donations sent abroad, or an individual sending

Key terms

Trade in services (also known as the **balance of trade in services**) – the difference between the value of invisible exports and the value of invisible imports

Invisibles – services and other products that are intangible (they do not exist in a physical form)

Primary income – earnings that come from a factor of production (land, labour, capital or enterprise)

Wages – the income an individual receives from their employer in return for mental or physical effort. Wages are the factor reward for labour.

Profit – the income a firm receives after expenses have been deducted (total revenue – total costs). Profit is the factor reward for enterprise.

Dividends – the portion of a firm's profit that is paid to shareholders, the owners of the business

money to family members in another country, would be recorded in the secondary income component of the current account. A net inflow of secondary income is when the current transfers flowing into a country are greater than those flowing out. A net outflow of secondary income, on the other hand, is when the current transfers flowing out are greater.

$$\text{secondary income: } \frac{\text{inflow of secondary}}{\text{income}} - \frac{\text{outflow of secondary}}{\text{income}}$$

$$\text{net inflow: } \frac{\text{inflow of current}}{\text{transfers}} > \frac{\text{outflow of current}}{\text{transfers}}$$

$$\text{net outflow: } \frac{\text{inflow of current}}{\text{transfers}} < \frac{\text{outflow of current}}{\text{transfers}}$$

By summing up all of the total inflows and outflows of money in each of these four components of the current account, it is possible to determine whether the overall current account of a country is in deficit or surplus.

- A **current account deficit** would indicate that the money flowing out of the country from trade in goods, trade in services, and primary and secondary income is greater than the money flowing in.

- A **current account surplus**, on the other hand, would indicate there is a net outflow of money from the current account.

$$\text{current account balance: } \frac{\text{trade in}}{\text{goods}} + \frac{\text{trade in}}{\text{services}} + \frac{\text{primary}}{\text{income}} + \frac{\text{secondary}}{\text{income}}$$

current account deficit: inflow of money from trade in goods, trade in services, and primary and secondary income < outflow of money from trade in goods, trade in services, primary and secondary income

current account surplus: inflow of money from trade in goods, trade in services, primary and secondary income > outflow of money from trade in goods, trade in services, primary and secondary income

Calculating a current account deficit or surplus

Current account deficit on the balance of payments for Country A

	Component section	Inflow of money into Country A		Outflow of money from Country A		Net balance
1.	Trade in goods	Value of visible exports	$14m	Value of visible imports	$34m	= −$20m (deficit)
2.	Trade in services	Value of invisible exports	$16m	Value of invisible imports	$7m	= $9m (surplus)
3.	Primary income	Inflow of wages, interest, profits, dividends	$9m	Outflow of wages, interest, profits, dividends	$8m	= $1m (net inflow)
4.	Secondary income	Inflow of current transfers	$1m	Outflow of current transfers	$5m	= −$4m (net outflow)
	Current account balance = −$20m + $9m + $1m − $4m					= −$14m (deficit)

2 Do the values in the table for Country A most likely indicate that this is a developed or developing country? Why?

Application task

Here is some information on the current account of the balance of payments of Country B:

Value of visible exports = $76m

Value of visible imports = $40m

Value of invisible exports = $28m

Value of invisible imports = $38m

Inflow of primary income = $30m

Outflow of primary income = $35m

Inflow of secondary income = $16m

Outflow of secondary income =$5m

1 Copy the table below into your exercise book. Use the information provided above to complete the table.

	Component section	Inflow of money into Country B	Outflow of money from Country B	Net balance
1.	Trade in goods			
2.	Trade in services			
3.	Primary income			
4.	Secondary income			
	Current account balance =			

2 What is the overall current account balance for Country B?

3 What is the main reason for the imbalance on this current account?

The other component of the balance of payments

The balance of payments of a country also includes a second component – the capital account (or financial account). The capital account of the balance of payments records the value of investments, such as foreign direct investment (FDI) and short-term capital flows of hot money, flowing into and out of the country.

Due to the complexity involved in recording all financial transactions between one country and all other countries, there are likely to be some mistakes and miscalculations, which are reflected in a balancing item called **net errors and omissions**.

Key term

Net errors and omissions – a balancing item included in the balance of payments which accounts for mistakes made in calculating inflows and outflows of money to and from a country

balance of payments = current account + capital account + net errors and omissions

Causes of current account deficit and surplus

A current account deficit or surplus could be the result of an imbalance in one or more of the four components of the current account. Causes of a current account deficit or surplus include:

- **Exchange rate changes**. A change in the value of the currency will influence the current account position of a country. For example, a fall in the value of the currency will reduce the price of exports and increase the price of imports. The resulting increase in the sale of exports and decrease in the purchase of imports should lead to an improvement in the current account balance over time.

- **Inflation**. The inflation rate affects the price of exports. For example, if the inflation rate of a country is higher than its trading partners, its exports will be less competitive while imports into the country will be more competitive. As a result, sales of exports are likely to fall and purchases of imports are likely to rise, worsening the current account balance over time.

- **Levels of consumer income**. Changes in consumer incomes may impact the current account position of a country. For example, higher consumer incomes resulting from rising economic growth are likely to lead to increased spending on imported goods, such as cars, TVs and brand name clothing labels, worsening the country's current account balance. Rising consumer incomes in the economies of trading partners, on the other hand, are likely to increase spending on exports, thus improving its current account position.

- **Protection policies**. The imposition or removal of trade barriers is likely to affect the current account position of a country. For example, a tariff imposed on imports will increase the price of imports, making home-produced goods more competitive. The resulting decrease in spending on imports over time should lead to an improvement in the current account.

- **Changes in productivity**. An improvement in productivity due to increased investment in training or automation (use of machinery) by domestic firms can lead to an increase in productivity and a fall in unit costs in the longer run. As a result, a country's exports will become relatively cheaper and imports relatively more expensive, leading to higher sales of exports and reduced spending on imports. This will have the effect of improving the current account over the longer run.

- **Operations of multinational companies (MNCs)**. MNCs setting up in a country are likely to result in an outflow of profits over time leading to a worsening of the current account. On the other hand, some MNCs may export their production to other countries, leading to an improvement in the current account. Whether MNCs contribute to a surplus or deficit on the current account therefore depends on which of these two effects is greater. The amount of profit flowing out of the country will depend on aggregate demand in the domestic economy. High aggregate demand is likely to lead to higher profits for MNCs and more profits leaving the country.

3 What would be the impact of the imposition of an import tariff on the current account of a county if the demand for imports were price inelastic?

Consequences of a current account deficit and surplus

A current account deficit or surplus that is *small* as a proportion of a country's GDP or *temporary* in nature is not necessarily a problem for an economy. Economists would consider this to be relatively stable. However, a current account deficit or surplus that is *large* as a proportion of the country's GDP and *persists* over a long period of time could have a destabilising effect on an economy.

Consequences of a current account deficit

A large and persistent deficit on the current account indicates that there is a net outflow of money from a country, usually due to excessive spending on imports by consumers, firms and the government. As export revenue is insufficient to cover spending on imports, the deficit must be financed (paid for) using other means. There are two main ways in which a current account deficit can be financed. The first is using the country's **foreign currency reserves** held at the central bank. The second is by borrowing money from abroad. As foreign currency reserves are limited, a country with a large current account deficit is likely to have to borrow in order to finance it.

A country that finances its deficit by borrowing must make regular **debt repayments** – payments to **creditors** that cover **interest** and **principal** (the borrowed funds) at frequent intervals. Provided the income (or GDP) of the country is increasing, it should be able to meet its debt repayment obligations.

Key terms

Foreign currency reserves – a store of foreign currency held at a country's central bank

Debt repayments – fixed amounts (consisting of principal and interest) paid to a creditor at regular intervals on a loan

Creditor – the lender of money

Interest – the cost of borrowing money which is paid to a creditor in addition to the principal

Principal – the total amount borrowed

However, if a country experiences a sudden fall in income, it may struggle to make the repayments. In this situation, a country may have to enter a period of **austerity**, in which spending is drastically reduced in the economy so that debt repayment obligations to creditors can be met. The government may also raise taxes in order to generate additional revenue to repay the money it owes. As a result, aggregate demand in the economy is likely to fall, which may lead to recession. Rising unemployment and falling incomes would make the country's debt even harder to repay.

If a country is unable to repay its debt, it may be forced to **default** on its loans. In this case, a large portion of the country's **assets**, including land and natural resources, will be sold off to foreign buyers to repay creditors. To avoid default, a country may go to the International Monetary Fund (IMF) for a **bailout loan**. The IMF will lend a country the money it needs to avoid default but will often set conditions, such as the imposition of strict austerity measures. South Korea received an emergency bailout loan from the IMF in 1997 and Greece required bailout loans from the IMF in 2010, 2012, 2015 and 2017 due to excessive debt, which it had accrued in part due to its large current account deficit.

Impact of a current account deficit on an economy

A current account deficit will affect all the main elements of an economy. These are outlined in the table below.

The impact of a current account deficit

Economic growth	The effect of a current account deficit on a country's GDP depends on the types of good a country is importing. If a large proportion of the goods imported into the country are consumer goods, such as cars and electronic gadgets, the living standards of the population are likely to be high. However, imported consumer goods will do little to increase the future GDP of the economy. If, on the other hand, a country is importing mostly capital goods (capital equipment and machinery), the productive capacity of the economy will increase. This should lead to more goods being produced in the future, thus increasing the GDP of the economy over time. 
Employment	High consumer spending on imports rather than home-produced goods is likely to lead to unemployment in domestic industries. This is because domestic firms are likely to experience falling sales as consumers purchase imports rather than locally made goods. Low foreign demand for a country's exports may also lead to job losses in export industries.

Inflation	A current account deficit is likely to lead to lower inflation. One reason for this is that low demand for exports is likely to reduce aggregate demand in the economy, leading to lower demand-pull inflation (see Unit 4.8). High domestic demand for imports rather than home-produced goods may also reduce aggregate demand, putting downward pressure on the domestic price level.
Foreign exchange rate	High spending on imports will lead to an increase in the supply of the domestic currency in the foreign exchange market. Low demand for exports will lead to a fall in the demand for the domestic currency (see Unit 6.3). The combination of these two effects will result in a depreciation of a country's foreign exchange rate over time.

Consequences of a current account surplus

A large and persistent surplus on a country's current account may occur because a government maintains a low fixed exchange rate (see Unit 6.3). This makes its exports more price competitive abroad, which over time is likely to result in higher export revenue. It also increases the price of imports, leading to a reduction in import expenditure.

Just as a country with a current account deficit is a net borrower, a country with a current account surplus is likely to be a net lender, using its surplus funds to provide loans to those countries with large deficits. These funds will be repaid in the future with interest, generating future income for the country.

However, there is an opportunity cost to a country with a current account surplus as the use of resources to produce exports for overseas markets means that there are fewer resources available for domestic consumption. As a result, living standards in the country are likely to be lower than they could be.

Impact of a current account surplus on an economy

A current account surplus will affect all the main elements of an economy. These are outlined in the table below.

The impact of a current account surplus

Economic growth	GDP in the economy is likely to rise as a result of high foreign demand for exports.	
Employment	High demand for exports is likely to create jobs in export industries, leading to lower unemployment. High demand for home-produced goods rather than the relatively more expensive imported goods is also likely to create employment opportunities in domestic industries. Domestic firms benefitting from higher sales will expand production, thus creating jobs and lowering unemployment.	

Inflation	High demand for exports and low demand for imports is likely to lead to an increase in demand-pull inflation.
Foreign exchange rate	High demand for exports will lead to an increase in the demand for the domestic currency in the foreign exchange market. Low demand for imports will lead to a fall in the supply of the domestic currency. The combination of these two effects will result in an appreciation of the foreign exchange rate.

Policies to correct a current account deficit

The government of a country with a floating exchange rate system may choose to allow the value of its currency to adjust automatically to correct a current account deficit. The combination of high spending on imports and low demand for exports will lead to a depreciation of the exchange rate. The effect of this is to make exports cheaper and imports more expensive. Over time, this should result in an increase in export revenue and a reduction in import expenditure, leading to an improvement in the current account.

Alternatively, a government may seek to improve a current account deficit through the use of policy measures. These include:

- **Exchange rate devaluation**. A devaluation of the exchange rate (see Unit 6.3) would make exports cheaper and imports more expensive. Increased sales of exports and reduced spending on imports over time should result in an improvement in the current account.

- **Subsidies paid to domestic producers**. Subsidies to domestic producers would lower their costs of production, enabling them to charge lower prices. Consumers would likely respond by substituting relatively cheaper home-produced goods for imported goods. The resulting reduction in spending on imports would lead to an improvement in the current account.

- **Imposition of tariffs or quotas**. Import restrictions could also help to improve a current account deficit. For example, the imposition of a tariff or import quota would increase the price of imports, making them less competitive in the domestic market (see Unit 6.2). As a result, consumers would switch away from imports to consuming more home-produced goods, leading to an improvement in the current account.

- **Improved productivity of domestic firms**. A government could use supply-side policy to increase the productivity of domestic firms in the long run (see Unit 4.5). For example, a subsidy on capital investment may encourage domestic firms to innovate and develop more efficient production processes, increasing productivity. The price of home-produced goods would therefore decrease relative

to the price of imports. As a result, spending on home-produced goods would likely rise as consumers switch away from the relatively higher-priced imports, thus improving the current account.

The effectiveness of these policies depends largely on the price elasticity of demand for exports and imports, which is likely to be inelastic in the short run and elastic in the long run (see Unit 6.3). The more elastic the demand for exports and imports, the more effective the policies will be. In addition to this, the effectiveness of protection policies to correct a current account deficit will depend on how trading partners respond to restrictions placed on their exports. If trading partners choose to retaliate by imposing trade barriers in kind, the effectiveness of these policies in improving the current account deficit would be significantly reduced.

Contractionary demand-side policies can also be used to correct a current account deficit by reducing consumer spending on imports. They include the following:

- **Contractionary monetary policy**. The central bank can take action to reduce a current account deficit by raising interest rates. Higher interest rates will increase the cost of borrowing in the economy, leading to a reduction in consumer spending. As a result, spending on imports will fall, improving the current account balance.

- **Contractionary fiscal policy**. A government could improve a current account deficit by reducing government spending or increasing income tax rates. A reduction in government spending on infrastructure or public services, for instance, will result in higher unemployment and lower incomes. As a consequence, spending on imports is likely to fall. Higher income tax rates will similarly reduce demand for imports as it will reduce the amount of disposable income consumers have to spend.

While demand-side policies can be effective in reducing a current account deficit, they may also have the undesirable consequences of higher unemployment and a slowdown in economic growth.

Policies to correct a current account surplus

A current account surplus could be corrected by allowing the domestic currency to appreciate in the foreign exchange market. A country with a surplus is likely to be selling a large volume of exports abroad. This would increase demand for the domestic currency, putting upward pressure on the exchange rate. As the currency appreciates, exports will become more expensive and imports cheaper. Over time, this is likely to lead to a fall in export revenue and a rise in import spending, reducing the current account surplus.

Economic growth in the domestic economy over time is also likely to reduce a current account surplus. As an economy grows, consumer incomes tend to rise, leading to increased domestic consumption of imported luxury goods, thus reducing a surplus on the current account.

Germany's record current account surplus

In 2016, Germany posted a current account surplus of €253 billion ($297 billion), overtaking China as the country with the world's largest surplus on its current account.

A relatively weak euro contributed to this, increasing the competitiveness of German exports, such as motor vehicles and machinery, and leading to a rise in export revenue. Secondly, with Germany's population ageing, individuals were net savers, saving more than they were spending as they prepared for retirement. Low domestic demand consequently led to German businesses investing abroad rather than at home.

As a member of the eurozone, Germany's currency (the euro) was unable to appreciate enough to correct its surplus. Thus, the German government turned to other policies, including raising the national minimum wage in 2015, increasing pensions to the elderly in 2016 and increasing government spending on areas including roads and digital infrastructure to correct the surplus.

1 Give two reasons for Germany's record current account surplus mentioned in the extract.

2 How might one of the government policies mentioned in the extract be effective in reducing Germany's current account surplus?

Applying

Project work

Using the internet, and following the steps below, prepare a brief report on specific reasons for a current account deficit and a current account surplus.

1. Identify a country with a current account deficit.

2. Explain one reason for the deficit.

3. Identify a country with a current account surplus.

4. Explain one reason for the surplus.

Be ready to share your research findings with your classmates in the next lesson.

Knowledge check questions

1 Describe the components of the current account. [8]

2 Explain a current account deficit. [4]

3 Explain **two** causes of a current account deficit. [5]

4 Explain the effect of a current account surplus on the foreign exchange rate of a country. [4]

5 Analyse how a devaluation of a country's currency could be used to correct its current account deficit. [8]

6 Other than a devaluation of the country's currency, analyse **two** other policies that could be used to correct a current account deficit. [7]

7 (E) Discuss whether a current account deficit is always bad for a country. [15]

Check your progress

Read the unit objectives below and reflect on your progress in each.

- Identify and describe the components of the current account of the balance of payments – trade in goods, trade in services, primary income and secondary income.

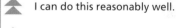 I struggle with this and need more practice.

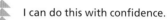 I can do this reasonably well.

I can do this with confidence.

- Calculate deficits and surpluses on the current account of the balance of payments and its component sections.

- Explain the reasons for current account deficits and surpluses.

- Analyse the consequences of a current account deficit and surplus – impact on GDP, employment, inflation and foreign exchange rate.

- Analyse the range of policies available to achieve balance of payments stability.

- Discuss the effectiveness of policies to achieve balance of payments stability.

Chapter review

Multiple-choice questions

1   Which of the following is an advantage of specialisation at national level?

    A   balance of payments instability

    B   diseconomies of scale for firms

    C   reduced choice and lower prices for consumers

    D   the economy's resources are put to their most productive use

2   Which of these is a potential advantage of multinational companies for a host country?

    A   an outflow of profits to the multinational's home country

    B   depletion of the country's natural resources

    C   higher prices for consumers

    D   increased competition for local businesses

3   What might be a benefit of free trade?

    A   a large and sustained deficit on the current account

    B   a large and sustained surplus on the current account

    C   an outflow of short-term capital (hot money)

    D   potential for economies of scale for domestic firms

4   What is the effect of an import quota on agricultural goods?

    A   higher prices for consumers

    B   increased choice for consumers

    C   increased tax revenue for the government

    D   increased transport costs for importers

5   One argument for the imposition of trade barriers is to protect infant industries. What is an infant industry?

    A   an industry that is benefitting from economies of scale

    B   an industry that is experiencing declining sales

    C   an industry that is emerging

    D   an industry that specialises in the production of a particular good

6   What is **likely** to cause a fall in the foreign exchange rate of Country A?

    A   foreign speculators buying Country A's currency

    B   increased demand for Country A's exports

    C   increased spending on imports in Country A

    D   the central bank in Country A raising interest rates

7 What is **likely** to be the effect of a fall in the demand for exports on the exchange rate of a country?

A

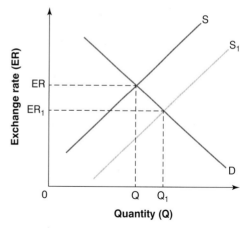

B

C

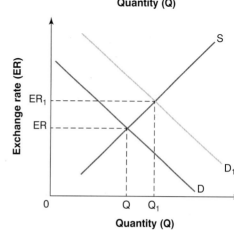

D

8 Which country had the largest surplus on the trade in goods component of its current account?

	Trade in services	Primary income	Secondary income	Current account
A	−$10m	+$10m	−$10m	+$20m
B	+$30m	+$20m	+$10m	+$40m
C	+$20m	−$20m	+$10m	+$30m
D	−$20m	−$20m	−$10m	−$80m

9 Which policy could be used to improve a current account deficit?

    A a raising of interest rates

    B a revaluation of the currency

    C an increase in government spending

    D the removal of subsidies from domestic firms

10   What might cause a country's current account deficit to worsen?

    A   a depreciation of the exchange rate

    B   a fall in domestic consumption

    C   increased demand for exports

    D   low domestic inflation relative to other countries

Structured questions

1   **Nigerian international trade**

Africa's largest economy, Nigeria, is also the most populous country in Africa with approximately 167 million inhabitants.

Over 90% of Nigeria's export revenue comes from petroleum and other petroleum products extracted and refined from its rich reserves of oil. Petroleum production makes up 40% of Nigeria's GDP and 80% of government revenue. Other exports include cocoa and rubber. Lower oil prices in 2016 resulted in a 1.7% fall in Nigeria's GDP and a significant fall in government revenue. Following this, the Nigerian government announced a plan to diversify the economy away from oil.

A large number of multinational oil companies have set up in the Niger Delta, Nigeria's main oil-producing region. Oil exploration in the region has caused significant environmental damage, including serious oil spills, which have had a devastating impact on local communities and wildlife in the area.

The Nigerian government imposes restrictions on imports and exports to protect local businesses in industries including meat, noodles, bagged cement, furniture and footwear. Import duties are also imposed on certain goods such as rice, which faces a tariff of 20%.

Nigeria's current account balance

Current account balance (in US dollars)

2015 est.	−$15.44 billion
2016 est.	−$2.856 billion

Balance of trade (in US dollars)

	Exports	**Imports**
2015 est.	$45.89 billion	$52.33 billion
2016 est.	$33.27 billion	$36.40 billion

In 2015, Nigeria's largest export market was India, which purchased 17% of the country's exports. In the same year, over a quarter of goods imported into Nigeria came from China.

Source: Data from the CIA *World Factbook*

(a) Calculate Nigeria's trade balance in 2016. [2]

(b) Using examples from the extract, explain what is meant by the term **factor endowments**. [3]

(c) Using information from the extract, explain **two** disadvantages of specialisation at national level. [4]

(d) Describe how Nigeria's current account balance changed between 2015 and 2016. [2]

(e) Give **two** reasons why the Nigerian government might impose protection policies on its footwear industry. [4]

(f) Identify the **four** components of the current account of the balance of payments. [4]

(g) Analyse the possible effects of a fall in oil prices on Nigeria's current account balance. [5]

(h) Discuss whether multinational companies are always bad for a host country. [8]

2   The establishment of the ASEAN Free Trade Area (AFTA) has resulted in the lowering of tariffs on products traded between the following members of the Association of South East Asian Nations (ASEAN): Brunei Darussalam, Indonesia, Malaysia, Philippines, Singapore, Thailand, Myanmar, Cambodia, Laos and Vietnam.

(a) Define tariff. [2]

(b) Give **two** reasons why a government may impose protection policies. [4]

(c) Analyse how the removal of tariffs may affect the balance of trade. [6]

(d) Discuss whether a free trade area always improves living standards. [8]

3   Following the 2016 Brexit referendum, in which a majority voted for the UK to exit the European Union, the value of the British pound fell more than 10% against the US dollar, from $1.50 USD to $1.33, its lowest level since 1985.

(a) Define exchange rate depreciation. [2]

(b) Give **two** factors that might cause a country's exchange rate to depreciate. [4]

(c) Analyse how an exchange rate depreciation can improve the balance of trade of a country. [6]

(d) Discuss whether a devaluation always results in reduced unemployment. [8]

4   In 2016, the USA recorded a current account deficit of $469.4 billion. China, on the other hand, recorded a current account surplus of $210.4 billion.

(a) Define current account deficit. [2]

(b) Give **two** causes of a current account deficit. [4]

(c) Analyse how an appreciation of a currency can help to reduce the rate of inflation. [6]

(d) Discuss whether a deficit on the balance of trade is always a problem. [8]

GLOSSARY

Absolute advantage – a situation in which a country is able to produce a particular good or service at a lower cost (using fewer resources) relative to other countries

Absolute poverty – a situation in which an individual does not have enough income to satisfy their most basic needs of food, clean water, clothing, shelter, education and healthcare

Age distribution – the proportion of people within a population who fall into certain age groups, for example, young (0–14 years), of working age (15–65 years) and old (65 years and above)

Ageing population – the increase in the median age of the population of a country over time

Aggregate demand (AD) – the total demand for all goods and services in an economy from consumption (C), investment (I), government spending (G) and net exports (X – M)

Aggregate supply (AS) – the total supply of goods and services in an economy

Allocation of resources – the way resources are allocated to the production of the goods and services most wanted by consumers

Appreciation – a rise in the value of a currency due to market forces

Assets – items of value, such as property and land

Austerity – a situation in which government spending is cut and taxes are increased in a country, usually to meet debt repayment obligations

Average cost (AC) – the cost of producing a unit (unit cost of production). It is calculated by dividing total cost by output or quantity.

Average fixed costs (AFC) – the fixed costs per unit

Average revenue (AR) – the revenue per unit sold

Average variable costs (AVC) – the variable costs per unit

Bailout loan – a loan provided in order to prevent payment default

Balance of payments – a record of the flows of money into and out of a country

Balance of trade – see Trade in goods

Balance of trade in services – see Trade in services

Balanced budget – revenue = spending

Barriers to entry – ways in which new firms are prevented from entering a particular industry

Barriers to trade – restrictions imposed by a government that prevent the free trade of exports and imports between countries

Barter – the act of trading goods or services between two or more parties without the use of money

Base rate (or bank rate) – the interest rate that a central bank will charge to lend money to commercial banks and on which other financial organisations base their interest rates

Base year – a year which is allocated a value of 100 index points against which other years are compared

Basic needs – what is needed for survival, such as food, shelter, water and clothing

Basic pay – the amount of money received before any additional payments are added or any deductions, such as income tax, are made

Basket of goods – a selection of goods and services normally purchased by a typical (ordinary) household which is used in the calculation of the consumer prices index to measure inflation

Birth rate – the number of live births for every 1000 people in a country in a year

Black market – an illegal market in which goods and services are traded without any government controls

Boom – a period of high and rising real GDP in the economy over time

Borrowing – being lent money with the requirement to pay it back in an agreed period of time, very often with interest

Budget deficit – spending > revenue

Budget surplus – revenue > spending

Business confidence – the extent to which businesses feel optimistic about the future: if business confidence is high, producers are likely to invest more in capital equipment to expand output

Business cycle – see Economic cycle

Capital – includes all man-made resources

Capital account (also called the **financial account**) – a record of the money flowing into and out of a country from investments, savings and foreign currency transactions to stabilise the exchange rate

Capital goods – equipment and machinery purchased and used by firms for the purpose of increasing production of goods and services

Capital intensive production – where a high level of investment is required, such as in machinery, equipment, vehicles, etc. compared to the other factors of production

Central bank – responsible to its government for controlling the country's money supply as the issuer of notes and coins and the level of reserves a commercial bank must hold. It also sets the rate of interest.

Ceteris paribus – all other things remaining the same

Claimant count – a measure of unemployment that is calculated by counting all individuals who receive an unemployment benefit as being unemployed

Collective bargaining – a process of negotiation over pay and conditions between a trade union, representing a group of workers, and employers

Commercial bank – financial institution in which individuals and firms can save their money and also obtain loans

Comparative advantage – a situation in which a country is able to produce a particular good or service at a lower opportunity cost (giving up fewer resources) relative to other countries

Competition – where different firms are trying to sell a similar product to a customer

Competitive market – where a large number of firms compete with each other to satisfy the wants and needs of a large number of consumers

Complementary good – a good that is consumed together with another good

Conditions of demand – factors other than the price of the good or service that lead to a change in position of the demand curve

Conditions of supply – factors other than the price of the good or service that lead to a change in position of the supply curve

Conglomerate merger – two firms with unrelated business activities join together

Consumer confidence – the extent to which consumers feel optimistic about the future: if consumer confidence is high, consumers are likely to spend more and save less

Consumer goods – final goods and services purchased and used by consumers

Consumer prices index (CPI) – a measure of the changes in the prices of a selection of goods and services normally purchased by a typical (ordinary) household

Consumer sovereignty – the power of consumers over how the market allocates resources through determining what is produced and for whom

Consumer spending – see Consumption (C)

Consumption (C) – the purchase of goods and services by households; also referred to as **consumer spending**

Contraction in demand – a decrease in quantity demanded as a result of a rise in price

Contraction in supply – a decrease in the quantity supplied in response to a decrease in price

Contractionary fiscal policy – a reduction in government spending and/or an increase in income tax rates in order to reduce aggregate demand in the economy

Contractionary monetary policy – the decrease in the money supply by the government, leading to a fall in aggregate demand

Corporation tax – a tax levied on a firm's profits

Corruption – the dishonest behaviour of people in power for their own personal gain

Cost of living – the day-to-day living expenses incurred by an individual

Cost-push inflation – an increase in the general price level in an economy due to an increase in firms' production costs

Creditor – the lender of money

Current account – a component of a country's balance of payments in which inflows and outflows of money from international trade and income flows are recorded

Current account deficit – the money flowing out of the country from trade in goods, trade in services, and primary and secondary income is greater than the money flowing in

Current account surplus – the money flowing into the country from trade in goods, trade in services, and primary and secondary income is greater than the money flowing out

Current transfer – a sum of money that is voluntarily given to another individual, business or government for which nothing of economic value is received in return. This is different from a **transfer payment**, which refers to a transfer of income, usually provided by the government to an individual or firm. The payment of unemployment benefits and subsidies to producers are examples of transfer payments.

Cyclical unemployment (also called **demand-deficient unemployment**) – unemployment that exists due to falling aggregate demand, which occurs when an economy enters a recessionary period in its economic cycle

Death rate – the number of deaths for every 1000 people in a country in a year

Debt repayments – fixed amounts (consisting of principal and interest) paid to a creditor at regular intervals on a loan

Declining industry (or **sunset industry**) – an industry that is experiencing falling sales due to a change in the structure of the economy

Decrease in demand – a leftward shift in the demand curve showing that a smaller quantity is demanded at each price than was previously

Decrease in supply – a leftward shift in the supply curve showing that a smaller quantity is supplied at each price than was previously

Default – failure to repay funds to a creditor (lender)

Deflation – the sustained fall in the general level of prices of goods and services in an economy over time

Demand – the quantity of a good or service that consumers are willing and able to buy at a given price in a particular time period

Demand curve – a graph plotting the quantities of a product demanded at a range of prices

Demand-deficient unemployment – see Cyclical unemployment

Demand-pull inflation – an increase in the general price level in an economy caused by an increase in aggregate demand

Demand schedule – a table that gives the quantities demanded at a range of prices

Demerit goods – a lack of information as to how harmful these products are for the consumer leads them to be overconsumed

Dependent population – the dependent population of a country consists of people who do not earn an income themselves and rely on others to provide them with the goods and services they need. It includes young children, the elderly, people who cannot work due to illness or disability, as well as those in full-time education

Depreciation – a fall in the value of a currency due to market forces

Deregulation – the removal of laws, rules and regulations, making it easier for a business to enter or operate in an industry

Derived demand – when a product or factor of production is not demanded for itself, but is dependent on the demand for the product it helps to produce.

Devaluation – a decrease in the value of a currency due to government intervention

Developed country – a country that has high income and living standards with most of its economic activity based in the tertiary sector

Developing country – a country that has a low income and is generally reliant on the agricultural industry for its employment and output

Direct tax – a tax on income or wealth

Diseconomies of scale – where an increase in the level of production results in a rise in the average costs of production

Disposable income – the income available to spend and save after direct taxes have been deducted and any state benefits added

Dividends (IPDs) – the portion of a firm's profit that is paid to shareholders, the owners of the business

Division of labour – the process by which workers specialise in, or concentrate on, one particular task

Dumping – the sale of imported goods at a price below what it cost to produce them

Earnings – the total amount received including additional payments

Economic cycle (also called the **business cycle** or **trade cycle**) – changes in the real GDP of an economy over time through periods of boom, recession, slump and recovery

Economic development – an improvement in the living standards and quality of life of the population of a country as it transitions from being reliant on the primary sector for employment and output towards the secondary and tertiary sectors

Economic goods – goods which are scarce relative to the demand for them

Economic growth – the change in the value of the goods and services produced within a country over time

Economic growth rate – the percentage increase in the value of goods and services produced in an economy over time (usually a year)

Economic resources – land, labour, capital and enterprise

Economies of scale – where an increase in the level of production results in a fall in the average costs of production

Effective demand – consumers' desire to buy a good, backed up by the ability to pay

Efficiency – how effective the firm is in using factors of production to generate its output

Embargo – a complete ban on the import of a certain product or all products from a particular country

Emigration – the movement of people out of a country to reside permanently elsewhere

Employment – the state of having paid work

Enterprise – brings all the other factors together to produce a good or service

Equal opportunities – the policies and practices in employment that prevent discrimination against someone on the grounds of race, age, gender, religion, disability or any other individual or group characteristic unrelated to ability, performance and qualification

Equilibrium price – the price at which the quantity that buyers want to buy is equal to the quantity that sellers are prepared to sell

Excess demand – see Surplus

Excess supply – see Shortage

Excise duty – a tax levied on goods that are manufactured in a country

Expansionary fiscal policy – an increase in government spending and/or a reduction in income tax rates in order to increase aggregate demand in the economy

Expansionary monetary policy – the increase in the money supply by the government, leading to a rise in aggregate demand

Export subsidy – a financial grant given to exporters by the government that does not need to be repaid

Exports – locally-made goods and services sold abroad

Extension in demand – an increase in quantity demanded as a result of a fall in price

Extension in supply – an increase in the quantity supplied in response to an increase in price

External benefits – the benefits to a third party from the production or consumption of a good

External costs – the costs to a third party from the production or consumption of a good

External economies – arise from factors outside the control of a firm and fall on all firms in the industry regardless of size

Factor endowments – the factors of production a country has available to produce goods and services

Factor immobility – the difficulties in transferring factors of production so that they may be used by an alternative industry

Factors of production – land, labour, capital and enterprise

Fertility rate – the average number of children per woman of childbearing age in a country

Final goods and services – goods and services that are ready to be used by the end consumer (both households and firms) when they are purchased, such as televisions, cars, pizza, etc.

Financial account – see Capital account

Finite resources – non-renewable resources that will eventually run out

Fiscal policy – the use of government spending and income tax rates to achieve certain macroeconomic objectives

Fixed costs (FC) – those costs which do not vary with output

Fixed exchange rate – a system where the value of the currency is controlled by government intervention in the foreign exchange market

Fixed exchange rate system – maintains a country's exchange rate within a very narrow band against other currencies

Fixed income earners – individuals who receive a set amount of income at regular intervals (weekly or monthly), for example pensioners and those who receive welfare payments

Fixed system – the value of a currency maintained at a certain level by the government

Floating exchange rate – a system where the value of a country's currency is determined by demand and supply

Floating system – the value of a currency determined by the market forces of demand and supply in the foreign exchange market

Foreign currency reserves – a store of foreign currency held at a country's central bank

Foreign direct investment (FDI) – money (capital) that flows into a country for the purpose of setting up business operations

Foreign exchange market – the place where buyers and sellers meet to trade foreign currencies

Foreign exchange rate (or exchange rate) – the price of one currency in terms of another currency

Formal economy – the official economy that is controlled by the government and subject to taxation

Free goods – resources that are supplied at zero cost because there are more than enough available to satisfy the demand for them

Free trade – the exchange of goods and services between countries without any government-imposed restrictions on volume or price

Free trade agreement (FTA) – an agreement between two or more countries to reduce restrictions on some or all products traded between them

Frictional unemployment – unemployment that exists when people are between jobs, moving from one job to another

Full employment – also referred to as **low unemployment,** this is a situation in which the vast majority of the labour force in an economy are in paid work

Gender distribution – the proportions of people in a country who are male and female

Geographical distribution – the way people are spread across a country or region, for example, the proportion of the population living in urban and rural areas

Geographical mobility – the ease with which an individual can change from one location to another for work purposes

Globalisation – the integration of local markets into a single global market

Goods and services tax (GST) – see Value added tax

Government budget – a plan of a government's future income and expected spending over a period of time (usually a year)

Government spending (G) – expenditure by the government

Grant – a sum of money that is given by the government which does not have to be repaid

Gross domestic product (GDP) – the total value of all final goods and services produced within a country over a year

Gross national income (GNI) – total income earned by the residents of a country (individuals and businesses) at home and abroad

Gross national income per head – gross national income averaged across the population of a country (GNI per head = GNI/population)

Health and safety – the laws and rules for identifying potential dangers and health problems at work and, also, the ways of preventing these issues and keeping people safe

Home country – the country in which a multinational company was originally established and where its headquarters are based

Horizontal merger – two firms at the same stage of production in the same industry join together

Host country – the country in which a multinational company operates that is not its home country

Household – a group of people who share the same living accommodation, who pool at least some of their income and who consume certain goods and services such as housing and food collectively

Human development index (HDI) – a measure of human development and wellbeing that takes into account the three dimensions of living standards, health and education

Human trafficking – the forced and illegal transport of human beings from one country to another

Immigration – the movement of people into a country to reside there permanently

Import quota – a limit on the quantity of a good imported into a country

Imports – foreign-made goods and services purchased locally

Income – the reward for the services provided by a factor of production, including labour

Income tax – a tax levied on a person's earnings from employment

Increase in demand – a rightward shift in the demand curve showing that a greater quantity is demanded at each price than was previously

Increase in supply – a rightward shift in the supply curve showing that a greater quantity is supplied at each price than was previously

Indirect tax – a tax on goods or services, such as sales tax or VAT

Industrial action – any measure taken by a trade union (or other organised labour) to try to enforce their demands or to address their complaints; this may take the form of strikes, overtime bans, go-slows, work-to-rules or sit-ins

Infant industry (or sunrise industry) – an emerging or newly established industry that is still too small to benefit from internal economies of scale and is therefore unable to compete with large foreign rivals

Infant mortality rate – the number of babies who die before their first birthday for every 1000 live births in a year

Inflation – the sustained rise in the general level of prices in an economy over time

Inflation rate – the percentage increase in the general price level in an economy over time (usually a year)

Informal economy – the unofficial economy, which is not taxed or controlled by the government

Infrastructure – facilities that are essential for an economy to function, including roads, a transport network, a communication network, electricity supply, etc.

Interest – the cost of borrowing money which is paid to a creditor in addition to the principal. Alternatively, the income received on money that is loaned out: the factor reward for capital

Interest rate – the cost of borrowing money

Intergenerational poverty – the continuation of poverty from one generation to the next, mainly due to lack of access to quality education

Internal economies – come from the growth of the firm itself, resulting in a fall in average costs (economies) or rise in average costs (diseconomies)

Investment (I) – the purchase of capital goods by firms to expand production

Invisibles – services and other products that are intangible (they do not exist in a physical form)

Labour – includes all human resources

Labour force – all individuals of working age (between the ages of 15 and 65 in most countries)

who are either employed or unemployed in a country

Labour Force Survey (LFS) – a measure of unemployment that uses data gathered from a survey of a sample of households to calculate the unemployment rate

Labour intensive production – where the production of a good or service depends more heavily on labour than the other factors of production

Labour productivity – output per worker per time period

Land – includes all natural resources

Law of demand – as the price of a good or service falls, the quantity demanded increases

Law of supply – as the price of a good or service falls, the quantity supplied decreases

Lender of last resort – where the central bank gives loans to banks or other eligible institutions that are experiencing financial difficulty and may not be able to quickly borrow money elsewhere

Life expectancy – the number of years a person in a country is expected to live

Living standards – the economic wellbeing and quality of life of members of a population

Living wage – a wage set at a level to enable workers to reach a minimum acceptable living standard

Loan – a sum of money that is given to a person or entity on the promise that it will be repaid at an agreed time in the future with interest

Long run – the time it takes to change the factors of production to expand and produce on a larger scale

Macro economics – the study of the whole economy

Macroeconomic aims – the goals a government wishes to achieve for the economy as a whole at a national and international level

Market – where many buyers and many sellers come together

Market disequilibrium – where the quantity demanded by consumers and the quantity supplied by producers are not equal

Market economic system – a system with prices that are based on competition between private sector businesses; markets are not controlled by the government

Market economy – also called a 'free market economy', an economy in which goods are bought and sold, and prices are determined by the free market without intervention by the government

Market equilibrium – where the quantity demanded by consumers and the quantity supplied by producers are equal

Market failure – a situation where the economy's resources are not efficiently allocated: the market does not produce the goods and services that consumers most want and in a quantity that is required

Maximum price control – prices are not permitted to rise above a certain level set by the government

Measure of value or unit of account – the idea that money allows the value of different goods and services to be compared

Medium of exchange – anything that sets the standard of value of goods and services and is acceptable to all parties involved in a transaction

Menu costs – the costs incurred by firms in changing their prices

Merger – the process by which two independent firms come together to form a new firm

Merit goods – a lack of information about how beneficial these products are for the consumer leads them to be underconsumed

Micro economics – the study of the economic behaviour of individuals and businesses

Minimum price control – prices are not permitted to fall below a certain level set by the government

Minimum wage – the lowest wage level that an employer may legally pay their workers

Mixed market system – an economy that has both private sector firms and government supplying goods and services

Mobility of factors of production – how easily any of the factors of production can be transferred to an alternative use

Monetary policy – when the government controls the money supply (usually by changing interest rates) in order to achieve certain macroeconomic aims

Money – anything that is generally accepted as a means of payment for goods and services

Money GDP – the total money value of the goods and services produced in an economy, not accounting for inflation (may also be referred to as GDP or nominal GDP)

Money supply – the quantity of money in circulation in the economy

Monopoly – the sole producer or seller of a good or service

Monopoly power – a single firm dominates the market and has the power to determine the market price

Multinational company (MNC) – a company that operates in more than one country

Nationalisation – the transfer of ownership (of property or a business) from the private sector to the government

Natural rate of unemployment – a certain amount of unemployment that will always exist in an economy as a result of people moving between jobs

Needs – goods or services necessary for survival

Net errors and omissions – a balancing item included in the balance of payments which accounts for mistakes made in calculating inflows and outflows of money to and from a country

Net exports (X – M) – the difference between the value of exports and the value of imports

Net migration – the difference between immigration into a country and emigration out of a country

Non-excludability – consumers who have not paid for a good (or service) cannot be excluded from benefitting from the consumption of that good or service

Non-rivalry – the consumption of goods by one individual does not prevent another individual consuming the good at the same time

Non-wage factor – something other than pay that influences choice of occupation

Occupational distribution – the proportion of people working in each of the primary, secondary and tertiary sectors of an economy

Occupational mobility – the ease with which an individual can change from one job in a particular field or industry to one in another field or industry

Opportunity cost – the next best alternative foregone when making an economic decision

Optimum population – a situation where a population is sufficient to ensure that all resources in a country are fully utilised and output is maximised

Overcrowding – an increase in the number of people to beyond what is comfortable due to lack of living space

Overpopulation – a situation where there are not enough resources to sustain the population of a country

Pensioners – individuals who are retired (no longer work) and receive a pension as their income

Planned economy – an economy in which all decisions concerning production, investment, prices and incomes are determined by the government

Population density – the number of people living in a certain area, usually one square kilometre

Population growth – the change (increase or decrease) in the number of people living in a particular geographical area

Population growth rate – the rate of change (expressed as a percentage) in the number of people residing in a country or a particular geographical area

Positive supply shock – a sudden increase in aggregate supply in an economy, such as a sudden fall in oil prices

Poverty cycle – a situation in which a developing country is unable to develop economically due to low income, leading to low savings, leading to low investment, leading to low productivity, leading to low economic growth and, thus, again leading to low income

Price elastic demand – the percentage change in quantity demanded is greater than the percentage change in price

Price elastic supply – the percentage change in quantity supplied is greater than the percentage change in price

Price elasticity of demand (PED) – the responsiveness of quantity demanded to changes in price

Price elasticity of supply (PES) – the responsiveness of supply to changes in price

Price inelastic demand – the percentage change in quantity demanded is lower than the percentage change in price

Price inelastic supply – the percentage change in quantity supplied is lower than the percentage change in price

Price mechanism – a system that enables buyers and sellers to trade with each other at an agreed price

Primary income – earnings that come from a factor of production (land, labour, capital or enterprise)

Primary sector – the direct use of natural resources; it is the extraction of basic materials and goods from the land and sea

Principal – the total amount borrowed

Private benefits – the benefits to an individual or business when they produce or consume a good

Private costs – the costs to an individual or business when they produce or consume a good

Private goods (or **private services**) – goods that it is possible to exclude individuals from consuming if they have not paid and there is rivalry in the consumption of these goods

Private sector – the part of the economy made up of individuals and businesses that make economic decisions

Privatisation – the transfer of ownership (of property or a business) from the government to the private sector

Product differentiation – setting one product apart from another by emphasising a particular aspect or aspects; it is used to increase consumer interest

Production – the total output of the goods and services produced by a firm or industry in a period of time

Production possibility curve (PPC) – shows the maximum possible output for two goods or services with a given amount of resources

Productive capacity (or **productive potential**) – the ability of an economy to produce goods and services if all factors of production are fully employed

Productivity – measures the contribution to production (total output) by each factor of production employed. It is one measure of the degree of efficiency in the use of factors of production in the production process. It is measured in terms of output per unit of input.

Profit – the income a firm receives after expenses have been deducted (total revenue – total costs). Profit is the factor reward for enterprise.

Profit maximisation – the greatest profit a firm can make is shown by where there is the most positive difference between TR and TC

Progressive taxation – a tax system that takes a higher proportion of income from the rich than the poor

Proportional taxation – a tax system that takes an equal proportion of income from all income earners (rich and poor)

Protection (or **protectionism**) – restrictions on imports and/or exports that are imposed by a government in order to safeguard jobs and domestic industries

Public goods (or **public services**) – goods that consumers cannot be excluded from enjoying even if they have not paid; everyone can equally enjoy consuming the good

Public sector – the part of the economy that is under the control of the government

Purchasing power – the value of money in terms of the quantity of goods and services it can buy

Quantitative easing (QE) – where a central bank buys financial assets from banks and other private sector businesses with new electronically created money

Quota – a physical limit on the quantity of a good that is allowed into a country

Rate of inflation – the persistent rise in the general price level over time

Rate of interest/interest rate – the cost of borrowing money from a lender, and the reward for saving

Real GDP – the total value for goods and services produced in an economy which has been adjusted to take inflation into account

Real GDP per head (real GDP per capita) – a measure of the average income of the population within a country

Real income – income taking the effects of inflation into account, so it is the purchasing power of income

Real output – the total value of goods and services produced in an economy after inflation (rising prices) has been taken into account

Recession – a sustained period of negative GDP in the economy over time; also defined as two consecutive quarters (three-monthly periods) of negative economic growth

Recovery – a period in which real GDP begins to rise as a result of rising aggregate demand in the economy

Redundant – a worker is made redundant when they lose their job because their skills are no longer needed by the business

Regional unemployment – when unemployment occurs in a particular geographical area

Regressive taxation – a tax system that takes a higher proportion of income from the poor than the rich

Regulation – the imposition of rules by the government, backed by the use of penalties that are intended to modify the behaviour of individuals and firms in the private sector

Relative poverty – a situation in which an individual does not have enough income to buy the goods and services normally consumed by members of the society in which they live

Remittance – a sum of money sent by a worker in a foreign country to relatives in their home country

Renewable resources – resources that can be replaced as they are used to produce goods and services

Retaliation – the imposition of protection policies by a government on imports from another country in response to protection policies imposed on exports from its country

Revaluation – a rise in the value of the domestic currency as a result of government intervention in the foreign exchange market

Salary – an annual sum of money usually paid in twelve equal monthly amounts

Sales (revenue) maximisation – where a firm increases market share and/or increases total revenue

Saving – that part of someone's income which is not spent on consumption

Scarcity – a lack of goods and services available to satisfy unlimited wants

Seasonal unemployment – unemployment that exists because the workers are not needed all year round

Secondary income – income received through current transfers

Secondary sector – all activities in an economy that are concerned with either manufacturing or construction

Shoe leather costs – the costs incurred by a business in searching for the best prices from suppliers

Shortage (or **excess demand**) – demand is greater than supply at a given price

Short run – an amount of time that is less than what is required for a firm to be able to expand and increase all of the factors of production. It is when at least one of the factors of production has not been changed

Short-term capital flows ('hot money') – the flow of money from one country to another on a temporary basis in order to earn income from changes in interest rates

Slum – an area in a city in which people live in poor conditions characterised by non-durable housing, unpaved paths, and lack of space, sanitation facilities and access to safe drinking water

Slump – a period of negative real GDP characterised by low aggregate demand in the economy

Social benefits – the private benefits plus the external benefits of producing a good

Social costs – the private costs plus the external costs of producing a good

Social optimum quantity – the level of output where the social costs equal social benefits: the market equilibrium reached fully takes into account all the costs and benefits associated with the production and consumption of the good

Social welfare – a firm being concerned about the welfare of its workers, society as a whole or local community

Specialisation – the process by which individuals, firms, regions and whole economies concentrate on producing those products in which they have an advantage

Spending – involves the use of money to purchase goods and services

Spillover effects – effects on a third party

Standard for deferred payment – enables people to borrow money and pay it back at a later date

Store of value – allows wealth to be stored in the form of money

Strategic industry – an industry that is important to the long-term wellbeing of a country

Structural unemployment – unemployment that exists due to a change in the structure of an economy, usually because it is becoming more developed

Subsidy – an amount of money given to a firm to lower the cost of supplying the good or service to the market

Subsistence economy – an economy in which people are self-sufficient, producing only enough to satisfy their own basic needs, including food, clothing and shelter, and the basic needs of their families

Substitute good – a good that is consumed as an alternative to another good

Sunrise industry – see Infant industry

Sunset industry – see Declining industry

Supply – the quantity of a good or service that producers are willing and able to supply at a given price in a particular time period

Supply curve – a graph plotting the quantities of a product supplied at a range of prices

Supply schedule – a table that gives the quantities supplied at a range of prices

Supply-side policy – a government action which leads to an increase in aggregate supply in an economy by improving either the quality or the quantity of resources

Surplus (or **excess supply**) – supply is greater than demand at a given price

Survival – the objective of remaining in business

Takeover – the process by which one firm buys another firm either by buying out the owner or by purchasing more than 50% of its shares

Tariff – a tax imposed on imported goods

Tax avoidance – the process of finding legal ways to minimise the amount of tax paid to the government

Tax evasion – illegal non-payment of taxes to the government

Tax revenue – the money a government receives from direct and indirect taxes

Technological unemployment – unemployment that exists because people are replaced by machines

Tertiary sector – all activities in the economy that involve the idea of a service

The economic problem – how can scarce economic resources be most effectively used to satisfy people's unlimited needs and wants?

Time lag – the period of time between an economic action and when it starts to take effect

Total costs (TC) – all the costs of the firm added together. TC = FC + VC

Total revenue (TR) – the total income of a firm from the sale of its goods and services

Trade cycle – see Economic cycle

Trade deficit – a situation where the value of imports of a country is greater than the value of exports

Trade in goods (also known as the **balance of trade**) – the difference between the value of visible exports and the value of visible imports

Trade in services (also known as the **balance of trade in services**) – the difference between the value of invisible exports and the value of invisible imports

Trade surplus – a situation where the value of exports is greater than the value of imports

Trade union – an organisation of workers that actively supports its members in a variety of ways, such as increasing wages and improving working conditions

Underpopulation – a situation where some of the resources of a country are left unused or wasted because there are not enough people to fully exploit them

Unemployment – the state of being without paid work but willing and able to work if a job becomes available

Unemployment rate – the percentage of a country's labour force that is without paid employment but actively seeking work

Unit elastic supply – the percentage change in quantity supplied is equal to the percentage change in price

Unit elastic demand – the percentage change in quantity demanded is the same as the percentage change in price

Unlimited wants – there is always something else that people would like and so people are never satisfied

Value added tax (VAT) – a tax levied on goods and services sold in a country calculated as a percentage of the sales price (also called a goods and services tax (GST) in some countries)

Variable costs (VC) – those costs which change as output changes

Vertical merger – two firms at different stages in the same industry join together; this may be forward or backward

Visibles – goods that are tangible (they exist in a physical form)

Voluntary unemployment – when an individual chooses to remain unemployed when they have the option of working

Wage – a payment for units of time or units of product

Wage–price spiral – the inflationary cycle of higher wages, leading to higher production costs, which in turn leads to higher prices and living costs, which lead again to higher wages, and so on

Wage rate – the amount of money paid to a worker per unit of time

Wages – the income an individual receives from their employer in return for mental or physical effort. Wages are the factor reward for labour.

Wants – goods or services not necessary for survival

Weighted average – the calculation of an average by multiplying each item by a factor indicating its importance; the total sum of the weightings in a calculation equals 1

Weighted price index – an index (with a base year of 100) in which the prices of goods are weighted according to their importance

Weighting – an indication of the importance of a good when calculating a weighted average; the more important the good, the higher the weighting it receives

Welfare services – financial support provided by the government to those most in need, including the elderly, children and the unemployed

Working-age population – the proportion of a country's population that is of working age, usually between the ages of 15 and 64

Index

Acknowledgements

The publishers wish to thank the following for permission to reproduce photographs. Every effort has been made to trace copyright holders and to obtain their permission for the use of copyright materials. The publishers will gladly receive any information enabling them to rectify any error or omission at the first opportunity.

(t = top, c = centre, b = bottom, r = right, l = left)

P 4br ALBERT GONZALEZ FARRAN/AFP/Getty Images, p 147br Natanael Pohan/ Pacific Press/ LightRocket/Getty Images
All other photographs used under licence from Shutterstock:
p. 1 Hans Verbug, p. 2c Nataliya Hora, p. 2cl geniusksy, p. 2cr denis kuznetsov, p. 3rb Cienpies Design, p. 3rt StockHouse, p. 4cl Gyvafoto, p. 4cr hagit berkovich, p. 6r Lukas Budinsky, p. 7tc Julia Jetta, p. 9tr Milan Kolovrat, p. 11brb bartxt, p. 11brt vuvu, p. 12brt Tony Baggett, p. 15tl FenlioQ, p. 15tr maradon 333, p. 17br Andrey_ Popov, p. 18br Leonard Zhukovsky, p. 19c gyn9037, p. 19cl humphery, p. 19cr estherpoon, p. 23 Vintage Tone, p. 24tr cla78, p. 26tr Trong Nguyen, p. 27bl dwphotos, p. 27bl eWilding, p. 27br charnsitr, p. 27tl Alexander Raths, p. 27tr Lucia Pitter, p. 30tl Bill45, p. 30tl kurhan, p. 30tr Nataliya Hora, p. 30tr Monkey Business Images, p. 31cr Pearl diver, p. 33cr NakarinZ, p. 34cr julie deshaies, p. 36tc HB511, p. 39tc Ken Wolter, p. 39tl Rob Wilson, p. 41cr Jery Lin, p. 43c Sangit Fuangnakhon, p. 43cl nimon, p. 47tr mailsonpignata, p. 48cr Trupungato, p. 49cr er ryan, p. 50cr pp1, p. 51rb Africa Studio, p. 51rt 1000 Words, p. 53cr Paolo Gallo, p. 53cr Valentyn Volkov, p. 54tc Svetlana Foote, p. 56cr er ryan, p. 57tl tgavrano, p. 58cr er ryan, p. 60cr DONOT6_ STUDIO, p. 62br Thampapon, p. 63tr 1989studio, p. 70cr bunyarit, p. 70tr Monkey Business Images, p. 71br Shulevskyy Volodymyr, p. 71tr Passakorn sakulphan, p. 73br symbiot, p. 79tc PhotoSky, p. 79tl Djelen, p. 79tr Eivaisla, p. 81cr NYCStock, p. 88tr ESB Professional, p. 92cr paulista, p. 92tr In The Light Photography, p. 93bl Caron Badkin, p. 95tc Andrey_Popov, p. 95tl Bumble Dee, p. 95tr Serp, p. 96cl manfredxy, p. 96cr ngaga, p. 96tr AeroFoto, p. 97cl Rawpixel.com, p. 97cr Have a nice day Photo, p. 97tr AVN Photo Lab, p. 100br Jan Martin Will, p. 100tr Denis.Vostrikov, p. 109br Chesky, p. 110br motorolka, p. 111brb Dionisvera, p. 111brt Antonova Ganna, p. 112tr yevgeniy11, p. 117tr seeshooteatrepeat, p. 118 Sasils, p. 120tc Athitat Shinagowin, p. 120tl Ivelin Radkov, p. 120tr tovovan, p. 121cr Peter Stuckings, p. 122br Curioso, p. 122tr Feng Yu, p. 123tr Olga Kashubin, p. 124cr Vlad Kochalaevskiy, p. 126tc Monkey Business Images, p. 126tl Monkey Business Images, p. 126tr anekoho, p. 128tr Pixel Embargo, p. 130cr Sayan Puangkham, p. 130tr Branislav Nenin, p. 134tc Frame China, p. 134tl Monkey Business Images, p. 134tr Monkey Business Images, p. 135cr ArtOfPhotos, p. 136cr Rob Marmion, p. 138br TOWANDA1961, p. 141cr Salvador Aznar, p. 143 Stanislaw Tokarski, p. 143 xieyuliang, p. 146br Rawpixel.com, p. 146tr ibreakstock, p. 147tr Don Fink, p. 149tr Xinhua /Alamy Stock Photo, p. 150cr ANADMAN BVBA, p. 152tl zhu difeng, p. 153tr View Apart, p. 154cr wavebreakmedia, p. 155br TTphoto, p. 157br Niloo, p. 159br Alexander Raths, p. 160br MAGNIFIER, p. 163tr Sergei Butorin, p. 165bl Dariush M, p. 167tr Zoran Karapancev, p. 168br Phaendin, p. 168cr Svend77, p. 168tr wavebreakmedia, p. 171br mady70, p. 173cr Duncan Andison, p. 174cr Madhourse, p. 175br Arina Habich, p. 178tr Zivica Kerkez, p. 181crb Nednapa Sopasuntorn, p. 181crt eFesenko, p. 183br northallertonman, p. 183cr Vladi333, p. 183tr catastrophe_OL, p. 184tr Andrey Khachatryan, p. 185cr JuliusKielaitis, p. 191 a-image, p. 192clb Monkey Business Images, p. 192clt degetzica, p. 192crb Syda Productions, p. 192crt Derek Gordon, p. 194cr Monkey Business Images, p. 194tr istanbul_image_video, p. 195br tcly, p. 195tr Galyna Andrushko, p. 197br testing, p. 197cr bodom, p. 197tr aldarinho, p. 200br Tyler Olson, p. 200tr tcly, p. 201c JohnKwan, p. 201cl Ekaterina_Minaeva, p. 202cr Joe Ravi, p. 204bc CandyraiN, p. 204bl Shcherbakov Ilya, p. 204br Steve Cordory, p. 205tr Dmitry Kalinovsky, p. 206br Rawpixel.com, p. 207br Andrey_Popov, p. 207c pixfly, p. 209brb Monkey Business Images, p. 209brt wavebreakmedia, p. 210br Zoriana Zaitseva, p. 211cr singh_lens, p. 216cr Ant Clausen, p. 217br Radu Bercan, p. 218cr Stockr, p. 218tr William Perugini, p. 220br Thanakrit Sathvornmanee, p. 220c Stokkete, p. 220cl Lucia Pitter, p. 221br I viewfinder, p. 223br BasPhoto, p. 223cr AlexLMX, p. 227bc mihalec, p. 227bl goodluz, p. 227br Phonlamai, p. 229cr bluedog studio, p. 229tt Matt Gibson, p. 230br Monkey Business Images, p. 230cr paul prescott, p. 233br Michal Knitl, p. 235bl Gwoeii, p. 235br QQ7, p. 236br Rawpixel.com, p. 240br Michaelpuche, p. 242bc Vlad Karavaev, p. 242bl Everett Collection, p. 243tr Skynavin, p. 244tr bibiphoto, p. 245tl sculpies, p. 245tr wavebreakmedia, p. 246br Ilia Torlin, p. 246c Loboda Dmytro, p. 246cl testing, p. 249br J2R, p. 249tr Cynthia Farmer, p. 251cr Monkey Business Images, p. 251tr marino bocelli, p. 252br Pressmaster, p. 252cr Rafal Chichawa, p. 252tr ChameleonsEye, p. 253cr Monkey Business Images, p. 253tr Jasminko Ibrakovic, p. 256cr Syda Productions, p. 256tr Andreas Semerad, p. 257cr ChameleonsEye, p. 258br Maximum Exposure PR, p. 259br Robert Cernohlavek, p. 260br InnaFelker, p. 262bc ESB Professional, p. 262bl withGod, p. 262br anucha maneechote, p. 265tl Minerva Studio, p. 265br Harper 3D, p. 267b Christher Halloran, p. 267cr Kzenon, p. 270c Kaspars Grinvalds, p. 272crb Matyas Rehak, p. 272crt Mocha.VP, p. 274br wavebreakmedia, p. 275tr Photographee.eu, p. 277tr IR Stone, p. 280br Taras Vyshnya, p. 282 Narit Jindajamorn, p. 283bc Spotmatik Ltd, p. 283bl Monkey Business Images, p. 283br everst, p. 286br Sergey Uryadnikov, p. 286cr MD_Photography, p. 287cr SAPhotog, p. 288brb Travel Stock, p. 288brt Rawpixel.com, p. 288cr wong yu liang, p. 289cr num_skyman, p. 290cr PhilipYb Studio, p. 292bl Avatar_023, p. 292br Halfpoint, p. 294br Kaikoro, p. 294tr gcelebi, p. 296trb Andrey Bayda, p. 296trt akturer, p. 297bl Riccardo Mayer, p. 297br Ananchai Phuengchap, p. 297tr Nuk2013, p. 298br R.M. Nunes, p. 298tr KingTa, p. 300bc 1000 Words, p. 300bl Orlok, p. 300br michaeljung, p. 301cr Bikeworldtravel, p. 301tr Istvan Csak, p. 303br Yury Birukov, p. 303tr saurabhpbhoyar, p. 305cr Kobby Dagan, p. 305tr africa924, p. 306cr 1000 Words, p. 307cr MD ZAKIER HOSSAIN SOHEL, p. 307tl Tyler Olson, p. 307tr 06photo, p. 308br Piyada Jaiaree, p. 308cr africa924, p. 309br Blend Images, p. 309tr Igor Drondin, p. 310cr pixelheadphoto digitalskillet, p. 311br Catalin Petolea, p. 312cr spass, p. 312tr Monkey Business Images, p. 313br paul prescott, p. 314tl LongJon, p. 315br MissRuby, p. 317tr Mark52, p. 319bl Vlad Karavaev, p. 319br Monkey Business Images, p. 320br Martchan, p. 320trb rweisswald, p. 320trt Parmna, p. 321tr myfavoritescene, p. 324br SantiPhotoSS, p. 325cr TierneyMJ, p. 325tr Valeriya Anufriyeva, p. 326tr ESB Professional, p. 330br Christher Meder, p. 332 BkkPixel, p. 333bl NinaMalyna, p. 333br Suriya99, p. 334br huafeng207, p. 334tr Frame China, p. 334tr sunun, p. 335bl bibiphoto, p. 336br melis, p. 336cl Nickolay Khoroshkov, p. 338bc Thinglass, p. 338bl Songquan Deng, p. 338br Michaelpuche, p. 339br walterericsy, p. 339cr KAE CH, p. 339tl John Keenan, p. 339tr Pierre-Yves Babelon, p. 340trb Settawat Udom, p. 340trt Grzegorz Czapski, p. 341cR TORWAISTUDIO, p. 341tl Sorbis, p. 341tr Igor Iakovlev, p. 342tc nui7711, p. 342tl humphery, p. 343brb paul prescott, p. 343brt franz12, p. 343tr Firma V, p. 345br marcin jucha, p. 346brb corlaffra, p. 346brc Orientaly, p. 346brt seyephoto, p. 347br Elena Elisseeva, p. 347tr michaeljung, p. 348cr l I g h t p o e t, p. 350cl Bankoo, p. 350cr AB Visual Arts, p. 352br pitchr, p. 353tr Sk Hasan Ali, p. 354brb Angelina Dimitrova, p. 354brt Gorodenkoff, p. 354trb Ivan Olianto, p. 354trt Jonathan Weiss, p. 355cr Leon T, p. 356br Vadim Ratnikov, p. 357br Studio Vlad, p. 359br D. Pimborough, p. 361tr I viewfinder, p. 363bl humphery, p. 363br tcly, p. 364br withGod, p. 365br Kdonmuang, p. 365tl Chittapon Kaewkiriya, p. 366cl ChameleonsEye, p. 368br Roman Tiraspolsky, p. 369tr Mark Yuill, p. 370bl Krivosheev Vitaly, p. 370tr Giannis Papanikos, p. 371br humphery, p. 372br FabrikaSimf, p. 372cr JP WALLET, p. 373cr Alick To, p. 374cr Gilles Lougassi, p. 378cr Bennian.